D0122477

UNDERSTANDING ADOLESCENCE

Current Developments in
Adolescent Psychology

UNDERSTANDING
ADOLESCENCE

Current Developments in
Adolescent Psychology

Edited by
James F. Adams

ALLYN and BACON, Inc.

BOSTON

Library of Congress Catalog Card Number:

68-14863

PRINTED IN THE UNITED STATES OF AMERICA

To

Our Adolescents

Past - Present - Future

Robert B. Adams	*George H. Carter, Jr.*	*Glen B. Johnstone*
Dorothy L. Adams	*Celia T. Carter*	*Aryl D. Kohrs*
James E. Adams	*Caroline A. Carter*	*Dorena D. Kohrs*
Marta L. Bell	*Paul S. Elkind*	*Richard A. Loomis*
Robin A. Bell	*Robert E. Elkind*	*Barbara M. Wendt*
Paul S. Beller	*Eric A. Elkind*	*Jo-Ann M. Vaugn*
Daniel R. Beller	*Cynthia C. Fizur*	*Keith L. Macomber*
Susan D. Block	*Karl C. Garrison, Jr.*	*David K. Nichols*
Jody L. Block	*Mary N. Haan*	*James E. Nichols*
David L. Block	*Peter A. Haan*	*Joshua H. Smith*
Carol A. Block	*John S. Hackman*	*T. Daniel Smith*
Carolyn J. Borow	*Patricia H. Kendall*	*Rebecca M. Smith*
Nancy J. Borow	*Eric C. Johnstone*	*J. Torquil Smith*

Preface

ORGANIZING A BOOK ON THE TOPIC OF "ADOLESCENCE," IS A FASCINATING
as well as a thought provoking task. It is probable that this will always
be true. The adolescent changes with his times and will be of interest
to the adults of each generation who find themselves in the process
of relinquishing the reins or being phased out by the next generation.
It seems such a short time ago that we were the "in group," and the
adult world was viewed as being in the archaic past.

This book was planned as a textbook for those who are interested
in understanding today's adolescent. It contains chapters which cover
topics which are of traditional concern (such as physiological development) as well as chapters which are of current concern (such as
activism and apathy in contemporary adolescents). It is probable
that this book could be read with profit by any interested and concerned adult; but, it has been written, in particular, for the student
who is preparing for his future role of parent, teacher, psychologist,
social worker, or, responsible citizen. The book should work well as
a primary text but should also prove useful as supplementary reading
to the more traditional adolescent texts.

I am indebted to many individuals who, over the years, have stimulated my interest in adolescence. These individuals include two professors of mine, Dr. James H. Elder and Dr. Wayne Dennis. Their
enthusiasm was contagious and I hope no cure is ever discovered for
this type of contagious disease. Next in line would be my three children who are now in this stage and who don't particularly like the
term "adolescence." However, since they couldn't agree on a better
term (I suggested "elderly children"), they have accepted the title
of the book and agree that *understanding* would help.

Certainly, I must express my appreciation to the authors of the
various chapters who, as a group, were very cooperative. Without their
knowledge and willingness to take the time to put their thoughts on
paper, there would have been no book. If the book is found to have
merit, it is primarily due to their efforts.

Lastly, there have been three individuals who have been of immediate assistance: Miss Ruth E. Simpkins who worked as my research

assistant for several years as I was developing the ideas for this book; secondly, Miss Joan R. Rubin who has been most valuable with her suggestions in the final preparation of the manuscript; and lastly, Mrs. Velma T. Carter who has typed this manuscript and who has been extremely helpful.

JAMES F. ADAMS, *Editor*
Temple University

❧ Contents ❧

CHAPTER 1

An Introduction to Understanding Adolescence

James F. Adams *

EVERY GENERATION OF ADOLESCENTS HAS HAD PROBLEMS WHICH WERE unknown to the previous generations. Conversely, previous generations have had difficulties of little concern to the adolescent of today. As adults we look at our young people and wonder how they will ever be able to cope with the impossible world we have produced and developed for their inhabitation. Undoubtedly, our parents had the same disquieting thoughts, and it is probable that our adolescents, in a few years, will go through the same cycle of disturbed thinking. Amazingly enough, the vast majority of adolescents will grow into productive, responsible, and reasonably happy adults. They do this year after year; sometimes in spite of, and not because of, the adult world's help. There are segments of the population for whom this process will be much more difficult (e.g., disadvantaged youth), but even within these segments, reasonable adjustments will be made. The term, reasonable, may be defined differently than you and I would like to have it defined; but it must be remembered that no one segment of society has a monopoly on semantics.

It would seem to me that a major share of the adult world's disturbance, with respect to the difficulties of the adolescent, comes from confused thinking. This confusion is purely and simply, ours and not the adolescent's. This is not to say that the adolescent doesn't have his share of confusion. He does. However, it would be safe to estimate that the overlap between these private domains is minor (although there may be a causal relationship at times).

✱ JAMES F. ADAMS is a Professor of Psychology and Educational Psychology at Temple University. In addition to this book he has edited or written: *Problems in Counseling: A Case Study Approach; Counseling and Guidance: A Summary View;* and journal articles on such topics as counseling, adolescent psychology, psychological testing, and the history of psychology.

The adult world derives its confusion from a fear that the chaotic world of today will be more chaotic in the future as a function of the next generation falling apart. Psychologists and psychiatrists contribute to this fear by calling to our attention the disturbed young people who pass through their offices. From this attention, the impression is conveyed to the public that all adolescents are disturbed. And, if you stop to think about it for a moment, this state of affairs is not too unexpected; after all, it is not the normal, reasonably adjusted adolescent who needs our help and who comes to our attention. In addition, in our literature, movies, and television, the disturbed or abnormal young person is of more interest. Abnormality has a greater market value and a greater news value. Further, there *are* things wrong in the adult world that the adolescent does not like and will not accept (as an adolescent). His protest is not always reasoned or reasonable. It may at times become violent and frightening. Is it surprising that we, in our culture, have developed a myth with respect to the universality of the disturbed adolescent?

Let us make it more personal. We have been talking in generalities and with respect to our culture at large. But now, as a present or future parent, assume you have an adolescent *within your own home.* I wonder if you have ever stopped to consider the fact that there is no such thing as a professional parent. We are all amateurs in our roles of raising children. By the time we have learned a little, our children are grown and we have already made our mistakes (and had our triumphs, hopefully). Reading about the raising of children can prove to be helpful, but we should never forget that while this literature may have been written by qualified educators, psychiatrists, psychologists and sociologists, when it comes to being parents we too are amateurs. Raising one, three or even a dozen children is just as personal with us as it is with you. We share, in spite of our professional training, the same fears, misgivings, joys, and hopes for our children. What we can contribute from our various disciplines is an objectivity about other people's children—not our own. Many of the writers of this book have spent their lives studying and trying to understand children and adolescents. All of us would quickly admit that having our own children has had a humbling effect on our expertise. However, by controlled study and experimentation, much has been learned which is true with respect to young people *in general* and even specifically (on occasion). This knowledge should make you a more intelligent parent, teacher or adult when it comes to working with or understanding the adolescent.

Let us return to that relative in your home. As a parent you are suddenly aware that you no longer have a child. The child has become a more or less independent young adult—the adolescent. Day by day you wonder if you have prepared him adequately for the new world he is facing. You may become suddenly concerned with his table manners (which you have been neglecting) and he, just as suddenly, becomes totally unconcerned. You find that there are times he is affectionate and that there are times he goes his own way without seeming to need the closeness that you once had together. As a parent, you try to comfort yourself with some old cliché such as "The love of a parent for a child is the one love that should grow toward separation." It does not help much. In short, you are a little confused with respect to this new state of affairs. Then, you suddenly become acutely aware of teenage problems, and they take on a new meaning. You hear of gang wars, drinking and "pot" parties. A young girl down the street is killed in an automobile accident while on a date. School grades become of increasing concern as the possibility of going to college approaches. Your son decides he should assert his grownup status by smoking. You hear of a friend's fifteen-year-old who is pregnant. The frequency of suicide increases on college campuses. Have you raised your son or daughter to cope with these pressures? You hope that you have, but there is a strong element of doubt in your mind. Do you now understand what I mean when I say that you have joined, or absorbed, the adult world's adolescent-confusion?

There is another side to the coin. The adolescent stands on the threshold of adult responsibility. He is beginning to think for himself and to question the wisdom of his parents. Sometimes he finds that his parents aren't too receptive to discussing issues, e.g., the time he should be home and the occasion involved. He looks at his school and his teachers differently. He finds that no one in the adult world is perfect—including his parents.

The adolescent finds that there is a discrepancy between what he has been taught as being right and how people conduct themselves. This young person lives in a world of high hopes and aspirations, but he finds that others (the adults) do not share either his enthusiasm or his ideals. He observes that as a congressman it is permissible to steal if you are relatively quiet about the matter. As a citizen, it is more laudatory to steal "big" than to steal "small." Americans admire private enterprise.

The adolescent may turn to educational institutions to find his answers. It doesn't take much of an investigation to find that education might be better called *hedgeucation*. He hears that learning for learning's sake is to be greatly admired. Then he observes that what adults are really interested in are those grades. He finds that education is great at *hedging* when he asks questions. Why is it so important to keep up with the Russians? Why does his school organize its teaching around the College Boards when they tell him they are preparing him for enlightened citizenship? What's so important about teaching calculus in the ninth grade? Just what is education, anyway? He sees some of his friends going to college to keep from being drafted. He hears his father say: "Where else can they do less harm for four years?" He reads that keeping young people in school is important because it keeps them off the labor market. His counselor tells him that if he goes to college he is likely to earn a quarter of a million dollars more in his lifetime. Is this what education is for—to make money? Why can't or won't adults give him a straight, honest, meaningful answer? It is not surprising that many adolescents decide to ignore the adult world and build their own private world within their peer groups; or, they may decide to try to change the world intellectually or overtly. Another group will passively join society and the system as they find it and "get theirs."

On top of all this, the adolescent has his own personal concerns. Socially, he may be ill at ease, but he is learning to converse in both an adult and heterosexual world. He wants to be accepted by the girls and boys of his peer group. There is a lot of verbal fencing and the trying on of roles for size.

Our adolescent finds that the adults (his parents become the representatives of this group) are strangely reticent to recognize his newly assumed maturity. When he acts grown-up, they convey to him that he is still a child. When he reverts to childhood behavior, they tell him to grow up. It is difficult to win in the adult game. He can usually handle the situation, but the rules are always changing. "The world is one vast, blooming, buzzing confusion."

I think that as adults, the burden of understanding reasonably rests upon our shoulders. As we learn more about the world of the adolescent, we should be better able to aid him in his transition to our complex adult world. As a function of this understanding, we should become more secure and efficient in our desire to help these youth in our roles as parents, educators and politicians. In short, at least some of the fog of confusion which exists in both camps (adults and adolescents) should be rolled away through our mature understanding. This is not to imply that *understanding* will ever completely insure our feelings of security as adults or parents. Living, itself, is not a secure proposition at best and there are no final proven answers to most of the important issues of life. However, understanding should help!

PERSONAL PROBLEM AREAS
FOR ADOLESCENTS

A few years ago, I became interested in the viewpoints of adolescents as they looked at themselves and their country. This was not a new venture for a psychologist or an adult. We have always been interested in the problems of adolescents. However, it was the beginning point for the organization of this book and its focus. So, let us take a look at the general findings of this study (Adams, 1963; 1964; 1966) and use them as a jumping-off place for the remaining chapters in which some of the crucial issues of adolescent development are discussed.

As we consider the personal problems of adolescents in this section, let us bear in mind that we are not emphasizing the *problem* aspect as being the private property of the adolescent. Children and adults also have personal problems. The focus is really on those matters which are *of concern* to the adolescent and how these matters change as a function of the age and the sex of the young person. First, a brief comment on the composition of the sample in my study. Most of these adolescents came from the Philadelphia suburban schools. A few came from smaller communities in neighboring counties and states. There was surprisingly little difference between the adolescents as a function of these variables. The total sample can best be described as being middle and upper middle class in composition.

"What problem do you have right now that you think is a big problem? In other words, what is the biggest personal problem which may be causing you some difficulty?" This is the first question that these young people were asked. Table 1-1 contains a summary, by category, of their responses. The interested reader will, by analyzing the Table, discover a number of interesting age and sex differences. To conserve space I shall only note that for the boys the major problem area involves the school and academic difficulties. In addition there are three secondary areas: Interpersonal Problems, Family Problems (usually with both parents), and Financial Problems. The girls present a somewhat different picture. Their problems, with about the same frequency, can be found in three major areas: the School, the Interpersonal, and

TABLE 1-1

PERCENTAGES OF MALES AND FEMALES WHO IDENTIFY VARIOUS PERSONAL PROBLEMS

Age	Sex	School	Inter-Personal	Matur-ity	Emo-tions	Work	Sports Rec.	Health	Ethi-cal	Fam-ily	Hab-its	Fi-nances	Un-classi-fiable	No An-swer	No Prob-lem	N
10	M	20	22	0	0	1	12	8	1	6	0	6	11	5	6	80
	F	38	11	2	3	1	8	2	0	19	0	1	11	1	1	88
11	M	28	14	0	1	1	7	6	1	12	0	5	8	7	8	263
	F	20	20	4	3	1	4	5	2	21	0	3	9	3	3	268
12	M	32	12	0	2	2	6	2	1	16	0	6	9	4	7	328
	F	20	18	3	3	1	4	6	1	26	0	2	7	3	4	287
13	M	38	13	3	1	2	1	3	0	12	1	5	9	6	2	251
	F	23	29	3	1	1	0	4	0	19	0	2	6	5	6	213
14	M	45	12	2	2	4	3	0	0	6	0	7	7	5	6	176
	F	20	22	4	5	0	2	6	3	22	0	2	4	1	8	170
15	M	39	15	2	1	8	2	3	1	6	1	11	7	2	2	190
	F	17	27	3	3	4	1	3	2	24	0	5	5	2	3	238
16	M	34	9	1	1	12	5	1	0	8	0	16	5	5	2	237
	F	22	15	1	3	9	0	2	4	24	0	8	5	3	2	207
17	M	33	6	2	3	13	3	1	2	7	0	15	9	4	1	280
	F	23	15	2	3	17	1	1	3	18	0	6	5	4	1	220
18	M	39	8	3	2	14	3	0	1	4	0	14	7	2	2	196
	F	27	12	3	9	10	0	2	2	14	0	4	9	4	2	127
19	M	38	8	4	10	10	0	4	0	4	0	10	2	6	4	50
	F	30	8	2	8	12	0	3	13	8	0	7	3	5	0	60
Total	M	34	11	2	2	6	4	2	1	10	0	10	8	4	4	2051
	F	22	19	3	4	5	2	4	2	21	0	4	6	3	3	1878

the Family (with the major difficulties involving the mother although, in addition, they exceeded the boys in problems which mentioned both parents). In order that the categories used will be more meaningful, I shall list them with a few explanatory comments as to the types of problems each category contains.

1. School—academic difficulties, extremely few negative comments about teachers
2. Interpersonal—getting along with one's peer group and other people
3. Maturity—recognition by others (mostly parents) and one's self
4. Emotions—lack of understanding one's emotions, moodiness, fluctuations
5. Work—finding a job, deciding upon a vocation
6. Sports and Recreation—athletics, dancing, driving, use of leisure time
7. Health—skin blemishes, weight problems, mental and physical health problems of self and family
8. Ethical—moral problems in dating behavior, religion (girls)
9. Family—parents, siblings
10. Habits—smoking, drinking
11. Finances—personal financial needs, family, college
12. Unclassifiable—very infrequent, e.g., "I robbed a store last night."
13. No Answer—did not give an answer
14. No Problem—stated that he or she had no problem, frequently apologetically

No effort was made to ascertain the severity of these problems so, again, it is best to view them as *concerns* of young people. Bearing this in mind, it is apparent that one of our major concerns as adults should be with the role of educational institutions in adolescent development. This is quite obviously not a simple issue; nor is it independent of other issues such as the responsibility of the home and the needs of society. It further presupposes that our schools have the information they need to understand and prepare the adolescent for his role in an adult world, e.g., an understanding of how thinking develops, how to provide for the creative individual, and to what degree can the environment modify or stimulate genetic potential? All of these questions are tied into larger issues concerning the values of society. What can or should the individual reasonably expect from life? What are our rights and re-sponsibilities as citizens? How does one decide on a vocation and what effect will our future industrial society have on limiting or expanding occupational opportunities? How should the educational institution cope with problems such as these?

As parents, teachers, and adults we must consider where our respon-sibilities reside: in the home, in the school, or in our churches. How do each of these institutions operate in such areas as sex education, the formation of values and education for citizenship? Let me quickly mention that this book will not answer all of these questions or even make an attempt to answer many of them. I am raising them to set the stage for the reader; a stage on which each of us will be a player at some point in our lives. I am hoping that if we consider these problems before the curtain goes up, we will give a more acceptable perform-ance for our respective audiences.

INTERNATIONAL AND DOMESTIC ISSUES

We have another important area to consider. In our world today, we can no longer afford the luxury of insulating and isolating ourselves in our own little communities. We are now, whether we like it or not, a world community. The fantastic advances in transportation and com-munication have stretched man's handshake to the four corners of the world; and, if we wish to keep that hand open in friendliness, rather than in a clenched fist, our young people will need wisdom in their roles as world citizens.

Are our young people aware of the problems they will one day face within this larger perspective? To find at least a partial answer to this question, I asked the young people we have been discussing: "What do you consider to be the major problem of your country?" It was con-venient to classify their responses on the *International* and *Domestic* levels. With respect to the international identifications of these youth, it is likely that many of the categories found in Table 1-2 could have been included under one heading, viz., Russia. It is also probable that the headings will have to be re-cast from time to time (e.g., Korea, China, Vietnam, Cuba, Africa, South America, etc.). In any case, these young people seemed to be remarkably aware of what was going on in their world. Examining Table 1-3 convinces me that these adolescents are correspondingly aware of the domestic issues perplexing their elders. There is at least one age trend which is worth reporting briefly.

TABLE 1-2

PERCENTAGE OF MALES AND FEMALES WHO IDENTIFY INTERNATIONAL PROBLEMS AS BEING
THE MAJOR CONCERN OF THEIR COUNTRY

Age	Sex	Russia & War	Disarmament	Communism	Cold War	Keeping Peace	Defense	Foreign Policies	Space Program	% Total N	Total N
10	M	52	01	02	00	02	00	10	12	81	80
	F	49	00	02	00	03	00	14	06	74	88
11	M	44	02	02	03	06	01	07	12	75	263
	F	50	01	03	01	03	01	11	04	74	268
12	M	41	01	04	02	03	01	06	07	65	328
	F	41	02	02	01	03	01	04	04	58	287
13	M	48	01	03	02	08	00	06	06	73	251
	F	44	00	05	01	05	00	07	05	67	213
14	M	36	01	02	01	06	02	07	07	62	176
	F	40	01	01	01	01	00	08	02	58	170
15	M	37	02	04	02	06	01	07	04	62	190
	F	34	00	02	01	08	00	08	06	60	238
16	M	23	02	09	02	09	01	08	06	60	237
	F	30	00	06	00	11	00	09	05	62	207
17	M	26	01	06	02	08	02	09	04	59	280
	F	30	01	06	01	12	01	10	02	63	220
18	M	22	01	10	05	09	05	10	00	63	196
	F	29	03	04	02	06	02	09	02	56	127
19	M	22	02	00	04	06	06	14	02	56	50
	F	27	00	02	00	18	00	23	00	70	60
Total %	M	36	01	05	02	06	02	08	06	66	2051
	F	38	01	03	01	07	01	09	04	63	1878

TABLE 1-3

PERCENTAGE OF MALES AND FEMALES WHO IDENTIFY DOMESTIC PROBLEMS AS BEING THE MAJOR CONCERN OF THEIR COUNTRY

Age	Sex	Racial	Edu-cation	Eco-nomic	Popu-lation	Juv. Delin.	Health	Crime	Moral & Rel.	% Total N	% No Ans. Unclass.	Total N
10	M	01	00	04	00	01	00	00	00	06	12	80
	F	00	01	07	01	03	02	04	01	20	06	88
11	M	02	01	07	01	03	00	00	00	14	11	263
	F	03	02	06	01	05	01	02	00	20	06	268
12	M	02	04	10	02	02	01	01	01	22	12	328
	F	05	04	10	04	06	01	01	01	31	11	287
13	M	04	03	07	01	02	02	01	02	20	07	251
	F	06	03	05	01	05	01	00	01	23	10	213
14	M	06	04	06	01	06	01	02	00	26	12	176
	F	16	04	05	00	07	00	02	01	34	09	170
15	M	10	05	05	01	02	00	04	02	28	10	190
	F	15	02	05	01	06	00	03	01	32	08	238
16	M	10	03	06	02	02	00	01	01	26	13	237
	F	16	03	07	00	03	00	02	02	33	05	207
17	M	08	03	05	02	04	00	02	04	28	14	280
	F	12	03	04	00	02	00	01	03	26	11	220
18	M	08	06	06	01	00	00	02	05	27	10	196
	F	13	06	05	00	01	00	02	04	30	14	127
19	M	10	06	08	00	04	00	04	00	32	12	50
	F	10	07	02	00	02	00	02	03	25	05	60
Total %	M	06	04	06	01	03	00	02	02	23	11	2051
	F	10	03	06	01	04	00	02	02	28	09	1878

Fifty per cent of the ten year olds viewed "Russia and War" as the major problem of their country. By age 19, this percentage has fallen to 25. There is a somewhat similar increase (with age) of emphasis on domestic difficulties, and girls are a little more involved with this area than are boys. It would be interesting to speculate on the reason (and the desirability) for this increasing focus on the domestic scene. I shall refrain from prolonging this introductory chapter by doing so and permit the reader to make his own "guesstimates."

If we disregard age and sex, approximately two thirds of the total group focused on the international scene and one fourth on the domestic scene. The important observation is, however, that young people of today are not blind with respect to the issues with which responsible citizens *should be concerned.* Having demonstrated that they are aware of these issues, I have not demonstrated the depth or intensity of their concern; nor do we know, at this point, their relative numbers in the general population of emerging adults. Where and how do we train these citizens in the assumption of their responsible roles in society? Or, do we continue to lock them out of the adult world by the age-old ploy of throwing their youth into their faces as an excuse for not listening? Ignoring these issues will not resolve them.

SUMMARY

In this introductory chapter, I have given you some of my thinking as I considered what chapters could profitably be included within this book. My primary goal was to include discussions of topics which would increase the reader's understanding of adolescence and adolescent behavior. I have thoroughly enjoyed the task I have set for myself. Lacunae in my own knowledge have been filled in by the chapter authors and I sincerely hope that the reader will have the same experience. It is quite possible that you will find certain chapters more important from your respective needs and viewpoints. Each author was encouraged to reflect his own opinions if he so desired. If the subject of the chapter needed little documentation (in other words, the literature is well known) less documentation has been used than in other chapters. If, when you have finished reading this book, you find that you have increased your understanding of adolescence, the book will have been partially successful. If, you find that you are able to translate this understanding in a positive sense into your contacts with adolescents, the book will have been entirely successful.

REFERENCES

Adams, J. F. Adolescent opinion on national problems. *Personnel and Guidance Journal,* 1963, *42,* 397–400.

Adams, J. F. Adolescent personal problems as a function of age and sex. *Journal of Genetic Psychology,* 1964, *104,* 207–214.

Adams, J. F. Adolescents' identification of personal and national problems. *Adolescence,* 1966, *1,* 240–250.

CHAPTER 2

The Transition from Childhood to Adolescence

Ruth Strang *

THE IMAGE OF THE CHILD AT THE THRESHOLD OF ADOLESCENCE, WITH ONE hand stretched toward childhood and the other toward adulthood, is a psychologically accurate symbol of this transitional period. It is a time of mixed feelings. As one fourteen-year-old boy described it:

> I don't know whether I like being a teenager or not. I get more allowance, and I can spend it my own way, instead of my mother telling me what to spend it on. I can go to more dances and parties and get to bed later than I used to. My mother fusses over me less as to what I should wear and who should be my friends, etc. I can go to more places without my mother.
>
> There aren't many disadvantages, but some of them are: I get more chores to do and I get lots more homework, so much in fact that I don't have time to go many places. I don't get into movies for half price any more.
>
> I think after all this is a nice age to be, even though I am looking forward to growing past this age.

Teachers and parents should understand the psychology of "the overlapping situation" in which preadolescents find themselves. While desiring to be fully independent and competent, they are, at moments, still in love with the security and irresponsibility of the very young. It

*RUTH STRANG is Professor Emeritus of the Teachers College of Columbia University. She is presently a Professor of Education at the University of Arizona. Her well-known books include: *The Adolescent Views Himself; An Introduction to Child Study; The Role of the Teacher in Personnel Work; The Improvement of Reading; Diagnostic Teaching of Reading;* and *Helping Your Child Develop His Potentialities*. Dr. Strang has also written many articles on child and adolescent psychology, mental health, and the gifted.

is not without regret and anxiety that they see the doors of childhood closing forever.

The shift from childhood to adolescence is one of the chief transitional stages in human development: the individual is faced with the task of putting away childish things and taking on an adult role.

One thing that complicates this shifting of roles is the ambiguous attitude that adults take toward children who are going through this in-between period. One moment they tell the child that he is too young to drive the car, and at the next, that he is too old to engage in childish antics. Misled by the physical maturity of many preadolescents, adults expect a corresponding social maturity. If their role were more clearly structured for themselves, their parents, and their friends, adolescents would be less vacillating in their behavior.

The transition from childhood to adulthood is most difficult in societies in which the status of the adolescent is undefined. Linton (1945, pp. 67–68) has admirably described this situation:

> In societies which recognize adolescents as a distinct category and ascribe to them activities suited to their condition, the period passes with little or no stress, and the transition from the roles of childhood to those of adult life is accomplished with little shock to the personality. Societies which choose to ignore the particular qualities of adolescence may elect to deal with the situation in either of two ways. They may extend the child category, with its ascribed attitudes and patterns of overt behavior, upward to include adolescents, or they may project the adult category downward to include them. In either case the adolescent becomes a problem for himself and for others. . . . Perhaps the thing worse than either of these methods is to do as we do and leave the social role of adolescents in doubt.

Being a member of a minority culture or a disadvantaged socioeconomic group can further complicate the problem. The following statement was written by a gifted girl shuttling between two cultures, and conscious also of the conflicting values of two generations:

> I am one of the new generation that is living under the threat of the Atomic Bomb—one of the post-war generation who is supposed to try and relieve the world of the problems it formed before I was born. Being in the higher section of my class scholastically and socially, I am a preordained leader of others.
>
> Being socially and scholastically higher than those of my race in this region, I find myself a loner. Other people don't seem to take

interest in my interests, nor do I show interest in theirs. For example, I am alone in enthusiasm for reading books, listening to semi-classical and classical music, preferring creative dancing to the latest steps others are doing.

Being an only child, I do not like to be alone, so I try to make friends in everything I do.

Other people of my race, I have heard, think of me as a "snob," "stuck up," "unsociable." To them, maybe I am, but if I were to venture into their world I would find myself at a complete loss.

This girl achieved a personal identity that was commensurate with her ability by resisting the cultural pressure to conform to the standards of her group.

It should be noted that the transition from childhood to adolescence is not in all cases a period of "storm and stress." Whether or not a particular individual finds it so depends upon (1) the demands and expectations of his environment, (2) the competencies that he has acquired, and (3) his attitude toward restrictions and frustrations. The transition into maturity should be comparatively comfortable and uncomplicated if the individual (1) has acquired the skills he needs to cope with the new experiences; (2) is introduced to these new experiences gradually; (3) is given as much responsibility as he is ready to assume at a given time; and (4) finds that his interests and needs are recognized, accepted, and met by adults. He faces the special problems created by physical changes and their accompanying emotional and social demands with a determination to solve them.

THE TRANSITION PERIOD DEFINED

Puberty is that time in the life cycle when the reproductive organs have developed sufficiently for the individual to become capable of reproducing his kind. The advent of puberty in girls is generally dated at the first menstruation, although its approach is heralded by a spurt in growth, a gradual change in figure—widening of the pelvis and development of the breasts—and the appearance of pubic hair. It is more difficult to date the exact arrival of puberty in boys. As Garrison discusses the physiological development in adolescence within a later chapter, I shall not comment further on these aspects.

The central tendency is for puberty to occur between the twelfth and the fifteenth years; it may occur anywhere from the ninth to the seventeenth years in girls, and one to two years later in boys. Most studies of boys have reported that the average for boys is somewhere between 13 and 16 years.

Over the past 100 years, the age of puberty has been showing a tendency to occur earlier. "The average age for menarche has dropped from seventeen to thirteen in the last one hundred years or so, and is still falling" (Lieberman, 1966, p. 45). This trend may have important implications for education, as well as a significant bearing on the social problems of adolescents.

The exact time at which a given child becomes pubescent is a matter of individual growth; it is affected by both internal and external factors. For example, low socioeconomic status, which frequently involves poor nutrition, illness, and an unfavorable environment, has been found to be associated with retardation of menarche.

The generally recognized instability of this transitional period is a function of both internal and external factors. The adolescent's desires are often intense but transient; his social and psychological fields are indefinite, uncharted, and unclear. This sense of uncertainty is well described in the following composition:

> Grownups say they remember how it was to be growing up; that they understand our problems. I disagree, as they forget the unpleasant memories; only someone who is going through the process knows what it is like to be growing up.
>
> Growing up is a time of confusion and uncertainty. You begin to question principles that you had always considered concrete fact. Ideas, all conflicting, pour in from all directions—parents, teachers, adult and teenage friends, movies, radio, TV, books, etc. You decide you are for one thing, then someone talks you into the opposite side. Adults are confused, too, but they have had time to form their opinions and standards, whereas we teenagers are floundering in a sea of indecision.
>
> While growing up, everything seems to be pressing down on you. Teachers want homework, parents want work around the house, friends want you to go here and there with them. Life seems so short and so fast. There is no time for the things you really want to do.
>
> During this period, there are many disappointments which will seem silly and trivial in ten years. But to us they are very real. If you don't make the team, don't have a date, fail a test, lose a friend, don't have an invitation to a party—these things can make life miserable. When you are older, you realize that life goes on and nothing like that really matters, but now they are earth-shattering.

Although there are many compensations in growing up, I think it is a hard time, and I shall not feel badly when it is over.

PRELUDE TO PUBERTY

By the time a child arrives at puberty, he has already acquired a central orientation, a style of life, or a radix of personality that is persistent and predictive of future behavior. This complex of attitudes, traits, and abilities develops very early, "partially as a function of genetic characteristics, of physical-physiological events, and of early inter-personal experiences—they set the broad limits of the repertoire of responses favored by the organisms and are responsible for the under-lying continuity of development" (Bronson, 1966, p. 126). The two orientations that seem most influential are those that affect patterns of withdrawal-expressiveness and reactivity-placidity. If an individual's behavior changes less than might be expected in the period between childhood and preadolescence, this may be due to the fact that pre-existing behaviors are intensified rather than changed. Such traits, for example, as vulnerability, lack of confidence, emotional dependence, uncertainty, and intellectual inertia may exert an increasing influence on the adolescent's behavior. This makes the period particularly diffi-cult for the emotionally withdrawn child.

The way children have been brought up during the 13 or more years prior to puberty and the external pressures to which they are subjected at puberty largely determine the nature of their adjustment at this critical time. Children who have grown up in an atmosphere of un-conditional permissiveness cannot be expected to have learned to take responsibility, to do work that must be done, or to abide by reasonable rules and regulations.

Children who have never learned in elementary school to love read-ing, to be intellectually curious, cannot be expected to have any qualms about cheating to get the marks that will "get them ahead," with a minimum of wisdom in their heads.

Children who have not developed individuality or originality of thought, action, and appearance must be expected to conform to what-ever is popular, whether it be good, bad, or indifferent.

Children who have had no training from their earliest childhood in habits of common courtesy and consideration for others can be ex-pected to antagonize their elders and widen the gap between the two generations.

Children whose parents have encouraged them to hold unrealistic aspirations, and whose teachers have neglected to help them appraise their abilities and achievements with reference to the abilities and achievements of others, can be expected to suffer a period of intense disillusionment.

Children whose parents and teachers are overprotective may be prevented from gaining independence and self-reliance.

Children who have been deprived of opportunities to make their own decisions and to select their own acquaintances may have serious difficulty in meeting the demands of approaching adulthood, leaving behind their childish ways, and moving on to increasing maturity. Opportunities for voluntary and deliberate choice contribute to maturity. The practice of limiting children's choices or giving them opportunities for choice without making sure that they have an adequate basis of knowledge and effective habits of thinking makes it more difficult for them to attain maturity. A 14-year-old girl appreciated the reasonable freedom she had been given in making decisions:

"I think that parents try to interfere with their children's problems too often. I think teenagers should try to settle their own problems unless it is absolutely necessary or if the teenager asks advice of the parent. I do not mean that every person is capable of being treated that way, but if a child thinks that he should be, and a mother knows that she can depend upon her son or daughter, she should let her child stand on his own two feet. It will help the teenager make important decisions later on in life. It will also place a good sense of responsibility with the person.

Another problem that often arises is that of dating. From my own experience I know that my mother thinks that I am too young to date, but she does let me go out occasionally (once a week or once every two weeks) depending on where I want to go. I do not mind it because I feel my mother knows more about these things than I do and I have learned to take her decision as final. Some people tell me that they think my mother is old-fashioned but I don't think it is true. When a mother treats a child the way my mother treats me, it is because she is interested and that she is looking out for my welfare."

If children have learned during childhood to accept and face both minor and major difficulties, they will be equipped to handle the special problems of growing up. They will welcome responsibility that they recognize as worthwhile and important. One boy said, during a flood, "I just love emergencies." In this emergency he had experienced the socializing effect that comes from serving, participating, and belonging.

The idea that freedom entails responsibility was well expressed by another 14-year-old girl:

"Growing up has many meanings to most people my age. To me, the most significant is being trusted by both my friends and my parents. For instance, at the age of fourteen, I would like my parents to have enough trust and faith in me and my intelligence to let me travel alone, like I did this summer. It was a wonderful feeling to be alone without mother or father watching over me all the time. I knew, too, that they were not sitting home worrying about me and regretting every minute that I was apart from them for fear I would meet with an accident.

Another important part of growing up is having many responsibilities, which my mother and father feel I can handle without too many difficulties. For instance, I am given two allowances. One is the weekly allowance which I may spend for my own needs even if I don't spend it wisely. Therefore, I have the feeling that mother and father believe I am mature enough to spend my money as I see fit, although sometimes my mother will give me advice on the subject. My second allowance is for clothing. I am allowed a certain sum of money a month to spend on clothes with my mother's guidance. Being able to handle a certain amount of money which my father works hard for gives me a wonderful feeling of growing up.

Another very important part of growing up to me is the increasing privacy which I am allowed at home. When I was younger, the door to my room was always kept open. On the other hand, now I am permitted to close my door and I am not questioned whether I did, or did not, do my homework. Although I do not think it is necessary to shut my door at any time, it is wonderful to know that I do have that privacy.

Thus I am very happy that my parents encourage my wish to be independent and take responsibility."

The child's way of dealing with major adolescent problems is affected not only by his parents' way of dealing with him and his problems of growing up, but also by their behavior toward each other. If his childhood experiences have convinced him that marriage is nothing more than a daily cat-and-dog fight, he will not look forward to marriage as a relationship of mutual love and respect. Moreover, if he receives all his ideas about sex from the mass media of communication, he will not know that extramarital relations are, in most cases, tawdry and unsatisfactory, or that they can destroy the mutual trust and wholeness that must prevail between husband and wife. Staton's chapter on sex education develops this theme further.

If a boy or girl approaches puberty lacking the security that arises from affectionate relations with parents, teachers, and friends, he will have difficulty in relating himself to others during adolescence. Childhood behavior should be guided by love rather than hate—except for hatred of things that are cruel and mean; this gives the child a firm foundation for the next stage of development. One of Anatole France's (1918, p. 198) characters summed up the responsibility of education in a simple sentence about his plans for his young ward: "I would make lovable to her everything I would wish her to love."

Our unconcern with what enters the minds of children is in marked contrast with Plato's educational philosophy. The young child is so impressionable that Plato would "establish a censorship of the writers of fiction" since "anything that he receives into his mind is likely to become indelible and unalterable: and therefore it is most important that the talks which the young first hear should be models of virtuous thoughts." Contrast this idea with our practice of letting children expose themselves to radio and TV programs. No one knows what subtle conditioning is going on in the mind of the elementary child who spends, on the average, 26 hours a week watching TV. When one mother asked her little boy what he had been watching, he replied nonchalantly, "Just murder." Values are a long time a-growing. The individual who does not acquire sound values in childhood will lack a sense of direction when he approaches the unmarked wilderness of conflicting adolescent behavior.

PERPLEXITIES IN THE PRESENT

During the transition to adolescence, children are confronted by numerous perplexities. Complications are caused by (1) radical physiological and physical changes; (2) more difficult academic requirements; (3) new social situations; and (4) conflicts between inner urges and environmental demands.

The tasks that the child must accomplish at puberty are probably thrust on him more abruptly than the tasks of any other transitional period. His expectations of himself can hardly keep pace with the demands of his environment. Nor is status clear. By some people he is treated as a child; by others, as an adult. Even this situation is subject to fluctuation: any adult may suddenly switch from one mode of treatment to the other, perhaps misled by the discrepancy between his physical and his social development.

Physical and Physiological Changes

Following a period of slow growth, children show a spurt of rapid growth about six months prior to puberty. Until about ten years of age, boys tend to be taller than girls. Between the ages of eleven and fourteen, girls tend to forge ahead. However, individual differences are concealed in average figures. Individuals whose growth is extremely accelerated or extremely retarded are the ones most likely to experience difficulties in adjustment. The growth spurt that precedes puberty may have mixed effects, depending upon its timing.

Boys, especially those who lag behind their peers, may be subject to particular tensions, worries, and insecurities. It should be comforting to these late maturers to know that, although they are not growing as fast as other boys, they may continue to grow over a longer period. There appears to be no relation between final height and rapidity of growth during this period. With both height and weight, there are great individual differences.

Individual differences in the advent of puberty are due to both heredity and to environmental conditions (see Nichols' chapter).

Personality differences are associated with the age at which one matures. "The boy whose pubescence came late is active and exploring with evidence of compensatory adaptations. In adulthood, he is insightful, independent, and impulsive . . . the late maturer has the ability to cope—with humor, with tolerance of ambiguity and of individual idiosyncrasies, with perceptiveness, and with playfulness in the service of the ego. However, this adaptability is accompanied by a certain fearfulness and vulnerability to threat" (Jones, 1965, pp. 899, 908).

The early maturing boy, who rapidly grows taller and heavier, has assets that are highly valued by the peer culture. He usually has an advantage in sports, and often in social status with his peers. "In adulthood the same success pattern continues. He is poised, responsible, achieving in conformity with society's expectations" (Jones, 1965, p. 899).

Jones' (1944) developmental study of a middle-class, urban, Western sample indicates the complexity of personal and social interactions that affect individual development.

The early maturing girl often has more serious problems of adjustment than the late maturing girl. In a study of 13-year-old girls (Stone and Barker, 1939), those who had menstruated were found to be more mature in many ways than those who had not. They were more interested in boys, had older friends, were more concerned with clothes and personal appearance, and were less eager to engage in vigorous games and activities than those who had not passed puberty.

> Prestige and the traits significantly correlated with prestige were most frequently ascribed to sixth grade girls who were "prepuberal" while in all three junior high school grades girls who were physically accelerated received the preponderance of favorable reputation scores. A discrepancy between rate of developmental change and rate of change in prestige-leading evaluations during adolescence was noted and was interpreted in terms of the different meaning which early and late development has for girls at different times during adolescence (Faust, 1960, p. 183).

The physical and physiological changes that occur during puberty are often accompanied by other problems. Periods of rapid and uneven growth are frequently marked by physical awkwardness and embarrassment in social situations. Tensions also arise from sexual maturation; growth of the breasts, and the psychic and physiological effects of menstruation may produce uncomfortable self-consciousness and a tendency to withdraw. There are also special physical disabilities that afflict many youngsters during this period—more rapid tooth decay, poor posture, and skin eruptions.

Physical and health education that helps girls to become more attractive and graceful, and boys to become skillful in the popular sports, helps to relieve some of the tensions felt by adolescents. It plays a useful part in educating their emotions. It is good social education, too: one's physical appearance evokes either favorable or unfavorable responses from other people. In one school for multiple-handicapped children special attention is given to physical appearance. Emphasis on good posture, attractive clothes, and simple but effective grooming helps to improve the self-concept of these children and increases their self-confidence. For girls the three chief motives for personal appearance seem to be (1) to look more grown up, (2) to look attractive to boys, and (3) not to look different from other girls.

For boys, athletic skills, good sportsmanship, and strength contribute to social acceptance. H. E. Jones (1944) noted that boys are twice as strong at eleven as they are at six, and that their manual strength increased 100 per cent between the ages of eleven and sixteen. At age 13 they show a marked advance both in weight and in strength of grip. This increase may be due in part to their greater physical activity at this age. Physiological maturity seems to parallel these increases in strength and motor performance.

For many young teenagers the physical aspects of recreation are not so important as the social. Recreation that gives them opportunities to assume healthy leadership and sets them good examples of sportsmanship has many values: it offers a means of temporary escape, an opportunity to express suppressed feelings, and a chance to develop useful social attributes through many experiences in cooperation.

Sexual maturation may be both welcomed and feared; which emotion predominates depends largely on the family's attitude toward the process and the degree to which the child understands its physiological aspects. Children taking their first course in biology often are disappointed when they get no further than the earthworm or when the study of the reproductive system is nervously and hastily passed over in the last two periods. Not only do the youngsters feel they have been left ignorant; they may also get the impression that acquiring sexual maturity is an anxiety-arousing process.

Scholastic Demands and Cognitive Development

Adjustment to the more difficult academic requirements of the junior high school is still a central problem for some youngsters. Here, more than in the other major aspects of adolescence, previous achievement—especially proficiency in handling the tools of learning—determines one's success, not only academically but in other relationships as well. After Sputnik pointed up the deficiencies in American education, academic requirements in many schools became more severe, and even the higher IQ group quickly began to complain about the burden of

excessive homework. Their complaints may well stem from the un-
stimulating nature of most assignments, the failure of teachers to coordinate their giving of homework, or the comparatively greater appeal
of extra-class activities.

Pupils show their anxiety about school work when they are asked
to express their feelings about getting report cards. In compositions
written by over 500 children in the upper elementary grades and in
high school, comments such as the following were common:

> I was scared because my mother and father said, "If you get a
> bad report card all your privileges will be taken away."
>
> When the teacher says she is going to give out report cards, my
> heart goes down into my toes. I feel shaky and scared.
>
> The day my report card is to be given to me, I become very nerv-
> ous. By the time the reports are given out, my fingernails are all
> chewed up.
>
> After I read it, I get a strange feeling in my stomach, like when
> you're high on a swing. I worry about what my father and mother
> are going to do with me.
>
> My parents are a pair who want perfection.
>
> My parents didn't say a word about the A's and B's but I thought
> they'd never stop harping about the C.
>
> When my parents see it, they always expect more than what I
> receive, and I'm very disheartened, because I know I've tried tre-
> mendously hard and I'd like to have some commendation from my
> parents, which I never get.

On the other hand, some children are thankful for understanding
parents who give them the help they need:

> I do not get jittery when the reports are being given out because
> my parents are understanding, and they will help me in whatever
> subject I'm behind in.
>
> If I bring home a good report card, I get praised. If I bring home
> a bad report card, my mother and father and I sit down and figure
> out why I got a bad report card and how I could improve in my
> studies.
>
> When my report card is exceptionally good, my parents commend
> me for my good work. If it is not up to my previous marks, my
> parents never discourage me by belittling the work I have done.
> They always tell me I should do my best and that is all they expect
> of me.

Some youngsters take a very mature attitude toward report cards:

When I get my report card, I wonder if I've done my very best and tried really hard.

I have to confess it was my own fault for not studying harder.

I am glad that we get report cards; then we know whether or not we're up to standards and what subjects we need help in.

Frankly, I think the report card is a good idea. Some of the subjects I thought I was doing pretty good in on my report card I found I wasn't as good as I thought I was.

The trouble with most report cards is that they make no allowances for individual differences in mental ability, or in habits of thinking, reasoning, and learning. Nor do they explain either to pupils or parents what the marks really mean and what can be done to improve a poor record.

Individuals of the same chronological age stand at different stages of cognitive development. Some succeed in reaching a goal but are quite unaware of the method they used or the reasons why it was successful. They do not look for reasons behind their reactions; they are more interested in taking action than in thinking about an action. Others have reached the second stage: they have "a vague global intuition" about the method by which they gained certain results, but they do not try to explain it. They may discover certain relationships, but they do not look for the reasons behind them. In the next stage of their progress in logical thinking, they make increasingly more accurate formulations of relationships. Finally, they look for and analyze the reasons for the relationships and discover the laws that govern the observed facts or actions (Inhelder and Piaget, 1958). Any child who is going through this transitional period may stand at any of these stages of cognitive development.

During these years, students should also be developing the more mature habits of reading that they will need to succeed in high school and college. By observing each student and asking him to write introspective reports, the teacher can help him appraise his progress toward the following goals:

Before beginning to read a given selection, does he stop to think about his purpose in reading it and to recall what he already knows about the subject?

Does he read with the intent to apply what he learns or does he "just read"?

Does he make the right responses without being aware of the method by which he has arrived at them? (Possibly he has learned a sound method and used it so long that it has become "second nature" to him, and he is not consciously aware of it.)

Does he recognize certain clues to meaning but fail to interpret them into a pattern of comprehension?

Mature habits of reading and studying enable children to meet the more exacting scholastic demands that they are subject to in this period of multiple adjustments.

Methods of teaching play an especially important part in this transitional period. Rousseau's description of it as an "in-between period" seems very modern. We would agree that children at this age show intensification of reason and self-consciousness, an enormous amount of physical energy, and a keen curiosity—if it has not been squelched. Rousseau emphasized the discovery technique, as many modern writers have done, especially in the study of science. "He [the child] is not to learn science; he is to find out for himself." Children pay better attention when they are finding things out for themselves rather than being told by the teacher. They are also more likely to remember things they have learned through the process of discovery.

Preadolescents have many complaints about school. One boy wrote:

> I go to school because I have to. So while I'm going to school I might as well learn something. A lot of the things we do in school I don't like, but I have to do them or fail. We should have more time to rest from work. We should go places like the great Ebbets Field where the world champions play. Sometimes we get bored listening to teachers, so I think we should be able to talk for a minute or so.

In a later section, the thoughtful reader will find Elkind's more extensive discussion of cognitive development of definite interest.

New Social Situations

Social development involves moving from the complete egocentricity of the infant to the compassionate social outlook of the adult. As the circle of social contacts grows even wider, the demands of the social organization become more and more complex. In this transitional stage the child often finds himself in social situations in which he does not know "the thing to do." A ninth grade girl expressed a desire to receive this kind of guidance from her parents:

> I believe that persons my age would like to be able to talk things over with their parents. If something goes wrong or something nice happens, we would like to tell our parents.
>
> But if they don't seem interested, we find someone else to talk to, most likely our friends. And they may often give us the wrong advice.
>
> Many children need help in their homework, but their parents are always "too busy" or "too tired" and so the children take less interest in their work.
>
> Children don't like to be told what friends they can or can't have. If a parent doesn't approve of a certain friend, they shouldn't forbid their child to be friendly with him or her.

They would like guidance on dating and make-up, allowance and clothes.

With respect to heterosexual relations, there has been a shift from encouraging early "going steady" to discouraging this precocious practice. However, the social problems that used to be associated with later adolescence have moved down to the younger age group. "The unwed mothers' division of the County Court of Philadelphia reports 2,677 petitions for the support of unwanted babies were filed by unwed mothers in 1964. Junior and senior high school girls represent 40 per cent of these applicants, and 11- and 12-year-olds, still in elementary school, have become a significant group" (Sacks, 1966, p. 80).

Sex education is a part of character education. It should not be set apart from the consideration of other interpersonal relationships. Adolescent girls should know that one can keep a boy friend by sharing interests, thoughts, moods, and concerns, as well as by allowing excessive petting. According to one eminent psychologist, there is no "sex instinct"; sexual response is activated by external stimuli. In our society today preadolescents are constantly exposed to sexual stimulation in advertisements, fiction, plays, movies, TV, dancing, and recordings of the latest popular music.

Adolescents are carried away by group contagion, as in the crowds of youngsters screaming and swooning over the Beatles or whatever the latest fad may be. Many preadolescents begin petting early, before they are in a position to recognize the problems involved, on the one hand, in going steady, early marriage, or the proper rearing of children by immature parents; or, on the other hand, in divorce, promiscuity, or the disposition of illegitimate children.

As a means of developing counter interests, the psychological process known as sublimation has long been advocated. It is a sound procedure. If the peer group approves a given activity, sublimation works well. Preadolescents can be interested in sports, in esthetic dancing—the ballet or folk dancing performed expertly; many of them are willing to practice endlessly to acquire any kind of skill. Boys are interested in body-building activities. Drama clubs, social service projects, and painting or sculpture appeal to many youngsters. One gifted parent, whose 13-year-old daughter was tremendously interested in dramatics, invited the neighborhood children to put on a musical performance in her yard. The children took the major responsibility, and she served as "counselor to the cast." They constructed the scenery, made the costumes, handled the lighting with the help of an electrician father, and produced two excellent performances—"Mary Poppins" one summer, and "The Sound of Music" the next summer. All seats were sold for the six performances. Appreciative audiences reinforced the children's feelings of success. Although there were some squabbles over the time and effort demanded by rehearsals, they learned to work together and to consider the consequences of failing to fulfill their obligations. By discussing the causes and consequences of their behavior, preadolescents learn to sort out their childhood habits and keep those that will be of permanent value in the adult world.

As an intermediate milieu between the worlds of childhood and adulthood the peer culture plays an important role. Recent studies have shown the increasing influence of the peer culture in shaping adolescents' interests, attitudes, and behavior. This increasing influence is accompanied by the decreasing influence of parents and teachers, which results in a widening of the gap between adolescent society and adult society. Too often parents submissively permit the peer group to set norms for questionable activities, late hours, drinking, and excessive intimacy, instead of getting together on a community-wide basis to insist upon structured guidelines for all the young people in the community.

Today's youngsters find it easy to achieve independence from the family. They earn money of their own and spend it as they please; they no longer contribute a large part of their earnings to the family, as in the days before high wages and widespread welfare aid. The automobile permits them to get miles away in a few minutes. As one boy said, "I could be ten miles from home and my mother would have no idea of where I was or what I was doing." With both parents out of the house much of the time, either employed or socially engaged, the child receives little supervision. Since he has no necessary work to do in or around the house, he seeks other ways to spend his time. Those who feel they have been rejected at home or at school turn to the peer group for acceptance and recognition. They conform to the standards of the peer group "just to be fellows"—to be accepted.

The youngster who depends upon his peers for companionship, support, and clarification of his role in this transitional period often finds that there are conflicts between his values and beliefs and those of his friends. It is because of these value conflicts that some preadolescents turn to adults for advice and for models of mature behavior. However, if the adults are aloof or unsympathetic, the child has no recourse but to return to his peers. He needs someone to recognize and reinforce his best self—the self he will further develop in the years ahead.

Development of the Self-Image

The transition modifies, without radically changing, the self-concept that has been developing through all the experiences of childhood. The self-concept tends to be persistent and pervasive. Although self-esteem is a relatively stable dimension of the self, social-personal orientation changes. At the preadolescent and adolescent levels, Carlson (1965) found no sex differences in the level of stability of self-esteem; however, six years later the girls were significantly more socially oriented than the boys.

Nevertheless, the instability of this period, with its invitation to discard childish ways of behaving and the physical and physiological changes that it brings, offers greater possibility of change than will ever occur again. It represents an opportunity to sort out one's several selves and to become the kind of person one most wants to be. Perhaps this is why so many youngsters who have had a sense of failure during the elementary school years enter junior high school with high hopes, as did Sam:

> Sam hadn't done so well in school. It just seemed as if he couldn't learn so well as the other kids. He had "stuck" twice, in the first grade and again in the fifth. But he was going to do better when he went to the junior high school on the hill. He'd study hard and make good grades. Then he'd send his brother Ernie a letter telling him about his good work in school and Ernie would be proud of him.

With these good intentions Sam came to junior high school. . . .

For the first month Sam was excited and pleased with his new school. He ate in the cafeteria, went to assembly, and took gym twice a week. He really enjoyed gym. Larger and stronger than the other boys, he could lead in that class, and the shower afterward certainly made him feel good.

But in other respects he did not fare so well. . . . (Strang, 1953, pp. 4–5).

To take full advantage of the opportunities for change in this in-between period, parents and teachers, and the children themselves, must give attention to (1) aspects of physical development which can be capitalized on, (2) reading and study skills that will be needed to succeed in an appropriate curriculum, (3) social skills that can be learned, and (4) emotional adjustments that need to be made.

Inner Urges vs. Environmental Demands

The intensification of self-awareness that occurs during this transitional period is due partly to the suddenness with which the child is expected to assume the role of the young adult. Since he lacks the skills with which to meet his new responsibilities, he has strong feelings of inadequacy. These feelings may have the positive effect of motivating him to achieve adequacy and personal effectiveness. He wants to be accepted and to feel that he belongs in his age group. The key to success is skill—social, physical, and intellectual.

Gradually decreasing adult protection should be balanced by gradually increasing personal competence. Competence in even one area is reassuring. For instance, if a boy is successful in sports, he will be more likely to attack his social tasks with an expectation of success. If he is overprotected, he does not develop the strengths he needs to meet the more exacting tasks ahead. If, on the other hand, he does not receive whatever degree of protection and support he may still need, his feelings of insecurity may deter him from attempting an appropriate task. If he is overpersuaded by either hope or fear, he may not make the progress now that will lead to further progress later.

Nothing succeeds like observed success. The memory of previous accomplishments and consequences of his acts strongly motivates the child to tackle new, more adult-like tasks—provided adult demands and expectations are not too far beyond his present competence. Each healthy adjustment that he makes in his present situation facilitates the making of further adjustments during adolescence and adult life.

The emotional turmoils of this period gradually diminish the directness and immediacy of the child's responses. He learns to develop defenses that the simplicity of his earlier life did not demand. He may show physical evidences of emotional turmoil—general restlessness, nail-biting, frequent minor physical complaints. There are usually emotional signs as well: day-dreaming, withdrawal, excessive anxiety over mistakes, inability to concentrate, uncontrolled laughing or crying, sudden attachments to older people, extravagant expressions of emotion. Boys are likely to show off, brag, bully, violently resent authority, or become generally destructive. The individual must resolve his inner conflicts before he is accessible to learning.

In his struggle with the often contradictory demands of his own inner urges and those of his environment, the individual may behave in ways that in a more stable period, would be considered neurotic. For this reason adolescent Rorschachs must be interpreted cautiously; in fact, special norms should be developed for adolescents. Both test results and behavior should be examined in the light of environmental conditions. For example, a 14-year-old girl who was referred to a guidance clinic because "she went all to pieces in a difficult situation" was actually making a good adjustment to a family that was far more seriously disturbed than she was. In an interview she admitted, "I know it's childish to have temper tantrums, but that's the only way I can get some of the things I really need." It is important for parents and teachers to know the nature of the adjustments that a given young person feels called upon to make, and to help him discover the reasons for the recurrent mistakes that have led him to take ineffective and inappropriate action.

It seems obvious that internal disorder can only be intensified by a disorganized family life, a lack a reasonable routine in school, or a cluttered physical environment. Organization of these external factors may help the confused child to organize his thoughts. In one school the basic treatment for emotionally disturbed children was to give them the experience of following a planned daily schedule.

In this unstable period, it also helps children to have a sense of identification with family traditions or with organized groups such as the Scouts, Camp Fire, 4-H, "Y," or church clubs.

The rural child has special environmental difficulties in making the transition from childhood to adulthood. The necessity to do chores at home deprives him of group experiences and friendships. Lack of experiences in social participation makes it more difficult for him to talk easily to people with whom he has no shared experiences. Farming does not have the prestige value of many other vocations. Ignorance of city ways and fashions may be another source of embarrassment. The child who has not learned to suppress his simple and direct responses to social situations is often ridiculed by his more sophisticated urban associates. The following was written by a rural child who succeeded in making a good adjustment:

> I had lived all my life in a small rural hamlet of 800 people . . . I loved the town where I lived. I liked my neighbors, my dog. My lifelong friends lived around me. . . .
> When my father thought it best to move, I was heartbroken.
> My first few weeks in a rather crowded apartment in the city were more than difficult. I was lonely and homesick. I didn't know a soul in my new high school. I even talked to my father about finishing the school year in the little town and staying with friends there. He convinced me that this would be unwise. So I decided to try to make new friends and find new interests here.
> I soon found the young people in the city high school just as friendly as any other group. My list of friends and interests increased tremendously after a month or two.
> I joined the Y.M.C.A., took part in school affairs, got acquainted with my teachers and neighbors, and became a member of a boys' club.
> I am now a senior and I find myself completely happy and contented in my present location.

Paths to Pathology

As the period of childhood is increasingly invaded by what used to be considered adult interests, and as demoralizing influences become more widespread, serious problems become more prevalent during the preadolescent period. For example, the problem of drinking which is associated with automobile accidents, sexual indulgence, and other aspects of juvenile delinquency, has become as common in well-to-do homes as in slum areas. Preventive measures have become necessary. Preadolescents are impressed, for good or ill, by statements made by older adolescents:

I really hate the taste of liquor. The only reason I drink is that I'm too chicken not to conform. I want to be one of the crowd. That's the only reason. You feel self-conscious being the only guy who doesn't drink.

Like most kids, I started drinking out of curiosity. Now I drink to hide the pain of failure: failure in sports, in exams, failure with girls, teachers, and parents.

A more mature and gifted adolescent analyzed the situation as follows:

> Then I started observing the other people in my crowd. The more I thought about it, the surer I was that they drink, not because they really like to, but because it gave them a thrill to indulge in something they thought wrong for teenagers, and because they didn't want to feel different from the group, as I had felt. I found that teenagers who drink were not the ones who were respected. I talked it over with several of the other kids in our crowd, and I was glad to hear that they shared my views on the subject. . . . I really believe that if every person who drinks would analyze his views on the subject and find out why he does and what he gets out of it, there would be fewer cases of teenage drinking in America today (Strang, 1957, p. 446).

In *The Republic*, Plato asserted that boys were too excitable to be allowed to drink wine until they were 18 years old. The fact that our society treats teenage drinking with amused tolerance may well prove to be a major factor in the increasing prevalence of alcoholic addiction.

It seems curious that preadolescents who generally resent adult authority and control do not see how they are being exploited by a small number of adults who profit by the sale of alcoholic beverages—who spend millions of dollars on advertising that subtly associates drinking with sports, popularity, and other things prized by teenagers, to promote the sale of a product that research has shown to be detrimental both to society and to the individual. An eminent psychiatrist, Harry Stack Sullivan, has made the statement that alcohol "definitely poisons the self-system progressively . . . [and] practically all the anxiety is experienced later, retrospectively" (1953, pp. 273–274).

Although it may seem premature to bring these problems to the attention of children who have not reached puberty, it would be an advantage to establish certain points of view early, before all the other decisions and conflicts of adolescence crowd in.

The problem of drug addiction is also moving down to the pre-adolescent age group. They are an easy prey for drug peddlers and older addicts. The ready availability of the drugs and the desire of this age group to identify with an older and daringly antisocial element combine to reinforce individual susceptibility.

Juvenile delinquency is also increasing among early teenagers. In fact, many adolescent offenders trace their delinquent tendencies to childhood experiences that occurred when they were seven or eight years of age.

THOUGHTS AND FEARS OF THE FUTURE

In general, youngsters express a more optimistic view of growing up at preadolescence than they do four years later. They tend to approach adolescence eagerly, as an opportunity to be free from many restrictions; they often ignore the responsibilities that freedom entails. They see only the advantages: being able to select and buy one's own clothes, drive a car, stay out late at night, go places alone. In pleading for more privileges, one youngster said, "But Mother, you must remember, I am now an adolescent."

However, the developmental tasks of adolescence still lurk as dim and sometimes threatening shapes beyond the portals of the present. These tasks have been well described by many writers and will be discussed more fully in later chapters (e.g., the chapter by Beller on theories of adolescence development) of this book. At the beginning of the twentieth century, G. Stanley Hall described the adolescent's four major problems as self-realization, sex channelization, social reformation, and a search for God or cosmic meaning. In 1928, Leta S. Hollingworth mentioned four adolescent tasks or problems, whose importance subsequent research has confirmed—each with a modern twist: gaining independence from the family, establishing heterosexual relationships, choosing and preparing for a vocation, and developing a philosophy of life. In 1952, Havighurst added several others: developing physical competence, achieving identity, achieving scholastic success, making sound educational plans, and developing socially responsible behavior. Most of these goals were mentioned by a ninth-grade boy in an essay on "How It Feels to Be Growing Up":

As I grow up, I notice that gradually I am having more responsibility placed upon me. People watch what I do and how I react to certain circumstances. This in a way is good because it keeps me aware of every move I make.

I also notice that at home my parents are not as strict as they used to be to me, and they also give me many more freedoms than any boy my age. They let me drive the car, they let me go on dates any night over the weekend, and they also place responsibilities upon me.

I'm in charge of the house when they're away; I'm in charge of my brothers when they're not around, and they talk to me as if I were an equal.

Boys of my age like to be treated as grownups, but many of them don't act mature enough to merit that treatment.

When a boy reaches his teens, he doesn't like to be led around by his mother's apron strings, and he wants freedom and likes to feel self-dependent.

It feels good when you can go to your parents and tell them that you are going out with a girl on Saturday night and they say allright and don't stop to say no or question you.

All and all it feels great to be growing up.

In complete contrast with this optimistic statement is that of a girl who clearly feels unsure of herself:

I know I have very little self-confidence and this has handicapped me in several ways. Even now in high school I am afraid to go over to talk to a group of girls because I am afraid I am not wanted.

I am very dependent upon my mother, and I think this is partly because I am an only child and partly because my mother does not give me enough responsibilities. I have always found it very hard to make decisions for myself. I especially remember how upset I was in my last term of public school because I did not know which high school to go to. I greatly feared a wrong decision.

But my uncertainty did not stop when I entered high school, for then I found I had to make even more decisions for myself. I am still unsure of my future, and I do not know whether I want to go to college or business school.

My parents have always said that I think too much about myself, and I know this is true. I know my faults and the things that trouble me, but I find it hard sometimes to iron out my disturbances.

A relatively new kind of insecurity is that which derives from an adult society of broken homes and unstable vocational fields and from a war-threatened world. Its result may be to produce a vast apathy toward things of importance and a vast enthusiasm for such trivia as each new style of dress, new dance, or new song. This situation can be combated only by courage and commitment. It requires confidence in one's power to think critically, to observe accurately, and to make or withhold judgments.

Children who have already arrived at certain values are likely to be committed to these values. Children on the threshold of adolescence can recognize that cruelty and destructive behavior are wrong, while behavior that strengthens one's own personality or that of others is right.

The modern emphasis is not on formulating a verbal philosophy of life but on achieving a sense of identity, an accurate self-concept and a commitment to certain values. In a later chapter, Eisenman gives these topics more intensive consideration.

In essays written spontaneously and anonymously, preadolescents expressed a wide range of attitudes toward themselves—from complete rejection to excessive self-satisfaction:

> I'm good for nothing.
> No one cares what happens to me.
> I feel I'm not really as good as I think I am.
> I feel all confused; anything I do for someone doesn't seem to be right.
> I'm not important to other people, but I am important to myself.
> I am a person who lives in dreams of what I want to be, but my grades won't get me there.
> I feel I'm not important right now, but I guess I will be when I get a little older.
> I feel I can do just as well as the other fellows.
> I like myself. I like the way I'm built.
> I can do what anyone else does—or better.
> I feel that I and all other teenagers in the world are very important, because we will be running the world in the future (Strang, 1964, p. 28).

Orientation toward a specific vocation may be premature at this point. The world of work is changing too rapidly for long-term predictions and, besides, the preadolescent has his hands full with other tasks. A general orientation to the world and a general appreciation of its significance are sufficient to give him the sense of direction he needs with respect to his immediate educational plans. Among several groups of girls, a common pattern of future planning includes spending two or four years as a secretary, nurse, telephone operator, etc.; then marrying and having a family. However, many girls are now skipping the intermediate job and getting married as soon as possible.

THE ROLE OF ADULTS

What can adults do to assist young teenagers in this growing-up process? There are three possible courses of action that adults can take:

1. Withdraw from the youngsters and their peer groups; leave them alone; let them make their own decisions regardless of their degree of competence, experience, and knowledge; let them learn from their failures. This is the extremely permissive attitude.

2. Insist upon their conforming to adult rules and standards; exercise a strict, authoritative control. This is the autocratic approach.

3. Try to understand the bewildering desires, demands, and expectations with which they are confronted and guide them, through and within the substructure, in reaching toward maturity.

The role of the adult is to:

- let them assume responsibility in their own way and at their own speed.
- be present at their meetings and give suggestions about how they can work harmoniously and successfully as a group.
- be ready to help when they ask for help. The presence of an adult at their meetings, in the role of counselor rather than a director, gives them a sense of security. They are often glad to have an excuse not to follow the extreme dictates of certain members.

Many young people are convinced that their parents do not understand much about them, especially the fact that they *are* growing up. A 14-year-old boy was quite emphatic about this; he suggested an explanation:

> Parents, it seems to us, worry too much about our welfare. But that is simply because they are under a false impression. We are grown up long before they have a chance to realize it. The children

today are more mature; therefore, they tend to feel independent. Of course, I am referring to children (or young people—I like that name better) as a whole. There are many exceptions to this rule, the majority of which consists of very sheltered children, or introverts. For my part, I think that this independent feeling, this state of being mature, should be recognized by parents and also accepted. For the world today is different than the world in which our parents lived. Everything is done faster and more efficiently. Therefore, is it not common sense that eventually growth too would increase in speed? The secret of growing up lies in one's surroundings.

Adults should not abdicate their responsibility for setting standards. They should be ready to point out better ways than the young people themselves have arrived at. For example, with respect to obscene words, it is often enough to say, "People don't like that word very much; this is the word most people use." Use of language is partly a matter of consideration for other people. It is the duty of parents to provide their children with a respectable and acceptable vocabulary, and to suggest substitutes for foul language used as a means of relieving tension or aggression.

"Actions speak louder than words." Adolescent boys especially prize integrity, trustworthiness, and forthrightness; they look for these qualities in their parents. They resent any adults who are "phonies." They are confused by vacillating parents or teachers. They look for leaders who have a maturely evolved viewpoint.

The effectiveness of any guidance depends largely on personal relationships. Some children do not accept their parents' values, often because of unsatisfactory personal relations. Rebellion of this sort is usually partly due to a breakdown in communications. While they resent attempts to pry into what they regard as their private lives, children want their parents to show an honest and sincere interest in their thoughts and feelings.

It is important to keep avenues of communication open. Skillfully led discussions can be most enlightening, both to parents and to young people. In any child-adult discussion group, the children are to be treated as equals. Indeed, they often bring up more pertinent and fundamental issues than do the adults, who may get bogged down in trivia and preconceived ideas. Each age group may gain more understanding of the other's points of view. Strangely enough, most children seem at ease in such a group. It is a new and healthy experience for them to be the center of attention—to have adults listen to what *they* have to say. Although it is difficult for both children and adults to see themselves objectively, both age groups can understand their own situations more clearly when they learn that someone else is faced with similar problems.

The self-sufficient, unabashed preadolescent rejects phoney guidance; guidance must contribute to the attainment of his goals. Adolescents have by now observed so many discrepancies between adult words and adult actions that they have come to distrust adult knowledge and values. They dislike having problems that are serious to them, minimized. They resent prying and incessant gratuitous advice. Quite justly they complain that adults do not listen to them or try to understand their points of view (Strang, 1957).

They appreciate adults who will explore troublesome questions with them—how to get along with certain people, how to deal with anger or other disturbing feelings. One 13-year-old girl expressed her idea of guidance in a characteristically frank and direct way: "I want guidance from adults so that I can be the kind of girl all the nice fellows like and want to date a lot. What to say and do on a date so that the boy will want to take me out again" (Strang, 1957, p. 524).

The role of the parents constantly changes between prepubescence and late adolescence. If they themselves are simultaneously going through a particularly trying time of life—overburdened by debt and worried about changing circumstances—they may be so preoccupied with their own problems that they either neglect their teenage children or make excessive demands upon them. When a child enters adolescence with unsolved emotional difficulties, he is in special need of parents who accept and stimulate him, but also furnish controls when his control system is in danger of breaking down (Strang, 1957).

The influence of teachers is second only to that of parents. These children want teachers who respect them. They want friendly teachers who understand the shifting self-perceptions that especially affect their behavior from day to day. With respect especially to school achievement, the preadolescent's concept of himself is a factor of repeated appraisals by his teachers. He sees through cajolery and resents manipulation. In his teachers he looks for sincerity, honesty, and genuine interest in all the students—no favoritism, no partiality to certain individuals, no cliques (Schmuck, 1965).

Schools are probably more to blame than parents for the underachievement of potentially able learners—children from favorable home environments who are not being intellectually challenged. In fact, certain teachers and certain classmates have a demoralizing influence on the sensitive preadolescent whose standards and values are much higher at the outset than those of his associates.

Young teenagers have a certain sense of immediacy which should be capitalized on. They can appreciate these years as a good time, on the whole, for learning as much as possible and living as fully as possible: "Yesterday is gone; forget about it. Tomorrow is ahead; don't worry too much about it. Today is here; do something!"

SUMMARY

"Time present and time past
Are both perhaps present in time future. . . ."
(Eliot, 1943, p. 3)

The past, the present, and the future are all involved in a child's transition from childhood to adolescence.

The past is constantly pressing against the portals of the present. If a child's previous experiences have made him feel insecure, he will be afraid to give up his old ways of meeting life situations. If he has stored up feelings of hostility, rejection, or inferiority from his experiences in early childhood and the elementary years, he will have difficulty in establishing new relationships. If he has accepted dependency on his parents as the easiest way out, he will have special difficulty in breaking his close ties with them. If, on the other hand, he has gradually gained an adequate degree of security and competence, he will find this transition period, as many youngsters do, exciting, exhilarating, and rewarding: he will enjoy the feeling of growing up.

But the present depends not only upon the child's given capacities and previously acquired competencies, attitudes, and values; it also depends upon the child's current circumstances and upon his ability to apply previous learnings to new situations. If he is not overwhelmed by too many demands and inappropriate expectations, he will gain confidence with each small success.

Although he is preoccupied with present problems, he is nevertheless influenced by hopes and fears of the future, uncertain as it now seems. Its very uncertainty necessitates a tentative approach. His plans must be general, but they must also be in accord with his interests, capacities, and previous achievement. For him, the present not only grows out of the past and is guided by future goals; to a large extent, it determines the future. As John Dewey said, "The best preparation for the future is to live most fully in the present."

To help preadolescents achieve a socially useful and personally satisfying future, adults should stop focusing their attention on the faults of youth. They should begin using timely suggestions, careful attention, and sincere approval to reinforce any moves young people make in the right direction. Behavior is changed by its consequences. If it is accompanied and followed by satisfaction, it tends to be repeated. This was E. L. Thorndike's "law of effect"; it is not very different from the modern psychological emphasis on "operant conditioning" and "reinforcement theory."

However, the changing of behavior is not as simple as these theories suggest; it is the preadolescent himself, with all his complex predispositions, skills, attitudes, knowledges, interests, and values who is changing himself. It is the responsibility of adults who have a respect for individual personality to provide each child the best possible conditions for different kinds of learning, and to make sure that the results are as rewarding as possible.

REFERENCES

Bronson, Wanda C. Central orientations: a study of behavior organization from childhood to adolescence, *Child Development*, 1966, 37, 125–155.

Carlson, R. Stability and changes in the adolescent's self-image. *Child Development*, 1965, 36, 659–666.

Eliot, T. S. *Four quartets.* New York: Harcourt, Brace, 1943.

Faust, Margaret S. Developmental maturity as a determinant in prestige of adolescent girls. *Child Development*, 1960, 31, 173–184.

France, A. *The crime of Sylvestre Bonnard.* New York: Dodd, Mead, 1918.

Havighurst, R. J. *Developmental tasks and education.* New York: Longmans, Green, 1952.

Inhelder, B., and Piaget, J. *The growth of logical thinking from childhood to adolescence.* New York: Basic Books, 1958.

Jones, H. E. The development of physical abilities. In: *Adolescence: Forty-third yearbook,* National Society for the Study of Education. Chicago: University of Chicago Press, 1944.

Jones, Mary C. Psychological correlates of somatic development. *Child Development,* 1965, *36,* 899, 908.

Lieberman, E. J. The urban adolescent. *Adolescence,* 1966, *1,* 45.

Linton, R. *The cultural background of personality.* New York: Appleton-Century-Crofts, 1945.

Sacks, Sylvia R. Widening the perspectives on adolescent sex problems. *Adolescence,* 1966, *1,* 80.

Schmuck, R. Concerns of contemporary adolescents. *The Bulletin of the National Association of Secondary School Principals,* 1965, *49,* 19–28.

Stone, C. P., and Barker, R. G. The attitudes and interests of premenarcheal and postmenarcheal girls. *Journal of Genetic Psychology,* 1939, *54,* 27–71.

Strang, Ruth. *The role of the teacher in personnel work,* Fourth edition. New York: Teachers College Press, 1953.

Strang, Ruth. *The adolescent views himself: A psychology of adolescence.* New York: McGraw-Hill, 1957.

Strang, Ruth. *Target tomorrow: An educational and vocational guide for teenagers.* New York: Dell, 1964.

Sullivan, H. S. *The interpersonal theory of psychiatry.* New York: W. W. Norton, 1953.

CHAPTER 3

Physiological Changes in Adolescence

Karl C. Garrison *

THE GROWTH OF AN INDIVIDUAL FROM BIRTH TO MATURITY COVERS AN extended period of time and involves continuous physiological changes which affect the entire organism. Simple physiological growth, then, plays a tremendously important part in a person's development. During the adolescent years significant physiological changes take place which involve the entire body, internally and externally, in both structure and in function.

Change goes on constantly in living cells. This is implied in the statement, "life is a process of changing." The growing child is repeatedly faced with new and different forces of two special types. One is organic, and is in essence the physiological process occurring in all living organisms by which energy is made available through the metabolic processes related to food assimilation. It is released through activity. The other force is man's environment, which continuously stimulates a reaction. Concerning the effect of these forces, Boswell states:

> Each living organism, in relation to internal as well as external changes and conditions, tends to maintain itself as an integrated whole, as do also social organisms and a wide range of animate things. Each is then not merely something happening, but is a complex, integrated, and unified system of activities. Thus, definite

*KARL C. GARRISON is Emeritus Professor of Education at the University of Georgia where he was Chairman of the Department of Educational Psychology. Dr. Garrison has had a most distinguished writing career and is well known for his articles and books in the area of developmental and adolescent psychology. He has authored or co-authored *The Psychology of Adolescence; Growth and Development; Educational Psychology; Psychology of Exceptional Children;* and *Child Psychology.*

internal changes are taking place within each living being in accordance with its character and mode of life; and all its mechanisms,
however varied, combine to maintain a uniform dynamic state or
"field" within each individual, in the face of fluctuating conditions
of internal and external stimulation (1947, p. 290).

Thus, it may be noted that the development of the individual is a
result of conditions set forth in the germ plasm and environmental
stimulation operating on the growing organism. From the moment
the egg is fertilized until death, we may say that an individual is
always responding to stimuli. His behavior may very well be considered as a series of responses to a continuous series of situations. It
is only by definition that we can separate the individual and his
environment.

STUDYING PHYSIOLOGICAL DEVELOPMENT

In the early part of the present century it was known that important
changes occurred prior to and following puberty. However, the early
students of adolescent psychology gave little attention to the physiological changes due to the lack of scientific knowledge relative to such
changes (Garrison, 1965). Although individuals differ in rate of development, we note that certain developmental patterns do exist for different organs and parts of the body. Today it is generally recognized that
the young child is not a miniature adult; likewise, that the adolescent
is neither a child nor an adult in his physiological development and
reactions.

Longitudinal studies are the best means for arriving at a valid index
of the rate and periodicity of physiological growth during childhood
and adolescence. However, since reliable and interpretable data on
changes in body chemistry are difficult to obtain, a relatively small
number of studies have been conducted in many areas of physiological
development. Nonetheless, those that have been made have furnished
useful scientific data and serve as a basis for understanding and guiding
growing boys and girls. For example, a study of the differences in the
rate of physiological development of boys and girls gives one a better
perspective on the earlier changes in social-sex interests on the part
of girls as they pass from childhood into and through adolescence.
Mental hygiene problems, behavior problems and disorders, and per-

sonal maladjustments can also be better understood by studying physiological changes that occur during late childhood and adolescence.

Physiological Changes

Children and adolescents frequently suffer from the "tyranny of the
norm," i.e., the expectation that at a particular chronological age
certain mental, physiological, and social characteristics should appear
or else they will not be normal. There are, however, no "normal"
physiological changes commensurate with each age level. Each person's
growth is not dependent on his chronological age, but rather on
physiological age, and the extent of his sexual development. Changes
in height, weight, body build, metabolism, blood pressure, and strength
all depend on the occurrence of puberty. And, although there is a
sequential order of the changes that occur, wide differences appear
in the time of the onset of puberty and in rates of changes. The
materials presented throughout this chapter are not for the purpose
of providing norms or standards for judging the physiological development of an individual, but rather to emphasize the nature of physiological changes that occur during the adolescent years.

Endocrine Factors in Relation to Development

Scientific studies show a close relationship between developmental
changes and hormones produced by the pituitary gland. Two hormones
from this gland are especially influential. One of these is the growth
hormone, which enables the healthy, well-nourished child to attain
his normal body size. If there is a deficiency of this hormone, normal
growth will be retarded, and a form of pituitary dwarfism will result.
On the other hand, if an excess of the growth hormone is produced
during the growing period, pituitary giantism will follow. The other
pituitary hormone of special importance in maturation is the gonad-
stimulating hormone. The action of these hormones in a normal healthy
child will cause the immature gonads to grow and eventually develop
into mature ovaries or testes. These hormones, furthermore, help to
sustain the normal function of the ovaries or testes of the individual
after maturity. A deficiency of these hormones during preadolescence
would interfere with the normal growth and development of the
ovaries or testes; an oversupply would tend to produce precocious
sexual development.

The gonad-stimulating hormones act upon the pituitary gland in such a way as to reduce the effects of the growth hormones and the rate of growth. The importance of properly timed action of the growth and gonad-stimulating hormones has been pointed out by Greulich:

> If the testes or ovaries begin to function at the requisite level too early in life, growth is arrested prematurely and the child ends up abnormally short. If, on the other hand, the adequate production of the ovarian and testicular hormones is unduly delayed, growth, particularly that of the limbs, continues for too long a period and the characteristic bodily proportions of the eunuch are attained. It appears, therefore, that normal growth and development are contingent upon the reciprocal and properly timed action of pituitary (growth) and gonadal hormones (1944, p. 16).

A number of studies have been conducted related to gonadotrophic hormone secretion in children. In general, these studies indicate that the excretion of gonadotrophic hormones in early childhood, in both sexes, is too slight to be detected by the methods which were used, and that measurable amounts first appear in the urine during adolescence. Data are reported by Greulich and others on the results of 120 urinary gonadotrophic assays performed on 64 boys. Concerning the significance of gonadotrophic excretion in adolescence, they conclude:

> The results show that with advancing age and with advancing developmental status there is a general tendency for gonadotrophin to increase in amount from the undetectable levels of early childhood to levels more characteristic of the adult . . . it seems reasonable to suppose that the primary changes of puberty, namely an increase in size of the testes and the initiation of spermatogenesis, are related to the action of this gonadotrophin upon the seminiferous tubules. Secondary sex changes related to the secretion of the steriod sex hormones may be ascribed to the action of the hormone upon the interstitial gland of the testes (1942, p. 62).

Nathanson and his collaborators (1941) have reported somewhat similar results. Average curves for boys and girls show that during the early years the amount of androgens secreted into the urine is only slightly less for girls than for boys. The difference becomes more pronounced after age eleven. Before the ages of ten or eleven boys and girls excrete measureable amounts of male and female hormones. Slightly greater amounts of the male hormones are secured from the boys; while a greater amount of the female hormones are obtained from the girls, although these differences are slight.

PUBERTY CHANGES

The most important changes that signify the beginning of adolescence involve the sex glands. Horrocks states: "The advent of puberty or sexual maturity is the most clear-cut and most dramatic line of demarcation between the child and the adolescent" (1954, p. 712). The hormones from the sex glands bring the reproductive organs to maturity, and the individual becomes potentially capable of reproduction. This point of life is called puberty. The first menstruation marks puberty for girls, but there is no single criterion to indicate puberty for boys. Some criteria frequently used are the occurrence of first ejaculation, the appearance of axillary hair (underarm) and pubic hair, and the appearance of other secondary sexual characteristics. Girls tend to judge a boy's sexual maturity by facial and body hair, and by change in voice; boys judge a girl's sexual maturity in terms of figure and breast development. Regardless of the method used for determining puberty, it is generally recognized that boys mature about two years later than girls (Garrison, 1965).

The Period of Maturity

Whereas puberty refers to a specific time signalling the beginning of adolescence, pubescence refers to a period of time during which a constellation of changes are taking place. Among the changes taking place during this period are those involving metabolic rate, blood pressure, pulse rate, skeletal growth, voice pitch, and axillary and pubic hair.

The range of puberty for girls may vary as much as ten years, although over 75 per cent of girls have their first menstrual period at 12, 13 or 14 years of age. Bryan (1954) gathered data on the sexual development of a group of 97 girls. He defined the immaturity point as the age at which the girls show changes associated with sexual development. From a careful analysis of the data obtained, Bryan found the average age of beginning breast development to be approximately 10.7 years; of pubic hair, 11.5 years; of axillary hair, 12.5 years; and of menarche, 13.1 years.

The age of sexual maturation seems, however, to be related to living standards. In the highly developed countries comprising Western civilization, the average age of first menstruation has steadily declined for several decades. Burrell and others (1961) conducted a study of girls of different races to determine possible gentic influences on the age of menarche. They found that, although significant differences existed between girls from different families, the incidence of menarche was heavily dependent on living conditions, including improved diet and medical care. A comparative study by Ito (1942) showed that Japanese girls who were born in Japan but reared in California from infancy or early childhood were one and a half years ahead of Japanese girls born in California but reared in Japan. With the improved living standards in Japan since World War II, one would expect that Japanese boys and girls mature earlier sexually today than in the late thirties and early forties. Michelson (1944) found that menarche occurs later among Negroes in the West Indies than among Negroes in the United States.

There is no scientific evidence that race differences exist. A comparative study of the age of menarche for Negro school girls in Alabama with that of white school girls in Georgia by Henton (1959) revealed no significant difference.

The influence of family heredity may be shown by the relationship of sexual age to the degree of blood relationship. I have frequently observed that children in some families mature earlier than children in other families. This may even be observed in the case of first cousins. However, environmental influences sometimes reinforce hereditary influences and sometimes cancel out such influences. Thus, a girl whose mother matured early may, because of deficiencies related to illness or poverty, mature late. On the other hand, there are many cases today of children being brought up in better circumstances than were their parents. These children are in general maturing earlier than their parents.

The problem of determining the exact age of puberty is more difficult for boys than for girls. No clearcut line of demarcation such as that provided by the menarche for girls is present for determining the exact period of puberty for boys. An early study reported by Ramsey (1943) furnishes one of the most complete analyses available. Complete sex histories were obtained through personal interviews of 291 boys between the ages of ten and 20 years. These boys were from the middle or upper socioeconomic strata of a midwestern city. The data obtained from this study showed that the different aspects of sexual development did not appear at the same time. However, the thirteen-year level was the modal age for the appearance of each of four characteristics studied—ejaculation, voice change, nocturnal emission and pubic hair. There was a distribution range for each of the four characteristics of from 10 to 16 years, with the voice change and the development of pubic hair showing distributions more nearly approximating the normal bell-shaped curve. Of these four characteristics of sexual development, nocturnal emission was latest for most of the boys studied, with over 50 per cent having their first nocturnal emission after age 13.

The beginning of menstruation does not mean that the girl has reached sexual maturity as measured by fertility. For most girls, menstruation begins before the ovaries are capable of producing ripe ova. The ovaries at the time of the first menstruation are relatively small compared to their weight at the time of complete physical maturity. Ovulation tends to occur before the uterus is sufficiently mature to support pregnancy (Ford and Beach, 1951). The pubescent period for girls is approximately three years, while that of the boys is more variable, being from two to four years. Also, girls are more nearly their adult size when they become sexually mature than are boys.

Growth in Height and Weight

Tables of averages for growth during childhood and adolescence are likely to be misleading, since children of the same age vary enormously in their rate of development. Such tables do furnish useful information about growth trends and about the average height at different age levels. They furnish no useful information about individual patterns of development (Bayley, 1956).

Just prior to the advent of puberty, the rate of growth in height increases. According to Nicolson and Hanley (1953) the average chronological age at which the largest increment in standing height occurs is 11.5 years for girls and 13.8 years for boys. The height records of 408 girls of known age at the time of menarche show that the mode of increase is 2.5 inches, with 17 per cent of the girls growing more than four inches after menarche (Fried and Smith, 1962). The average yearly increments for weight show a somewhat different picture. Beginning around the fifth year, there is a gradual and progressive increase in gain each year, with the girls having a greater increase than the boys. The average 13-year-old girl is both heavier and taller than her male contemporary (Martin, 1955). The growth in weight during the early teen years is frequently followed by a falling off in weight on the part of many girls (Bayley, 1956). The emphasis upon slenderness as the ideal physique for the teenage girl is no doubt responsible for this early stabilization of weight in girls. However, Meredith and Knott concluded from a comparison of girls in the United States in 1960 with those of 1880 that "13-year-old schoolgirls are shown to be larger today than eighty years ago by four inches in mean stature and over twenty pounds in mean weight" (1962, p. 294).

The only adequate way to measure acceleration in growth is with longitudinal studies extending a few years before and after the advent of puberty. This was done in a study involving 1817 girls, ages 6 to 17 years, and 1884 boys, ages 6 to 18 years (Richey, 1937). The subjects were divided into three maturity groups on the basis of objective criteria. Some conclusion from this study are:

1. Differences in the height-weight relationship suggest differences in the body build of the members who made up the three groups.

2. Growth as measured by height and weight is slightly accelerated before puberty.

3. No significant differences are found in the heights of different female maturity groups after 15 years, or in those of different male maturity groups after 17 years.

Skeletal Development

Skeletal development, also referred to as anatomical development, is associated with the development of the bones. It consists of growth in size of the bones, and change in number and composition of the bones. This follows the same general pattern as that described for growth in height and weight; that is, rapid changes occur during the early childhood years, followed by a decelerated rate of growth, which in turn is followed by the early adolescent growth spurt.

The ossification of the bones, as an indicator of maturity, was used by Baldwin and others as early as 1928 for measuring the anatomical development of children and adolescents at different age levels. These studies revealed that after age five or six, girls show more advanced ossification than boys. Osseous development has been found useful in predicting puberty as well as other aspects of development (Harding, 1952). By the age of 13, the average girl will have about 70 per cent ossification of her wrist area.

Both skeletal age and tooth eruption are closely tied to the onset of puberty. Normal skeletal development will not occur in the absence of adequately functioning gonads. A study of somatic and endocrine changes associated with puberty was carried on by Greulich and his coworkers (1942) over a period of several years at Yale University. The skeletal status of 476 private school boys was compared with the degree of the development of various sexual characteristics. The boys were divided into five maturity groups representing successive stages in sexual maturity from prepuberty to late adolescence. Skeletal age was found to increase with advancing maturity regardless of chronological age.

The Development of Strength

The most satisfactory study of the development of strength during childhood and adolescence is one that makes use of longitudinal data gathered on children over a period of years. Data by Jones (1949) reveal that the development of strength follows a pattern somewhat similar to that of weight. There is a gradual increase until about the age of 12, followed by a much increased rate of development. There is also a significant relationship between strength and sexual maturity. Jones (1944) presents data from the California Adolescent Growth Study which compares the strength of two groups of girls representing contrasting extremes of age at menarche. Among these girls, the early maturing group shows a rapid rise in strength of grip prior to age twelve. The late maturing group is relatively retarded in strength from age eleven to age 15.8. The two groups eventually reached the same level of manual strength. The greatest increment for each group occurred near the time of menarche.

The results of a study by MacCurdy (1953) support the general findings and conclusions of Jones; i.e., that a significant relationship exists between the development of strength and sexual development. MacCurdy noted that in boys strength grows gradually to age twelve— then quite rapidly, reaching a maximum point around age 18. An early study by McCloy (1935) confirms the fact that the most rapid increase in strength for boys is between 13 and 16 years. In girls the most rapid increase is between 12 and 14 years, there being no increase recorded for the average of girls after age 15.

Thus, we note that as with height and weight, body strength is closely related to sexual maturity. This has an important bearing on the adjustments of activities of boys during the teen years, since strength is closely identified with the masculine role and so much emphasis is given to competition involving different kinds of physical performances which demand strength and agility. During the pre-adolescent and early adolescent years there are wide variations in body size, physiological maturity, and strength. Age groupings are at this period frequently most unfair to the immature boy who is unable to compete successfully in physical performances. I recall the case of an immature boy whom no group wanted on their team because he could not carry his part of the load toward winning. He was frequently found playing with smaller and younger youngsters whom he could bully more readily. This condition is perhaps more prevalent among lower and lower middle class boys than among upper middle and upper class boys, since fighting and other activities demanding strength have more prestige value among lower class boys. However, body size and strength are important aspects of the masculine physique and generally have prestige value among all groups of boys. In a seven year longitudinal study of boys reported by Jones (1949), the ten highest in strength had greater social prestige and fewer adjustment problems; whereas the ten lowest in strength suffered from low social prestige and feelings of inferiority.

BASAL METABOLISM, CIRCULATORY, RESPIRATORY, AND DIGESTIVE CHANGES

While the numerous changes involving body size are taking place, other developments are occurring involving basal metabolism, circulation of the blood, respiration (vital capacity), and digestion. These changes are closely associated with the development of sexual maturity and are vitally important in the development of adolescent boys and girls.

Age Changes in Basal Metabolism

Probably the most striking non-sexual physiological change appearing at the time of puberty is the rather sudden decline in basal metabolism (Shock, 1944). There is a continuous decrease in basal metabolism throughout the teen years for both boys and girls. Individual curves show a marked increase just before or at puberty for girls, followed by a significant decrease. There are, however, cases which do not conform to this pattern. The individual slump in metabolic rate exists among both boys and girls. However, the metabolic rate of boys is above that of girls relative to the surface area of the body. This may be due to the greater mesomorphy of boys—the muscles having a greater resting oxygen consumption than fat, and muscular children having a greater oxygen consumption than fat children (Garn, *et al.*, 1953).

Differences in body size and muscle mass do not account for all the sex differences which occur at puberty. Garn and Clark (1953) have shown that boys have a higher oxygen consumption per body weight even when compared with girls of the same muscular bulk from puberty or slightly before. It seems then, that the male acquires a specific metabolic stimulus which is most likely derived from the androgenic steroids.

Blood Pressure, Heart, and Pulse Rate

The growth of the heart, like that of other organs of the body, follows a course of its own. During the adolescent years its weight almost doubles, and its transverse diameter increases by almost 50 per cent (Marsh, 1953). During most of childhood, boys' hearts are slightly larger than girls'; then from approximately 9 to 14, the girls' are larger. After age 13 boys' hearts continue to grow at a rapid rate; girls' hearts, on the other hand, grow slowly during this period.

The basal heart rate falls gradually throughout the entire period of growth, with perhaps a check to this decrease about the time of peak stature growth. There is also a sex difference established at adolescence which persists during early adulthood (Iliff and Lee, 1952). This difference may be a result of the greater size of the male's heart, or it may arise simply from the difference in basal body temperature. The mouth temperature of girls and boys shows a gradual decrease during childhood, although this decrease in girls seems to stop around the age of ten or eleven. The heart rate is fairly closely related to body temperature in healthy persons. Thus, the difference of about 0.7° F. between boys' and girls' temperature at age 17 may account for the difference of about five heart beats per minute at the same age.

Systolic blood pressure rises steadily throughout childhood, but at adolescence the rise becomes more rapid and adult values are quickly reached (Downing, 1947; Schwenk, *et al.*, 1955). There is also a rise of pulse rate during the preadolescent years, with the maximum for girls being reached during the years prior to the menarche. A marked change in both blood pressure and pulse rate can be found at physiological maturity. The relation of these changes to sexual development may be seen most easily in girls, since their menstrual period furnishes conclusive evidence of sexual maturity at a particular time. There is no single criterion to provide a specific date for sexual maturity in boys. Shock (1944) presented data on 50 girls tested every six months for many years, for both blood pressure and pulse rate. A tabulation of the data with reference to each girl's first menstrual period and without respect to chronological age showed that blood pressure rose sharply during the three years before puberty and for six months afterwards. It then settled to a new level of about 106. Apparently, sexual maturity operates to stabilize the upward trend of blood pressure and to reverse that of pulse rate. After the menarche, there is a gradual decline in pulse rate.

It is mainly because of red cell growth that the blood volume increases more in boys than in girls at puberty; consequently, in childhood there is no sex difference when the blood volume is considered in relation to height or weight, whereas after puberty the male value is higher (Sjöstrand, 1953). However, not all the blood volume growth is attributable to an increase in cells; there is also a greater increase in plasma volume in the male than in the female (Morse, *et al.*, 1947; Russell, 1949).

Respiratory Changes

The lungs grow steadily during childhood, followed by a much accelerated rate of growth during adolescence. This is especially true for boys. A common measure of lung growth is vital capacity which consists of the amount of air that can be exhaled from the lungs after one has drawn a deep breath. Most girls fail to develop their maximum capacity, since they do not engage in vigorous activities. Growth data for liters of air exhaled, presented by Ferris and others (1952, 1953), of boys and girls from ages 5.5 to 17.5 years shows that boys excel girls during the first 9.5 or 10 years. At that age level, there is no significant sex difference noted. Beginning at about age 11.5, vital capacity of boys exceeds that of girls, and the difference increases during the growing years from 11.5 to 17.5 years. This increased difference is affected by both the larger lungs of the boys as well as their greater amount of activity.

The Digestive System

There are also pronounced changes in the organs of digestion during adolescence. The stomach increases in size and capacity and undergoes qualitative changes. The increased size of the stomach is related to the nutritional needs during adolescence. There are two fundamentally different kinds of food needs which are referred to as *energy requirements* and structural requirements. Energy is required for maintaining such activities as the beating of the heart, digestion of food, glandular secretion, and muscular activity. There is also an energy requirement for growth. These requirements are obtained chiefly from carbohydrates and fats.

Energy requirements. The amount of energy needed in terms of calories will vary considerably from adolescent to adolescent since it is dependent upon a number of variables. It differs with the size of the individual as is indicated from the caloric requirements set forth for different age groups in Table 3-1. The 12–15 year-old boy with a weight of 98 pounds needs 600 more calories than his brother in the 9–12 year-old category who weighs only 72 pounds.

TABLE 3-1

RECOMMENDED DAILY DIETARY ALLOWANCES (CALORIES)[a]

	Age	*Weight (pounds)*	*Height (inches)*	*Calories*
Boys	9–12	72	55	2400
	12–15	98	61	3000
	15–18	134	68	3400
Girls	9–12	72	55	2200
	12–15	103	62	2500
	15–18	117	64	2300

[a] National Academy of Sciences–National Research Council, *Recommended Dietary Allowances*, Revised, 1963. Washington: National Academy of Sciences–National Research Council, 1964.

The caloric requirement will also depend upon the rate of activity of the body processes while at rest—the basal metabolic rate. The faster the metabolic rate (heart beat, respiration, etc.) the greater will be the number of calories used in a given period of time. Energy requirements will also differ in accordance with the efficiency of the body in using food. In some individuals, foods are digested and turned into energy more readily than in others. Furthermore, the need for calories will depend on the rate of growth. During the early adolescent years, when growth is rapid, there will be an added need for food. According to Johnston (1957), the caloric requirements for the preadolescent and adolescent girl parallels her rate of growth.

Structural requirements. Structural requirements include the needs for materials that go to make up tissues and regulate the function of those tissues. The adolescent's body does not require all the chemical substances in a ready-made form; his body can provide some of these if the necessary materials are provided. What is most needed is a balanced diet of "protective foods"—foods rich in essential ingredients.

The vitamins as regulators of body processes are essential for physical health and development during the adolescent years. Vitamins A, D, C, K, thiamine, riboflavin, niacin, folic acid, B_6, and B_{12} are recognized as contributing to the health and growth of children and adolescents (Breckenridge and Lee, 1965).

Minerals serve as constituents of tissue; e.g., calcium and phosphorous are responsible for the rigidity of the bones. An inadequate amount of these minerals during childhood and adolescence would produce, among other things, poor teeth. Phosphorous and iron are essential components of all living cells. The importance of phosphorous for muscle, glandular, and nerve tissue is well known. Iron and copper are essential for the function of the lungs and the life activities of all the tissues.

Changes in nutritional needs and the actual assimilation of food elements that make up muscle and bone parallel the growth rate. Since the rate of growth varies from one person to another, food requirements also vary (Johnston, 1948). Burke and others (1962) have noted wide variations in adolescents of the same sex. Usually the individual's appetite serves as a natural guide for fulfilling nutritional requirements (Maroney and Johnston, 1937). However, psychological and societal factors also enter into the consideration of the topic of food. These include such things as the stringent dieting on the part of some teenage girls or the overeating on the part of the maladjusted adolescent.

SECONDARY SEX CHARACTERISTICS

The secondary sex characteristics are the physical features which distinguish the male from the female. Unlike the sex organs, they have no direct relationship to reproduction. However, like the sex organs, they follow a predictable pattern of development. At the beginning of puberty, when the primary sex characteristics have a growth spurt, the secondary sex characteristics likewise begin to develop.

Sexual Development and Body Build

Age of puberty is markedly influenced by body build. The child with an endomorphic build—broad hips and relatively short legs, is likely to mature earlier than the average, while the child with an ectomorphic build—slender body, broad shoulders, and long legs—usually matures later than the average. In a similar fashion to the endomorphic child, the mesomorphic child (whose build is muscular and compact) reaches maturity at a slightly earlier age than the average. Obese children as a group reach puberty about a year earlier than their age-mates whose weight is more nearly the average (Kralj-Cereck, 1956). Kralj-Cereck collected data from girls born in the northeastern region of Slovenia. The girls were divided into three groups: Baroque-"pyknic," broad, feminine; Renaissance-medium; and Gothic-"linear" or "boyish," angular. Comparisons of the three groups showed that the Baroque type had their first menstrual period earlier than the Renaissance girls, and the Gothic girls had the latest menstrual beginning.

When these results about the relationship of physique and sexual maturity are considered along with results from studies of the relationship between socioeconomic status and sexual maturity, the findings become very confusing. The relationship between physique and rate of maturation is presumably genetically determined; yet, all the evidence suggests that adverse environmental conditions slow the rate of physiological development. However, the results of a study by Dupertius and Michael (1953) suggest that for mesomorphs and ectomorphs the somatotype remains relatively constant throughout childhood. The evidence seems overwhelming that girls who mature earlier than the average are more endomorphic in body build during adolescence than girls who mature at an average age or slightly later than the average age (Zuk, 1958; Acheson and Dupertius, 1959).

Changes in Hair

Throughout the growing period there is a gradual darkening of the hair of the head, but at adolescence this becomes more marked (Grimm, 1952). Very likely, the adolescent darkening is due to the increase in adrenal androgens; for in the adrenogenital syndrome, the hair tends to darken. Not only is there a change in the darkening of the hair, there is also a change in the structure of the hair. The *vellus*, down hair, which persisted through childhood is replaced by terminal hair which becomes the dominant hair type in the adult. This replacement is greatly accelerated during puberty.

There is also a distinct change in the shape of the hairline on the forehead as the individual begins to mature. The hairline of immature boys and girls follows an uninterrupted bow-like curve. In a longitudinal study of the refractive index of head hair from birth to age 20, Duggins (1954) found a slow drop in the index until adolescence, at which time a much sharper index appears. In mature males, the curved hairline is interrupted by a wedge-shaped recess on each side of the forehead. This characteristic is usually a late rather than an early development feature.

Facial hair.   There are no marked sexual differences during childhood in the vellus of the upper lips, cheeks, and chin. Among boys, the downy hairs at the corners of the upper lip become noticeable about the time of puberty. This development extends medially from each corner of the upper lip and eventually forms a mustache of rather fine hair which is perceptibly larger, coarser, and darker than the downy hair it replaces. The mustache becomes progressively coarser and more heavily pigmented following puberty until complete maturity is reached. During the period when the mustache is developing, the vellus over the upper part of the cheeks increases in length and diameter. This hair persists as long, coarse down until the early juvenile mustache is fairly well developed. Somewhat later, a thin growth of long, fairly coarse, pigmented hairs appear along the sides and lower parts of the chin and on the upper part of the face just in front of the ear. These, too, gradually become coarser and form a beard which covers a large area of the face. The nature and extent of the facial hair are in part genetically determined.

Pubic hair. Pubic hair is a secondary characteristic that appears during puberty. However, it is not until the growth of the genitals are well under way that the terminal hair appears to replace the vellus hair. The extent of the development of pubic hair has been used to assess the sexual development of the individual. There are some who associate the amount and extension of terminal hair over the body with the existence of masculinity. However, there is no indication that a close association exists, in the case of boys, between the degree of masculinity in terms of sexual potency and the amount of hair on the body. Rather, it seems that the amount and extension of the hair over the body are primarily genetically determined.

Axillary hair. The axillary hair does not usually appear until the development of the pubic hair is nearly complete. The lateness of the appearance of axillary hair during pubescence may be noted in the sequence of changes that occur. According to Shuttleworth (1939), the order of development in girls is: enlargement of the breasts; appearance of straight, pigmented pubic hair; age of maximum growth; appearance of kinky pubic hair, menarche, and growth of axillary (underarm) hair. In boys the following order is found: beginning of growth in the testes, first pubic hair (straight, pigmented), early voice changes, first ejaculation, kinky pubic hair, age of maximum growth, axillary hair, marked voice changes, and development of beard.

Among boys, the development of terminal hair on the limbs and trunk begins to appear during the early stages of adolescence, with growth rather rapid at first. The development of terminal hair on the limbs begins on the upper part of the forearm, later on the sides of the lower arms, and still later on the back of the hands.

After the transition from long down to terminal hair has made considerable progress, a similar process begins on the distal half of the leg. The hair growth gradually extends upward toward and beyond the knee. The extension of the hair-covered areas from the centers on the trunk and limbs proceeds at different rates of speed in different boys, depending primarily upon their rate of sexual development and the genetic factors affecting the development of hair over their body. By the age of 18 or 19, the growth of hair on the arms is fairly heavy for the majority of boys. Also, there is a moderate growth of terminal hair over the legs, thighs, and buttocks as well as a varying amount on the ventral surface of the trunk. While lack of a beard frequently presents a problem during late adolescence for boys, heavy eyebrows and excessive underarm hair presents problems for some adolescent girls.

The Skin Glands

Marked changes take place in the structure of the skin and the operation of the skin glands as the individual matures sexually. The soft, delicate skin of childhood becomes thicker and coarser, and the pores become enlarged, a development sometimes associated with skin disturbances during adolescence.

There are three different kinds of skin glands, each of which is separate and somewhat distinct from the others. These are: (1) the *merocrine glands,* which are scattered over most of the skin surfaces of the body; (2) the *apocrine sweat glands,* which are limited to the armpits, mammary, genital, and anal regions; and (3) the *sebaceous glands,* or the oil-producing glands of the skin.

Merocrine and apocrine sweat glands. The merocrine and apocrine glands become increasingly active during adolescence. This is true even before the growth of axillary hair. Their secretion is a fatty substance with a pronounced odor that is usually not observable in boys prior to puberty, but becomes more pronounced during the early adolescent years. Among girls, the apocrine sweat glands appear to undergo a cycle of secretory activity during the menstrual period.

Sebaceous glands. The increased size and activity of the sebaceous glands is thought to be closely associated with skin disturbances during adolescence. These glands seem to develop more rapidly than the ducts. This produces a disproportionate relationship between the size and activity of these glands and the size of the ducts. They frequently become plugged and turn black as a result of the oxidation of the dried oil when it is exposed to the air. The well-known "blackhead" is the result. They are most frequently found on the nose and chin and are a constant source of annoyance to adolescents.

The sebaceous glands are associated with hair follicles and are not present in some regions of the body where there is a lack of hair, such as the palms of the hands. During pubescence, the sebaceous glands are associated with disproportionately small hairs. This may cause a temporary imbalance and is perhaps the major cause of acne. There is some evidence that an excess of male hormones may also be an important factor in the cause of acne.

Case studies of acne sufferers reveal that there is frequently a relation between emotional upsets and acne as well as other skin problems. For example, a boy may have a bad case of acne after an emotional episode in the home, such as a violent argument with his father. Again the chemical imbalance resulting from the emotional upset seems to furnish an overstimulation of the oily glands of the skin. Washing the affected parts with strong soap only serves to aggravate the condition. However, washing with a milder, medicated soap has been recommended as a means for helping the individual. Of course, in moderate to severe cases this cannot be offered as a substitute for a specialist.

Fat Thickness and Developmental Status

There is a pronounced reduction in the amount of fat over the thorax, abdomen, and back during childhood. The reduction is less marked in girls than boys, and the fat over the abdomen continues to develop during childhood. The fat gradually increases in boys after about the tenth year. The amount over the back, the thorax, and especially the abdomen increases in girls more than in boys in later years.

A study by Reynolds (1950) furnishes some quantitative information about the amount and distribution of subcutaneous fat in different regions of the body. Differences in growth patterns for the various areas may be noted, although the similarities are striking. Another observation resulting from this study involves sex differences. Girls display a greater pattern of fat thickness in all the areas studied than did boys. The continuous rise in mean values for girls, and the drop at adolescence for boys, are in harmony with the results obtained from other investigators.

In view of the "super-nutrition" and growth status of American children, it is very important for us to consider the relation between fatness and developmental status during childhood and adolescence. Since calories are growth-promoting, one would expect to find fatter children both taller and developmentally more advanced than leaner children.

A study reported by Garn and Haskell (1960) furnishes evidence that fatness during childhood is related to height and maturity status. The study consisted of data from serial radiographs, anthropometric measurements, and maturational information on 259 clinically healthy children. A consistent positive relationship was found between fat thickness, size, and skeletal age, especially between the ages of 8.5 and 12.5. Thereafter the relationship regresses toward zero in both sexes.

Since the data collected by Garn and Haskell were longitudinal in nature, it was possible to study the long-term effects of fat. The fat thickness in prepubertal girls (8.5 years) and prepubertal boys (9.5 years) was correlated with age of menarche and tibial union* for girls and with the age of tibial union for boys. These correlations show that fatness has long-term effects. The investigators conclude: "Thus, fatness results in accelerated growth and advanced maturation in both sexes" (p. 748). The investigators suggest that fatter children are neither taller nor shorter as adults, since fat-size correlations tended to regress toward zero after the twelfth year.

Voice Changes

Closely connected with muscular development are the obvious changes of voice during adolescence. This occurs in both sexes, with the voice becoming lower in pitch and more resonant. The changes are much more evident in boys and constitute one of the external signs of the advent of puberty. In the case of boys, the larynx or "Adam's apple" becomes enlarged, and the vocal cords within it increase in length (approximately doubling their former length) with a consequent drop of an octave in pitch. Girls' voices do not show such an outright change. At maturity their pitch may be a little lower than in childhood although girls' voices at this time become richer and fuller. Boys' voices not only change in pitch, but become more pleasant to the listener because of the increased volume. The sequence of physiological changes cited earlier shows that it takes two or more years for boys to achieve control in the lower register, and during that time the roughness of their tones may become a source of embarrassment. This can be observed in boys whose shifts of pitch suddenly jump from a deep bass to a high squeak (Curry, 1949).

The voice change is a poor indicator to use in judging the develop-

---

* Tibial union refers to the year during which the proximal epiphysis of the tibia fused with the diaphysis.

mental status of a boy, since there is no satisfactory way to evaluate the nature and amount of change objectively. If a recording device were used for comparing the different qualities of the voice at various stages of development, progressive changes would be observable and thus furnish a basis for judging the developmental status of the individual. As Garrison has pointed out, "it is the progressive deepening of the voice, rather than the absolute pitch, that is significant as an indication of progress toward maturity, since the voices of young men at maturity will vary widely in pitch and other qualities" (1965, pp. 70–71).

SUMMARY

Adolescence is a period marked by important physiological changes, the most significant being those related to sexual development. In the case of girls it begins with menstruation and extends over several years; in the case of boys, sexual development begins about two years later than girls. Changes in height, weight, body build, metabolism, blood pressure, and strength are closely related to the occurrence of puberty. There is considerable variation in the time of onset of puberty and the rate of changes occurring during this period.

There is a close relationship between developmental changes and hormones produced by the pituitary gland. The growth hormones enable the healthy, well-nourished child to attain his normal body size. The gonad-stimulating hormones act upon the pituitary glands so as to reduce the effects of the growth hormones. If the testes or ovaries begin to function at the required level too early, growth is arrested prematurely, and the child ends up abnormally short. If, on the other hand, the adequate production of the sex hormones is unduly delayed, growth, particularly that of the limbs, continues for too long a period and the child ends up with very long limbs. Secondary sexual changes related to the functioning of the sex glands also appear during adolescence. These seem to follow a sequential order with the development of the breasts occurring during the early stages among girls; an enlargement of the penis occurs during the early stages among boys.

The age of sexual maturation is in part genetically determined and in part related to living standards. In countries where high standards of living exist, the average age of first menstruation has steadily declined. In certain areas of the world, children are maturing sexually considerably earlier than their parents. The average age of first menstruation for girls in the United States is about 13 years. The pubescent period for girls is approximately three years, while that of boys is more variable being from two to four years. Just prior to the beginning of adolescence, there is a pronounced increase in rate of growth in height and weight. Girls are more nearly their adult size when they become sexually mature than boys. Skeletal development follows the same general pattern as that described for height and weight. The development of strength follows a pattern similar to that of weight, with a pronounced growth taking place after age twelve for most boys and girls.

Other physiological changes occurring during adolescence involve basal metabolism, circulation of the blood, respiration (vital capacity), and digestion. There is a continuous decrease in basal metabolism throughout adolescence for both boys and girls—there being a marked increase about the time of puberty for girls, followed by a significant decrease. During the adolescent years, the weight of the heart almost doubles, and its transverse diameter increases by almost 50 per cent. The basal heart rate falls gradually throughout the growth period. Systolic blood pressure rises steadily throughout childhood; at adolescence the rise becomes more rapid and adult values are soon reached. Sexual maturity operates to stabilize the upward trend of blood pressure. There is an accelerated rate of growth of the lungs (vital capacity) during adolescence, especially for boys. After about age 11.5, the vital capacity of boys develops considerably faster than that of girls, partially because of their larger lungs and partially because of a greater amount of physical activity. The stomach increases in size and capacity and undergoes qualitative changes during adolescence. Changes in nutritional needs and the assimilation of food elements that make up muscle and bone parallel the growth rate. Wide variations exist in caloric needs with the needs of boys becoming increasingly greater than that of girls after age twelve.

The secondary sex characteristics are the physical features which distinguish the male from the female. These, too, begin to appear with puberty and are closely related to sexual development. There is a change in both the color and texture of the hair with puberty; the hair becomes darker and the downy hairs of the corners of the upper lips and cheeks become noticeable. This development eventually forms a mustache of coarse and more heavily pigmented hair among males. Pubic hair appears during puberty after the ovaries and testes are well underway. Axillary hair does not usually appear until the development of the pubic hair is nearly complete. With puberty, marked changes take place in the structure of the skin and the operation of the skin glands. The soft, delicate skin of childhood becomes thicker and coarse and the pores become enlarged, a development sometimes associated with skin problems. The amount of fat over the back, the thorax, and especially the abdomen increases in girls more than in boys after childhood.

In both sexes, there are voice changes, with the voice becoming lower in pitch and more resonant. This is much more evident in boys than in girls and is one of the external signs of the advent of puberty, although the early changes are not as evident as later changes. The larynx of boys becomes enlarged and the vocal cords within it increase in length with a consequent drop of an octave in pitch; the voice of girls becomes richer and fuller. However, voice change is a poor indicator of the extent of sexual development.

All in all, adolescence is a period of great physical change and development. Most young people move through it quite nicely. However, for some adolescents, physical change can present real physiological and psychological problems. These adolescents will need the help and understanding of mature adults.

REFERENCES

Acheson, R. M., and Dupertius, C. W. The relationship between physique and rate of skeletal maturation in boys. *Human Biology,* 1959, *29,* 167–193.

Bayley, Nancy. Individual patterns of development. *Child Development,* 1956, *27,* 64–65.

Boswell, F. P. Trial and error learning. *Psychological Review,* 1947, *54,* 290.

Breckenridge, Marian E., and Lee, V. E. *Child development.* Philadelphia: W. B. Saunders, 1965.

Bryan, A. H. Methods for analyzing and interpreting physical measurements of groups of children. *American Journal of Public Health,* 1954, *44,* 766–771.

Burke, Bertha S., *et al.* A longitudinal study of the calcium intake of children from one to eighteen years of age. *American Journal of Clinical Nutrition,* 1962, *10,* 79–88.

Burrell, J. W., Healy, M. J. R., and Tanner, J. M. Age at menarche in South Africa Bantu schoolgirls living in the Transki Reserve. *Human Biology*, 1961, *33*, 250–261.

Curry, E. T. Hoarseness and voice change in male adolescents. *Journal of Speech and Hearing Disorders*, 1949, *14*, 23–25.

Downing, M. E. Blood pressure of normal girls from 3 to 16 years of age. *American Journal of Diseases of Children*, 1947, *73*, 293–316.

Duggins, O. H. Age changes in head hair from birth to maturity. IV. Refractive indices and birefringence of the cuticle hair of children. *American Journal of Physical Anthropology*, 1954, N. S. *12*, 89–114.

Dupertius, C. W., and Michael, N. Comparison of growth in height and weight between ectomorphic and mesomorphic boys. *Child Development*, 1953, *24*, 212–213.

Ferris, B. G., and Smith, C. W. Maximum breathing capacity and vital capacity of female children and adolescents. *Pediatrics*, 1953, *12*, 341–353.

Ferris, B. G., Whittenberger, J. L., and Gallagher, J. R. Maximum breathing capacity and vital capacity of male children and adolescents. *Pediatrics*, 1952, *9*, 559–570.

Foll, C. A. Physical development of school girls in upper Burma. *Archives of Diseases of Childhood*, 1958, *33*, 452–454.

Ford, C. S., and Beach, F. A. *Patterns of sexual behavior.* New York: Paul B. Hoeber, 1951

Fried, R. K., and Smith, E. E. Postmenarcheal growth patterns. *Journal of Pediatrics*, 1962, *61*, 562–565.

Garn, S. M., and Clark, L. C. The sex difference in the basal metabolic rate. *Child Development,* 1953, *24*, 215–224.

Garn, S. M., Clark, L. C., and Portray, R. Relationship between body composition and basal metabolic rate in children. *Journal of Applied Physiology*, 1953, *6*, 163–167.

Garn, S. M., and Haskell, Joan A. Fat thickness and developmental status in childhood and adolescence. *American Journal of Diseases of Children*, 1960, *99*, 746–751.

Garrison, Karl C. *Psychology of adolescence,* Sixth edition. Englewood Cliffs, N.J.: Prentice-Hall, 1965.

Greulich, W. W. Physical changes in adolescence. *Forty-third yearbook of the national society for the study of education*, Part 1. Chicago: Department of Education, University of Chicago, 1944, Chap. 2.

Greulich, W. W., *et al.* Somatic and endocrine studies of puberal and adolescent boys. *Monographs of the Society for Research in Child Development*, 1942, 7, No. 3.

Grimm, H. Eine menarchestatistik, von Berliner Schulabgangen. *Zbl. Gynäk*, 1952, 74, 1743–1745.

Harding, V. S. V. A method of evaluating osseous development from birth to 14 years. *Child Development*, 1952, 23, 247–271.

Henton, C. L. A comparative study of the onset of menarche among Negro and white children. *The Journal of Psychology*, 1958, 46, 65–73.

Horrocks, J. E. The adolescent. In: Carmichael, L. (Ed.) *Manual of child psychology*. New York: Wiley, 1954, 697–734.

Hunt, E., Cooke, E. G., and Gallagher, J. R. Somatotype and sexual maturation in boys: a method of developmental analysis. *Human Biology*, 1958, 30, 73–91.

Iliff, A., and Lee, V. A. Pulse rate, respiratory rate, and body temperature of children between two months and eighteen years of age. *Child Development*, 1952, 23, 237–245.

Ito, P. K. Comparative biometrical study of physiques of Japanese women born and reared under different environments. *Human Biology*, 1942, 14, 279–351.

Jacobsen, L. On the relationship between menarcheal age and adult body structure. *Human Biology*, 1954, 26, 127–132.

Johnston, J. A. Adolescence. In: McQuarrie, I. (Ed.) *Brennemann's practice of pediatrics*, Vol. 1. Hagerstown, Md.: W. F. Prior Co., 1957.

Johnston, J. A. Nutritional problems of adolescence. *American Medical Association Journal*, 1948, 137, 1587–1588.

Jones, H. E. California adolescent growth study. *Journal of Educational Research*, 1938, 31, 561–567.

Jones, H. E. The development of physical abilities. *Forty-third yearbook of the national society for the study of education*, Part 1. Chicago: Department of Education, University of Chicago, 1944, Chap. 6.

Jones, H. E. *Motor performance and growth*. Berkeley, Calif.: University of California Press, 1949.

Jungck, E. C., Brown, N. H., and Carmona, N. Constitutional precocious puberty in the male. *American Journal of Diseases of Children*, 1956, 91, 138–143.

Kralj-Cereck, Lea. The influence of food, body build, and social origin on the age at menarche. *Human Biology*, 1956, 28, 393–406.

MacCurdy, H. L. *A test for measuring the physical capacity of secondary school boys.* New York: Harcourt, Brace & World, Inc., 1953.

Maroney, J W., and Johnston, J. A. Caloric and protein requirements and basal metabolism of children from four to fourteen years old. *American Journal of Diseases of Children,* 1937, *54,* 29.

Marsh, M. M. Growth of the heart related to bodily growth during childhood and adolescence. *Journal of Pediatrics,* 1953, *2,* 382–404.

Martin, W. E. *Children's body measurements for planning and equipping schools.* Special Publication No. 4. Washington: U. S. Department of Health, Education, and Welfare, 1955.

McCloy, C. H. The influence of chronological age on motor performance. *Research Quarterly,* Association of Physical Education, 1935, *6,* 61–64.

Meredith, H. V., and Knott, Virginia B. Descriptive and comparative study of body size of the United States schoolgirls. *Growth,* 1962, *26,* 283–295.

Michelson, N. Studies in physical development of Negroes. IV. Onset of puberty. *American Journal of Physical Anthropology,* N. S. 1944, *2,* 151–166.

Morse, M., Schlutz, F. W., and Cassels, D. E. Blood volumes of normal children. *American Journal of Physiology,* 1947, *151,* 448–458.

Nathanson, I. T., Towne, L. E., and Aub, J. C. Normal excretion of sex hormones in childhood. *Endocrinology,* 1941, *28,* 851–865.

Nicolson, A., and Hanley, C. Indices of physiological maturity: deviations and interrelationships. *Child Development,* 1953, *24,* 3–38.

Ramsey, G. V. The sexual development of boys. *American Journal of Psychology,* 1943, *56,* 217–223.

Reynolds, E. L. The distribution of subcutaneous fat in childhood and adolescence. *Monographs of the Society for Research in Child Development,* 1950, *15,* 1–189.

Richey, H. G. The blood pressure in boys and girls before and after puberty. *American Journal of Diseases of Children,* 1931, *42,* 1281–1330.

Russell, S. J. M. Blood volume studies in healthy children. *Archives of Diseases of Childhood,* 1949, *24,* 88–98.

Schwenk, A., Eggers-Hohmann, G., and Gensch, F. Arterieller blutdruck, vasomotorismus und menarchetermin bei mädahen im 2. Leben sjahrzchnt. *Arch. Kinderheilk,* 1955, *150,* 235–249.

Shock, N. W. Physiological changes in adolescence. *Forty-third yearbook of the national society for the study of education,* Part 1.

Chicago: Department of Education, University of Chicago, 1944, Chap. 4.

Shuttleworth, F. K. The physical and mental growth of girls and boys age six to nineteen in relation to age at maximum growth. *Monographs of the Society for Research in Child Development*, 1939, 4, No. 3.

Sjöstrand, T. Volume and distribution of blood and their significance in regulating the circulation. *Physiological Review*, 1953, 33, 202–228.

Wolff, O. H. Obesity in childhood: a study of the birth weight, the height, and the onset of puberty. *Quarterly Journal of Medicine*, 1955, 24, 109–123.

Zuk, G. H. The plasticity of the physique from early adolescence through adulthood. *Journal of Genetic Psychology*, 1958, 92, 205–214.

CHAPTER 4

Theories of Adolescent Development

E. Kuno Beller ✳

IT WILL BE EVIDENT, FROM THE OTHER CHAPTERS IN THIS BOOK AND FROM the literature in general, that an abundance of empirical data has been accumulated and that adolescence has been accepted as a clearly delineated and important period. Yet, theory has taken a less central place in the research and discussions on adolescence than it has in the study of other phases of human development. One reason for this might be that the study of human development reaches its most complex stage during adolescence. In most societies, the onset of puberty is marked by pronounced changes in many areas of functioning. Although the rate of change varies from area to area and from individual to individual, by and large, the human being at this stage of development poses a problem to himself, to his family and to the larger group of which he is to become a member. Biologically, intellectually, the adolescent approaches maturity at a rather rapid rate. Psychologically and socially, he often interrupts the course of gradual development and deviates in a variety of ways both from his somewhat younger peers and from his elders. This disparity in the rate and direction of change between adolescence and the other phases of development also presents special problems when one attempts to integrate the data contributed from differing disciplines, such as biology, psychology and sociology. However, the very difficulties that have interfered with the formulation of theories of adolescence, point clearly toward the need for a theoretical framework which will make the disparities and deviations that characterize development during adolescence meaningful and predictable.

✳E. KUNO BELLER is a Professor of Psychology at Temple University. Prior to this he was the Director of Research of the Child Development Center in New York City. Dr. Beller has published a number of articles on child psychology, motivation, perception, and psychopathology. In addition has has written *Clinical Process*.

The different theories of adolescence to be discussed in this chapter will be grouped as follows: biological, psychological, psychosocial, sociological, psychoanalytic and anthropological. Since the imitations of space do not permit an exhaustive discussion of the several theories (as in Ausubel, 1954; Blos, 1962; and Muuss, 1962), an attempt will be made here to reduce the overlap and repetition which exist in abundance from theory to theory, and to highlight instead the unique features of each.

BIOLOGICAL THEORIES OF ADOLESCENCE

Practically all theories which we will undertake to examine accept adolescence as a unique phase in human development and agree on the central biological and physical changes of puberty which mark its onset. However, they differ widely with regard to the importance and influence of these biological changes on the psychological processes. Furthermore, there is a frequent use of the same, or very similar empirical facts, as evidence for, or illustrative of, quite different theoretical models.

Hall: Recapitulation

It is of historical interest that the father of a "psychology of Adolescence," namely G. Stanley Hall (1916), was also the founder of the approach to adolescence as a separate and distinct phase in human development. Following Darwin's concept of evolution, Hall introduced a theory of recapitulation which assumed that the experimental history of the race becomes a part of the genetic constitution of the individual. According to this view, each individual passes through stages which repeat the history of mankind. The direction of development in general, and of adolescence in particular, is thus seen, as essentially controlled by internal forces.

In animals, phylogeny is recapitulated before birth. In human beings, infancy represents a re-enactment of the prehistoric stages of the human race. During infancy, the development of vegetative, sensory and motor functions are dominant. The early part of middle childhood represents a re-enactment of the cave-dwelling culture of early history. The later part, namely, preadolescence, which lasts from 8 to 12 years of age, parallels that phase of early history at which discipline marked the major progress of mankind. At this stage of development, the child is amenable to mechanical training; that is, training which involves those skills necessary for sensory, motor, perceptual and cognitive functioning. Adolescence itself is a period of rebellion which, in terms of recapitulation, corresponds to a time when the human race was in a transitional stage. Historically, Hall chose *Sturm und Drang* (storm and stress) as the model for temperament and mentality that characterizes adolescence. Furthermore, adolescence is frequently characterized by extremely contradictory tendencies which make this phase of development one of instability and one in which the individual may fluctuate between emotional, social and ideological extremes. Thus, it is only in late adolescence that the individual begins to settle down and reach his maturity. This phase of development represents a recapitulation of the beginning of modern civilization.

Since Hall considered adolescence, as he considered all other stages of development, to be primarily biologically determined, there was little room in his system for environmental factors to influence adolescent phenomena. Consistent with this point of view, Hall considered it best not to interfere with the natural course of development, since he believed it to be inevitable and determined by inner forces.

Hall might be taken as a prototype of those later biological approaches to human development which assume, in a general way, that the direction of psychological development recapitulates the evolutionary development of the strata in the human brain. A common characteristic shared by these biological approaches is that they do not postulate basic psychological principles for predicting developmental changes. The only principles provided to account for such changes are drawn from biology and bio-genesis. For the realm of psychological development, these theories provide descriptive concepts for the ordering of the experiences and behaviors that characterize each of the successive stages of development.

Gesell: Morphogenesis and Spiral Growth

Arnold Gesell is best known for his observational work on human development from birth to adolescence (1940; 1946b; 1956). His descriptions of age trends have been accepted by many parents in the United States as norms of what to expect in their developing children. Gesell's biological orientation, with respect to the predetermined stages of maturation, reflects rather clearly the points made in the previous paragraph. On a level of theory, Gesell offered the general formulation that mental growth is a progressive morphogenesis, that is, a process of differentiation and integration. According to this view, environmental factors may facilitate or inhibit growth; but, the basic direction of growth is laid down by maturational forces. In order to account for changes between developmental stages, Gesell employs the model of a spiral (1946a). Growth consists of oscillation along a spiral course toward maturity. The child frequently reverts to earlier forms of behavior before he is able to surpass his previous performance. Thus, progression and partial regression, until further progression takes place, characterize the course of developmental change.

Like Hall, Gesell saw adolescence as a transitional period between childhood and adulthood. Unlike Hall he did not conceive of adolescence as a period of storm, contradictions and extremes. However, in his generalizations which are derived from his empirical observations, Gesell does place stress on the differences which appear in the adolescent from year to year. This is really similar to Hall's *Sturm und Drang* —an aspect of development which Gesell had de-emphasized in his theorizing. The ten-year-old is described as stable, well-adjusted to his family, and altogether fond of company. At the same time, he is intrigued by secret societies and is supersensitive to the fairness of adult authority. With regard to peers, he prefers to associate with his own sex. In contrast to the ten-year-old, the eleven-year-old is moody, quarrelsome, rebellious and argumentative. This turbulence has disappeared in the twelve-year-old who is more sensible and tolerant than he was at eleven. The twelve-year-old is concerned with social recognition and more interested in the opposite sex. This greater peace with social environment changes again at thirteen. The thirteen-year-old turns inward; he is more critical of himself and his family. In line with his rapidly changing body structure and body chemistry, he is more tense, more aware of himself, and less secure than he was in the preceding year. At fourteen, the adolescent goes through a phase of reversal toward extroversion and frequently becomes enthusiastic. He is self-confident and more at ease with himself. He has begun to make definite choices of his ego ideals, and he identifies closely with his heroes from folklore and from other sources. This trend is again reversed in the fifteen-year-old who manifests increased tension, hostility and rebellion against authority. He is again self-conscious and, in addition, perfectionistic. The rebellious trend at this age level makes the youth vulnerable to delinquency, particularly because he is eager to move away from home and to disassociate himself from family and authority. In sharp contrast to the picture presented by the fifteen-year-old, the sixteen-year-old gives evidence of emotional integration and balance, a high degree of social adjustment and self-control. He is friendly, outgoing, and independent in a self-confident sort of way.

The foregoing brief descriptions indicate that adolescence is conceived of as a phase of glaring contradictions within adjacent age levels with alternating stages of calmness and storm. They also reflect normative generalizations with regard to restricted age levels. These cannot be easily conceptualized in terms of the relative effects of biological, psychological, and cultural factors. It is for these reasons, together with the inferences that parents have drawn with respect to the meaning of their child's deviations from the norms, that Gesell came under the fire of considerable criticism. Notwithstanding such hazards, and in spite of the methodological criticism justly leveled against Gesell's work, he has provided us with a host of ideas which provide fertile ground for conceptual probing and empirical research.

Kretschmer: Body Types

A different biological approach to adolescent development has been formulated by the followers of Ernst Kretschmer (1951). They have employed his theory of body types to explain the direction of developmental change. Kretschmer focuses our attention on three basic body types: the pyknic, athletic, and asthenic. He held that each of the body types represents a predisposition to certain major psychological tendencies. For example, schizoid tendencies are said to appear more frequently in people with slender and tall or athletic body build, whereas manic-depressive or cycloid tendencies are said to appear more frequently in people with a stocky body constitution. Adolescence was characterized by Kretschmer's followers as a developmental phase with "schizoid" characteristics. Moreover, the degree of turbulence experienced by the adolescent was hypothesized to be correlated with his body type. This means that a youth with a lean and slender body type would already have a tendency toward a schizoid personality and would, therefore, experience adolescence as a turbulent period. A child with a stocky body constitution, who is inclined toward cycloid personality characteristics, would not experience adolescence as a very disturbing phase in his development. There is, as yet, very little empirical evidence to support or refute these speculative assertions.

Zeller: Body Gestalt

The approach of Wilfried Zeller, a follower of Kretschmer, is actually closer to the theorizing of Gesell since Zeller (1951) postulates relationships between changes in body constitution and changes in psychological functions. For each stage in psychological development, there is a specific *body gestalt* (body gestalt refers to the total structure and composition of the body) that corresponds to it. Although changes appear most clearly in one or another of the body areas, functions, or organs, Zeller emphasized that these changes only signify a total change of the body gestalt, which would also be reflected by a similar change in the psychological sphere. For example, children lose their first tooth and gain their first permanent tooth between five and one-half and six and one-half. Such a specific change is indicative of a much broader change in both the physique and personality of the child. This change also coincides with the child's introduction to formal schooling. Similarly, the appearance of secondary sex characteristics at puberty (see Garrison's discussion within this volume) involves a much broader, more comprehensive change of the body structure and hormonal dominance. The broader change in body structure is a beginning disharmony that occurs at the onset of the puberal phase. In early adolescence this increased disharmony of the body gestalt is reflected in a sudden increase of impulsivity, nervousness, and in a more critical attitude. This is directed at the adolescent's body, as well as toward his inner psychological world. Zeller presents a number of empirical observations in support of his theory. He maintains that changes in body gestalt cannot be measured totally by means of quantitative methods. Certain aspects of these changes are qualitative, and for that reason the observer has to rely on intuitive judgments to grasp changes in the gestalt quality. It is interesting to note in this context that Sheldon (1940) has made similar statements with regard to judgments of body types.

The application of typology to development represents one of the two major biological approaches to adolescence in contemporary Germany. The major biological approach is represented by a stratification theory of personality. This theory holds that psychological functions are embedded in layers of the brain. The more elementary affective functions are thought to have their root in the cerebellum while the more cognitive and intellectual functions originate in the cerebrum. The stratification theory makes the assumption that a direct relationship exists between the evolution of the brain, its structure and stratification, and the development of personality.

Remplein: Personality Strata

Heinz Remplein (1956) has been singled out as a representative of this orientation because his approach is essentially a biological one. Remplein's theory of development follows closely a genetic concept of brain development. Innate dispositions determine the direction of development. They also determine the limits of influence that environmental forces can have on the development of personality. The lowest layer of personality, involving dispositions which are necessary for survival, is the most resistant to environmental influences. Those innate dispositions of development which are part of the higher layers of personality reflect the newer layers of the brain and are more open to environmental pressures.

Remplein emphasizes the need for psychological development to follow the structure of layers of personality and hypothesizes that premature pushing beyond the developmental levels expected may lead to such negative consequences as an arrest in development since the psychological energies are used up too early.

In Remplein's system, the lowest layer of personality consists of those psychological processes that are related to the body functions which preserve life, in body needs for comfort, and in the psychological functions that are closely related to body organs. The second layer of personality is the endothermic stratum which is the seat of emotions. The third and highest layer of personality is the personal stratum which is represented by ego functions, e.g., cognition and volition. This layer of personality organizes and directs the elements of the lower layers into specific forms of behavior.

Following closely his biological model, Remplein does not consider developmental change as continuous, but rather as the superimposition of new layers on older ones. The old layers do retain some autonomy, even through the conscious functioning of the individual is dominated by the new layers. A developmental source of maladjustment may result from a failure of the newly developing strata to integrate properly with the older one. This hierarchical process of integration is particularly vulnerable to maladjustment during the transition from early to middle childhood and from middle childhood to adolescence. These periods of transition are characterized by negativism. The first period of negativism occurs between two and four and involves the integration of the two lower personal strata (the vital needs stratum and the endothemic stratum). This integration must occur before their subordination to the newly rising personal stratum. The child becomes conscious of his ability for self-determination and, through negativism, he facilitates the process by which the personal stratum acquires dominance over the two lower psychic strata.

The second period of negativism occurs during the transition from middle childhood to adolescence, that is, from ten to thirteen years of age. Changes in endocrinological secretion, brought about by the onset of puberty, lead to a resurgence of new drives. These take the form of adventure seeking and the acting out of sexual and aggressive urges. The adolescent experiences these resurging drives as a desire for self-determination and independence while his environment perceives them as forms of negativism and rebellion. In reality, this negative phase, like its earlier forerunner, represents a transition which makes possible a new integration between the strata of personality (e.g., sexual impulse emanating from the lowest strata and love emanating from the second strata). In addition, there is a renewed attempt of the third personal strata to assert its leadership on a higher level of psychological functioning than was previously possible.

Since these periods of negativism are necessary for the restructuring of relationships between the strata of personality, it is important to be tolerant of the emotional instability, disobedience, and exaggerated self-assertion that are characteristic of these transitional periods in normal development.

PSYCHOLOGICAL THEORIES

We have selected Oswald Kroh, Edward Spranger and Kurt Lewin as representatives of the psychological approach in the study of adolescence. Their theories represent a movement away from biological models. In spite of differences between these theorists, they all share a focal interest in the psychological processes as the central factor in adolescent development. Specifically, these three theorists concentrate on various aspects of experience, such as consciousness, perception, values, inner conflict and stress. They all build their theories on the basis of their study of individual human experience rather than on the structure of the brain.

Kroh: Phase Structure

Oswald Kroh's (1951) approach resembles, in some ways, the formulations of personality stratification theorists. In fact, his work and writings have influenced the thinking of Remplein. Kroh broke away from using the structure and evolution of the human brain as a model for his theory of psychological development. He was primarily concerned with the psychological aspects of consciousness at different stages of development. Kroh advanced the concept of *phase structure* which emphasized the wholeness of personality along the lines of Gestalt theory. Kroh's influence on Zeller can be seen in the latter's concept of body gestalt which was discussed earlier in this chapter.

Kroh formulated two major developmental trends. The first trend referred to the expansion of the child's concept of the world. In this, Kroh comes closer to Heinz Werner's (1940) concept of physiognomic perception. At first, the child expresses magical thoughts concerning objects in the external world. This is followed by a period of a more realistic perception of the world beginning with the elementary school years. The onset of adolescence marks the emergence of a theoretical view of the world which enables the individual to reach a deeper understanding of life. The second developmental trend bears some similarity to Piaget's formulations. This developmental trend extends from reflex action to motor control and purposeful action, followed by foresight and planning, and finally reaches the point of causal cognition and creative production (see the chapters by Elkind and Piers).

Kroh was the originator of the idea of negativistic periods which separate the three main stages of development from one another. His formulations on the nature and function of negativism during transitional periods have been taken over by Remplein.

Spranger: Value Hierarchy

Edward Spranger (1955) also dissociates himself from biological speculations in formulating his theory of adolescence. He is entirely committed to a psychology of understanding which does not deny certain effects of endocrinological change, but maintains that psychological change cannot be explained by physiological states. Moreover, he proposes that the methods employed to study psychological change are not the same as the methods employed by natural science to investigate physiological change. His methodological approach is one of understanding rather than of causal explanation and prediction. Spranger emphasizes the totality of the psychic structure. This is more akin to Gestalt psychology and phenomenological psychology than to the structural psychology of Wundt and Titchener.

Adolescence is conceived of as a period of transition during which a hierarchy of values is established. This hierarchy of values is the basis of Spranger's theory of personality types. Differences in the value hierarchy will affect different patterns of change. Spranger distinguishes three such patterns of adolescent development. The first pattern consists of radical and dramatic changes which accompany a shift in the individual's perception of himself. The second pattern refers to a slow and continuous change in which the individual gradually adopts cultural values that are held by his society without basic alteration in his personality. The third pattern refers to a growth process in which the adolescent achieves his goals through self-discipline and active efforts.

The discovery of the ego as a self is a central concept in Spranger's formulation of structural change during adolescence. The ego is now experienced by the adolescent as separate from the external world. The result is in feelings of loneliness and a heightened need to experiment with the newly-discovered self in the adolescent's search for a life plan and a definite identity. The adolescent begins to examine previously unquestioned ideas and relationships. This may result in rebellion against institutionalized traditions of society. It may also result in an increased need for social recognition and new interpersonal relationships. The predominance of one or another of these trends will be determined by the value hierarchy or typology that characterizes an individual adolescent.

Although Spranger had due regard for influences of social and environmental conditions on adolescent development, he was concerned primarily with inner determinants and with the individual's experience and perception. Spranger is essentially a phenomenologist for whom the primary task of the psychologist is the study of the content and structure of inner experience. In this he shared the preoccupation of a third important theorist, Lewin. Lewin's approach is also essentially psychological and phenomenological, although environmental determinants played a larger role in his theorizing than in Spranger's.

Lewin: Field Theory

Kurt Lewin (1935; 1939; 1948) was more interested in analyzing the subjective world of the adolescent than in the individual differences between adolescents. He applied his concepts of field theory to accomplish this task. The basic psychological law of field theory is that behavior (B) is a function (F) of the person (P) and of his environment (E) or $B = F(P \; E)$. The sum of all interacting environmental and personal factors is called the life space or the psychological space. Within the life space, there are positive and negative goals to which the individual feels either attracted or repelled. These goals are called *valences*. An individual moves either toward or away from the goals in his life space, and this movement is termed *locomotion*. A very important variable in this conceptual framework is the existence of barriers that interfere with the individual's locomotion and with his reaching his goals.

According to Lewin, the life space of the child depends on the stage of his development. The growing child is increasingly able to distinguish between the real and the unreal, hopes and realistic expectations, and falsehood and truth. Thus, a result of increased differentiation is the growing organization of the child's life space.

Several conditions in the development of a child will affect the degree of structure and organization of the child's life space. If the parents do not provide a sufficient amount of structure for the child in the early stages of development, his personality will lack integration. However, as the child grows older and as his life space becomes more differentiated, he needs freedom to advance into new regions and to have new experiences. Thus a reduction in the amount of direction as well as in the restrictions legislated by the parents is indicated.

Rate of change is a second condition that will affect the degree of increasing differentiation in the developing child. If change is gradual, it will facilitate organization. If changes are rapid and sudden, they are likely to result in periods of stress and crisis. Adolescence is characterized by relatively rapid change in the structure of the life space and, therefore, results in stress and in disorganization within the life space. Lewin does not attribute the stress which results from biological changes during puberty to the amount of change that takes place objectively, but rather to the central position of the body in the life space of an individual. Thus, it is the subjective meaning of the body to the adolescent that determines for him many of the consequences of the perceived changes in the body at the time of puberty.

A third condition that will affect differentiation is the presence of conflicting forces at various points in development. The conflicting forces may originate in the child's organism, or in the environment as the child perceives it. The analysis of the heightening of conflicting forces during adolescence forms an important basis for Lewin's approach to the understanding of adolescence. For example, if the child has been highly dependent on his family, then cultural demands for increased self-sufficiency at puberty will conflict with the dependency, and puberty will be experienced as a period of violent change. Another source of conflict and stress for the adolescent in our society results from the ambiguous way in which he is treated by adults. For instance, certain childish forms of behavior and goals which still have strong positive valences for him are no longer accepted as appropriate by adult society. However, the adolescent is not permitted to replace these childish behaviors with adult forms of behavior such as driving a car, drinking liquor, and having sexual relations which also have strong positive valences.

Lewin has compared the marginal position of the adolescent in transition to the position of a minority group member who tries to dissociate himself from his background and to enter the majority group. The adolescent wishes to dissociate himself from his childhood background and to enter the adult society which he perceives as the powerful majority group. If the minority group member is only partly successful in establishing relationships with the privileged group, he becomes a marginal man in both groups. This applies equally to the experiences of the adolescent. Both are plagued by an increased amount of emotional tension, and both are extremely sensitive to the shortcomings of the background from which they try to dissociate themselves.

Lewin offers certain interesting formulations concerning the ideological instability and extremism that often characterize adolescents. The adolescent experiences an expansion of his life space which is accompanied by uncertainty and by conflicting pressures, and therefore has the consequences of emotional and ideological instability. Moreover, in taking a radical position with regard to social ideology, the adolescent moves through fewer regions than the adult. This is so because the perception of the political arena is much more differentiated for the adult than it is for the adolescent. The adolescent distinguishes only between the left and the right, whereas the adult distinguishes more steps between the extreme right and the extreme left. The ease with which adolescents take extreme positions is also a function of the lack of differentiation in the adolescent's political ideology compared to the differentiation that exists in the political life space of the adult individual. On this point, the Haan, Block, and Smith chapter within this book will be of interest to the reader. Still another reason for the adolescent being an easy prey for ideological extremists comes from changes in the fantasy-reality balance in development. The adolescent is increasingly under greater pressure from the adult society to relinquish his "lack of realism" in favor of the reality of the adult world. This often has the consequence of accentuating the conflict of the real with the ideal and of leading to an intensive desire of the adolescent to structure, or rather to overstructure, his field of values and ideals. It may account for the readiness of the adolescent to follow anyone who offers a definite pattern of values. Extremists, of course, have the least doubt and the least self-criticism with regard to the values they hold.

Lewin's position with regard to adolescence may be summed up as follows: (1) The adolescent phase of development involves a widening of the life space, especially socially, and in time perspective. This change has the consequence of a sharp decrease in cognitive structure. The adolescent has less direction as well as more conflicting pressures for his behavior than either the child or the adult in our society. (2) The adolescent occupies a position between the child and the adult similar to a marginal member of an underprivileged minority group in our society. (3) Puberty, as a new experience of the adolescent with his own body, can be represented as a baffling change of a central region in the established life space. From these three postulated characteristics of adolescence follow certain predictions concerning social behavior and emotional experiences. The adolescent will be overly-sensitive and will fluctuate between extremes of shyness and aggressiveness. The adolescent will experience extreme conflict between social and moral values, between ideologies, and between different styles of living. Finally, the experience of conflict will set up tensions which will throw the adolescent into positions of extreme attitudes and actions.

PSYCHO-SOCIAL AND SOCIOLOGICAL THEORIES

The psychological theorists discussed in the previous section, particularly Lewin, did not ignore the importance of the social environment as a determinant of adolescent development. They merely placed their emphasis on intrapersonal psychological processes and on experience. Similarly, the social psychologist does not ignore nor neglect the importance of personality mechanisms and intrapsychic factors. However, his emphasis is on the influence of the social environment and on the role of the interacting processes between the adolescent and his society.

Davis: Socialization

We find the concept of socialization the key concept employed by Allison Davis (1944). Davis approaches adolescent development as being a continuous process of social reinforcement and punishment. Society designates behavior as acceptable by reinforcing or rewarding it and designates other behavior as unacceptable by punishing it. Anticipation or fear of punishment, after repeated experiences, brings about "socialized anxiety" which then becomes a key factor in the socialization process. Socialized anxiety functions as a tool for the individual in his attempt to adapt to the demands of his culture. Once the child develops this anxiety, he will acquire behavior which mitigates or reduces it. It should be noted that socialized anxiety is different from neurotic anxiety since neurotic anxiety is irrational and not adaptive. Similarly, if socialized anxiety is too strong, or too intensive, it will have an inhibiting and disorganizing effect.

Society defines what goals, values and behaviors are acceptable and to be acquired. In our society, socialized anxiety increases with the onset of adolescence, particularly in a middle-class youth. This is because he faces increased demands from society to accept social responsibilities and because society asks him to delay and generalize the gratification of such pressing needs as sex and aggression. With this increased pressure, and with the heightening of socialized anxiety, the adolescent becomes aware of the values of his culture and depends increasingly upon social acceptance, prestige and status.

Lower-class adolescents have different experiences in the areas of gratifying sex and aggression. The basic difference in the lower-class adolescent is that he does not develop the socialized anxiety which in turn motivates him to achieve and to postpone immediate gratification for the sake of long-range goals. Kohrs considers this point in his chapter on *The Disadvantaged and Lower Class Adolescent*. Moreover, the lower-class adolescent learns that he is not likely to receive symbolic rewards such as status and social acceptance for inhibiting sexual and aggressive behavior.

Havighurst: Developmental Task

While Davis was primarily concerned with the role of social anxiety in adolescent development, Robert Havighurst (1951) formulated and investigated the concept of developmental tasks. These tasks are defined in relationship to those goals and criteria which society expects fulfilled or met at the different stages of development. Developmental tasks can be defined then as the skills, knowledge and attitudes which a child has to acquire at successive points in his development. The mastery of these tasks depends on physical maturation, as well as on personal effort. Developmental anxiety is a motivational and reinforcement process which facilitates the acquisition and mastery of developmental tasks. The mastery of developmental tasks on any one age level prepares the individual for mastering new tasks at the next age level. Havighurst suggests that failure in a given developmental task will result in maladjustment, social disapproval, increased anxiety and subsequently greater difficulty in mastering future tasks. Each developmental task has its critical period within which it must be learned. This emphasis by Havighurst should remind us of the formulations by the theorists of the German school. In particular Kroh, and the personality stratification theorists come to mind. However, Havighurst places a greater emphasis on the socializing agents and upon the methods of reinforcement which society uses in an attempt to help the individual at a given age level. He also emphasizes the cultural relativity that determines the nature of the developmental tasks. The more dominant the cultural element of the task is (over the biological element), the more likely it will differ from culture to culture.

Havighurst defines developmental tasks for each age level. For adolescence, he defines such tasks as accepting one's physique and sex role, relations with peers of both sexes, emotional independence of parents, partial attainment of economic independence, making vocational choices, acquiring intellectual competence and socially responsible behavior, preparing for marriage and family life, and the building of values which are in harmony with the world picture of the society to which the adolescent belongs.

SOCIOLOGICAL THEORY

Sociological theories of adolescence focus clearly on social institutions and on the position of the individual in society, that is, on the adolescent's role and his status as the determiners of his development. Even though sociological theory is at the other end of the biological-social dimension, it is interesting to note that sociologists pay considerable attention to the interacting effects of biological, physical, and social factors in adolescent development. The same cannot be said for biological theorists who deal much less systematically with the social environment as a determinant of developmental change.

Kingsley Davis: Sociological Theory

We have selected Kingsley Davis (1960) as a representative advocate of sociological theory. Davis maintains that in a complex Western society, adolescence represents a phase in development in which physical maturation and maturity move far ahead of social maturity. In terms of physical strength and mental capacity, full maturity is attained shortly after puberty.

Socially, the adolescent has a long way to go before he reaches a mature status. In most societies, power and status are dependent on social position and experience rather than on brute strength or even on mental capacity. However, social position and experience come with middle or old age rather than with adolescence. Thus, despite his physical or even mental equality to his elders, the adolescent is placed in a socially subordinate position. This presents a source of conflict between the generations. It is probable that the learning process would have a better chance if physical and mental maturity would come between 30 and 35 years of age instead of between 15 and 20 years of age. As it is, especially in modern society, the individual must keep on learning after his capacity to do so has begun to decline. Knowledge, judgment, insight and self-reliance are generally far from their peak when mental capacity has already reached its peak. In a physical sense, society does not utilize its great men until they are past their prime. However, in a social sense, society does utilize its men at the peak of their administrative or sociological maturity. That is to say, it utilizes them when they have hopefully accumulated the greatest know-how for making political decisions of far-reaching consequences.

From a sociological point of view, adolescence is the phase in development in which the lag of social development behind physical development first becomes pronounced. From this point of view, one might anticipate that as society becomes more complex, the lag will become greater and adolescence will be prolonged further into organic adulthood. Specifically, the position of adolescence is determined sociologically by four factors: occupational placement, reproductive control, authority organization and cultural acquisition.

Occupational placement. Selection of individuals for occupational placement may be made by conscription or by choice. If the selection is made by choice, it follows that the earlier the choice is made, the more intensive can be the training. The later the choice is made, the more it may rest on an accurate evaluation of personal talent and preference (see Hackman's chapter on vocational counseling with the adolescent). The more complex societies defer the final decisions until adolescence and provide most of the specialized training during that period. Primitive societies need not defer the decision until adolescence. They can make their choice much earlier and provide the training during childhood because division of labor is so slight. If training starts early, as is the case in a simple society, and extends through childhood, adolescence will not stand out occupationally as a period of any particular importance. By the time the individual reaches adolescence, he is practising his occupation and accepted by his society as an adult. If, on the other hand, as is the case in a complex society, occupational choice and training is centered in adolescence, the strain in this phase of development will be greater. Finally, if standards for occupational status are determined by achievement and not by social class and caste, the level of general achievement in the culture is raised, but the status of the adolescent is lowered by putting him at the bottom rung. This makes adolescence a period of strain and, in some societies, a period of deprivation.

Reproductive control. In every society, reproductive capacity first appears at the inception of adolescence. However, the control of reproduction and of sexual behavior is exercised differently in different societies. Each society is confronted with three basic questions concerning reproduction and sexual gratification. First, whether the adolescent shall be permitted to enter normal heterosexual intercourse, or whether he should be forced or encouraged to postpone such behavior. Second, whether marriage should be permitted with the onset of sexual maturation. Third, whether marriage should be the result of free choice or whether it should be controlled by others. Also, should marriage establish a separate household or merely an extension of their parental menage. This last question is an issue which primitive and modern societies face together. Until recently, one common characteristic was shared by most societies. The adolescent was permitted to exercise both his sexual and reproductive functions; however, society carefully controlled the exercise of these functions.

In our society, the ideal of pre-marital chastity is upheld. The postponement of marriage, as well as the independence and separateness of the wedded couple, is also advocated. The adolescent is permitted to associate closely with the opposite sex, but is put on his honor to remain virtuous. The adolescent is permitted to choose his own mate independently, but his or her parents retain veto rights in many areas. Both Bell and Staton discuss these problems in separate chapters so we will not consider them further here. Of course, the competitive struggle for status in the occupational area also gets entangled with the competitive system in the courtship and dating area. This does little to lessen the problems of the adolescent period.

Authoritarian organization. The next major sociological issue concerning adolescence is that of the child's emancipation from the authority of his family. In our society, adolescents believe that obtaining a job and becoming married entitles a person to independence. In other societies, the authority of parents continues after adolescence, and adolescence does not stand out as a significant period of change in an individual's relationship to authority. In our society, in the absence of publicly-accepted practices for emancipation from authority, wide individual variations exist from family to family and each family must settle the matter in its own way. In many instances the adolescent craves the protection of his family, but he rebels against its authority. He is torn by the conflict of dreading to leave the careless existence of childhood and accepting the burdensome responsibility of adult life. The nature of this conflict and its possible consequences were discussed in some detail in the presentation of Lewin's theory. It is also discussed by Strang in her introductory chapter to this book. This whole issue will be taken up again when we turn to the psychoanalytic theory of adolescence.

Let us examine more closely some of the sociological determinants of the conflict between parental authority and adolescence. One of these determinants is the rate of social change. The more rapid the social and technological change in a society, the greater will be the difference in the cultural content experienced by two different generations at the same stage of development. The parent learns that his adolescent experiences are outdated when he assumes the responsibility of transmitting his background experience to his own child. The problem of cultural lag, on the parents' part, is aggravated in modern society by the fact that the child is exposed to competing authorities. Professional educators usually teach ideas which are in advance of their own culture and, thereby, they widen the intellectual gap between parent and child.

It is interesting to raise the question as to why parental authority generates so much more conflict than other institutions of authority. One of the factors determining this difference is that society defines clearly those selective areas in which it assumes authority. In contrast, parental authority includes most aspects of a child's life. Often parents are glad to relinquish their authority over the adolescent child and to grant him independence. However, a child's social status is identified with parental status and parental status is socially identified with the child's conduct. Therefore, parents often wish to insure proper conduct on the part of their offspring by prolonging parental authority.

A related phenomenon bearing on adolescent conflict is the combination of *concentration and dispersion* that characterizes our family system. The smallness of the family unit in our society makes for intensity of family feelings. Most of the day's schedule takes place outside the home and this makes for dispersion of activities. This dispersion of activities away from home isolates and increases the intensity of the affectional bonds within the home. The major share of the family sentiment is directed toward a few individuals who are so important to emotional satisfaction that complexes easily develop. There is less sentiment to go around and, therefore, we are left with youth who are emotionally deprived.

Cultural acquisition.   A fourth issue that defines the adolescent period is that of cultural acquisition. The more primitive the culture, the earlier the child can be taught its rudiments. Highly civilized societies require specialized educational establishments. The universal and specialized school system, as we know it, becomes a necessity. However, the school system concentrates on teaching abstractions which are often divorced from the facts and experiences of real life. Thus, the adolescent emerges from his school with knowledge which does not help him to handle concrete everyday situations. This incongruence tends to produce problems of motivation. The existence of the long interval of time between learning and its vocational application also contributes to the problem of academic motivation. Davis (1960) suggests certain modifications in the school system which would reduce the problem it currently produces. The school system should make greater efforts to introduce inventions of new educational technology and to overhaul the incentive mechanism. For example, recent methods of improving reading habits may shorten the absorption of the same amount of knowledge.

The current incentive mechanisms might be greatly improved by introducing vocational and occupational training earlier. This would permit the adolescent to carry out rewarding functions in society simultaneously with his continued schooling.

PSYCHOANALYTIC THEORY

Psychoanalytic theory is being presented separately because it cannot be put into any one of the previous headings without distortion. Biological, psychological and social processes and concepts occupy equally central positions. In its early stages, psychoanalytic theory was heavily weighted toward biological factors and evolutionary ideas. Very early in its development, however, the clash between the biological-constitutional vs. the social-environmental orientation was worked out by two psychoanalytic theorists who broke away and developed their own theories. Of course I am referring to Carl Jung and Alfred Adler. The former went in the direction of extreme emphasis on a constitutional typology and evolutionary recapitulation of human experience, whereas the latter elevated the family and other social factors to a position of central importance. As psychoanalysis developed, Freud (1936) himself shifted toward a greater emphasis on external reality. Later, Anna Freud (1948), in her concern with the educational process and particularly with defense mechanisms of the ego, anticipated the developments of ego psychology. Finally, studies in cultural anthropology carried out by psychoanalysts such as Abraham Kardiner (1939) and

Erik Erickson (1950; 1959) have elevated culture and environment to central positions in psychoanalytic theory.

Infantile Sexuality

For many centuries, and until relatively recently, it was assumed that puberty marked the onset of sexuality. With the advent of Sigmund Freud (1953) the concept of infantile sexuality and of psychosexual development replaced the traditional concept of puberty. Infantile sexuality refers to those pleasurable experiences which are associated with the stimulation and gratification of the basic needs relating to food intake, elimination and genital excitement. These occur prior to the onset of puberty. The organization and course of infantile sexuality during early and middle childhood determine how adolescence is experienced and expressed. Briefly, some of the structural formations of childhood may be described as follows.

Early Childhood

The psychic apparatus of the infant is dominated by the pleasure-pain principle. The dominance of this principle diminishes as a result of two important factors. First, as the infant develops trust in his mother's ability to allay his tensions, he becomes correspondingly less dominated. The second factor is the child's growing control over internal tension and his mastery of the stimulation from his external environment. This process contributes to a shift in the child's position from passivity to activity. The child learns to manipulate others and the physical world to gain his own ends.

The child's feelings of self-confidence derived from his mastery and from his shift to an active position are absorbed in the next phase of development, namely, the phallic phase. This is particularly true in the boy in whom they take on the form of exaggerated fantasies of power. During the phallic phase, the child begins to develop fantasies of possession and intimacy toward the parent of the opposite sex; this period is the oedipal stage. The oedipal conflict is wrought with sexual and aggressive wishes that take on frightening proportions. The child resolves this conflict between forbidden impulses and authority by identifying with the authority figure and thereby erecting a built-in censor of his own forbidden impulses. This is the beginning of conscience and superego. The experience of this conflict and its resolution usher in the period of middle childhood which has been called the *latency period.*

Middle Childhood

The particular importance of the latency period for adolescence is the sharp increase on control over the impulses which occur during this period. The increased control is facilitated by the development of a conscience based on the internalization of and the identification with parental authority. With it, the child's respect for law and order assumes a dominant place. The internalization of parental authority has another consequence, as well. The child's dependence on parental praise and approval for feelings of self-worth is replaced by those inner sources of assurance which we call self-esteem. Another important consequence is the child's greater independence from the parent. As a result of this greater independence, the child is less likely to be frustrated by the parent and this lessens his mood fluctuations and produces more emotional stability.

The formation of the superego and the strengthening of the ego represent an increased differentiation of the personality. It is further facilitated by a separation of verbal and motor expression. This in turn permits rapid strides forward in the development of language and symbolic activity. This differentiation is particularly important in enabling the child to tolerate conflicting demands from within as well as from the external environment.

As mentioned earlier, the mother-child relationship is important for the development of the structural formations of childhood that survive and determine the course of adolescence. At first, the infant experiences both parents as dispensers of comfort or frustration. Mother's role is not primarily feminine, but rather that of an active person. The child is in a passive position of getting or not getting. By identifying with his mother as a source of nurturance, the child acquires not only some independence, but also some of his mother's active position.

For the boy, the mother continues through childhood to be the object of his affection. What changes in the little boy is his position from passive receptivity to active mastery. The latter reaches its first peak in the phallic phase of development. Here the little boy identifies his power with masculinity. Excessive masturbation, which may arise both during this period and in puberty, is interpreted as a defense against regressing to a passive position. The boy discovers sex differences, and in his fantasy, he interprets the difference as an injury to the opposite sex. Psychoanalytic theory relates this interpretation to the contempt and fear with which our culture treats femininity in boys. The male's contemptuous attitude toward the female sex often harbors his deep-seated fear of regressing to his earlier passive receptive position in infancy. The boy's identification with his father helps him to combat this fear. Identification with the father is facilitated by the fear consequences of the boy's rivalry with his father for the affection of his mother. The fear is resolved by identifying with the father. These changes toward masculine identity-formation, or a failure of such changes and an alternative course of regression to a passive position, are of utmost importance as a background for the developmental trends which occur during adolescence.

The formation of feminine identity is different and equally important for the adolescent phase. At first, the girl shares with the boy a passive position toward her mother as a provider. When the girl enters a phase of independence and of an active position, unlike the boy, she not only changes her position toward her mother, but she also changes her love object from mother to father. Her continued identification with the mother as a provider will reinforce her active position and will conflict with the girl's imitation of her mother's passive position toward her father. The active position the girl takes persists for a long time throughout childhood. There are very strong psychological, social and practical reasons for the persistence of this active position. The little girl is greatly rewarded for being self-sufficient; she envies boys for their physique and status; a girl is not criticized as much for being a tomboy as a boy is criticized for being a sissy; the active position is a satisfying one to any child regardless of his sex; finally, the role of the woman is that of a nurturant-giving person which certainly entails an active position. It is not until much later in the course of development that the girl begins to take a passive position toward men and to identify more fully with her mother in the mother's passive position toward the father. Thus, we find that the course of the development of masculine identity for boys is simpler than the development of the feminine identity for girls. The boy not only retains the same love object (the mother), he also develops in one direction, namely from passivity to activity. The girl, on the other hand, changes from a passive to an active position, then back again to a passive position.

The latter must differ considerably from the early infantile passivity shared by boys and girls alike. These, then, are the structural formations of childhood which survive into adolescence.

Adolescence

At the onset of adolescence, both boys and girls give signs of experiencing stress and of giving up some of the accomplishments in education and social conformity that were achieved during the latency period. The degree and direction of regression will have common elements. It will also be greatly affected by pre-adolescent development, as outlined, up to this point. The adolescent not only manifests regressive tendencies, but also a variety of defensive maneuvers to ward off the regressive pull.

An important development at the onset of adolescence, as seen by psychoanalytic theory, is the moving away from the love objects of early childhood. This is a continuation of the move in the same direction which occurred during latency. A certain amount of affection becomes liberated as a result of the dissociation from early love objects and goes in search of new love objects outside the family. With it occurs a weakening of the parental authority which formed the backbone for superego development. This weakening of the superego is further reflected in feelings of loneliness, inner turmoil and depressed moods. Adolescence has been described as a phase in which mourning and being in love dominate the affective life of the young person. The rebellion against, and separation from, the parent, involves a real loss and results in experiences of emptiness, grief and sadness which are a part of all mourning. The working through of such mourning is an important task of adolescence.

Friendship acquires an enormous importance for adolescent boys and girls. Not only do friendships gain in importance, but they also acquire a new quality, namely, an idealization of the friend. The idealized image of the friend supplements the earlier idealized image of the parent. The relationship between the loss of early love objects and the formation of intensive relationships, such as friendships and crushes during adolescence, can be seen in the reactions to the loss of an idealized friend when such a disappointment or loss results in depressions or in going-on-eating binges. The fact that these relationships are often transitory and of short duration betrays an ulterior purpose of these friendships. The friendship has been a search for a replacement of the abandoned parent.

Heterosexual relationships. Now, turning to heterosexual relationships, psychoanalytic theory points to striking differences between boys and girls in their reactions to the opposite sex at the onset of puberty. The boy first turns away from heterosexuality and escapes into his male peer groups. He is preoccupied with defending himself against regressive tendencies and the feared consequences of such tendencies. The girl does not react in the same way at the onset of puberty. She goes through a stage of exaggerating her active position in life without turning away from heterosexuality. In contrast to the boy, her defense against regression (to an infantile passive position and to infantile sexuality) is an exaggeration of heterosexual interest and experience. She does not assume a feminine role, but acts as the active, aggressive partner in the pseudo-love game. Related to this turn of events is the fact that girls mature more rapidly than boys during this period and experience more violent and painful changes in their physiological functioning. Evidence from psychoanalytic therapy on the adolescent acting-out of girls suggests that the excessive active and aggressive role in the frantic attempt to relate to men represents an over-compensation in the adolescent girl. This is a counter against the strong regressive pull to be fondled in the same passive manner as the infantile girl was fondled by her mother. Instances of adolescent infatuation with much older men may represent a giving in to this regressive pull.

Defense mechanisms. As indicated earlier, the adolescent employs a variety of defensive maneuvers in his reaction to the inner impoverishment he experiences, and to other sources of stress and conflict. One fairly common defensive reaction consists of a self-induced heightening of ego states. In this category belongs self-induced exertion. Pain and exhaustion are fairly common phenomena among adolescents. These self-induced ego states of affective and sensory intensity allow the adolescent to experience a heightened sense of self. They enable the adolescent to discharge tension which comes from the stress and conflict he experiences.

Sometimes specific defenses against anxiety and conflict function under an umbrella of a socially-accepted form of behavior. An example of this may be seen in the sharing of a code of behavior which permits the adolescent to divorce his feelings from his actions. This may occur because the behavior is public and because he does not have to take the responsibility for it. Under such circumstances, the adolescent can act out, without having any strong feelings about his action. The specific defense mechanisms hidden in this type of socially sanctioned acting out are denial and isolation. The adolescent denies his feelings and isolates feeling and awareness. He is fully aware of what he does without having any feelings. Conversely, due to his submerging himself in the peer code, he may experience feelings of anger or act aggressively without any awareness of what the source and target of his anger is, or without awareness of the aggressive consequences of his behavior.

The peer group and social belonging. Erickson (1959) points toward the positive value of the gang for the adolescent and the ways in which the clique helps the adolescent form his ego identity. The adolescent who rebels against the dominance of his parents, against the dominance of their value system and their intrusion into his life, has a desperate need for social belonging. The peer group and the gang help the adolescent find his own identity. The adolescent relies on his peers for comfort by stereotyping himself at a time when his body image changes radically and when he is confronted with pressures which threaten to overwhelm him. This is one of the reasons why totalitarian systems are so attractive to the adolescent. They supply convincing and suitable identifications. Democratic identity involves freedom of choice and does not supply an identity as readily. The democratic group requires that the person have sufficient ego identity to tolerate ambiguity. The adolescent who has to question his own identity at every moment welcomes membership in the totalitarian peer group which relieves him of his painful search and provides emotional crutches until he can learn to stand on his own two feet.

ANTHROPOLOGICAL THEORIES

Anthropology, more than any other discipline, has cast doubt on the validity of biological theories of personality development. Ruth Benedict (1950) has suggested that very few human traits are universal. Moreover, the universal existence of certain human traits would not represent scientific evidence that such traits must be biogenetically determined. Similarly, anthropologists do not consider many problems to be inherent in adolescent development. Cross cultural studies have shown that a good many of the problems which have been described

and discussed earlier in this chapter may not exist at all in some societies, and may be solved at different age levels in other societies. Even
physiological maturing, such as the onset of puberty, will acquire
different meanings in different cultures and, therefore, will result in
different reactions and behavioral changes during adolescence. For
example, as Margaret Mead (1952) has shown, it has been found in
primitive tribes that menstruation may be interpreted as dangerous by
one tribe because the menstruating girl could dry up the well, and as
good in another tribe because the menstruating girl could improve the
crops and increase the food supply. Instances have also been found in
which no taboos and rituals are connected with menstruation. In such
instances, the girls are not even forbidden to prepare food or mix freely
with other members at the onset of menstruation.

Cultural anthropology challenges the universality of the specific
stages in human development which are an essential part of most of
the theories discussed in this chapter. The majority of anthropologists
hold that specific patterns of cultural conditions determine whether
development takes place in stages or is continuous. Gradual and abrupt
changes before and after adolescent development vary widely from
culture to culture and no single rate of change, within development,
can be considered universal. The cultural prescriptions for age and
stage grading in Western society may be contradictory, but they are
definitely there and they strongly reinforce stages in development.

Observers of adolescents in modern society are more likely to be
impressed with the unique sources of developmental change that characterize adolescence than are the observers of primitive cultures. The
rules, sanctions and taboos for conduct in primitive cultures are more
directly related to the patterns and changes of behavior during adolescence than is the case in our complex modern society. Thus, the role
of the social environment in adolescent development emerges more
clearly in primitive societies than it does in a modern society. This
more direct and explicit influence of cultural conditioning on adolescence may well be related to the greater continuity between the
parent and the growing child in the primitive society. Conversely,
the more indirect and complex relationship between cultural conditioning and adolescent development, as well as the presence of the
conflicting and ambiguous standards in modern society, may have
facilitated the widening gap between the parent and the growing child.
By comparison with primitive societies, it is clear that the adolescent
in modern society conforms increasingly more to peer group standards
and has become less responsive to parental values and expectations.

Other reasons for the widening gap between the generations have been discussed earlier in this chapter, particularly in the section on sociological theory.

Most anthropologists who have studied primitive cultures are impressed with the beneficial effects of gradual change and continuity in development, particularly for the period of adolescence. One anthropologist (Leta Hollingworth, 1928), has gone so far as to describe the position of characterizing adolescence as a period of inevitable storm and stress, from which new and different personalities emerge, as a survival of the ceremonial rebirth folklore which constituted the initiation of primitive youth into manhood and womanhood. She also describes those attempts to explain psychological changes during puberty as a result of biological and organic change, as a survival of the sudden change in social status that occurred as the result of puberty initiation rites among primitive people. The biological theorists have clung to their belief in the biological determinants of psychological changes during adolescence with extreme tenacity. Contrasting this with the extreme paucity of convincing evidence, Hollingworth's suggestion becomes even more intriguing. However, in fairness, it must be remembered that the more recent biological theorists have left ample room for individual differences in biological predispositions. This allows for a wide range of different effects of organic change on adolescent development. An example of this can be seen in the discussion of followers of Kretschmer who have held that differences in body type will affect differences in the amount of storm and stress experienced by the adolescent.

SUMMARY

The present writer shares some of the expressed concerns of the anthropologist with respect to biological theories of adolescence. The evolutionary speculations of G. Stanley Hall and the biological speculations of Remplein are post facto analogies which seem mainly an attempt to reconcile biological and psychological development. They are found lacking as a conceptual framework for the organization of the psychosocial phenomena of adolescence. This is particularly true when it comes to understanding, prediction, and control. Gesell's concept of spiral growth and of an oscillation between progression and regression in development may be useful and may have helped Gesell to organize his empirical observations. However, the validity of this concept, when applied to psychological change, does not hinge on demonstrating a direct link between oscillation in biological development and psychological development. Learning theory has found this fluctuation in conditioning and habit formation and has been quite successful in discovering psychological mechanisms and processes to account for these phenomena. Similarly, Piaget's concept of equilibration and Anna Freud's concept of the interaction between progression and regression in developmental change, provide models of oscillation in development without any reference to biological processes. As in the case of learning theory, both Piaget and Anna Freud use psychological mechanisms to account for this oscillation. These mechanisms are both plausible and testable.

Some of the biological variables and processes that have been suggested appear to have considerable promise for facilitating systematization of the psycho-social phenomena during adolescence. As indicated earlier, the concept of body build (proposed by Kretschmer) the reference to endocrinological changes have considerable promise for understanding the fluctuations in mood and anxiety during adolescence. This is true because these particular psychological variables are more closely linked to biological processes than many other aspects of human experience.

Finally, it should be apparent to the reader of this chapter that much fruitful thinking and many profitable ideas are to be gained from a greater familiarity with European theories. To the present time these theories have not received a receptive ear in the psychological circles of the United States. It is hoped that the brief introduction to adolescent theories provided in this chapter will encourage the student to continue to familiarize himself with the writings of Spranger, Kroh, Zeller, and the other psychologists who have much to offer toward an understanding of adolescence.

REFERENCES

Ausubel, D. P. *Theory and problems of adolescent development.* New York: Grune and Stratton, 1954.

Bendict, Ruth. *Patterns of culture.* New York: The New American Library, 1950.

Blos, P. *On adolescence.* Glencoe, Free Press, 1962.

Davis, A. Socialization and adolescent personality. In: *Adolescence:*

Yearbook of the national society for the study of education, 1944, 43, Part I.

Davis, K. Adolescence and the social structure. In: Seidman, J. (Ed.) *The adolescent.* New York: Holt, Rinehart and Winston, 1960.

Erikson, E. H. *Childhood and society.* New York: W. W. Norton, 1950.

Erikson, E. H. Identity and the life cycle: Selected papers. *Psychological Issues Monograph Series,* I: No. 1. New York: International Universities Press, 1959.

Freud, Anna. *The ego and the mechanism of defence.* Baines, E. (Trans.) New York: International Universities Press, 1948.

Freud, S. *Three essays on the theory of sexuality.* London: Hogarth, 1953.

Gesell, A., *et al. The first five years of life.* New York: Harper, 1940.

Gesell, A. The ontogenesis of infant behavior. In: Carmichael, L. (Ed.) *Manual of child psychology.* New York: John Wiley, 1946.

Gesell, A., and Ilg, Frances L. *The child from five to ten.* New York: Harper, 1946.

Gesell, A., Ilg, Frances L., and Ames, Louise B. *Youth: The years from ten to sixteen.* New York: Harper, 1956.

Hall, G. S. *Adolescence.* New York: Appleton, 1916.

Havighurst, R. J. *Developmental tasks and education.* New York: Longmans, Green, 1951.

Hollingworth, Leta S. *The psychology of the adolescent.* New York: Appleton-Century, 1928.

Kardiner, A. *The individual and his society.* New York: Columbia University Press, 1939.

Kretschmer, E. *Korperbau und Character.* Berlin: Springer Verlag, 1951.

Kroh, O. Psychologie der entwicklung. In: *Lexikon der Paedagogik,* Vol. II. Bern: A. Francke, 1951, 438–447.

Lewin, K. *A dynamic theory of personality.* New York: McGraw-Hill, 1935.

Lewin, K. Field theory and experiment in social psychology: Concepts and methods. *American Journal of Sociology,* 1939, 44, 868–897.

Lewin, K. *Resolving social conflict.* New York: Harper, 1948.

Mead, Margaret. *Adolescence in primitive and modern society.* In: Swanson, G. E., Newcomb, T. M., Hartley, E. L., *et al.* (Eds.) *Readings in social psychology.* New York: Henry Holt, 1952.

Muuss, R. E. *Theories of adolescence.* New York: Random House, 1962.

Remplein, H. *Die seelische Entwicklung in der Kindheit und Reifezeit.* Munich: Ernst Reinhard, 1956.

Sheldon, W. H. *Varieties of human physique.* New York: Harper, 1940.

Spranger, E. *Psychologie des Jugendalters.* Heidelberg: Quelle and Meyer, 1955.

Werner, H. *Comparative psychology of mental development.* New York: Harper, 1940.

Zeller, W. Ueber de Entwicklungstypus. *Psychologische Rundschau,* 1951.

CHAPTER 5

Nature and Nurture in Adolescence

Robert C. Nichols *

THE NATURE-NURTURE ISSUE, AS IT APPLIES TO ADOLESCENT PSYCHOLOGY, concerns the extent to which adolescent behavior is dependent on inherited characteristics, passed from one generation to the next by genetic mechanisms, and the extent to which it is dependent on the individual life experiences of the adolescent. The major dimensions of human behavior, those things that distinguish man from other animals, are obviously genetically determined; while the specific form they take (the particular language spoken, the type of clothing worn, the kinds of tools that are used) is just as obviously, culturally determined. This seems to be true of the period of adolescence itself. The physiological changes and the growing capacity for independent action are dependent on maturation of genetically determined characteristics, while the specific behaviors resulting from these changes (e.g., rebellion, self-consciousness, peer orientation, and initiation rites) are conditioned by the culture. In this broad fashion heredity and environment are both necessary and interdependent determinants of all behavior.

The situation is much less obvious, however, when we consider the relative importance of heredity and environment as determinants of individual differences in behavior within a given culture. The people in the United States, for example, compose a common cultural group that is becoming increasingly homogeneous with the increasing equality of educational opportunity and the increasing penetration of

* ROBERT C. NICHOLS is the Director of Research for the National Merit Scholarship Corporation. He has written a chapter in *Methods and Goals in Human Behavior Genetics* and has published widely on such topics as the gifted, birth order and intelligence, academic aptitude and success, and the influence of hereditary factors.

the mass media. Yet, there are great differences in the typical behavior of individual adolescents, all of whom have been exposed to this common culture. There are differences in abilities, differences in interests, differences in temperament and personality. What is the origin of these individual differences? To what extent are they due to genetic differences and to what extent are they due to differences in experience?

In the first third of the 20th century, psychologists were greatly preoccupied with this question. Individual psychologists tended to take extreme positions, and there were violent polemics between the hereditarians on the one hand and the environmentalists on the other. Like many arguments in the history of science, this issue was never resolved but concern with it simply died away as the major proponents reached retirement age and younger psychologists became interested in other problems.

Recently there has been a renaissance of interest in behavior genetics, and it is once again becoming a lively area of research. The current concern is not so much with showing the pre-eminence of either hereditary or environmental factors, but with gaining an understanding of the way in which behavior is influenced by genetic mechanisms. The proportion of the variance of a trait that is attributable to genetic differences has no absolute validity, but instead is specific to a given population at a given time. If all people of a given group are exposed to the same environmental circumstances, any differences in behavior among the people in this group will be attributable to heredity. At the other extreme, any differences in behavior observed among people with the same genetic characteristics, such as identical twins, can be attributed to differences in experience. Since all behavior is affected to some extent by both heredity and environment, the *heretability* (the proportion of the total variation attributable to heredity) of particular traits perhaps tells more about the diversity of hereditary and environmental influences in the population than it does about the relative importance of heredity and environment in any absolute sense. Thus, heretability estimates are of relatively little enduring scientific importance, although they do contribute to the understanding of behavior patterns within a given culture at a given time. Our understanding of adolescent behavior will be enhanced by a consideration of the degree to which individual differences among adolescents in Western culture are due to differences in environmental experiences and the degrees to which they are due to hereditary differences. For example, Elkind in a later chapter has discussed the development, among adolescents, of intellectual ability; and Piers discusses the topic of creativity. To what extent is development along these lines due to different family and school experiences and to what extent is it due to inherited ability?

INTELLIGENCE AND ACADEMIC ACHIEVEMENT

The trait that has received the most intensive study from the heredity-environment point of view is intelligence. This is due primarily to the fact that individual differences in ability are large and have pervasive influences on life and school success. There are also much better measures of individual differences in intelligence than there are of other behavioral characteristics. So we will first examine the evidence concerning the role of hereditary and environmental factors in bringing about differences in ability among adolescents. Students are usually keenly aware of the fact that there are great individual differences in measured ability, even among such relatively homogeneous groups as the student bodies of the more selective colleges. Some students seem consistently to make top grades with ease while others are able to compete only by long hours of arduous study. What is responsible for these differences?

There are three main types of variables that seem likely to have an important influence on ability and school achievement. These are the *school factor* or organized educational influences, the *family factor* or all of the social influences of family life on a child, and the *genetic factor*. In addition to these three main influences one might also add nutritional factors, peer influences, and community influences.

The separation of the effects of the major types of influences on ability has proved to be difficult, and all of the research so far has not resulted in unanimously accepted conclusions. This is due primarily to the fact that in human society most good things tend to go together. All other things being equal, the most intelligent parents, i.e., those with the best genetic potential, tend to provide the most comfortable and intellectually stimulating home environments for their children, and they also tend to send their children to the most affluent and well-equipped schools. Thus, the ubiquitous correlation between family socioeconomic status on the one hand and test performance and school achievement on the other is ambiguous in meaning, and isolating the independent contribution of the various factors involved is difficult. An additional complicating factor is that there are still strong emotionally motivated attitudes and vested interests concerning the heredity-environment issue that have tended to inhibit dispassionate, objective evaluation of the available evidence.

The School Factor

It seems almost self-evident that there should be a large school effect on measures of ability and academic achievement. Obviously, universal education in the United States has been largely responsible for producing the highly literate and capable population we see today. Without continued educational efforts we would undoubtedly regress to more primitive levels. But the very fact that education is so widespread and so obviously successful may reduce its importance as a source of individual differences in ability in this country.

Recent studies of school effects have tended to emphasize that differences in school experiences have little relationship to differences in student performance after all the relevant background factors have been controlled. For example, there are large differences among colleges in such respects as the average Graduate Record Examination scores of their graduates, the proportion of their graduates planning to enter various careers, and the proportion later entering graduate school. Early studies tended to assume that these differences between graduates were mainly due to the different experiences of the students at the various colleges; and "PhD Productivity," the proportion of a college's bachelor level graduates who eventually obtain a PhD, was widely considered to be an index of college quality (Knapp and Goodrich, 1952; Knapp and Greenbaum, 1953). However, subsequent studies (Astin, 1962), have shown that the differences between colleges in PhD productivity are almost entirely due to differences in the characteristics of the students entering the colleges as freshmen. Similar dependence of college output on student input has been found for career choice (Astin, 1965), Graduate Record Examination scores (Nichols, 1964), and personality and interest scales (Nichols, in press). Jacob (1957) reviewed the available literature and concluded that colleges have little differential effects on attitudes and values.

One might say that large school effects should not be expected for students of college age. By the time a person is 17 years old the major influences have already been operating for a long time, and students have likely developed defenses against noxious stimuli and methods of compensating for environmental inadequacies. It seems reasonable to assume that we should look to earlier ages for substantial school effects.

A recent large scale study of equality of educational opportunity by the U.S. Office of Education (Coleman, *et al.*, 1966; Nichols, 1966b) focused on the period from the first through twelfth grade, where school effects might more reasonably be expected. Over 600,000 students in a representative sample of more than 4,000 public schools took tests of verbal and non-verbal ability and of school achievement. There were substantial differences in the average performance of students in the various schools, as might be expected, but these differences among schools were associated with measures of the students' home background rather than with characteristics of the schools, *per se.* When family background was controlled statistically, the students' ability and achievement scores were found to be correlated, not with measures of school quality, but with the socioeconomic characteristics of the other students in the school. This finding suggests that peer influences may be more important determiners of achievement than are school and teacher quality. These and other results led the authors to conclude that "variations in school quality are not highly related to variations in achievement of pupils. . . . The school appears unable to exert independent influences to make achievement less dependent on the child's background" (Coleman, *et al.*, 1966, p. 297). Thus, the same rationalization of negative results that we used for colleges is also used here: the really formative influences have already taken place; enduring individual differences in ability are already established before students enter first grade.

This sort of reasoning was probably one of the major justifications for the Head Start program to provide preschool educational experiences for deprived children in the U.S. Since compensatory education programs for older disadvantaged students have not in general resulted in dramatic improvements in performance, it seemed reasonable to introduce a preschool program to reach the children in the formative period before the maladaptive behavior patterns had become solidified. Early studies of the results of the Head Start experience seem to be finding that the gains from this program tend to be temporary and that the head start may be lost during the first semester of first grade. Again an educational experience does not seem to produce enduring individual differences in ability and our attention is directed toward even earlier events.

The largely negative results of studies of school effects suggest that in the United States, where some sort of education is available to everyone and the mass media continually bombard us with seductive conceptual material (in other words, where very few suffer really drastic educational disadvantage), the family factor and the genetic factor are likely the major sources of individual differences in ability.

The Family Factor

Perhaps the best evidence for the importance of early experience for later intellectual development comes from studies of animals. Hebb (1949) suggested that animals reared in a stimulus-rich environment should show enduring superiority in adaptive response and perceptual capacity over animals deprived of this early stimulation. This hypothesis has been well substantiated in a variety of experiments (Denenberg, 1962). Even very brief handling experiences of infant rats, if they occur at fairly sharply defined critical periods, will affect the animals' learning performance in adulthood. It is interesting to note that infantile stress appears also to result in earlier sexual maturation (adolescence) in both animals (Morton, Denenberg, and Zarrow, 1963) and humans (Whiting, 1965).

The human situation is undoubtedly much more complicated than that of rats and mice, and it is dangerous to generalize from animal studies more than the gross principle that early experience can be very influential on later behavior, and perhaps that there are critical periods when certain experiences are more salient than they are at other times.

We have very little information about what early experiences may be critical in human development. This is a field that deserves much more attention that it has received, and fortunately a number of good researchers are now becoming interested in this problem.

The literature concerning environmental effects on intelligence was reviewed by Bloom (1964), who concluded that the maximum effect on intelligence of extreme environmental differences was around 20 IQ points (about 1.25 standard deviations). Bloom also noted that environmental effects appear to be greater early in life, particularly during the preschool years, than they are at older age levels. It is interesting to note that 20 IQ points is the average difference found by Salzberger and Jarvik (1963) between pairs of identical twins when one twin had been deaf since early in life.

The classic study by Lee (1951) of Negro children who were born in the South and moved to Philadelphia is an example of the sort of evidence considered by Bloom. Negro children born and raised in Philadelphia had a constant average ability level from the first through ninth grade relative to normative groups of their age, while Negro children born in the South and enrolled in the Philadelphia school system showed a steadily increasing average ability level during their first nine years of school. The Negro children who entered Philadelphia schools in the first grade showed a greater increase than did those who entered at later grades. It might well be assumed that Negro children in the South suffer a greater degree of environmental and educational deprivation than they do in the urban environment of Philadelphia, and that the increasing performance of the children moving to Philadelphia is the result of exposure to the more stimulating environment.

Another example of the sort of evidence that points to the importance of early experience for the development of intelligence is the study by Wolf (1965) of specific early environmental experiences and later achievement. He reasoned that if the typical correlation between family socioeconomic status and student achievement of .40 to .50 is mediated in part by differential experiences of children in families at different socioeconomic levels, then the correlation should be higher if a direct assessment were made of the child's environment rather than indirectly through characteristics of the parents. Ratings of environmental stimulation based on parental reports were found to correlate .69 with measured intelligence and .80 with school achievement. These correlations, which seem almost too high to be true, suggest that differential early stimulation accounts for part of the differences in performance of students from different socioeconomic levels.

A clue to the importance of a particular configuration of early experiences comes from studies on the effects of birth order (which is a particularly felicitous variable for research since valid information about it is easily obtained at almost any age) and it reveals a great deal about the early life of the person. For example, the typical early family experiences of two brothers, two years apart, are quite different. Altus (1966) has reviewed the literature on birth order, which suggests that earlier born (the older) siblings in a family tend on the average to be more intelligent, more likely to attend college and more likely to achieve eminence. This phenomenon has also been observed in the National Merit Scholarship competition. Among Merit Finalists from two-child families there are about twice as many first-born as second-born. In three-child families there are about as many first-born as second and third-born combined, and the second-born outnumber the third-born. This same trend holds true for four- and five-child families.

There are three possible explanations for these findings: (1) Some physiological effects of the more difficult birth or younger age of the mother of earlier born children may influence intelligence, (2) the differential family environment of early and later born children may affect the development of intelligence, or (3) the relationship may be an artifact of varying birth rates, differential participation in scholarship programs or some other spurious influence.

To study these problems further the 800,000 students who took the National Merit Scholarship Qualifying Test in 1965 were asked to indicate the number, age and sex of their siblings, which made it possible to study the relationship of the test score to birth order, sex of siblings and spacing. The yet unpublished results of this study confirm the findings concerning birth order among Merit Finalists. The earlier born the students were in their family, the higher their average test score; and this relationship held for all family sizes for both boys and girls regardless of the sex or spacing of the siblings. For a given family size and birth order, the sex of the sibling had little relationship to the test score for either boys or girls, but spacing of the siblings was quite important. For a given family size, the closer in age the nearest sibling, the lower the test score tended to be; and this tendency was more pronounced if the nearest sibling were older than if he were younger.

The relationship between birth order and test score among all participants in the National Merit tests seems to indicate that the excess of early born among Merit Finalists is not an artifact of greater participation of the older children in a family or of varying birth rates; and the relationship of sibling spacing to test score seems to favor a psychological rather than a physiological explanation for the birth order findings. The available data offer no hint as to whether it is the greater parental attention often devoted to the first born children in a family, the competitive interaction between the siblings themselves, or some other factor in the situation that puts the younger sibling at a developmental disadvantage. However, the birth order findings do suggest that the family factor is important, and they provide some vague hints concerning the kinds of experiences that may be salient.

Thus, there are clear indications that the family factor is an important source of individual differences in ability, but as yet we do not know just what the critical experiences are or much about their timing, except that the most important events occur early in life, probably before three or four,

The Genetic Factor

In contrast to the scant information about the family factor, there is fairly convincing evidence that the genetic factor is a major determinant of individual differences in ability. Erlenmeyer-Kimling and Jarvik (1963) have prepared the chart shown in Figure 5-1 to summarize the results of the 52 studies they were able to find in the literature concerning the relative similarity in measured intelligence of people with varying degrees of genetic relationship.

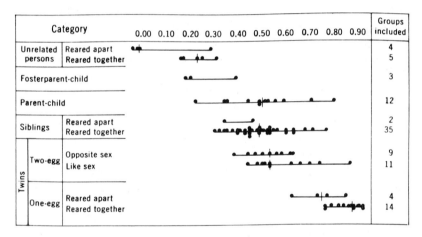

Fig. 5-1.* Correlation coefficients for "intelligence" test scores from 52 studies.* Some studies reported data for more than one relationship category; some included more than one sample per category, giving a total of 99 groups. Over two-thirds of the correlation coefficients were derived from I.Q.'s, the remainder from special tests (for example, Primary Mental Abilities). Midparent-child correlation was used when available, otherwise mother-child correlation. Correlation coefficients obtained in each study are indicated by dark circles; medians are shown by vertical lines intersecting the horizontal lines which represent the ranges.

The figure shows that the similarity in intelligence of pairs of people increases steadily as their genetic relationship increases. The orderliness of these results is all the more compelling when we consider that

* Erlenmeyer-Kimling, L. and Jarvik, Lissy F. Genetics and intelligence: A review. *Science*, 1963, *142*, 1477–1479. Copyright 1963 by the American Association for the Advancement of Science. Used by permission.

the studies were conducted over a period of several generations in several different languages on several different continents, and that results were included from studies with serious methodological defects.

Twins are of particular significance for the study of hereditary influences because they form a natural experiment in which the two kinds of twins are alike in the similarity of their environmental experiences but differ in hereditary similarity. *Fraternal or dizygotic* (DZ) twins develop from separate ova fertilized at about the same time by separate spermatozoa. The resulting two individuals have about half their genes in common, the same genetic relationship as ordinary siblings. *Identical or monozygotic* (MZ) twins, on the other hand, develop from a single ovum fertilized by a single spermatozoon that separates into two parts during the early stages of cell division. Each part develops into a separate individual, both of which have identical genetic endowment. The *zygosity* of twins (whether they are MZ or DZ) is best determined by analyses of blood samples. There are a number of genetically determined characteristics of the blood which make almost completely accurate diagnoses possible. However, highly accurate diagnoses can also be made on the basis of similarity of easily observable external physical characteristics. Such characteristics as eye color, hair color and texture, facial features, shape of ear lobes, height, weight and fingerprints have a large hereditary component. Nichols and Bilbro (1966) have shown that sets of twins who are similar in all of these characteristics are almost always MZ, while twins with a substantial difference in any one of these characteristics are usually DZ.

To the extent that a trait is genetically determined, identical twins would be expected to be more similar than are fraternal twins. Table 5-1 shows the degree of similarity in intelligence of the two kinds of twins observed in several studies. The fact that the correlation for identical twins is less than the typical reliability of the tests used (which in most instances is between .90 and .95) suggests that differential environmental experiences of the twins have affected the development of ability. The fact that fraternal twins show considerably less similarity than identical twins suggests that the greater genetic similarity of identical twins is responsible for their greater similarity in ability. In an attempt to correct partially for the possibly greater similarity of experience of MZ twins, Nichols (1965) discarded from his analysis those sets of twins who reported periods of separation, major illnesses, or other important differences in experience. The effect of discarding these cases was to increase both the MZ and the DZ

TABLE 5-1
SUMMARY OF RESULTS OF STUDIES OF THE INTELLECTUAL
RESEMBLANCE OF TWINS

Study	MZ Twin Sets Intraclass Correlation	N	DZ Twin Sets Intraclass Correlation	N	Test
Holzinger (1929)	.88	50	.63	52	Binet IQ
Newman, Freeman, Holzinger (1937)	.91	50	.64	50	Binet IQ
Newman, Freeman, Holzinger (1937)	.92	50	.62	50	Otis IQ
Blewett (1954)	.75	26	.39	26	PMA Composite
Husén (1959)	.90	215	.70	416	Swedish Military Induction Test
Husén (1960)	.89	134	.62	180	Reading Achievement
Husén (1960)	.87	134	.52	181	Arithmetic Achievement
Erlenmeyer-Kimling and Jarvik (1963)	.87	14[a]	.53	11[b]	Various Intelligence Measures
Nichols (1965)	.87	687	.63	482	NMSQT Composite

[a] Median of 14 studies.
[b] Median of 11 studies.

correlations by about the same degree, indicating that differences in experience do not account for the greater similarity of MZ twins.

Several formulas have been proposed for calculating the heritability of a trait from twin correlations (Holzinger, 1929; Nichols, 1965). When applied to the twin correlations in Table 5-1 these formulas yield estimates that approximately 70 per cent of the variation in intelligence is attributable to hereditary factors. This is somewhat lower than the 88 per cent arrived at by Burt (1958) using a different method of calculating heritability. These calculations are based on so many tenuous assumptions that they should be considered only *rough estimates* of heritability. However, they do suggest that a substantial proportion of the variation in ability is due to genetic influence.

Studies of adopted children provide a different line of evidence relevant to the question of the relative importance of the family factor and the genetic factor in determining the widely observed family resemblance in intelligence. Intelligence test scores of children raised with their true parents show increasing correlation with their mothers' education (a good substitute for intelligence tests on the mother) as the children grow older. The curve starts with a correlation near zero at age 1 or 2 and levels off at a correlation near .35 at about age 6 or 7. There are at least two possible explanations for the child's increasing similarity to his mother with increasing age: (1) greater length of exposure to the psychological influence of the mother and (2) better measures of the child's true intelligence with increasing development of verbal skills. Adopted child studies offer a way to separate these two effects. To the extent that a family factor is important the adopted child's intelligence should become increasingly similar to that of the foster parents with increasing age in a manner similar to that for children raised with their true parents. To the extent that the genetic factor is important the adopted child's intelligence should increasingly resemble that of his true parents from whom he is separated. Honzik (1957) has brought together data from two longitudinal studies which show these relationships quite clearly. The correlation of adopted children's test scores with the education of their true mothers (whom they have never seen) follows a pattern identical to that just described for children raised with their true parents, and the curve also levels off at a correlation of about .35. The correlation of the adopted children's test scores with the education of their foster mothers (who actually raised them) never reached a point higher than .10. Similar results were obtained for the relationship of the child's intelligence with the education of their true and foster fathers. These findings suggest that the genetic factor plays a greater role than the family factor in producing the correlation between the ability of children and the socio-economic status of their parents.

Still another line of evidence for the importance of the genetic factor comes from animal breeding experiments. If a behavioral trait is to some extent hereditary, selective breeding should produce strains that differ in regard to the trait. Tryon (1942) selected rats for their performance in running a maze, breeding together those with the best maze scores to produce a "maze-bright" group and those with the worst maze scores to produce a "maze-dull" group. After eight generations of such selection there was practically no overlap in the maze scores of the two groups.

Tryon's pioneering study was widely interpreted as showing the inheritance of "intelligence," however further studies of Tryon's "maze-bright" and "maze-dull" strains, which have been maintained as separate breeding populations, suggest that their differences in "brightness" are specific to maze-running and do not generalize to other measures of ability. Searle (1949) compared the two strains on a number of measures and concluded that the "maze-bright" strain was more strongly motivated by food and water deprivation and was less fearful of mechanical apparatus than was the "maze-dull" strain. Thus, Tryon seems to have produced strains that differ more in temperamental traits than in intelligence.

We might summarize this discussion of factors producing individual differences in intelligence by making a rough ordering of the major factors in terms of the degree of their contribution to individual differences in ability among adolescents in the United States. The evidence seems to indicate that the genetic factor is responsible for the largest portion of variability, followed by the family factor, and that the school factor makes the smallest contribution to individual differences. It is interesting to note that this is exactly the reverse order from a ranking in terms of the amount of effort and attention devoted to these factors in attempts to improve the performance of young people in this country. Indeed, it is probably this very distribution of effort that has resulted in the findings we have discussed. The more we succeed in equalizing the effects of a particular factor in the population, the less important that factor will become as a source of individual differences.

COMPONENTS OF INTELLIGENCE

So far we have considered intelligence as a unitary trait, which is a useful fiction, since almost all ability measures are positively correlated and verbal reasoning ability plays a large part in almost all cognitive tasks. However, factor analytic studies have shown that there are a number of components of ability that can be measured independently. Are these ability components the result of environmental experiences that facilitate the development of some abilities but not others or are they due to independent genetic mechanisms? The evidence on this interesting issue is far from conclusive, but several studies suggest that there are a number of independently inherited abilities. Blewett (1954) and Vandenberg (1962) have studied the resemblance of twins on the Thurstone Primary Mental Abilities test, an instrument designed to measure separately several components of ability. Both studies concluded tentatively that more than one ability component is dependent in part on genetic factors. Nichols (1965) reached a similar tentative conclusion from studies of twin resemblances in the subtest pattern of the National Merit Scholarship Qualifying Test. Perhaps the best evidence on this point has just recently been reported by Schoenfeldt (1967), who studied 523 sets of twins participating in Project Talent, a national survey of the abilities of approximately 400,000 high school students. By factor analytic studies of the 60 ability tests included in Project Talent, Lohnes (1966) developed a measure of general verbal ability and separate measures of 10 specific abilities. The specific abilities were measured in such a way that they were uncorrelated with general ability and with each other. The heritability coefficients for each of Lohnes' eleven factors are shown in Table 5-2.

TABLE 5-2

TWIN RESEMBLANCE IN SPECIFIC ABILITIES MEASURED INDEPENDENTLY OF GENERAL INTELLIGENCE (ADAPTED FROM SCHOENFELDT[a])

Factor	Heritability[b]	
	Males	Females
General Intelligence	.55**	.62**
Differential Aptitudes		
Visual Reasoning	.35*	.43**
Perceptual Speed and Accuracy	.34*	.28*
Memory	.40**	.29*
Educational Achievements		
English Language	.36*	.28*
Mathematics	−.05	.32**
Special Knowledge		
Simple Information	.21	.01
Information about Hunting and Fishing	.15	.05
Information about Colors and Food	.24	.09
Information about Etiquette	.21	.15
Information about Games	.32*	.32*

** Difference in similarity between MZ and DZ twins statistically significant (P < .01).

* Differences in similarity between MZ and DZ twins statistically significant (P < .05).

[a] Schoenfeldt, L. F. The hereditary components of the Project Talent two-day test battery. Paper presented at the American Research Association Meeting, February 16, 1967. Used by permission.

[b] The heritability coefficient reported is an index of the degree to which MZ twins were more similar than were DZ twins, and is an estimate of the proportion of variability attributable to genetic factors.

Schoenfeldt did not report intraclass correlations so his results for general intelligence cannot be compared directly with the results shown in Table 5-1. However, the coefficients in Table 5-2 provide a basis for comparing the relative heritability of the various factors. These results are consistent with previous studies in showing that general intelligence has substantial dependence on genetic mechanisms. What is new is the finding that differential aptitudes and educational achievements, when measured in such a way that they are independent of general ability, are also dependent in part on heredity. Special knowledges appear to have little if any genetic component. The data seem to indicate that the genetic component of differential aptitudes and educational achievements is smaller than that of general intelligence, but Schoenfeldt did not indicate the extent to which differences in the reliability of his measures could have produced the apparent differences in heritability.

Another, somewhat more indirect, line of evidence concerning genetic influence on the components of intelligence is provided by Fifer's (1965) study of ability patterns of racial and ethnic groups. Since such groups are to a degree independent breeding populations, it is to be expected that they will differ on many genetically determined traits. However, it cannot be concluded that all behavioral differences between racial groups are genetic, because they also differ in typical child rearing patterns, average socioeconomic status, and other environmental influences. In an attempt to separate the effects of these two influences on ability patterns, Fifer administered tests of four specific abilities to middle-class children and to lower-class children from four racial or ethnic groups. The samples of children were representative of all first grade children in the New York City schools of the particular racial group and socioeconomic level. First grade children were used because they were old enough to provide stable test results, but had not yet been exposed to common school experiences. It might be argued that if the ability profiles of these groups are due primarily to childhood experience they would differ at the different socioeconomic levels, since child rearing patterns are greatly influenced by socioeconomic status (Sears, Maccoby and Levin, 1957). However, if the ability profiles are due primarily to genetic factors, they should remain relatively constant for each racial group at the two socioeconomic levels.

Figure 5-2 shows the mean ability profiles for the various groups. For each ethnic group the children from middle-class homes scored substantially higher than did children from lower-class homes, reflect-

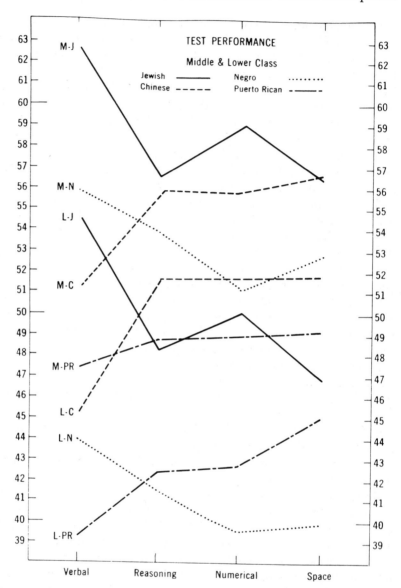

Fig. 5-2.*   Mean test profiles of lower and middle class first grade children of four ethnic groups. Each profile is the average performance of 20 boys and 20 girls. The tests were specifically constructed to measure these specific abilities at this age level.

* Fifer, G. Social class and cultural group differences in diverse mental abilities. In: *Proceedings of the 1964 Invitational Conference on Testing Problems.* Princeton, New Jersey: Educational Testing Service, 1965. Used by permission.

ing the well known correlation between family socioeconomic level and a child's ability. Each of the four ethnic groups had a distinctive profile shape that held for both middle-class and lower-class children. For example, the figure shows that Jewish children were relatively high in verbal skills and relatively low in spatial perception while Chinese children showed the reverse relationship. These patterns were little affected by socioeconomic status, even though the overall ability level varied greatly from one socioeconomic level to the other.

PERSONALITY AND INTERESTS

The results of studies of hereditary and environmental influences on intelligence are relatively clearcut and unambiguous when compared with studies of nonintellective traits. This discrepancy is due in part to the lack of satisfactory measures for temperament, and it may also be due in part to the sensitivity of personality traits to transient environmental influences.

Personality and Interest Scales

Researchers working with twins have consistently noticed that identical twins are quite similar in personality, temperament and interests. However, studies of twin resemblance on personality and interest scales have proved to be difficult to interpret. Carter (1932), Vandenberg and Kelly (1964), Nichols (1966a), Vandenberg and Stafford (1967), and Schoenfeldt (1967) have all found that identical twins have more similar interests than do fraternal twins. Studies of twin resemblance in personality (Nichols, 1966a; Schoenfeldt, 1967; Gottesman, in press) have also found that identical twins are more similar on various personality scales than are fraternal twins. The difficulty in interpreting these findings comes from the fact that there is little agreement from one study to another in the traits showing the greatest differences in similarity between the two kinds of twins. Some studies, for example have found the largest differences in similarity between MZ and DZ twins on measures of introversion-extroversion, and some writers have stated definitely that this major personality dimension has a large genetic component. However, other twin studies have found other traits to have substantially greater heritabilities than introversion-extroversion.

Another difficulty that has been encountered in twin studies of nonintellective traits is that frequently the differences between the two kinds of twins are larger than would be expected from the genetic model. The maximum difference between MZ and DZ twins that would be expected if individual differences in a trait were completely dependent on heredity can be calculated, and Nichols (1966a) has pointed out that twin studies often find differences in similarity between the two kinds of twins greater than this theoretical maximum. This suggests that something other than the greater genetic similarity of identical twins is contributing to their greater similarity on personality and interest tests.

Still another difficulty with twin studies of nonintellective traits is the failure to find agreement between the results for boys and those for girls. Most studies that have reported results separately for the two sexes have found essentially no correlation between the rank order of the heritabilities of personality and interest scales for boys and the corresponding rank order for girls.

This complicated situation makes it advisable to defer judgment concerning twin-similarity in personality until more consistent results are available. However, the consistent lack of agreement between studies and between sexes does pose a challenging problem for interpretation. One possibility is that twins talk to each other about their attitudes, opinions and interests (the sort of material that is included in personality scale items) and come to some common agreement about their opinions. Since identical twins are typically closer and spend more time together than do fraternal twins, they may arrive at a more common body of opinion than do fraternal twins. This would account for the greater similarity of identical twins and still allow twins of different sexes and twins in different geographical areas to arrive at quite different bodies of common opinion.

MENTAL DISORDER

Another line of evidence concerning the heritability of personality traits comes from the extensive body of research on the inheritance of mental disorder. Some theorists hold that the various mental disorders represent extreme forms of the motives and defense mechanisms that make up the personality differences between people in the normal range. To the extent that this is true, information about the heritability of mental disorder should also be applicable to the normal personality. However, it is also possible that mental disorders result from biochemical imbalances of a different order from the sources of normal variation in personality. This later possibility seems particularly likely in the case of schizophrenia, which is the mental disorder that has been most widely studied from the genetic point of view.

Kallmann (1953) has conducted extensive investigations of the mental health of relatives of hospitalized mental patients. A summary of his results for schizophrenia is shown in Table 5-3. The increasing

TABLE 5-3

RISK OF SCHIZOPHRENIA FOR RELATIVES OF SCHIZOPHRENICS[a]

(AFTER KALLMANN, 1946, 1950)

Class	Percentage Risk of Schizophrenia
Children of two non-schizophrenic parents (general population)	0.9
Relatives of adult schizophrenic index cases—	
Not consanguineous— Step sibs	1.8
Not consanguineous— Spouse	2.1
First cousins	2.6
Nephews and nieces	3.9
Grandchildren	4.3
Half-sibs	7.1
Parents	9.2
Full-sibs	14.2
Dizygotic co-twins	14.5
Dizygotic co-twins of same sex	17.6
Children with one schizophrenic parent	16.4
Children with two schizophrenic parents	68.1
Monozygotic co-twins	86.2
Monozygotic co-twins living apart for at least five years	77.6
Monozygotic co-twins not so separated	91.5

[a] From Shields and Slater (1961).

concordance of schizophrenia in pairs of people with increasing genetic relationship is convincing evidence for the importance of the genetic factor in determining the incidence of this disorder. This conclusion is supported by the observation that the incidence of schizophrenia is relatively constant in all human societies, even those with widely varying child rearing practices and sources of environmental stress.

Recent twin studies of schizophrenia using perhaps more complete samples of all twins in the population (Gottesman, 1966; Kringlen, 1966) have found lower concordance rates for identical twins than that reported by Kallmann, but the difference in concordance between the two kinds of twins was still substantial.

Most other mental disorders also show greater concordance for MZ than for DZ twins as is indicated by the typical results of twin studies shown in Table 5-4. These results would lead us to believe that there

TABLE 5-4

SUMMARY OF TYPICAL RESULTS OF TWIN STUDIES OF MENTAL DISORDERS
(ADAPTED FROM SHIELDS AND SLATER [1961])

Disorder and Reference	MZ Twin Sets Concordance[a] N		DZ Twin Sets Concordance N	
Schizophrenia				
Kallmann (1953)	86	268	15	685
Manic-depressive Psychosis				
Fonseca (1959)	75	21	38	39
Epilepsy (without brain damage)				
Lennox and Jolly (1954)	88	51	13	47
Neurosis, Psychopathic Personality				
Slater and Shields (1955)	53	38	25	32
Alcohol Addiction				
Kaija (1957)	65	26	30	58
Juvenile Delinquency				
Rosanoff et al. (1935, 1941)	85	42	75	25

[a] The concordance is the percentage of cases in which the disorder occurs in both twins of a set of all cases in which the disorder occurs in either twin of a set.

is a substantial genetic component in most mental disorders. However, it is not at all clear whether or not this same genetic component is also a determinant of normal variation in personality traits.

For additional details about the heritability of mental disorders see Fuller and Thompson (1960) and Shields and Slater (1961).

Animal Studies

The importance of genetic factors in determining temperamental traits of animals has already been suggested in the discussion of Tryon's selective breeding experiment. Hall (1938) performed a selection study, similar to Tryon's study of maze performance, in which rats were selected for 12 generations for high and low emotionality. A commonly accepted definition of emotionality in the rats was used: frequency of urination and defecation in a large, brightly lit open field. By the twelfth generation there was essentially no overlap in emotional response between the emotional and the nonemotional strains.

The temperamental differences typically found between different strains of animals are also evidence of the importance of the genetic factor. Inbred strains of rats and mice show large differences in activity level, emotionality and sociability (Fuller and Thompson, 1960). Scott and Fuller (1965) have described differences among five breeds of dogs in some 30 major test situations that furnished data on emotional reactivity, dominance, aggression, motivation, problem-solving and special capacities. Dog fanciers will not need to be told that large breed differences were found.

Animal studies have also shown that experience, particularly events occurring early in life, are important determinants of temperamental traits. Denenberg (1966) has reviewed studies in this area which show that a major effect of early stimulation is to reduce emotional reactivity to stress later in life. This reduced emotionality may be either adaptive or maladaptive depending on the test situation.

It should be pointed out that, while animal studies offer important clarifications of the mechanisms by which behavior is determined, they are of little help in understanding the relative effects of nature and nurture on adolescent personality. They merely show what we assumed to be true at the beginning of this chapter: that both heredity and environment are essential determinants of all behavior. An assessment of the relative importance of nature and nurture in producing the individual differences in adolescent personality observed in Western culture must await better studies at the human level.

HEREDITY-ENVIRONMENT INTERACTION

We have so far considered heredity and environment as if they were independent influences on behavior; however, recent evidence suggests that for many traits there is a large interaction between hereditary and environmental factors. In other words, the way in which a given genetic characteristic will be manifested may depend on environmental circumstances, and the effect of a given environmental experience may vary depending on the genetic characteristics of the experiencing organism.

An example of the way in which the manifestation of a genetic characteristic may be influenced by the environment in which it develops is provided by the treatment of phenylketonuria, a type of mental deficiency, by a special diet. Phenylketonuria is a recessive genetic defect resulting in a reduced ability to convert phenylalanine, an essential amino acid, into tyrosine because of a lack of the appopriate enzyme, phenylalanine hydroxylase. Without special treatment to toxic effect of the accumulation of phenylalanine or some of its derivatives results in mental deficiency. However, Armstrong and Tyler (1955) have reported a greatly reduced degree of mental deficiency in cases maintained on a low phenylalanine diet.

A number of recent animal studies have shown that the effects of environmental experiences are different, and sometimes in the opposite direction in different strains of animals (McClearn, 1964). For example, King and Eleftheriou (1959) found that early handling experience resulted in an *increased* number of responses in a shock-avoidance conditioning situation for one subspecies of deermice and a *decreased* number of responses in the same test situation for another subspecies of deermice.

Not a great deal is known as yet about the interaction of the hereditary and environmental influences that bring about the normal variation of intelligence and personality at the human level, but this appears to be a promising area for future research. As knowledge increases it may be possible by environmental manipulation to gain some control over the manner in which genetically determined traits are manifested. Also the effectiveness of educational and psychotherapeutic experiences may be greatly enhanced when we know enough to be able to tailor these environmental influences to the characteristics of the individual for whom they are intended.

SUMMARY

Individual differences among adolescents are caused in part by differences in native endowment, in part by family and peer influences, and in part by differences in educational opportunities. The available evidence suggests that in the United States, inherited differences are the most important and educational differences are the least important (of these three categories of influence) in bringing about individual differences in intelligence and academic achievement. Environmental experiences occurring early in life have greater effects than do those occurring later in life.

The various components of intelligence, in other words, the pattern of abilities, also seem to be determined in part by heredity.

The evidence concerning the relative importance of hereditary and environmental factors in bringing about individual differences in personality does not yet lead to a definite conclusion.

Both heredity and environment are important determinants of all behavior. In many instances heredity and environment interact in that the effect of the hereditary characteristics depends on the environment in which they develop; and the effect of environmental experience varies depending on the genetic characteristics of the experiencing organism.

REFERENCES

Altus, W. C. Birth order and its sequelae. *Science,* 1966, *151,* 44–49.

Armstrong, M. D., and Tyler, F. H. Studies on phenylketonuria. 1. Restricted phenylalanine intake in phenylketonuria. *Journal of Clinical Investigation,* 1955, *34,* 565–580.

Astin, A. W. "Productivity" of undergraduate institutions. *Science,* 1962, *136,* 129–135.

Astin, A. W. Effect of different college environments on the vocational choices of high aptitude students. *Journal of Counseling Psychology,* 1965, *12,* 28–34.

Blewett, D. B. An experimental study of the inheritance of intelligence. *Journal of Mental Science,* 1954, *100,* 922–923.

Bloom, B. S. *Stability and change in human characteristics.* New York: Wiley, 1964.

Burt, C. The inheritance of mental ability. *American Psychologist,* 1958, *13,* 1–15.

Carter, H. D. Twin similarities in occupational interests. *Journal of Educational Psychology,* 1932, *23,* 641–655.

Coleman, J. S., Mood, A. M., Campbell, E. Q., *et al. Equality in educational opportunity.* Government Printing Office, Washington, D.C., 1966.

Denenberg, V. H. The effects of early experience. In: Hafez, E. S. E. (Ed.), *The behavior of domestic animals.* London: Bailliere, Tindall & Cox, 1962.

Denenberg, V. H. Animal studies on developmental determinants of behavioral adaptability. In: Harvey, O. J. (Ed.) *Experience, structure and adaptability.* New York: Springer, 1966.

Erlenmeyer-Kimling, L., and Jarvik, L. F. Genetics and intelligence: A review. *Science,* 1963, *142,* 1477–1479.

Fifer, G. Social class and cultural group differences in diverse mental abilities. In: *Proceedings of the 1964 Invitational Conference on Testing Problems.* Princeton, New Jersey: Educational Testing Service, 1965.

Fonseca, A. F. Da' Anàlise heredo-cliniça das perturbacoes afectivas atraves de 60 pares de gemeos. Oporto: Faculdade de Medicina, 1959.

Fuller, J. L., and Thompson, W. R. *Behavior genetics.* New York: Wiley, 1960.

Gottesman, I. I. Schizophrenia in British twins. Paper presented at the Second Invitational Conference on Human Behavior Genetics, Louisville, Kentucky, April 30, 1966.

Hall, C. S. The inheritance of emotionality. *Sigma Xi Quarterly,* 1938, *26,* 17–27.

Hebb, D. O. *The organization of behavior.* New York: Wiley, 1949.

Holzinger, K. J. The relative effect of nature and nurture influences on twin differences. *Journal of Educational Psychology,* 1929, *20,* 241–248.

Honzik, M. P. Developmental studies of parent-child resemblance in intelligence. *Child Development,* 1957, *28,* 215–228.

Husèn, T. Psychological twin research. Vol. 1. *A methodological study.* Stockholm: Almqvist & Wiksell, 1959.

Husèn, T. Abilities of twins. *Scandinavian Journal of Psychology,* 1960, *1,* 125–135.

Jacob, P. E. *Changing values in college.* New York: Harper Bros., 1957.

Jones, H. E. Perceived differences among twins. *Eugenics Quarterly,* 1955, *5,* 98–102.

Kaija, L. Drinking habits of twins. First International Congress on Human Genetics, Part 5, *Acta Genetica,* 1957, *7,* 437–441.

Kallmann, F. J. The genetic theory of schizophrenia. *American Journal of Psychiatry,* 1946, *103,* 309–322.

Kallmann, F. J. The genetics of psychosis: An analysis of 12,232 twin index families. *Congr. Int. Psychiat.,* Paris, Hermann, Rapports: 1950, *6,* 1–27.

Kallmann, F. J. *Heredity in health and mental disorder.* London: Chapman & Hall; New York: Norton, 1953.

King, J. A., and Eleftheriou, B. E. Effects of early handling upon adult behavior in two subspecies of deermice, Peromyscus maniculatus. *Journal of Comparative and Physiological Psychology,* 1959, 52, 82–88.

Knapp, R. H., and Goodrich, H. B. *Origins of American scientists.* Chicago: University of Chicago Press, 1952.

Knapp, R. H., and Greenbaum, J. J. *The younger American scholar: His collegiate origins.* Chicago: University of Chicago Press, 1953.

Kringlen, E. Schizophrenia in Norwegian twins. Paper presented at the Second Invitational Conference on Human Behavior Genetics, Louisville, Kentucky, April 30, 1966.

Lee, E. S. Negro intelligence and selective migration: A Philadelphia test of the Klineberg hypothesis. *American Sociological Review,* 1951, 16, 227–233.

Lennox, W. G., and Jolly, D. H. Seizures, brain waves and intelligence tests of epileptic twins. *Research Publication of the Association of Nervous and Mental Disease,* 1954, 33, 325–345.

Lohnes, P. R. *Measuring adolescent personality.* Pittsburgh: University of Pittsburgh, Project Talent Office, 1966.

McClearn, G. E. Genetics and behavior development. In: Hoffman, M. L., and Hoffman, L. W. *Review of child development research.* New York: Russell Sage, 1964.

Morton, J. R. C., Denenberg, V. H., and Zarrow, M. X. Modification of sexual development through stimulation in infancy. *Endocrinology,* 1963, 72, 439-442.

Newmann, H. H., Freeman, F. N., and Holzinger, K. J. *Twins: A study of heredity and environment.* Chicago: University of Chicago Press, 1937.

Nichols, R. C. Effects of various college characteristics on student aptitude test scores. *Journal of Educational Psychology,* 1964, 55, 45–54.

Nichols, R. C. The National Merit twin study. In: Vandenberg, S. G. (Ed.) *Methods and goals in human behavior genetics.* New York: Academic Press, 1965.

Nichols, R. C. The resemblance of twins in personality and interests. *NMSC Research Reports,* 1966, 2, No. 8. (a)

Nichols, R. C. Schools and the disadvantaged. (A review of Coleman, J. S., et al. *Equality of educational opportunity.*) *Science,* 1966, 154, 1312–1314. (b)

Nichols, R. C. Personality change and the college. *American Educational Research Journal,* (In press).

Nichols, R. C., and Bilbro, W. C. The diagnosis of twin zygosity. *Acta Genetica et Statistica Medica*, 1966, *16*, 265–275.

Rosanoff, A. J., Handy, L. M., and Plesset, I. R. The etiology of child behavior difficulties, juvenile delinquency and adult criminality, with special reference to their occurrence in twins. *Psychiatric Monographs*, 1941, No. 1.

Salzberger, R. M., and Jarvik, L. F. In: Rainer, J. E., *et al.* (Eds.) *Family and mental health problems in a deaf population.* New York: New York State Psychiatric Institute, 1963.

Schoenfeldt, L. F. The hereditary components of the Project Talent two-day test battery. Paper presented at the American Educational Research Association meeting, February 16, 1967.

Scott, J. P., and Fuller, J. L. *Genetics and the social behavior of the dog.* Chicago: University of Chicago Press, 1965.

Searle, L. V. The organization of hereditary maze-brightness and maze-dullness. *Genetic Psychology Monographs*, 1949, 39, 279–325.

Sears, R. R., Maccoby, E. E., and Levin, H. *Patterns of childrearing.* Evanston, Illinois: Row, Peterson & Co., 1957.

Shields, J., and Slater, E. Heredity and psychological abnormality. In: Eysenck, H. J. (Ed.) *Handbook of Abnormal Psychology.* New York: Basic Books, 1961.

Slater, E., and Shields, J. Twins in psychological medicine. Paper read to the British Association, reported in: Relation of genetics to population studies, *Nature*, 1955, *176*, 532–533.

Smith, R. T. A comparison of socioenvironmental factors in monozygotic and dizygotic twins, testing an assumption. In: Vandenberg, S. G. (Ed.) *Methods and goals in human behavior genetics.* New York: Academic Press, 1965.

Tryon, R. C. Individual differences. In: Moss, F. A. (Ed.) *Comparative psychology.* Englewood Cliffs, New Jersey: Prentice-Hall, 1942.

Vandenberg, S. G. Innate abilities, one or many? *Research Report No. 3 from the Louisville Twin Study*, University of Louisville, 1962.

Vandenberg, S. G. and Kelly, L. Hereditary components in vocational preferences. *Acta Geneticae Medicae et Gemellologiae*, 1964, *23*, 266–277.

Vandenberg, S. G. Contributions of twin research to psychology. *Psychological Bulletin*, 1966, *66*, 327–352.

Vandenberg, S. G., and Stafford, R. E. Hereditary influences on vocational preferences as shown by scores of twins on the Minnesota

Vocational Interest Inventory. *Journal of Applied Psychology,* 1967, *51,* 17–19.

Whiting, J. W. M. Menarcheal age and infant stress in humans. In: Beach, F. A. (Ed.), *Sex and behavior.* New York: Wiley, 1965.

Wolf, R. The measurement of environments. In: *Proceedings of the 1964 Invitational Conference on Testing Problems.* Princeton, New Jersey: Educational Testing Service, 1965.

CHAPTER 6

Cognitive Development in Adolescence

David Elkind ✳

IN THE MOST GENERAL SENSE, COGNITION HAS TO DO WITH KNOWLEDGE and the mental processes involved in its acquisition and utilization. As this definition suggests, cognition covers a wide range of psychological phenomena; and a full presentation of the topic, even when limited to cognition in adolescence, is beyond the scope of a single chapter. Accordingly, the present discussion will not attempt to be encyclopedic, but rather will present material which illustrates, in depth rather than in extent, two major approaches to the study of cognitive development. While such a presentation runs the risk of omitting relevant issues, it has the virtue of confronting the student with some of the complexities of the subject and with some of the lacunae in present day theory and research pertaining to cognition.

The chapter is divided into two sections. The first section deals with the quantitative or mental test approach to the study of cognitive development, and aims to present four mental test issues which have particular relevance for cognitive growth during the adolescent period. These issues include: the course of cognitive growth; the differentiation of abilities in adolescence; the constancy of the IQ in adolescence, and sex differences in cognitive achievements during adolescence. All of these topics are true issues in the sense that a certain degree of controversy still centers about them. Consequently, it will not always be possible to draw final conclusions with respect to the issues in

✳ DAVID ELKIND is a Professor of Psychology at the University of Rochester. Prior to this, he was the Director of the Child Study Center at the University of Denver. Dr. Elkind has been a prolific writer in the child and adolescent development areas. He is the editor of *Six Psychological Studies* by Jean Piaget.

question. While this situation is perhaps less satisfying than one might wish, it nonetheless reflects the true state of our knowledge at the present time.

In the second section of the chapter, an attempt will be made to deal with the qualitative or developmental approach to cognition in adolescence. The aim of this section will be to describe and to illustrate the nature of adolescent thought and its differences from, as well as its similarities to, child thought. An attempt will also be made to show the close interdependence of cognitive and affective phenomena in adolescence. Of necessity, the tone of the second section will be more descriptive and impressionistic than the first section which is avowedly experimental.

It should be said, perhaps, that the qualitative and quantitative approaches to the study of cognitive growth do not contradict but rather complement one another. The quantitative, or mental test, approach is concerned with what remains more or less constant in mental functioning across the life span, and this is the individual's relative brightness with respect to his age group. The qualitative or developmental approach, on the other hand, focuses upon what changes with age, i.e., the mode of cognition at different age levels. The mental test approach does not deny that modes of thought differ with age and, in point of fact, the content of intelligence test items for different age levels reflects awareness of the fact that different processes are available at older age levels than are found at the younger age levels. Likewise, the developmental approach does not deny that individual differences in relative brightness exist, and such differences are used to account for the finding that some children attain particular mental abilities either before or after the majority of their age mates. Thus the mental test and the developmental approaches to the study of cognitive growth are both concerned with individual differences *and* with age group differences. They differ primarily with regard to the *kinds* of differences they choose to emphasize.

QUANTITATIVE ASPECTS OF COGNITIVE GROWTH IN ADOLESCENCE

The advent of intelligence tests and widespread intelligence testing has revealed several phenomena which appear to be unique to the adolescent period. Adolescence seems, for example, to be the period during which the capacity to acquire and to utilize knowledge reaches its peak of efficiency. It also seems to be the period, although there is considerable dispute on this point, during which particular mental abilities become relatively more differentiated than they were during childhood. Another disputed phenomenon has to do with the constancy of the IQ during adolescence. Finally, and here there seems to be more agreement, adolescence appears to be the age at which sex differences in cognitive achievements become the most prominent. In the following pages we will take up each of these issues in turn.

First, however, it may be well to make some remarks about the measurement of mental abilities in general. Such measurement is burdened with all sorts of confounding factors, some of which reside in the subject to be measured and some in the measuring instrument itself. With respect to the subject of measurement, an individual, unlike a physical object, is changed by the very fact of having been measured. The same individual, tested twice on the same instrument over a short period of time, will do better on the second testing by virtue of the practice gained during the first administration. Moreover, an individual's performance at any given time will fluctuate as a function of his overall mental state, his degree of fatigue, his level of anxiety, his attitude toward the examiner, and many other conditions. The individual's performance is thus always affected by numerous factors which are only indirectly related to his level of mental ability.

The mental test itself, however, is also different from a physical measuring instrument. Any given test samples only a limited number of mental abilities and may give precedence to some mental abilities over others. Most intelligence tests, for example, are heavily weighted in favor of verbal abilities. In addition, the tests of mental ability are likely to be different at different points in the scale so that performances at different age levels may not always be directly comparable. These are only a few of the measurement problems present in mental tests but should suffice to indicate that the mental test is far from being a perfect instrument and is subject to many kinds of error. Such tests are, nonetheless, useful and enable us to predict success with greater precision than we could without them. But the difficulties inherent in mental testing make it difficult to be dogmatic about such things as the constancy of the IQ or the differentiation of abilities in adolescence. All we can really do is reach some general statements which are valid to the degree that we can rely upon our measuring procedures.

The Course of Mental Growth

Perhaps the most famous study dealing with the course of mental growth across a long age span was an investigation published three decades ago by Jones and Conrad (1933). The study was instigated in part by the statement, made shortly after the First World War, to the effect that the mental ability of the average white draftee was equal to that of a thirteen-year-old child. This statement contradicted the notion that the mental ability of the average adult was comparable to that of a sixteen-year-old as indicated by the Terman (1916) revision of the Binet Scale. The aim of the Jones and Conrad study was to answer the question as to the peak of mental growth in a more systematic way than had hitherto been attempted.

In this carefully controlled and executed investigation, the Army Alpha Intelligence Test was administered to 1191 subjects who ranged in age from 10 to 59. For our purposes the most important finding was that mental growth increased rapidly until about the age of sixteen, after which the rate of growth became much slower. After the age of 21 the curve for mental ability began to move downward. In interpreting their results, Jones and Conrad took into account many nonintellectual factors that might possibly have affected their findings. They considered, for example, the fact that older persons might be handicapped with respect to younger ones because the Alpha is primarily a speed test and because older people tend to work more slowly than do younger people. Jones and Conrad were able to show, however, that the results held even for tests where no time pressure was involved. In summary, for the abilities tapped by the Army Alpha and for the populations studied (mostly persons from rural towns in New England), these findings with respect to the curve of mental growth would seem to have a certain measure of validity, and they have been supported in a general way by Shock (1951).

More recent work has, however, suggested that these initial findings have to be qualified in several ways. As Jones (1955) himself is quite willing to concede, the decline of intellectual functions will vary with the educational level of the subjects and with the nature of the mental abilities in question.

In a study by Thorndike (1948) it was found that mental test scores for individuals who are attending school continue to increase at least until the age of 20. Similar findings have been reported by Burns (1966), who retested 80 university graduates who had been tested on two previous occasions—during teacher training in 1930–33 when their age was 22½, and again in 1955 when their age was 47. The mean age at the third testing was 56. In general, Burns found that verbal skills such as vocabulary showed very little deterioration with age while number skills did show deterioration. Burns comments on the fact that the verbal skills may have been maintained because at least 60% of the subjects were engaged in teaching—which supposedly would serve to provide exercise for verbal skills.

These findings suggest that those persons who continue in intellectual pursuits during their adult lives may show less deterioration in some mental abilities than those adults who are not so engaged. This finding is probably complicated by the fact that the pursuit of an academic career is usually associated with higher intelligence and that persons of better than average ability may show less deterioration with age than persons of average ability. In this regard the findings of Owens (1953) with college graduates and of Bayley and Oden (1955) with gifted adults suggest that high intelligence as well as an academic profession is a hedge against the deterioration of some mental abilities.

All these studies are consistent in showing that verbal skills tend to deteriorate less rapidly than mathematical skills. An interesting hypothesis to account for the different developmental and decline patterns of varied mental abilities has been offered by Trembly (1964). He argues that each mental ability shows a period of rapid early growth after which it reaches a plateau and then proceeds to decline. In addition, each mental ability shows a distinct rate of growth, age of maturity, age of decline and rate of decline. Trembly argues further that those mental abilities which appear earliest in individual development show longer plateaus and less rapid decline at older age levels than do later appearing mental abilities. In support of this position, he cites tonal memory, which has a plateau of 30 years, and contrasts it with inductive reasoning, which appears much later in development and manifests a plateau of only three years.

This hypothesis is in keeping with the position of Jones (1955), who argues that those abilities that are maintained with little deterioration tend to reflect "the mere accumulation of verbal or factual inventories" while the abilities which show decline with age, such as mathematical reasoning and analogies, have more to do with high level mental processes. In this connection Jones (1955) cites Whitehead, "The imagination is most active between the ages of 19 and 35 and we mostly keep going thereafter, on whatever fizz we have experienced then." Such a view is supported by the fact that in science and in the arts the really great discoveries and creations are most often the work of young men.

The Differentiation of Abilities

One of the debates that seems to be perennial within developmental psychology is whether growth proceeds by differentiation or by integration. This debate has been carried on at the biological, physiological, and psychological levels without ever having been completely resolved at any level. In some cases the debate revolves more around a definition of terms than upon different interpretations of the data. Differentiation, for example, can mean either specialization of function or increased complexity of functioning or both! Likewise, integration can refer either to the unity of an organization or to its simplicity or to both at the same time. With respect to the issue of differentiation vs. integration of intelligence with age, the debate would appear to be factual as well as verbal.

In order to make clear the issue of differentiation with respect to intellectual functioning, it is necessary first to recall Spearman's (1923) theory of intelligence. According to Spearman, performance on any mental task involves a general or g factor present in all mental operations plus specific s factors unique to the mental operations called forth by different types of tasks. The issue with respect to the differentiation of abilities in adolescence concerns the relative amounts of g and s factors involved in specific mental tests at different age levels. Although these factors are extracted by the rather complex mathematical procedures of factor analysis, we need not understand those procedures to grasp the issues involved.

One of the first investigators to advocate the differentiation hypothesis with respect to adolescent intelligence was Burt who wrote:

> With younger children, and particularly, it would appear, with younger girls, one can demonstrate little but the existence of the general factor (i.e., g); with older school children and particularly with college students, little but specific talents or specialized interests (Burt, 1962/1921, p. 359).

This statement was based on factor analytic data which showed that the amount of the general factor in tests of verbal, arithmetical and manual ability decreased markedly with age while the reverse held true for the specific factors.

Support for this differentiation point of view came from Garrett (1946), who was primarily concerned with the nature of mental organization. In one study reported by Garrett (1946) 9, 12 and 15-year-old children were tested for memory, verbal, and number abilities. The degree to which the general or g factor was involved in these tests dropped from .31 among the youngest boys to .12 among the oldest boys, and for the girls the amount of g dropped from .31 among the youngest to .19 among the oldest. Garrett also reports other studies (which suggested comparable results) and postulated the following hypothesis: "Abstract or symbol intelligence changes in organization as age increases from a fairly unified and general ability to a loosely organized group of abilities or factors" (Garrett, 1946, p. 373).

Other investigators have found similar trends. Balinsky (1941) tested subjects ranging in age from 9 to 59 and found that the number of factors increased between the ages of 9 and 29 but declined thereafter. Thurstone and Thurstone (1941) also obtained evidence for differentiation with age. These investigators found six primary mental abilities among kindergarten children, seven among seventh grade children, and nine such factors among college students. Although arrived at by somewhat different methods and tests, these results are in general agreement with those of Burt (1962/1921) and Garrett (1946) with respect to the differentiation of mental abilities during adolescence.

Unfortunately, at least for those who like their science neat, other investigators have obtained evidence which contradicts the differentiation hypothesis in the sense that it points toward the motion that intelligence becomes more integrated with age. Cohen (1959), for example, tested children aged 7–6; 10–6, and 13–6 with the Wechsler Intelligence Test for Children (WISC) and found no evidence for the differentiation hypothesis. He argues that the same factors appear in the intellectual functioning of children and adults, and that adults show more of the general factor than do children. Likewise, Cropley (1964) tested 10 and 12-year-old children on the WISC and found comparable factor structures and a tendency for increasing integration with age. While these results might be questioned (on the basis of the methods used to extract the factors), as they stand they raise difficulties for the differentiation hypothesis. Perhaps a theory which postulates a general to specific to general development across the whole life span (Green and Berkowitz, 1964) may help resolve the problem. In addition, the utilization of uniform methods for extracting factors and uniform criteria for interpreting them would be helpful.

It is not possible at the present time to come to any clear-cut conclusion about the differentiation of abilities in adolescence although the bulk of the evidence seems to favor differentiation over integration at least during the adolescent period. All that we can do, as a parting shot at the problem, is to present a statement by Burt which helps to clarify the issues involved and provides a cautionary note as well:

> Judging from my own data, I should readily agree that, after the age of puberty, it is not easy to find evidence for further differentiation of *abilities*, though a differentiation of *interests* is often discernible. That, however, cannot affect the hypothesis with which we are here concerned—namely, that between late infancy and early adolescence, there is a definite increase in specialization in ability due, not to education, but to maturation. At the same time, *it would be a gross oversimplification to describe mental development in terms of a single sweeping principle—whether of increasing differentiation or increasing integration—or to assume that any such principle must hold good of all mental processes and of every individual.* (our italics) (Burt, 1954, p. 85)

The Constancy of the IQ from Childhood to Adolescence

On the surface, it might seem that an answer to the problem of whether or not the IQ remains constant over long time periods would be relatively easy to answer. All one needs to do is test the same subject as a child and again as an adolescent and then compare the results of the two examinations. In fact, however, the problem is complicated by many different factors, some of which come from the nature of the tests and some from the nature of the subject. Let us first consider the difficulties which are inherent in the tests.

The kinds of defects inherent in mental tests which make difficult the comparison of the performances of the same individual are illustrated by the 1937 revision of Stanford Binet (Terman and Merrill, 1937). Pinneau (1961), for example, has shown that by virtue of the way in which the test was constructed, a person who maintained the same relative standing with respect to his age group from childhood to adolescence would nonetheless have attained a different IQ score in adolescence than he did in childhood. The reason is statistical and has to do with the fact that the amount of variability at the two developmental periods differs. In addition, the correlation between the scores obtained by the same person on a particular intelligence test will vary as a function of the ages at which the examinations were given and as a function of the time interval between the examinations. Scores attained during the pre-school period, for example, tend to correlate less highly with scores attained during adolescence than do scores attained during the elementary period (Honzik, MacFarland and Allen, 1948).

Another major consideration in attempting to evaluate the constancy of the IQ is the kinds of experiences the individual has undergone. Since the IQ measures achievement as well as underlying capacity, any factors which affect achievement will also affect the IQ. Environmental experiences which make for self-confidence, which provide or deprive the individual of ample and effective stimulation for learning, may markedly affect the extent of the young person's intellectual achievements. Environmental circumstances, moreover, do not remain constant throughout childhood and adolescence. The family may move, the young person may become a member of a group which is for or against school, or he may encounter a teacher who sets a spark to his intellect or who, contrariwise, kills his interest in learning. All of these factors and more can and do affect performance on intelligence tests and make it difficult to say how stable the IQ will remain from childhood to adolescence.

For all these reasons, changes in IQ with age are probably the rule rather than the exception. It is also true, however, that a certain amount of constancy does occur. Correlations between IQ's attained in childhood and those attained in adolescence are on the order of .60, and the correlations between IQ's attained in adolescence and adulthood on the order of .80 (Bradway and Thompson, 1962). While the knowledge of the IQ of a child may not be sufficient to predict exactly what his IQ will be as an adolescent, it does enable us to make a better than chance guess as to what his relative standing in adolescence will be. And, in general, the more extreme the IQ at childhood, whether in a low or high direction, the more accurate will be the prediction. The greatest changes in IQ occur among those who score in the average range between 90 and 110, but even though there is an absolute change in score, the chances are that the person will remain in the average category. Put differently, if we think of IQ standing in terms of gross categories such as above average, average and below average, rather than in terms of absolute scores, then the IQ does remain relatively stable from childhood through adolescence. It is only when we think of the IQ in terms of absolute numerical scores that we must reject the notion of IQ constancy. The reader will also find Nichol's chapter, on the issue of the contributions of heredity and environment, a valuable supplement to his thinking in this area.

Sex Difference in Intelligence and Mental Ability

The literature on differences between boys and girls in intelligence in general and in cognitive abilities and interests in particular is enormous, and no attempt will be made to survey that material here. In a comprehensive summary of the findings up to 1954, Terman and Tyler made the following points which appear equally valid today:

1. If there are differences in general intelligence between the sexes, they cannot be identified by means of our present tests.
2. Girls tend to excel on verbal types of problems, boys on quantitative or spatial problems.
3. School marks almost universally indicate superior achievement for girls. Achievement tests, however, while they show girls to be superior in all kinds of language material, show boys to be superior in science and mathematics.
4. Vocational aptitude tests show boys as higher in mechanical, girls in clerical, aptitudes.
5. Ability differences are most apparent at the older age levels in children. Most of these differences do not show up in the pre-school period. (Terman and Tyler, 1954, p. 1068. Slightly modified version of original wording)

From the point of view of our particular focus, cognitive development in adolescence, Terman and Tyler's last point is of particular interest. Although sex differences in achievement appear prior to adolescence, they become particularly prominent during this age period. This is especially true in the areas of scientific knowledge and achievement. The performance of high school students on science tests has repeatedly shown that boys perform at a much higher level on these tests than do girls (Jordan, 1937; Edgerton and Britt, 1944, 1947). These differences are much less marked at the elementary school level. The writer, for example, found no sex differences between elementary school boys and girls with respect to certain quantity concepts (Elkind, 1961a) but significant differences between the sexes on quantity concepts among high school and college students (Elkind, 1961b, 1962). The differences among the older groups were consistently in favor of the boys. In the same vein, King (1963) examined the responses of 5–17 year old children to twenty science questions and found no sex differences for elementary school children but significant sex differences for secondary school children.

In all likelihood, these sex differences in scientific achievement which appear in adolescence reflect differences in interest rather than differences in mental ability. In one of the aforementioned studies of the writer (Elkind, 1962) it was found that the girls had higher mean IQ's than the boys even though they had more primitive quantity concepts. The results of Project Talent point in the same direction. Flanagan found, for example, that high school "boys did better than girls in physical science information, but their superiority was not nearly so great as in related nonacademic areas such as electricity and electronics." (Flanagan, 1964, p. 3–116). Flanagan argues that, "Boys did better than girls on the mechanical reasoning test (an aptitude measure) but not as much better as would have been commensurate with their superiority in mechanical information if the latter superiority had been wholly attributable to differences in aptitude." (Flanagan, 1964, p. 3–116). The adoption of adult sex roles in adolescence could thus serve to channel interests and activities and could help account for the divergence of the sexes with respect to scientific achievement. In summary we can conclude with some assurance that adolescence is a period during which differences in certain areas of academic achievement become the most marked.

QUALITATIVE ASPECTS OF COGNITIVE GROWTH IN ADOLESCENCE

The rapid physical and physiological changes that mark the advent of adolescence (as Garrison describes in detail), together with the inner emotional turmoil and outward defiance that mark this period, tend to obscure the truly remarkable changes which occur in cognitive ability. It would be hard to overestimate these changes since it is only during adolescence that the young person becomes capable of the kind of experimental thinking upon which modern society is based. In this section an attempt will be made to trace the evolution of adolescent thinking and to describe some of its manifestations and affective consequences. We will first refer back to the thinking of the child in order to show in what respects adolescent thought is an improvement over what was previously present.

In our discussion of the qualitative aspects of cognitive growth we will lean heavily upon the work and theory of the Swiss psychologist Jean Piaget and his colleague, Barbel Inhelder (Inhelder & Piaget, 1958). This will be done for two reasons. First of all, Piaget and Inhelder have provided the most comprehensive theory about the development of adolescent cognitive activity currently available. Secondly, almost all of the current research on the thinking of adolescence in one way or another takes the work of Piaget and Inhelder as a starting point. Accordingly, we will first review the general theory of cognitive development as outlined by Piaget (1950) and Inhelder & Piaget (1958) and then present the research work of other investigators within the general context of this theory.

From Concrete to Formal Operational Thinking

According to Piaget (1950), thought evolves from the gradual internalization of action. From this point of view, true thought does not emerge before the age of 6–7 when actions become fully internalized and organized into systems. The system of thought which is present during childhood (ages 6–7 to about the age of 10–11) differs from the system of thought which emerges during adolescence (after the age 12). To understand the differences between these two systems we need to consider the kinds of thinking of which the elementary school child is capable. Only then can the achievements of adolescent thought be truly appreciated.

The system of thought which is present during middle and late childhood is characterized by Piaget as the period of *concrete operations*. An operation is an internalized action which is part of a system of actions that manifests certain rules or properties. The properties manifested by the operational system during childhood, however, differ from those which are manifested by the operational system during adolescence and this is the reason for dubbing it *concrete* in opposition to the operational system in adolescence which is called *formal*. Let us consider some of the properties of the concrete operational system and some of the achievements which this system makes possible.

The concrete operational system can be conceived of as analogous to a logical group in the sense that it involves a set of elements (objects, relations, dimensions) and operations (addition, subtraction, etc.) and rules for their combination. One of these rules or properties is *commutivity*. This rule states that no matter how elements in the set are combined the results will be the same. For example, $A + (B + C) = (A + B) + C$. A second rule is that of *identity*. This rule states that for every element in the set there exists an identical element such that $A - A = 0$ or $A = A$. A third rule is *composition*, or that the combining any two elements of the set will result in a third element which is also a member of the set, or $A + B = C$. Finally, the fourth rule of the concrete operational system is that of *reversibility*, which states that for every operation in the set there is a second, inverse operation which can exactly annul the effects of the first. To illustrate, $A + B = C$, but $C - A = B$ and $C - B = A$. Reversibility means that one can always get back to the starting point of a series of operations.

The presence of this system of concrete operations makes possible a kind of reasoning that does not appear in the pre-school child. It is only with the advent of this concrete operational system that the child can deal effectively with classes, relations and quantities. It enables the child to nest classes, to seriate relations and to conserve quantities. To illustrate these achievements we will consider concrete examples of each of them in turn.

With respect to classes, the concrete operational child can deal with a large class and its subclasses at the same time. To illustrate, if a nursery school child is asked whether there are "more boys or more children" in the classroom, he will respond, "there are more boys than girls." For the young child, as soon as he deals with the subclasses the larger class is destroyed, since he cannot conceive that one and the same youngster can belong to two classes at the same time. The child of six or seven, however, has no trouble with this problem (Elkind, 1961c). He is now capable of the composition: Children = boys + girls, and of deducing from that the conclusion that since: Children — boys = girls, ∴ children ≠ boys. In a word, the presence of concrete operational thought makes possible deductive reasoning.

We come to the same conclusion when we look at how the pre-school and school age children handle the problem of seriating relations (Piaget, 1952; Elkind, 1964). If a nursery school child is shown a set of eight size-graded slats arranged in the form of a staircase and is then given a second set of slats, whose sizes are intermediate to those of the first set, and is asked to insert them into the staircase, he cannot do it. He builds a second staircase alongside the first or, if he does insert, he makes glaring mistakes. The child who has attained concrete operations, however, has no trouble with the problem. He correctly inserts the second set of elements, say *a,b,c,d,e,f,* within the first, say A,B,C,D,E,F. The older child can do this because he can compose the relations $D < d > E$ and recognize that d must be both larger than E and smaller than D if it is to be correctly fitted into its place. The young child fails because he cannot compose these relations and recognize that one and the same element can stand in two different relations at the same time.

The results of concrete operational thinking are equally clear in the realm of quantity. It is only around the age of six or seven, for example, that the child becomes aware of the fact that an amount of liquid poured from a big glass into two smaller glasses remains the same (Piaget, 1952; Elkind, 1961d). Prior to this age, the child judges that the amount of liquid changes with a change in its appearance. The concrete operational child solves the problem by taking account of *both* the width of the container and the levels of the liquids at the same time. He thus comes to realize that for every change in the level of the liquids there is a corresponding change in the widths of the containers which exactly compensates for change in level. This awareness of reversibility, thanks to the concrete operational system, allows the child to discover the conservation of quantities.

Despite these increments in mental power afforded the elementary school child by the emergence of concrete operations, his thinking is still quite limited in comparison with the thought of the adolescent or the adult. In the first place, the child can only reason about those things with which he has had direct personal experience. He has difficulty as soon as he has to deal with any hypothetical or contrary-to-fact proposition. In addition, while he can deal with two classes, relations, or quantitative dimensions at the same time, this is about the limit of his capabilities. As soon as more variables than two have to be taken into account in a systematic way, he flounders because he lacks an operational system appropriate to such situations. This is the fundamental deficiency of concrete operational thought.

With the advent of adolescence, however, a new kind of operational system emerges. This is a second order operational system in the sense that it takes the concrete operational system as its object. Put differently, the adolescent can take his own thought as an object and reason about it. What this means is that the adolescent can take the combinations or compositions that he was able to form at the concrete operational stage and combine these compositions as if they were elementary classes, relations or dimensions. The result is that the adolescent arrives at many combinations which might not occur in fact. At this stage he thus becomes able to deal with possibilities, or hypotheses as well as with facts. Furthermore, while the child's concrete operational system enables him to distinguish between reality and appearance, between how things look and how they really are, formal operational thought enables the young person to distinguish between truth and falsity, i.e., to judge hypotheses against fact (Inhelder and Piaget, 1958).

To make the potentialities of formal operational thinking more concrete, consider the following example. Suppose that one has four pieces of plastic, one of which is blue, another red, a third green, and a fourth yellow. Suppose further that these pieces of plastic are given to elementary school children and adolescents with the request that they be put together in as many different ways as possible. What one finds is that the child will at best combine only two of the pieces of plastic at a time, and if he goes beyond this he becomes bewildered and cannot proceed in any systematic way. The adolescent, on the other hand, easily comes up with the following system of sixteen combinations:

1) none of the pieces	2) R	6) RG	12) RGB	16) RGBY
	3) G	7) RB	13) RGY	
	4) B	8) RY	14) RBY	
	5) Y	9) GB	15) GBY	
		10) GY		
		11) BY		

The ability to generate all possible combinations within a system is thus a unique feature of adolescent thought and underlies many different types of accomplishment which we will detail in the next section.

In the foregoing example we have shown how adolescent thought goes beyond the thought of the child with respect to concrete materials, i.e., with respect to single elements. The adolescent can also do the same thing with compositions of two elements taken together even when these are expressed as propositions. Consider the following set of propositions suggested by Peel (1960):

it is raining and cold $(p.q)$
or (v) it is raining and not cold $(p.\bar{q})$
or (v) it is not raining and cold $(\bar{p}.q)$
or (v) it is not raining and not cold $(\bar{p}.\bar{q})$

These four propositions (p.q; p.q̄; p̄.q; p̄.q̄) can then be combined in a manner directly analogous to the ways in which the four pieces of colored plastic were combined. Depending upon the nature of these combinations they tell us different things about the relations of p and q to one another. For example:

a) pq v p̄q v p̄q̄ (pq̄ false) is equivalent to *p implies q.*
b) pq v pq̄ (p̄q and p̄q̄ false) is equivalent to *p is independent of q.*
c) pq̄ v p̄q (pq and pq false) is equivalent to *p is incompatible with q*
   (Peel, 1960, p. 127).

The possibilities which the ability to combine propositions opens up to thought should be immediately obvious. This is the mode of thinking which is present in all scientific endeavor. In any experiment, the investigator holds certain variables constant and changes others to determine their effects. It is only through combining variables in all these possible ways and comparing the results of the combinations with the experimental findings that he is able to draw his conclusion about their relatedness or their independence.

Before considering some of the ramifications of this form of thinking, it might be well to say a word or two about why this form of mental activity, which all of us engage in more or less regularly, looks so formidable in print. The major reason probably lies in the fact that as thinkers we are aware only of the products and not of the processes of our thought. It is only in retrospect that we reconstruct the processes that we *must* have gone through in arriving at particular conclusions. Thus, when it is shown that we have been thinking in the formal operational way, we are as amazed as Moliere's famous doctor when he discovered that he had been speaking "prose" all of his life!

Cognitive Manifestations of Formal Operational Thought

Let us now consider some of the cognitive manifestations of formal operational thinking and some of its affective consequences.

Differentiation of thought and external world. The growth of thought from infancy through adolescence is marked by a progressive differentiation of thought and reality. At each level of development this differentiation poses a unique problem and a unique solution. The infant begins, for example, by treating objects as if they no longer existed when they were out of sight. By the end of infancy, on the other hand, he shows, by his active search for hidden objects, that for him objects now have a permanence which is independent of their immediate sensory presence or absence (Piaget, 1954). From about the age of 2 to 6, the child begins to deal with subject-object differentiation at a new level. This period begins with the use of symbols and signs but without a clear understanding of the relation between signifier and what is signified. The pre-school child thinks that the name of the object resides in the object and has always been the name of the object.* He also believes that an object can have only one name and has difficulty understanding how people can call his baby brother "Robert" when in fact his name is "Bobby." Towards the end of this period the child discovers that names are arbitrary designations, as shown by the advent of *name calling* during the elementary school period. Thus a new level of subject-object differentiation has been reached, this time on the plane of the symbol and its referent.

During the period of concrete operational thinking (ages 6–7 to 11–12) the child encounters the problem of subject-object differentiation on still another plane. The advent of concrete operations makes possible elementary deductive thinking and hence the construction of concrete hypotheses about reality. At this stage the child does not recognize the hypothetical character of his conclusions and assumes that they have a measure of physical fixedness while reality has a degree of hypothetical arbitrariness. At this stage the child does not recognize that his notions have to be tested against the evidence and instead behaves as if the facts must be made to fit the hypotheses. Towards the end of childhood and the beginnings of adolescence, however, one sees a new subject-object differentiation. The adolescent recognizes the arbitrariness of his hypotheses and the necessity of testing them against the evidence.

Some concrete experimental data may help to illustrate the differences between the thought of children and adolescents in this regard. In an experiment by the writer (Elkind, 1966), children (8–9 years of age) and adolescents (13–14 years of age) were presented with a concept attainment task. The materials were pictures of wheeled and non-wheeled tools and wheeled and non-wheeled vehicles. The pictures were presented in pairs such that a wheeled tool or vehicle was

---

* The child at this stage behaves in the manner of the scholar who when asked why noodles are called noodles replied, "Well, they are white like noodles, soft like noodles and they taste like noodles."

always coupled with a non-wheeled tool or vehicle. Choice of a wheeled tool or vehicle always made a light go on, whereas the choice of a non-wheeled tool or vehicle never resulted in the light going on. The task for the subject was to find the kind of card which would make the signal light go on every time.

The results clearly illustrate the difference between adolescent and child thought. Only half of the children were able to arrive at the notion that it was the choice of wheeled objects which made the light go on. Furthermore, it took those children who did succeed almost all of the allotted 72 trials to arrive at the correct solution. On the other hand, *all* of the adolescents solved the problem and many did so in as few as 10 trials. The reason for this difference was quite clear from the spontaneous verbalizations made during the course of the trials. Adolescents raised hypotheses such as "maybe it's transportation" and then "no it must be something else, I'll try . . ." By constantly raising hypotheses and checking them against whether or not the light went on they quickly solved the problem. The children, however, seemed to get fixated on either the tool or vehicle hypothesis which was so strongly suggested by the pictures. These subjects kept trying to find ways they could reconcile this hypothesis with the cards that made the light go on. Moreover, when asked what the rule was that made the light go on, even those children who failed on the majority of trials still gave a rule as if it were a correct one. To test the strength of this hypothesis some children were shown a negative instance, for example if they said "things that move" they were shown a horse and a wheelbarrow where the choice of horse did not make the light go on and the choice of wheelbarrow did. Under this circumstance a common reply was, "Well, the horse moves in a different way."

It was clear, then, that the child stuck with his hypothesis and would not give it up in the face of the evidence. Indeed, the evidence was reinterpreted to fit the hypotheses! These findings support the view that the child, as compared to the adolescent, does not clearly differentiate his hypotheses from reality. Other data which support this conclusion have been provided by Weir (1964). In Weir's investigation, subjects from nursery school through high school were confronted with an apparatus on which there were three knobs. They were instructed that when the correct knob was pressed, a reward would drop into a small chute beneath the knobs. The machine was so adjusted that only one of the knobs "paid off" and this only 66% of the time. The *best* or maximizing solution was thus the simplest, "keep pushing the knob which paid off before."

The results differed from what is usually found in developmental investigations in the sense that there was not a regular improvement with age. In fact, the nursery school children were the most successful of all, although the adolescents ran them a close second. The elementary school children, however, had the most difficulty with the problem. Weir's examination of the qualitative aspects of the situation made clear what was going on. The young children simply persevered on the knob which paid off regardless of whether or not it paid off on a particular trial. The adolescents, on the other hand, initially adopted complex strategies in the sense that they assumed there were elaborate patterns of knob pressing to be discovered. They soon gave these strategies up, however, and began pressing only the pay-off knob. The difficulty encountered by the elementary school children resulted from the fact that they adopted a strategy—"if you win you shift and if you lose you shift"—from which they did not deviate despite the fact that this strategy did not succeed!

As in the previous study, the results of Weir's investigation strongly suggest that while the elementary school child raises hypotheses about physical events, he does not test these against the facts. Indeed, he seems unaware of the hypothetical quality of his strategy and seems to feel that it is imposed from without rather than constructed from within. It is for this reason that the child appears to be more rigid than the adolescent in certain problem-solving tasks. The adolescent, with his awareness of the arbitrariness of his hypotheses and of their mental quality, is ready to give them up to produce others. This ability to discriminate between thought and reality is derived from the capacity to take all of the possibilities in the situation into account, and it is the awareness of *possibility* that marks the true differentiation between thought and reality.

Utilization of abstract concepts. One of the most regular observations with respect to adolescent thought is that it is more abstract than that of the child. In this context, *abstract* usually means thinking which is more general and more divorced from immediate experience than is the thought of the child. This difference is most clearly illustrated in the kinds of definitions children and adolescents give for the same terms. With respect to a concept like *time*, for example, a ten year old youngster is likely to define it in a static, specific sense, as "it is something that the watch tells," or as "time means the clock" or as "a clock tells time." By the age of 15, however, time is defined as, "time is stable, it is what we don't have too much of," or "time is sort of like an interval of space" (Gesell, Ilg, and Ames, 1956). Comparable differences in definition have been observed with respect to a wide variety of vocabulary items (Feifel and Lorge, 1950).

Differences in level of abstraction between adolescents and children can also be observed when they are asked to deal with complex class concepts such as the concept of religious denomination. In one study (Elkind, 1963) elementary school and junior high school children were asked a variety of questions about their religious denomination which in this case was Protestant. One of the questions asked was, "Are all boys and girls in the world Protestant?" The routine answer of the children was "no" and this was usually explained by a statement such as, "Well, some of my friends are not Protestant," or "I know a boy who is not Protestant." By the age of twelve and thirteen, however, the typical response was usually, "No, because there are different religions in the world."

Although the differences between the replies of children and of adolescents to such questions are intuitively clear, it might be well to spend a few words on making these differences more explicit. If one looks at the child's explanations closely, it becomes immediately obvious that while they are correct as far as they go, they are incomplete. It is true enough that not all boys and girls in the world are Protestant and that acquaintance with non-Protestants is evidence for this conclusion. This explanation, nonetheless, does not take into account all of the *possible* non-Protestant children. To say, on the other hand, that there are "other religions" does take care of all the other children in the world. The same incompleteness can be seen in childen's definitions of most concepts as in their definitions of the concept of time, mentioned earlier. While it is true "that a clock tells time," it is also true that a calendar tells time. The definitions of the older children with respect to time attempt to provide notions which will take into account all the different kinds of time measures.

The major difference, then, between the definitions given by children and those given by adolescents is that the definitions of the adolescents take into account all of the instances and non-instances of the concept whereas the definitions of children take account of only some of the positive and negative instances. The completeness of definitions given by adolescents would seem to derive from their capacity for formal operational thinking. It is combinatorial logic which enables the adolescent to deal systematically with all of the possible positive and negative instances of a concept and thus to arrive at a definition which is both complete and precise.

Interpretation of literary and graphic materials. Still another way in which formal operational thought is manifested is in the interpretation of literary and graphic materials. The usual procedure in investigations of this kind is to present subjects of different ages with literary passages or graphic materials and then to question the subjects about them.

In a study by Peel[*] the following passage was read by children from 8 to 15 years of age who were also shown a picture of the Stonehenge site.

> *Stonehenge*
> Stonehenge is in the south of England, on the flat plain of Salisbury. There is a ring of very big stones which the picture shows. Some of the stones have fallen down and some have disappeared from the place. The people who lived in England in those days we call Bronze Age Men. Long before there were any towns, Stonehenge was a temple for worship and sacrifice. Some of the stones were brought from the nearby hills, but others which we call Blue Stones, we think came from the mountains of Wales.
>
> The questions asked of the children were as follows:
> Question 1: Do you think Stonehenge might have been a fort and not a temple? Why do you think that?
> Question 2: If the stones were rolled into position, what do you think has become of the rollers?
> Question 3: What do you think has happened to the missing stones?

Here are some of the replies from children at different age levels:

> A: aged 7:7
> 1) A temple (Why?) Because people live in it.
> 2) They've fallen down. People might have knocked them down. (Explanation of rollers) They'd broken.
> 3) They've fallen down. People have rolled them somewhere. (Why?) So they could live in them.

[*] Peel, E. A. *The Pupil's Thinking*. London: Oldbourne Press, 1960, pp. 117–120. Used by permission.

B: aged 9:1

1) I think it might have been to stop the enemy charging through. (Why do you think that?) It looks like it. The bricks would stand up. The enemy could not force through quick enough and they'd be killed.

2) They've thrown them away in a little river to the big sea. (There isn't a river there.) They carried them to the river and got sunk.

3) They must have sunk in the ground. (They dug around there and they couldn't find any.) They must have been used by the people that came after.

D: aged 14:0

1) I think it would be a temple because it was a round formation with an altar at the top end, and at a certain time of the year, the sun shines straight up a path towards the altar, and I think that it was used for the worship of the sun god. There was no roof on it so that the sun shines right into the temple. There is a lot of hard work and labour in it for a god and the fact that they brought the blue stones from Wales.

2) The rollers would be wooden and they probably rotted away by now.

3) The wear of the weather, the wind and sun have crumbled them to dust in the ages. (Do you think anything else might have happened?) A warring tribe might have come and knocked some down and took some away. (What for?) Just to get revenge on the tribe.

E: aged 14:11

1) I doubt it. I shouldn't think so. I seems rather open for a fort. It doesn't seem large enough either. It does seem rather small. You wouldn't need a fort in the middle of Salisbury Plain. Its deserted. There's not many people about. There's not likely to be any trouble around there.

2) It depends if they were made of wood they might have rotted and maybe if they were circular stones they may have been buried. I doubt if they would have been taken away. They would have had to shape stones. I think they would have used wood.

3) They may possibly have worn away through weather. I don't mean completely worn away but worn down like the small ones in the picture. There are a lot of stones lying down. There might have

been enough to make up the circle. (Some have disappeared.) Maybe some have been taken away to be examined to see how long its been standing. Is it proved that it was completed? (People think it was completed.)

If one compares the responses of the children with those of the adolescents several differences can immediately be seen. First of all, the child does not deal with the situation as a whole, but rather focuses upon one dominant feature of the situation. To illustrate, the child (B) who said that Stonehenge was a fort explained this solely on the basis of the fact that the "stones would stand up." The adolescent, on the other hand, considers the situation from many different points of view simultaneously, as (E) said, "it seems rather open for a fort. It doesn't seem large enough either . . . You wouldn't need a fort on Salisbury Plain . . ." Thus, while the child bases his interpretation on one or at most a few concrete aspects of the situation, the adolescent bases his judgment on many different considerations, some of which are far removed from the actual data presented.

Another difference between the responses of the children and the adolescents is reflected in the language with which they express their answers. The child expresses himself as if he were stating a fact. One child (B) says of the rollers, "They've thrown them away in a little river to the big sea. . . . They carried them to the river and they went to the sea and they got wet and sunk." Although this is just an hypothesis, the child states it as if it were a fact. The adolescent, on the other hand, states his conclusions in much more tentative language. D says, "the rollers would be wooden and they probably rotted away by now." These differences in the responses made to literary material by children and adolescents show in still a different way the effects of formal operational thought in enabling the adolescent to deal with all the possibilities in the situation and to differentiate between thought and reality. Similar results have been found with materials and questions dealing with the social sciences (Case and Collinson, 1962) and with religion (Goldman, 1965).

One observes comparable differences between adolescent and child thought in the interpretation and production of graphic materials. In an early study, Shaffer (1930) presented children and adolescents with political cartoons and asked them to write about what the cartoons meant. Shaffer found that it was not until the age of 12-14 that children got beyond the literal meaning of the cartoon to its metaphorical meaning. The inability of young children to deal with metaphoric expression has also been demonstrated in their reactions to poetry (Pyle, 1935).

Why should children have difficulty in dealing with metaphor when adolescents can take it in their stride? In metaphor, one and the same word or figure takes on a double meaning. In political cartoons, for example, the donkey and elephant symbolize much more than animals, and the same holds true for the "bears" and "bulls" or stock market cartoons. The grasp of metaphor presupposes the ability to recognize parallels between quite disparate things such as political parties and donkeys and elephants. It also presupposes that the figure can be separated from its literal representation. This ability, to see the many possible meanings of a concrete figure, no matter how removed these meanings may be from its literal interpretation, is once again a product of the combinatorial potential of formal operational thought.

The findings with respect to the interpretation of realistic pictures and the drawings of young people parallel the results obtained with cartoons and other metaphoric materials. Vernon (1948) has shown that the reactions to realistic pictures can be grouped according to three age related stages. Young children (4–6 years) merely *enumerate* the elements of the picture; somewhat older children (7–10) *describe* the picture in the sense of attempting to relate the elements of the picture to another in an objective way. It is only towards adolescence, however (11–12), that children begin to truly *interpret* the pictures in the sense of attributing motives and feelings to the depicted characters. With respect to graphic productions, Harris (1964) among others has shown that as children get older, their drawings become more differentiated in the sense that more and more details are taken into account. Here again, both with respect to the interpretation and production of realistic pictures, we see that the adolescent tends to take account of all, or at least most, of the possibilities present in graphic materials while the child focuses primarily on one or several salient aspects of the configuration.

The effects of formal operational thought, the ability to deal with all the possibilities in the situation, can thus be seen in the differentiation between thought and reality in the definitions given to concepts and in the interpretations of literary and graphic materials. Formal operational thought has consequences for the affective side of adolescence as well, and it is to these consequences that we will next direct our attention.

Affective Consequences of Formal Operational Thought

Up until this point we have dealt with cognitive development as if it were more or less unrelated to the affective side of adolescent behavior. Nothing could be farther from the truth. Much of what is considered typically adolescent in the way of emotionality can only be fully understood in the context of formal operational thought. This is true because it is formal operational thought which allows the young person to enter the world of ideals, theories, and possibilities in general. It is the adolescent's capacity for comparing the possible with the actual in many different compartments of his life that underlies, at least in part, the incessant conflicts which characterize this age period. In the following pages we will see how the advent of formational thought sets the stage for conflicts between the adolescent and his social milieu and between the adolescent and himself.

The adolescent and his world.   The child, for the most part, lives in the here and now. His concerns are with the world as it exists at present and with learning how to function in this world. With the advent of adolescence, however, and the emergence of formal operational thought, all of this changes. The adolescent is now able not only to grasp the immediate state of things but also the possible states they might or could assume. This new awareness of the discrepancy between how things are and how they might be—at home, at school, with themselves—probably underlies many of the recurrent adolescent feelings of depression and dissatisfaction (Weltschmerz). It is only in adolescence, for example, that adopted children feel compelled to seek out their real parents. Likewise, it is only in adolescence that previously happy, cheerful and "gutty" handicapped and crippled children experience their first real depression.

The awareness of the discrepancy between the actual and the possible also helps to make the adolescent a rebel. He is always comparing the possible with the actual and discovering that the actual is flagrantly wanting. Not unlike the child, who always finds another child's toys more appealing than his own, the adolescent finds possible situations enviable and his own situation unbearable. Much of this rebellion is, however, purely on the verbal level. The adolescent voices humanitarian causes, but does little to implement them. Likewise, his acute dissatisfaction with his parents does not, in most cases, cause him to break from them and to go out on his own. It is just because of this discrepancy between the adolescent's ability to conceptualize ideals and his lack of awareness as to what implementing these ideals entails in the way of action, that he is able to be so adamant (and apparently hypocritical) in his demands. Only towards the end of adolescence, when ideals get tied to appropriate action, does the young person take a less militant and more understanding stance towards society in general and his parents in particular.

The adolescent and himself. In the preceding section we dealt with the effects of formal operational thought upon the adolescent's attitude towards the societal and familial world about him. But this new form of thought has equally important consequences for his attitudes regarding himself. He now turns these new powers of thought upon himself and becomes introspective. He undertakes self analysis and criticism. This he does with a certain equanimity since he now recognizes the private character of thought and that he need not share the results of his self examination with others. In contrast to the child, he can now wear a facade which masks his real feelings and presents a different face to the world than the one which he himself confronts.

This new concern with himself is initially quite exaggerated and even projected upon others. He feels that others are as concerned with his behavior and with evaluating him as he is himself. Whenever he is in social situations, the adolescent feels as if he is on stage, and that everyone is watching and evaluating his behavior. He is thus constantly performing for an audience which is, in part at least, of his own making. It is this feeling that others are as concerned with him as he is with himself that is the substance of adolescent *egocentrism*. The child is egocentric in the sense that he is unable to take another person's point of view. The adolescent, on the other hand, takes the other person's point of view to an extreme degree. He is so concerned with the point of view of others and how they regard him that he often loses sight of his own point of view, i.e., his own best interests.

Adolescent egocentrism has several consequences that it might be well to chronicle. For one thing, this egocentrism accounts, in part, for the power of the peer group during this period. The adolescent is so concerned with the reactions of others towards him, particularly his peers, that he is willing to do many things which are opposed to all of his previous training and to his own best interests. At the same time, this egocentric impression that he is always on stage may help to account for the many and varied adolescent attention-getting maneuvers. Such things as long hair, tight pants, etc., as well as loud and booming sound, meet many different adolescent needs, and one of these is the egocentric need to be noticed and evaluated by others.

Still another consequence of adolescent egocentrism is that interpersonal relations during this period are often shallow and short lived. The adolescent "crush" frequently derives from the desire to idealize someone, and its brief duration results from the fact that no human person is ideal and that this is soon discovered. This discovery, however, does not prevent the adolescent from forming new crushes. Friendships during this period are often formed on the basis of self definition and self interest rather than on the basis of mutuality of interests and concerns. A pretty girl, for example, may befriend a plain girl who sets off her good looks while the plain girl takes vicarious satisfaction in the conquests of her "friend."

Towards the end of adolescence, this form of exploitative egocentrism gradually declines. The young person comes to realize that other people are much more concerned with themselves and their problems than they are with him and his problems. With the decline of adolescent egocentrism, there is a renewal of individuality and a new freedom from the conformity imposed by the peer group. Interpersonal relations are now based on mutuality of interest rather than on the basis of self interest. At the same time the young person becomes increasingly reconciled with both society and his family. This is generally accomplished through the engagement in productive work, which is the only effective bridge between the real and the possible. It is productive work which reunites thought and action and which enables the young person to keep looking toward the future without despairing of the present. The engagement in productive work thus marks the passage from adolescence to adulthood, which is to say, from personal isolation to social integration.

SUMMARY

The present chapter has attempted to selectively summarize two major approaches to the study of cognition in adolescence. One of these approaches, the mental test approach, is concerned with the quantitative assessment of mental abilities. A review of four of the issues raised by this approach suggests the following conclusions: a) that for those abilities measured by mental tests, adolescence appears to be the period during which such abilities reach their peak of efficiency; b) the bulk of the evidence suggests that there is an increase in the differentiation of abilities between childhood and adolescence; c) sex differences in intellectual achievement become most prominent in adolescence and d) other things being equal, the IQ, considered as a ranking, stays relatively constant from childhood through adolescence.

The second, qualitative or developmental, approach to cognition was described with special reference to the work of Inhelder and Piaget. Some of the characteristics of adolescent thought were pointed out, such as the ability to deal with propositional logic, to grasp metaphor, and to conceptualize and reason about thought itself. Several of the affective consequences of these new intellectual achievements, such as adolescent self-consciousness and superficial interpersonal relations, were also noted. From the developmental point of view, therefore, cognition in adolescence must be regarded as intimately involved with all aspects of adolescent experience and behavior.

REFERENCES

Balinsky, B. An analysis of the mental factors of various age groups from 9 to 60. *Genetic Psychology Monographs*, 1941, *23*, 191–234.

Bayley, N., and Oden, M. H. The maintenance of intellectual ability in gifted adults. *Journal of Gerontology*, 1955, *10*, 91–107.

Bradway, Katherine P., and Thompson, Clare W. Intelligence at adulthood: A twenty-five year follow-up. *Journal of Educational Psychology*, 1962, *53*, 1–14.

Burns, R. B. Age and mental ability: re-testing with thirty-three years' interval. *British Journal of Educational Psychology*, 1966, *36*, 116.

Burt, C. The differentiation of intellectual ability. *British Journal of Educational Psychology*, 1954, *24*, 76–90.

Burt, C. *Mental and scholastic tests*. London: Staples Press, 1962/1921.

Case, D., and Collinson, J. M. The development of formal thinking in verbal comprehension. *British Journal of Educational Psychology*, 1962, *32*, 103–111.

Cohen, J. The factorial structure of the WISC at ages 7–6; 10–6; and 13–6. *Journal of Consulting Psychology*, 1959, *23*, 285–299.

Cropley, A. J. Differentiation of abilities, socio-economic status, and the WISC. *Journal of Consulting Psychology*, 1964, *28*, 512–517.

Edgerton, H. A., and Britt, S. H. Sex differences in the Science Talent Test. *Science*, 1944, *100*, 192–193.

Edgerton, H. A., and Britt, S. H. Technical aspects of the Fourth Annual Science Talent Search. *Educational and Psychological Measurement,* 1947, 7, 3–21.

Elkind, D. Children's discovery of the conservation of mass, weight and volume. *Journal of Genetic Psychology,* 1961, 98, 219–277. (a)

Elkind, D. Quantity conceptions in junior and senior high school students. *Child Development,* 1961, 32, 551–560. (b)

Elkind, D. The development of the additive composition of classes in the child. *Journal of Genetic Psychology,* 1961, 99, 51–57. (c)

Elkind, D. The development of quantitative thinking. *Journal of Genetic Psychology,* 1961, 98, 37–46. (d)

Elkind, D. Quantity conceptions in college students. *Journal of Social Psychology,* 1962, 57, 459–465.

Elkind, D. The child's conception of his religious denomination III: The Protestant child. *Journal of Genetic Psychology,* 1963, 103, 291–304.

Elkind, D. Discrimination, seriation and numeration of size differences in young children. *Journal of Genetic Psychology,* 1964, 104, 275–296.

Elkind, D. Conceptual orientation shifts in children and adolescents. *Child Development,* 1966, 37, 493–498.

Feifel, H., and Lorge, L. Qualitative differences in the vocabulary responses of children. *Journal of Educational Psychology,* 1950, 41, 1–18.

Flanagan, J. C. *Project talent: The American high school student.* Pittsburgh: University of Pittsburgh, 1964.

Garrett, H. E. A developmental theory of intelligence. *American Psychologist,* 1946, 1, 372–378.

Gesell, A., Ilg, F. L., and Ames, L. B. *Youth: the years from ten to sixteen.* New York: Harper & Row, 1956.

Goldman, R. J. The application of Piaget's schema of operational thinking to religious story data by means of the Guttman scalogram. *British Journal of Educational Psychology,* 1965, 25, 158–170.

Green, R. F., and Berkowitz, B. Changes in intellect with age: II. Factorial analysis of Wechsler-Bellevue scores. *Journal of Genetic Psychology,* 1964, 104, 3–18.

Harris, D. B. *Children's drawings as measures of intellectual maturity.* New York: Harcourt, Brace and World, 1964.

Honzik, M. P., MacFarlane, J. W., and Allen, L. The stability of mental test performance between two and eighteen years. *Journal of Experimental Education,* 1948, 17, 309–324.

Inhelder, Bärbel, and Piaget, J. *The growth of logical thinking from childhood through adolescence.* New York: Basic Books, 1958.

Jones, H. E., and Conrad, H. S. The growth and decline of intelligence. *Genetic Psychology Monographs,* 1933, *13,* 223–298.

Jones, H. E. Age changes in adult mental abilities. In: Conrad, H. S. (Ed.) *Studies in human development.* New York: Appleton-Century-Crofts, 1966.

Jordan, A. M. Sex differences in mental traits. *High School Journal,* 1937, *20,* 254–261.

King, W. H. The development of scientific concepts in children. *British Journal of Educational Psychology,* 1963, *23,* 240–252.

Owens, W. A., Jr. Age and mental abilities: A longitudinal study. *Genetic Psychology Monographs,* 1953, *48,* 3–54.

Peel, E. A. *The pupil's thinking.* London: Oldbourne Press, 1960.

Piaget, J. *The psychology of intelligence.* London: Routledge & Kegan Paul, 1950.

Piaget, J. *The child's conception of number.* London: Routledge & Kegan Paul, 1952.

Piaget, J. *The construction of reality in the child.* New York: Basic Books, 1954.

Pinneau, S. R. *Changes in intelligence quotient: Infancy to maturity.* Boston, Mass.: Houghton Mifflin, 1961.

Pyle, W. A. An experimental study of the development of certain aspects of reasoning. *Journal of Educational Psychology,* 1935, *26,* 539–546.

Shaffer, L. F. *Children's interpretations of cartoons.* Contributions to Education, No. 429. New York: Teacher's College, Columbia University, 1930.

Shock, N. W. Gerontology (later maturity). *Annual Review of Psychology,* 1951, *2,* 353–370.

Spearman, C. *The nature of "intelligence" and the principles of cognition.* London: Macmillan, 1923.

Terman, L. M. *The measurement of intelligence.* Boston: Houghton Mifflin, 1916.

Terman, L. M., and Merrill, Maud A. *Stanford-Binet Intelligence Scale.* Boston: Houghton Mifflin, 1937.

Terman, L. M., and Tyler, Leona E. Psychological sex differences. In: Carmichael, L. (Ed.) *Manual of child psychology.* New York: Wiley, 1954.

Thorndike, R. L. Growth of intelligence during adolescence. *Journal of Genetic Psychology,* 1948, *72,* 11–15.

Thurstone, L. L., and Thurstone, Thelma G. Factorial studies of intelligence. *Psychometric Monographs*, 1941, No. 2.

Trembly, D. Age-curve differences between natural and acquired intellectual characteristics. *American Psychologist*, Abstract, 1964, *19*, 546. Paper delivered to the APA's 72nd Annual Convention, Sept. 4–9, 1964, Los Angeles.

Vernon, M. D. The development of imaginative constructions in children. *British Journal of Psychology*, 1948, *39*, 102–111.

Weir, M. W. Developmental changes in problem solving strategies. *Psychological Review*, 1964, *71*, 473–490.

Adolescent Creativity

Ellen V. Piers *

INTEREST IN AND SPECULATION ABOUT CREATIVITY IS NOT NEW, BUT efforts to approach it scientifically have expanded vigorously in the past 15 years. It is an area where there are far more questions raised than answers given: yet, it is in raising questions that the scientist frequently pinpoints the problem. Before we focus on *adolescent* creativity, let us take a brief look at the current status of the field as a whole. This will give us the background to understand the major problems when we narrow the focus to the adolescent himself.

THE STATUS OF CREATIVITY

One way to cover the field of creativity is to ask the questions that the psychologist asks; or, for that matter, the questions that the reader might ask. Such a plan might be more useful than presenting another review of the literature, a task which has been carried out most recently by Barron (1963), Golann (1963), Taylor (1964) and Mackler and Shontz (1965). So, let us begin at the beginning and raise the issue of:

What is Creativity?

Theories and definitions of creativity have been legion. Only a few of the most influential will be dealt with here, beginning with the psychoanalytic conception of "regression in the service of the ego." This oft-quoted phrase was presented by Kris (1952, p. 177) and

* ELLEN V. PIERS is an Associate Professor of Psychology at the Pennsylvania State University. She was formerly the Chief Psychologist for the Nashville City Schools. Dr. Piers has written a chapter in *School Psychological Services: Theory and Practice* and has authored several articles on the self concept and on creativity.

159

elaborated by Schafer (1958). It is described as a momentary, at least partially controlled, level of psychic functioning, where constructive use is made of more primitive, drive-dominated, non-logical (primary process) modes of thought. According to this view, the inspirational phase of creativity involves regressive thought processes, but in the service of final production so that control is not lost (as in psychotic thinking). In the elaborative phase of creativity the more conventional and logical (secondary process) modes of thought prevail. Considerable research has been carried out more or less related to this concept, and other theoretical statements have been made, supporting the idea that the creative process involves both more primitive and more realistic types of thinking.

In contrast to this psychoanalytic view is that of Carl Rogers. Creativity for Rogers is self-realization, and the motive for it is the urge to fulfill oneself. In his words, it is "the tendency to express and activate all the capacities of the organism, or the self" (1961, p. 351). The three inner conditions of creativity are: (1) openness to experience, which implies flexibility and tolerance of ambiguity; (2) an internal locus of evaluation; (3) an ability to "toy with" elements and concepts.

Rogers is using the term creativity in two senses here: what Maslow has designated as "special talent creativeness" and the broader "self-actualizing creativeness" (1959, p. 85). This latter sense implies a sound and integrated personality or one moving toward that state under the proper conditions, one of which might be psychotherapy.

Bruner (1962) takes as the hallmark of a creative enterprise an act that produces *effective surprise*. He describes some of the conditions that affect the creative process, but which, when taken together, may seem paradoxical. These include such conditions as detachment along with commitment, passion as well as decorum, a freedom to be dominated by the object, and immediacy along with deferral. He feels that what he calls the "internal drama," the working out of the conflict and coalition within the set of identities composing the person, is the source of much creativity.

Many definitions have been used in the recent attempts to study creativity scientifically. Taylor reported that the Fourth National Research Conference on Creativity at the University of Utah found two definitions most useful: Ghiselin's proposal that "the measure of a creative product be the extent to which it restructures our universe of understanding," and "the extent of the area of science that the contribution underlines," used by Lacklen of the Space Agency. Taylor also quotes Stein's definition that a process is creative when it results in "a novel work that is accepted as tenable or useful or satisfying by a group at some point of time" (1964, p. 6).

These definitions are social and stress the contribution, or solution to a problem. Accepted by some, but not all, is the additional concept of individual creativity. From this point of view, the individual who makes something that others, unknown to him, have made before, should also be called creative.

Guilford (1965), who deals in factors involved in creative thinking, focuses more on the abilities themselves, such as fluency, flexibility and originality. He does not require that creative output be socially useful or desirable, since science does not deal with values in this sense. His critics point out that by omitting this social aspect, the usual distinction between creative productions and pathological productions (which are frequently original but not often useful) becomes lost.

Part of the confusion lies in the fact that the students of creativity have emphasized one or another of its various aspects: the process, the product, or the person. One might speculate that focusing on the creative process would lead to a more individualistic view than focusing on the creative product. As for the creative person, no one really expects him to be creative 100 per cent of the time!

In trying to determine what creativity is, it is also important to establish what it is *not*. Taylor (1964) says it is necessary to distinguish between creativity and productivity, since productivity implies quantity and creativity implies high quality of a particular kind. Research findings suggest that they overlap at least to a limited degree, but the mistaking of one for the other should be avoided, particularly where a group such as research scientists are rating each other.

Flanagan (1963) goes one step further and distinguishes creativity from both productivity and ingenuity. In his definitions *productivity* is shown by bringing forth many ideas and solutions. It emphasizes both quantity and contribution. *Creativity* is shown by bringing something new into being. The emphasis is on the newness and lack of previous existence of the idea or product. *Ingenuity* is shown by inventing or discovering a solution to a problem. Here the emphasis is on the existence of a problem, and the demonstration of a quality of genius in solving it in an unusually neat, clever, or surprising way. It is thus a more limited concept than creativity. Most investigators, however, would probably include ingenuity as an aspect of creativity.

In general, the concepts of novelty and originality (or a novel rearrangement) and resulting social contributions are the most frequently mentioned in connection with creativity. But some, like Taylor, are content to say we do not yet know what creativity is, and that the definition need not come first. As with intelligence, construct validity for measures of creativity must be built up slowly by exploration and examination. Of course the choice of a criterion measure or measures, which is conceded to be the current major problem in creativity research, requires some type of definition.

What is the Relationship between Creativity and Intelligence?

This question is of particular concern to those who work with children and adolescents, and it has led to considerable research and controversy. Unfortunately, the interpretations and generalizations which have sprung from some of the work in this area have been accepted much too uncritically, and valid criticisms have been ignored. Let us consider some of the issues.

Guilford, who began analyzing intellectual abilities in general through his Aptitudes Project several years ago, soon included systematic studies of creative abilities. As he developed his *Structure of Intellect* model (1959) he differentiated two productive operations, convergent thinking and divergent thinking. Convergent thinking involves the giving of a well-determined answer as in a routine mathematical problem, while divergent thinking involves the generation of a variety of things, where there is no one correct answer. (One aspect of this is thinking of "what might be" rather than "what is.") Within the context of his model, Guilford found that most of the abilities that (presumably) contribute to creative thinking or performance fall into the divergent production category. As such, he considers that they are a *form* of intellectual ability, but of a much broader concept of intelligence than is usually held. They are not included, as others have also noted, in most intelligence or achievement tests, which stress only a few kinds of intellectual abilities such as cognition, memory, or other types of convergent thinking.

The question then is, to what extent are convergent and divergent thinking independent abilities? Are they sufficiently so to justify speaking of intelligence *and* creativity, or intelligence *versus* creativity?

Many of the studies have reported little or no correlation between the two. MacKinnon (1962) for example, at the Institute for Personality

Assessment and Research (IPAR), found very low correlations with intelligence in his group of creative architects. Holland (1961) concluded that intelligence has little or no relationship to creative performance in arts and science at the high school level (also see Welsh, 1966). Yamamoto (1964) obtained a correlation of .30 in high school between IQ and an index of creativity. Getzels and Jackson (1962) reported low correlations with their individual measures and based most of their (unfortunately) widely quoted study on similarities and differences between their High IQ-Low Creative groups (mean IQ 150 on a variety of tests) and their Low IQ-High Creative groups (mean IQ 127). Torrance (1960) did eight partial replications of the Getzels and Jackson study. In all of these, by emphasizing only two groups, the impression was given of different, almost mutually exclusive, abilities.

Barron (1963), also reporting on the IPAR work, suggests that the relationship between intelligence and creativity might depend on the type of creativity being considered. He feels that creative writers who produce original work in large quantities have mean IQ's around 140 or higher. Also, where the subject matter itself requires high intelligence for the mastery of its fundamentals, as in mathematics or physics, he feels the correlation with creativity is probably higher than it is for artists. In a somewhat sweeping generalization, he estimates that over the total range of intelligence and creativity a low positive correlation exists. This is probably in the neighborhood of .40. However, beyond an IQ of 120, measured intelligence is a negligible factor in creativity, and motivational and stylistic variables become more important.

The most vocal critics of the conclusions relating to intelligence from these and other studies have been DeMille and Merrifield (1962), Ripple and May (1962), Thorndike (1963), McNemar (1964), and Wallach and Kogan (1965). Rather than going through their individual criticisms, perhaps we can summarize the main points:

1. Any restriction of range, such as is found when "highly intelligent" and "highly creative" groups are used, will automatically lower the correlation between them. This is an elementary statistical fact of which many people seem to remain blissfully unaware. While we can assume that most authors who report the low correlations in these cases are aware that the range has been restricted (and in some cases say so), the fact nevertheless remains that the correlations are picked up by other people, and incorrect generalizations to the whole range are made.

2. Any attempt to separate *intelligence* and *creativity* into two relatively independent domains requires that the tests used to measure intelligence be more highly correlated with each other than they are with the tests used to measure creativity. Many of the tests originated by Guilford and adapted by Getzels and Jackson, Torrance, and others, have not fulfilled these requirements. We find that, in case after case, some divergent thinking tests correlate as highly with the intelligence measures, on the average, as they do among themselves.

3. The question is also raised whether we are justified in pooling divergent test scores, which may have an average intercorrelation as low as .18 or .24, and calling the results "creativity." (I did it myself once . . . see Piers, Daniels & Quackenbush, 1960.) These low intercorrelations, as opposed to averages of .50 to .60 obtained from traditional intellectual measures, argue either that the divergent thinking tests used are too diverse to be brought together under the general term "creativity" or that the domain itself is too diffuse to be considered as a unit.

4. The separation of groups into "High" and "Lows" (sometimes at the mean, sometimes as in the Getzels and Jackson study on the basis of the top 20%) can be very misleading, unless the relativity of these terms is stressed. We can agree that a mean IQ of 150 is high, but how many would agree that a mean IQ of 127 is low! Exaggerating the problem has been the emphasis on "Low-High's" and "High-Low's," to the exclusion of the other two possible groups, particularly the "High-High's," from whom we might ultimately expect the greatest contribution. Characteristics reported for the High Creative-Low Intelligence groups are thus becoming generalized to High-Creative individuals in general, which may or may not be justified.

Having made many of these points, Wallach and Kogan (1965) published an extensive study with fifth grade children, designed to establish definitively the degree to which the domains of creativity and intelligence can be separated meaningfully. Concluding that time limits and a test-like atmosphere interfere with creative responses and blur the distinctions, they eliminated these, and used visual and verbal tasks of good internal consistency in a play-like atmosphere with no time limits. The average intercorrelation among the creativity measures was .41; among the intelligence (and achievement) measures it was found to be .51; and between the creativity and intelligence measures it was .09. They thus achieved the separation they were seeking, and established that the creativity measures could legitimately be pooled to yield a creativity index score.

The authors then divided their groups at both means (for each sex), obtaining the familiar High-Lows and Low-Highs, but also using the remaining cells of High-Highs and Low-Lows, and compared the four groups on the many personality measures they had also obtained. Results of the analyses of variance at first seem rather random and uninterpretable; but the authors have managed, quite ingeniously, to pull together the results into the following generalizations:*

High creativity-high intelligence: These children exercise within themselves both control and freedom, both adultlike and childlike kinds of behavior.

High creativity-low intelligence: These children are in angry conflict with themselves and with their school environment and are beset by feelings of unworthiness and inadequacy. In a stress-free context, however, they can blossom forth cognitively.

Low creativity-high intelligence: These children can be described as "addicted" to school achievement. Academic failure would be perceived by them as catastrophic, so that they must continually strive for academic excellence in order to avoid the possibility of pain.

Low creativity-low intelligence: Basically bewildered, these children engage in various defensive maneuvers ranging from useful adaptations such as intensive social activity to regressions such as passivity or psychosomatic symptoms (Wallach and Kogan, 1965, p. 303).

After examining the research evidence, what can we say in general about the relationship between intelligence and creativity? In this connection I like Freehill's (1961, pp. 83 and 103) distinctions between (a) genius . . . "Superlative and recognized achievement . . . an exalted kind of mind which leads to original work of such quality that it is permanent and has nearly universal influence"; (b) talent . . . "remarkable ability falling short of the superlative . . . narrower cleverness . . . may or may not be original, may or may not have universal effect, and is of notably less transcendent proficiency"; (c) giftedness . . . used as a general term for all superior performance as well as more specifically for high intellectual ability (high IQ).

By definition then, geniuses are our most creative individuals, and

* It should be remembered that once again these Highs and Lows simply refer to above and below the mean of the group, which was largely upper middle class.

from Cox (1926) and others we estimate that they are also of very high intelligence. Johnson (1955) says there is little doubt that virtually all the persons who have made major creative advances in science and technology in historic times have possessed very great problem-solving powers.

The intellectually gifted may or may not be creative. One of the better-accepted facts is that many people with high IQ's who learn easily and who may be productive and successful are not necessarily original.

The talented also may or may not be creative in the sense of marked originality which makes a lasting social contribution, but they are probably more creative than the average person. The intelligence of the talented has been estimated as being above average, but not necessarily very superior.

To sum up, creativity and intelligence are not synonymous. They are positively correlated, but the degree of correlation apparently varies from slight to substantial, depending on the type of creativity. They *can* be separated, with some individuals scoring relatively higher or relatively lower on one or the other. High intelligence as measured by our traditional tests is certainly no guarantee of creativity, but many of our greatest contributions have come, and probably will continue to come, from those few who are high on both.

How is Creativity Distributed?

The assumption among psychological researchers is that most people have creative potential but that there are wide individual differences in degree. This differs from the idea of many lay people who feel that one either has or has not the potential to be creative. Gardner Murphy wrote: "We know from watching children in progressive schools that the desire to create must be almost universal, and that almost everyone has some measure of originality which stems from his fresh perception of life and experience, and from the uniqueness of his own fantasy, when he is free to share it" (1947, p. 453). And Fliegler says: "All individuals are creative in diverse ways and different degrees" (1961, p. 14). Lowenfeld (1959) distinguished between actual and potential creativity, the former being that potential which is already developed and functioning. But Kneller (1965) warns against the assumption that variations in creative achievement represent simply the degree to which it has been expressed or developed. As with intelligence, we must assume that variations are primarily due to a wide range of potential. In an earlier chapter, Nichols discusses the influence of heredity on measured intelligence and achievement. Because of the measurement difficulties, remarkably little interest has yet been focused on the relationship between heredity and creativity and the issue continues to reside in the speculative domain. Even how closely creativity follows the normal probability curve has not been established.

Can Creativity be Developed?

From some of the statements in the preceding section, it is obvious that many people feel that creativity can be developed. But this development can take place only within the limits of an individual's potential. In other words, a child with limited potential will probably not become extraordinarily creative even with considerable stimulation and training, although he may do better than he did before. The point that is usually stressed is that our educational efforts have emphasized convergent thinking and the learning of facts, and neglected the stimulation of creative thinking for all ranges of potential. The assumption is that if we do emphasize divergent thinking, we can achieve an enormous increase in the actual creativity of all levels of the population.

Only a few studies have been carried out to measure the effects of specialized training in creativity. One of the more extensive of these has been the group of studies conducted at the University of Buffalo (Parnes, 1962), results of which seem to warrant the postulate that the gap between an individual's innate creative talent and his lesser creative output can be narrowed by deliberate education in creative thinking.

Maltzman (1960) found that he could increase originality through training. His studies involved the repeated presentation of a list of stimulus words in a modified free association situation accompanied by instructions to give a different response to each stimulus. This training also resulted in an increased number of responses to the Unusual Uses Test, whereas specific training in unusual uses did not.

Other studies on training for creativity have taken place in industrial settings, and report at least some positive results. There are still many unanswered questions, however, including what training is best for what areas, how long effects last, and how much change can actually be effected.

How Can We Identify High Creative Potential?

It would be helpful if we could identify early the individuals who have the greatest potential. Such identification involves the establishment of predictors of future creativity. Considerable research has been done in this area, although it is recognized that in order for these characteristics to have true predictive validity, they should be used in longitudinal or follow-up studies in which they are compared with actual creative performance. Since the criterion problem of what constitutes creative performance is still not settled, and very few longitudinal studies have been made, we cannot assume that long-range predictive validity has been established for many of our indicators. Instead we have been forced, in the main, to rely on factorial or concurrent validities. In too many cases, the problem of validity has been ignored entirely, and conclusions are drawn from results with measures which have no claim to be measuring creativity other than the author's intent.

We do know that some of our traditional measures have not worked. Such things as school grades, traditional IQ tests, and sheer mastery of knowledge are not efficient predictors. So we have turned to many other sources of information in our efforts to identify the potentially creative person. The person himself has been asked to perform on certain tests, to do certain tasks, or to fill out forms on which he describes or rates himself in various ways. Teachers, peers, supervisors, and family members have been asked to rate him. Tangible products or accomplishments have been noted.

Modes of approach have also varied. Some (Cox, 1926) have looked at the early lives of individuals who later proved to be geniuses. The IPAR investigators and Anne Roe (1951, 1953a, 1953b) have studied the characteristics of groups who currently are rated as creative. Guilford has attempted to devise tests which have factorial validity, that is, which consistently cluster together in his divergent thinking areas.

These Guilford aptitude tests have attracted so much attention and have been adapted by so many other investigators that they should be discussed in some detail. They were developed in the 1950's and represent one of the first efforts at validation of creativity measures. Guilford and his co-workers regarded the establishment of factorial validity as the preliminary step in validational procedures, the second being the correlation of factor measures with practical criteria. By making up many tests designed to fill the squares of his Structure of Intellect model, and by refining these through successive factor analyses, Guilford believes he has found the basic traits in creative thinking. These include, for verbal tasks, three fluency factors (ideational, associational and expressional), two flexibility factors (spontaneous and adaptive, earlier called originality) and an elaboration factor. These all fall under divergent production. Guilford feels that creative thinking, though primarily divergent, also includes some convergent production abilities.

Examples of divergent thinking tests are Alternate (or Unusual) Uses, where the subject is asked to give, in a given time limit, all the uses he can think of for a newspaper or other object; Consequences, which asks the subject to consider what would happen "if. . . ."; Plot Titles, which asks the subject for titles to a narrative paragraph, and many others involving figural and symbolic information as well as verbal. Most are scored for both quality and quantity.

Apart from the numerous adaptations by others of the Guilford tests, which may or may not contain similar factorial validity, one other device which has shown some promise is Mednick's Remote Associates Test (1962), which calls for three-way associations. While some believe that this test involves more convergent than divergent thinking since there is a correct answer, it does require the generation of many associations in order to select the correct one.

Taylor (1964) reviewed the results from the various classes of measuring devices and feels that enough research has been done to enable a crude ordering to be made in terms of predictive efficiency. He ranks the various classes tentatively as follows, noting at the same time some individual exceptions:

1. Biographical items and past achievements
2. Self-ratings and direct expression of goals and aspirations
3. Originality and personality inventories
4. Aptitude and intelligence measures
5. Parental attitudes

He finds that ratings by teachers appear to have little value for predicting creative performance, but ratings by supervisors and peers seem to show promise in some settings. No evidence for the validity of other special devices and tests, or of physical measures and effect of drugs, is currently available.

If Taylor is correct, the personality inventories and especially the creative aptitude measures which attract so many investigators are running a poor third and fourth on the above list. One reason for this may be that they frequently have been compared with a measure such as teacher ratings whose validity itself is in doubt. Another reason for lower concurrent validity might be that they were compared with a different kind of creativity, for example, some of Guilford's verbal tests being compared with artistic productions. In any case, until such time as their predictive validity is improved, we should regard with a great deal of caution the conclusions drawn by the investigators using them. Meanwhile we should continue to try to improve our selection of biographical items, past achievements, and other promising predictors.

What Are the Characteristics of Creative People?

Too many characteristics of creativity have been enumerated to be very meaningful. In part this has been a function of the wide variety of measures used. It has also been a function of the confusion created by adding those characteristics uncovered by the sometimes doubtful measures purporting to identify *potential* creativity, to those which are characteristic of persons judged currently creative, or creative historically. We shall try to concentrate on those characteristics which have been reported fairly consistently.

There appear to be many more or less distinct intellectual components of creativity. Guilford's several divergent thinking factors which he feels operate along with convergent thinking in creative work have already been discussed. In other studies, physical scientists who were judged creative rated themselves high on cognition, discrimination of value, flexibility, academic achievement, and intuition. They were also characterized by early interest in intellectual activities and above-average breadth of interest.

Non-intellectual factors are also important for all types of creativity and may play a greater part than do the intellectual in some of the more artistic forms. Motivation, for example, seems to be one of the important non-intellectual components. Most studies mention high drive, involvement, curiosity, persistence, and dissatisfaction with the status quo.

Other personality characteristics frequently mentioned are high self-sufficiency, autonomy, and independence of judgment; self-confidence; self-acceptance; humor, intuition, desire for complexity; and tolerance of ambiguity. Creative males score toward the feminine side in some of their interests and in characteristics such as awareness of their impulses and sensitivity.

Characteristics which have been found to be negatively related to creativity include attitudinal rigidity, premature judgment, and defensiveness. More low creative people describe themselves in terms such as contented, gentle, conservative, patient, virtuous, and concerned for others.

Some characteristics seem relevant to different types of creativity. Type of interaction with parents, liking for ideas versus people versus things, tendencies toward socialization and interpersonal involvement, introversion versus extroversion, and suppression versus expression of impulses may vary according to different fields of interest. For example, Roe (1953) reported that social scientists' interaction with their parents involved overprotection, whereas physical and biological scientists developed early a way of life not requiring personal interaction.

To sum up, let us describe the personality attributes which Crutchfield (1961) feels tend to characterize creative individuals in general. In cognitive areas they are more flexible and fluent; their perceptions and cognitions are unique. In their approach to problems they are intuitive, empathic, perceptually open, and prefer complexity. In emotional-motivational spheres they are free from excessive impulse control, achieve through independence rather than conformity, are individualistic, and have strong, sustained, intrinsic motivation in their field of work.

What Do We Know About Creativity in Childhood?

Until recently there has been very little research on creativity in young children. Our knowledge has come chiefly from anecdotal accounts of the outstanding creative achievements, at an early age, of many of our geniuses. One of the few specific investigations was that of Andrews (1930) who studied the development of imagination in the pre-school child. Using a variety of methods and observations she came to the conclusion that total imaginative scores are highest between four and four and a half, with a sudden drop at age five when the child enters kindergarten. Griffiths (1945) also studied young children and felt that fantasy had an important function in helping to solve developmental problems. From various investigations it would appear that two of the most powerful inhibitors to creativity in early childhood are premature attempts to eliminate fantasy and the "holding-back operations" that keep children from learning until they are "ready" to learn.

At the elementary school age, greatest attention traditionally has been given to manifestations of creativity such as creative writing and art. Recently there have been developed a few more materials and attempts to measure creative capacities systematically, but it is difficult to say just where we stand. Much of the work at this level has come from Torrance and his associates at the University of Minnesota. Starting with adaptations of Guilford's tests, they soon left his measures of single factors for more complex tasks, and developed the Minnesota Tests of Creative Thinking. While many of these tests seem ingenious and attractive to children, it is not always clear what type of validity they claim, to take the place of the factorial validity they gave up.

This is, of course, where the danger lies. Starting with commendable efforts to investigate a difficult field and with admissions that results are tentative, it is easy to get carried away and to build up a series of conclusions from work with children who score low or high on tests, conclusions which are then labelled conditions and correlates of creativity. There are at least three points in this process where one can go astray: first, as was just mentioned, the validity of the tests themselves; secondly, the results which are partly a function of the design and statistical analysis of the study; and third, the interpretations of and generalizations from these results.

Torrance (1964) quotes test-retest reliabilities of about .85 in the intermediate grades and a range of .45 to .70 in the primary grades for his Creative Thinking Tests. Attempts to determine concurrent validity have resulted in the following list of characteristics for children who score high on his tests: a larger number of ideas in small group situations; reputations for having wild or fantastic ideas; drawings or other products judged to be unusual or original; and work characterized by humor, playfulness and lack of rigidity. In other studies by this group, high scorers were rated higher on strength of self-image, ease of early recall, humor, availability of Oedipal anxiety, and uneven ego development. Rorschach responses were interpreted as being more sensitive and more independent.

Many of these studies involved teacher ratings. On the other hand, Taylor, in the same volume (1964), states that teacher ratings have not been found useful for predicting creative performance. Piers, Daniels and Quackenbush (1960) found that correlations between various teachers' ratings (taken two at a time) of junior high school students averaged only .23, and the correlations between teacher ratings and creativity tests were −.02 with fluency and .23 with originality. Torrance himself states that the most urgent research need in relation to the elementary school years is the standardization of one or more batteries of tests for assessing creativity. Standardization implies, of course, further evidence of validity.

Besides test validity, there exists the question of whether results using these same tests can be replicated by others. Wodtke and Wallen (1965) for example, in testing the validity of some of the generalizations made by Torrance concerning the classroom behavior of "creative" students, found that teacher and observer ratings of fourth and fifth grade students did not correlate, the teacher ratings always being correlated with intelligence. In addition, high scorers on the Torrance tests exhibited no more "objectionable" behavior than did low scorers, and behavior of children under low and high control teachers did not differ on the dimensions rated. The authors concluded that too many recommendations for teachers of "creatives" have been made without systematic research to support them.

With respect to generalizations made from studies, it has already been pointed out that the exclusion of the "high-high" groups in the intelligence-creativity studies gives an erroneous impression, as does calling a mean IQ of 127 "low." McNemar (1964) takes specific exception to the Getzels and Jackson (1962) emphasis on the fact that the High Creative-Low Intelligence group performed as well on achievement as did the High Intelligence-Low Creativity group, and their subsequent implication that creativity is more important for ordinary school achievement than is the IQ. He suggests an alternative way of interpreting their data: namely, that the high IQ and the high creative groups did equally well in school achievement despite a (unreported) difference in mean creativity that is of the same order as the much stressed difference in IQ. Using the same faulty logic, the implication would then be that creative ability is not as important as IQ for school achievement—just the opposite of their position. The achievement issue could be minimized except that Torrance continues to make a great deal of it, and has adopted the so-called "threshold hypothesis" which he attributes to J. E. Anderson. In this instance, the concept suggests that below some critical point (estimated to be at about 120 IQ) differences in IQ are considered to be the major determiners of differences in academic achievement. Above this critical point, differences in creativity may be more closely related to differences in achievement.

Both Getzels and Torrance apparently interpret their work as supporting the hypothesis. However, several recent studies have failed to confirm their results. Edwards and Tyler (1965) found that ninth grade groups high on both creativity and intelligence scored no higher on achievement tests than did those high only on intelligence. They conclude that a scholastic aptitude test like the SCAT is still a more dependable predictor of school achievement than are creativity tests. A more extensive study by Cicirelli (1965), working with the Minnesota tests and sixth grade pupils, also failed to support the hypothesis either for a minimum or maximum IQ threshold, except for the possibility of a maximum IQ threshold at IQ level 130-139 in the case of language achievement. While the relationship between creativity and achievement was a weak one, Cicirelli found that the form of the relationship was such that IQ and creativity were additive and linear in their effect on academic achievement.

Other approaches to the measurement of creativity in children have typically involved attempts to adapt Guilford or other adult instruments (such as the Myers-Briggs Type Indicator, 1962) to younger age levels. Besides their work on creativity and intelligence, Wallach and Kogan (1965) have opened up several new areas with their studies of the effects of anxiety and defensiveness on creative performance, as well as their emphasis on a play-like atmosphere and extended time limits. This latter condition makes use of an extension of Mednick's (1962) theory, which defines creative thinking as the "forming of associative elements into new combinations which either meet specified requirements or are in some way useful" (1962, p. 221). Since it is proposed that more frequent associations will occur earlier and more unique associations later in a sequence, obviously it is important to allow sufficient time for the unique responses to occur. The theory also permits the testing of hypotheses about various methods of training.

To sum up, systematic research on creativity in childhood is in a very preliminary stage. It would be unwise to draw conclusions or make generalizations at this point. The criterion problem is especially evident at this level, and only longitudinal studies will definitively answer the question of whether adult creativity can be predicted with any degree of accuracy during the early school years.

CREATIVITY IN ADOLESCENCE

It has taken us a long time to get to the specific subject of this chapter, and now that we are here, it will be discouraging to find that while encouragement in such areas as creative writing and art have been present for a long time, and such projects as Science Fairs have become increasingly popular, the high school years have been the most neglected of all the age levels when it comes to systematic research on creativity. Most of the publications have dealt with the intelligence-creativity controversy, starting with the Getzels and Jackson (1962) study and followed by replications or modifications which supported or failed to support their position. (An interesting exception to this statement may be found in the 1966 Trowbridge and Charles investigation of creativity in art students.) This continued emphasis on the degree to which "Creativity" rather than IQ accounts for academic achievement, seems to me to be quite misplaced. It is rather ridiculous to spend so much time and effort trying to prove that scores on divergent thinking tasks predict convergent learning better than do convergent thinking tasks. It is as though there is a curiously emotional (almost fanatical) determination to replace the IQ, rather than just to accept the idea that we have neglected divergent thinking and need to promote it for many reasons besides the effect it might or might not produce on an achievement battery in the eleventh or twelfth grades.

A more useful approach is Guilford's (1961) attempt to establish whether the same factors appear in samples younger than his original groups of Air Cadets. Apparently sixth and ninth graders do show essentially the same factors, although a few specific tests should be carefully watched since they tend to change in nature over the different age levels. It is fortunate that Guilford confirmed the general similarities since many investigators were already using his tests for junior and senior high school groups. Results of the studies with these tests, however, have not added a great deal to our knowledge so far, perhaps because, as was suggested before, they are inappropriately used.

Predictive studies have been relatively short-term. Best-known of these have been the studies by Holland (1961), Holland and Astin (1962), and Nichols & Holland (1963), etc. on National Merit Scholars. In the 1963 study, predictors of academic achievement and extra-curricular achievements in science, art, writing, dramatics, music and leadership during the first year of college were studied with a sample of 1033 Merit Finalists. One hundred fifty-four potential predictors were used including aptitude scores, originality scales, self-ratings, life-goals, personality and interest scales, home background variables, and child-rearing attitudes of the students' parents.

With so many measures being correlated it is difficult to summarize results. The authors concluded that a variety of non-intellective predictors exist. Measures of creativity, orginality, interests, personality factors such as extroversion and social dominance, and measures of past performance, related to a variety of artistic and leadership criteria. Scholastic aptitude was, of course, non-predictive in this very selected sample.

Such large-scale programmatic research does not give us immediate answers but is a good beginning. Gradually the better short-term predictors can be narrowed down, at the same time that the careers of the Merit Scholars can be followed into adulthood and longer-range predictors identified. It should be noted that there is no question here of intelligence *versus* creativity. Instead, the predictors of creative performance are being sought within the group of high school students with the highest scholastic aptitude.

Another large-scale study which should eventually yield much valuable data is J. C. Flanagan's Project Talent, in which background information is being gathered on thousands of high school students along with results of an extended battery of tests. As these students are followed, important variables can be identified which will be used to predict later criteria of creativity.

What Can the Schools Do to Foster Creativity?

In spite of all our unanswered questions concerning the nature, development and measurement of creativity, there is a consensus that our schools can and must do more to foster it. In the past, we have concentrated on the transmission of information as one of the chief goals of education. While this is still a necessary goal, it is too often transmitted in a way which stifles creativity.

Anderson (1965) contrasts *Open* and *Closed* systems in education. The Open system is a system of relating which is both stimulating to the person and accepting of uniqueness in his perception and his thinking. Examples are found in the seminar, the class discussion, the term paper, the original experiment, or the student project. To Anderson this system constitutes a propitious environment for creativity.

The Closed System has two types. In the Personally Closed system one individual tends to restrict the expression of uniqueness, obstruct or inhibit creative interaction. Domination and usurpation are involved, which use force, threat, or the symbolic expressions of force in shame, guilt and other techniques for the stifling of individual differences and for producing conformity. Children and adolescents are still victims of these practices, both at school and at home. The Impersonally Closed system refers to the limiting of education to the experience of others, without leaving enough room in the curriculum for individual discovery, individual rearrangement or reorganization. Both Closed systems constitute an unpropitious environment for creativity, according to Anderson.

Rogers (1966) maintains that today the most important conceivable goal of education is learning how to learn or learning how to change, and to adopt new goals in our present-day world situation. This, he thinks rates far above any type of static knowledge. To do this will require increased flexibility of thinking.

Although we know very little about how to accomplish this goal, several types of suggestions have been made. Guilford (1966) says we need to decide what has to be learned, what it takes to be creative, and which contributing qualities respond best to training. Since there is always some degree of transfer in every act of creative thinking, he recommends that the *general* aspects of information be emphasized, and strategies be learned that have *general* application in connection with new information. An assumption, verbalized by Guilford and others, is that in whatever field of information the individual aspires to be creative, it is important to have a good fund of information of that kind in his memory storage. MacKinnon (1966) puts it that the more items of information the person has, the more likely it is, on purely statistical grounds, that he will be creative. So the approach certainly does not argue for *less* information, but rather for more and for different ways of using it.

The teacher, of course, is held to be the most important single influence. In the life histories of their creative adults, the IPAR group repeatedly found subjects testifying to the importance of some one teacher in the nurturing of their creative potential. Provus (1966) says that teachers, not materials or media, produce (or fail to produce) creative learning. But when given opportunities to construct creative learning materials, he found that only about 2/5 of the teachers became involved, while 1/5 fled from the experience and 2/5 remained passive. Even those who were interested took many months to change their style of teaching.

Although what constitutes a creative teacher has not really been defined, it is assumed that a creative teacher fosters creativity in children. This assumption may be mistaken—at least in the one or two studies done, there seemed to be no correlation between the creativity of the teacher and the creativeness of the children. Perhaps there is a difference between a teacher being creative *personally,* and knowing how to *teach* creatively.

Wallach and Kogan (1965), who emphasize learning in a spirit of associative play, feel that Burner's "inductive teaching" or the "discovery method" holds promise. A variation of this has been conducted by Crutchfield and Covington (1963) with an autoinstructional training program consisting of simplified detective stories which the children solved by being given successively more clues and information.

Finally, while it is felt that all children would profit from training in creative thinking, we may need different methods for different groups, and there is some disagreement about which groups to concentrate on first. Wallach and Kogan (1965) maintain that their high intelligence-low creativity child would be the most promising, while MacKinnon (1966) states that special attention should be given to groups who do not do well verbally or on verbal intelligence tests. In any event, he would de-emphasize group participation with its demand for conformity and provide maximum opportunity for potentially creative students to work out their own interests. He reminds us that his most creative adults were not "well-rounded" but had "sharp edges" to their personalities. They did not all have particularly smooth childhoods, and some suffered much anxiety and confusion. MacKinnon feels that many students who will eventually be identified as creative adults, will, as adolescents, be troubled and disturbed, experiencing conflicts of roles, possibly crises in religious beliefs, uncertainty with respect to a multiplicity of life goals, and so on. For these he recommends casual and inconspicuous guidance toward more and more sources of knowledge out of which the students can find answers they need. The general role of educational institutions in adolescent development has been discussed in detail by Macomber in another chapter so we will not carry the topic further here.

SUMMARY

Creativity is usually defined in terms of novelty and originality (or a novel rearrangement) and resulting social contributions. It can be studied as a process, a product or a person. All people possess creative potential but in different amounts and of different kinds. Creativity is related to, but different from, intelligence as we ordinarily measure it, and very bright people may be creative or non-creative.

Work on the identification of creative potential in children and adolescents is just beginning, and only longitudinal studies and more definitive criteria will tell us whether our present measures are in fact predicting who will be a creative adult.

Since we feel that creative thinking can be developed to a much greater extent than it is at present, there is much to be done to modify our present system of education so that more creative potential will be realized.

REFERENCES

Anderson, H. H. On the meaning of creativity. In: Anderson, H. H. (Ed.) *Creativity in childhood and adolescence.* Palo Alto, Calif.: Science and Behavior Books, 1965.

Andrews, E. G. The development of imagination in the pre-school child. *University of Iowa Studies of Character,* 1930, 3, (4).

Barron, F. *Creativity and psychological health.* Princeton, N.J.: Van Nostrand, 1963.

Bruner, J. E. The conditions of creativity. In: Gruber, H. E., Terrell, G., and Wertheimer, M. (Eds.) *Contemporary approaches to creative thinking.* New York: Atherton, 1962.

Cicirelli, V. G. Form of the relationship between creativity, IQ, and academic achievement. *Journal of Educational Psychology,* 1965, 56, 303–308.

Cox, C. M. The early mental traits of three hundred geniuses. In: *Genetic studies of genius:* Vol. II. Stanford, Calif.: Stanford University Press, 1926.

Crutchfield, R. S. The creative process. In: *Conference on the creative person.* Berkeley: University of California Institute of Personality Assessment and Research, 1961.

Crutchfield, R. S., and Covington, M. V. Facilitation of creative thinking and problem solving in school children. Paper presented at the AAAS convention, Cleveland, Ohio, 1963.

DeMille, R., and Merrifield, P. R. A review of Getzels, J. W., and Jackson, P. W. *Creativity and intelligence: Explorations with gifted students. Educational Psychological Measurement,* 1962, 22, 803–808.

Edwards, M. P., and Tyler, Leona. Intelligence, creativity and achievement in a nonselective public junior high school. *Journal of Educational Psychology,* 1965, 56, 96–99.

Flanagan, J. C. The definition and measurement of ingenuity. In: Taylor, C. W., and Barron, F. (Eds.) *Scientific creativity: Its recognition and development.* New York: Wiley, 1963.

Fliegler, L. Dimensions of the creative process. In: Andrews, M. (Ed.) *Creativity and psychological health.* Syracuse, New York: Syracuse University Press, 1961.

Freehill, M. *Gifted children.* New York: The Macmillan Co., 1961.

Getzels, J. W., and Jackson, P. W. *Creativity and intelligence.* New York: Wiley, 1962.

Golann, S. E. Psychological study and creativity. *Psychological Bulletin,* 1963, 60, 548–565.

Griffiths, Ruth. *A study of imagination in early childhood.* London: Routledge, 1945.

Guilford, J. P. Three faces of intellect. *American Psychologist,* 1959, 14, 469–479.

Guilford, J. P. A psychometric approach to creativity. In: Anderson, H. H. (Ed.) *Creativity in childhood and adolescence.* Palo Alto, Calif.: Science and Behavior Books, 1965.

Guilford, J. P. Basic problems in teaching for creativity. In: Taylor, C. W., and Williams, F. E. (Eds.) *Instructional media and creativity.* New York: John Wiley and Sons, Inc., 1966.

Guilford, J. P., Merrifield, P. R. and Cox, A. B. Creative thinking in children at the junior high school levels. *Reports of the Psychological Laboratory* No. 26, Los Angeles: University of Southern California, 1961.

Holland, J. L. Creative and academic performance among talented adolescents. *Journal of Educational Psychology,* 1961, 52, 136–137.

Holland, J. L., and Astin, A. W. The prediction of academic, artistic, scientific, and social achievement of undergraduates of superior scholastic aptitude. *Journal of Educational Psychology,* 1962, 53, 132–143.

Johnson, D. M. *The psychology of thought and judgment.* New York: Harper, 1955.

Kneller, G. F. *The art and science of creativity.* New York: Holt, Rinehart, 1965.

Kris, E. *Psychoanalytic explorations in art.* New York: International University Press, 1952.

Lowenfeld, V. Creativity and art education. *School Arts,* 1959, *2,* 5–15.

MacKinnon, D. W. The nature and nurture of creative talent. *American Psychologist,* 1962, *17,* 484–495.

MacKinnon, D. W. Instructional media in the nurturing of creativity. In: Taylor, C. W., and Williams, F. E. (Eds.) *Instructional media and creativity.* New York: John Wiley and Sons, Inc., 1966.

Mackler, B., and Shontz, F. C. Creativity: Theoretical and methodological considerations. *The Psychological Record,* 1965, *15,* 217–238.

Maltzman, I. On the training of originality. *Psychological Review,* 1960, *67,* 229–242.

Maslow, A. H. Creativity in self-actualizing people. In: Anderson, H. H. (Ed.) *Creativity and its cultivation.* New York: Harper and Row, 1959.

McNemar, O. Lost: Our intelligence? Why? *American Psychologist,* 1964, *19,* 871–882.

Mednick, S. A. The associative basis of the creative process. *Psychological Review,* 1962, *69,* 220–232.

Murphy, G. *Personality.* New York: Harper and Row, 1947.

Myers, I. B. *Manual of the Myers-Briggs Type Indicator.* Princeton, New Jersey: Educational Testing Service, 1962.

Nichols, R. C., and Holland, J. L. Prediction of the first year college performance of high aptitude students. *Psychological Monographs,* 1963, 77 (7, whole 570).

Parnes, S. J., and Harding, H. F. (Eds.) *A source book for creative thinking.* New York: Scribners, 1962.

Piers, Ellen V., Daniels, Jacqueline M., and Quackenbush, J. F. The identification of creativity in adolescents. *Journal of Educational Psychology,* 1960, *51,* 346–351.

Provus, M. M. Some personal observations on creativity. In: Taylor, C. W., and Williams, F. E. (Eds.) *Instructional media and creativity.* New York: John Wiley and Sons, Inc., 1966.

Ripple, R. E., and May, F. B. Caution in comparing creativity and I.Q. *Psychological Reports,* 1962, *10,* 229–230.

Roe, Anne   A psychological study of physical scientists. *Genetic Psychology Monographs*, 1951, *43*, 121–239.

Roe, Anne   A psychological study of eminent psychologists and anthropologists and a comparison with biological and physical scientists. *Psychological Monographs*, 1953, *67*, No. 2. (a)

Roe, Anne   *The making of a scientist.* New York: Dodd, Mead, 1953. (b)

Rogers, C. R. *On becoming a person.* Boston: Houghton Mifflin, 1961.

Rogers, C. R. (participant). In: Taylor, C. W., and Williams, F. E. (Eds.) *Instructional media and creativity.* New York: John Wiley and Sons, Inc., 1966.

Schafer, R. Regression in the service of the ego: the relevance of a psychoanalytic concept for personality assessment. In: Lindzey, G. (Ed.), *Assessment of human motives.* New York: Rinehart, 1958.

Taylor, C. W. (Ed.) *Creativity: Progress and potential.* New York: McGraw-Hill, 1964.

Thorndike, R. L. Some methodological issues in the study of creativity. In: *Proceedings of the 1962 invitational conference on testing problems.* Princeton, N.J.: Educational Testing Service, 1963.

Torrance, E. P. Educational achievement of the highly intelligent and the highly creative: Eight partial replications of the Getzels-Jackson study. (Research Memorandum BER-60-18). Minneapolis: Bureau of Educational Research, University of Minnesota, 1960.

Torrance, E. P. Education and creativity. In: Taylor, C. W. (Ed.) *Creativity: Progress and potential.* New York: McGraw-Hill, 1964.

Trowbridge, Norma and Charles, D. C. Creativity in art students. *Journal of Genetic Psychology*, 1966, *109*, 281–289.

Wallach, M. A., and Kogan, N. *Modes of thinking in young children.* New York: Holt, Rinehart, 1965.

Welsh, G. S. Comparison of D-48, Terman CMT, and Art Scale scores of gifted adolescents. *Journal of Consulting Psychology*, 1966, *30*, 88.

Wodtke, K. H., and Wallen, N. E. Teacher classroom control, pupil creativity and pupil classroom behavior. *Journal of Experimental Education*, 1965, *34*, 59–63.

Yamamoto, K. Role of creative thinking and intelligence in high school achievement. *Psychological Reports*, 1964, *14*, 783–789.

✖ CHAPTER 8

Values and Attitudes in Adolescence

Russell Eisenman *

ANYONE CONCERNED WITH THE SUBJECT OF ADOLESCENCE WILL SOONER or later find himself examining the values and attitudes which are characteristic of this stage in human development. Values and attitudes reveal themselves in behavior and, for this and other reasons, are of considerable interest and importance. To clarify our discussion of this important topic, let us first attempt to define and differentiate between values and attitudes. Although the distinction is imperfect, *values* generally refer to more general, abstract concepts (e.g., freedom, equal opportunity for all, education is important) while *attitudes* are less general and possibly inconsistent with one's values.[1] Examples of attitudes might be: Communists are bad, Mexicans are inferior, our school has the best football team, etc. It can be seen that the statement "Communists are bad" could also be considered a value, since this general belief of the culture provides a basis for forming opinions. At the same time, if the reasoning is that freedom is the most important value and that Communists oppose freedom (therefore Communists are bad), it would appear that the negative view of Communists represents an attitude more closely than it does a value. Perhaps the distinction between values and attitudes is unimportant.

* RUSSELL EISENMAN is an Assistant Professor of Psychology at Temple University. He has authored a chapter in the *Psychology of Modern Art* and has written numerous articles on such topics as moral judgments, attitudes, creativity, birth order and personality.

[1] A more formalized presentation of the difference between attitudes and values may be found in English and English (1958) who define an attitude as "an enduring, learned predisposition to behave in a consistent way toward a given class of objects . . ." A value may be considered to be the worth or excellence ascribed to something; or, an abstract concept which defines desirable ends or means. Additional definitions and uses of these terms are also given by English and English.

It should be readily apparent that the distinction is not always obvious. Nevertheless, we shall encounter a situation later in this chapter in which the failure to make such a distinction has led to an overly negative and stereotyped view of adolescence. Although it often seems vague and arbitrary, there is some utility in the value vs. attitude distinction.

IDEALISM AND REALISM

One of the most interesting characteristics of adolescents is their mixture of idealism and realism. On the one hand, the adolescent may live in what his parents consider an unrealistic dream world, with concern for world peace, absence of graft in politics, and other idealistic conceptions. On the other hand, the adolescent may have a cynical, "don't-kid-me-Mac,-I-know-the-score" outlook, which would seem to cast scorn upon all idealism. These seemingly contradictory outlooks must be viewed in the context of adolescent development and also within the framework of contemporary social phenomena.

Let us first consider idealism within the developmental framework. One way of explaining this idealism is to say that the adolescent is trying to find himself. In seeking his definition of himself he also seeks to define the world around him. Thus, he generalizes from his question of "What should I be like?" to "What should the world be like?" and comes up with idealistic answers which he will eventually discard (perhaps unfortunately). Activist youth are good examples of this idealism and are discussed in detail in the following chapter by Block *et al.*

A second explanation, also within the developmental context, is the one given by Stone and Church (1957) as one of several bases for adolescent idealism. Their explanation consists of what I call "the old switcheroo" approach. The prototype of the old switcheroo is the Freudian notion of reaction formation, in which the person does just the opposite of what his basic feelings would seem to demand. For example, the extremely hostile person may fear his hostility and outwardly become a very peaceful person. However, the hostility resides beneath the surface, and may explode under the proper circumstances. The old switcheroo concept emphasizes that things are not what they seem. With regard to the Stone and Church explanation, they suggest that adolescent idealism may constitute, in part, resistance to growing up. Thus, the idealism is not basically a concern with truth, beauty, and goodness. Rather it represents a defense in which the adolescent resists development into adulthood, with all of the implied responsibilities, including recognition of the world as a not-so-perfect place.

A third explanation also incorporates the old switcheroo notion, and is similar to the Stone-Church viewpoint. Adolescence represents a great change from childhood in physical and sexual development. We might suspect that the adolescent is threatened by his new found sexual interests and ability. This is especially true since our society exerts taboos against premarital intercourse, but at the same time emphasizes sexuality in general attitudes and values (e.g., in news-papers, movies and television). One way of resolving this conflict would be to retreat into idealism. Some support for such a viewpoint can be found in Peskin's (1967) research which has shown that early physical maturation in boys leads to decreased curiosity and explora-tory behavior and to increased social conformity. The implication is that early physical maturation automatically places the boy in conflict with a society which demands sexual and other kinds of inhibition at this age. The way out of this dilemma is general conformity to society which brings about a loss of personal curiosity. The interested reader should look at Peskin's research in detail since his work somewhat contradicts the studies which have presented a very negative image of the late maturing male.

We have now considered three possible explanations of adolescent idealism. All explanations emphasize characteristics which are con-sidered to be more or less unique in the adolescent. It should be noted, however, that the culture to a marked degree defines *what is* and *what is not* adolescent behavior. When we say something is peculiar to adolescence we imply, knowingly or not, that this some-thing is largely due to physical growth and maturational change. It is increasingly being recognized that many of the characteristics associated with adolescence may really reflect the particular demands of the culture for young people within a particular age range. Thus, it may have more to do with the culture of adolescence, than with the physiology of adolescence. Here we are getting into the theory and physiology of adolescent development. As Beller and Garrison discuss both of these subjects in separate chapters, we will not pursue them further. It should be noted that the question of the relative contributions of heredity and environment in adolescent development now comes into focus. Nichols considers this interesting issue, in detail, in an earlier chapter. For our purposes, let us make the safe assumption that many characteristics of adolescence are due to both physiological and cultural pressures. In particular, we shall concentrate on the influence of cultural pressures on the development of adolescent values and attitudes.

CYNICISM AND REBELLION

What makes adolescents so cynical at times? First, it may be that cynicism is part and parcel of the previously mentioned attempts at self-definition. Thus, cynicism can be seen as a kind of rebellion in which the adolescent says, "Your standards and values do not interest me. I know yours are phony and don't work and you know where you can take them. Don't give me that baloney." In attempting to find values of his own, the adolescent then rejects the ready-made values which his parents are trying to impose upon him. Self-definition, independence, and other high sounding terms are probably reflected in this rebelliousness and cynicism of adolescence. You may wonder, could not the adolescent seek his own values without rebelling so strongly against those of his parents and his society? It may be possible, but parents and society make such rational behavior very difficult, since parents and society are seldom very rational about their behavior. As I have pointed out in two articles on scapegoating (Eisenman, 1965; Eisenman, 1967a), societies tend to be quite conservative and deal harshly with those who would like to be different in any way. Thus, the adolescent is opposed by strong, irrational pressures toward socialization and he fights these pressures with an equally stubborn and hostile attitude. Seen in this perspective, it is not so surprising that the resistance by the object to the pressures of socialization, is irrational. In fact, it would seem strange for someone to say in a rational, intellectual manner, "You, my parents, as representatives of society, have chosen to impose certain standards upon me. However, I do not wish to abide by these standards, and therefore wish a conference to discuss possible changes." Such parental-adolescent peace talks are not likely to occur in most instances.

A second basis of adolescent cynicism has to do with the social scene in general. In a complex society such as ours the individual usually is not in a position to effect major changes. In fact, as Mills (1951) has emphasized, in our economic system today, there is less room for the entrepreneur. It is more likely that someone will make his living by working for someone else, and not as an independent businessman. Out of such a pattern of "massness" comes cynicism, or the conviction that nothing can be done; that all is in the hands of someone or something else. Powerlessness and alienation are often considered important aspects of our contemporary society. It is easy to understand how the member of such a society could develop a highly cynical or doubtful view on a number of topics. As an example of this, Jerome J. Platt and I recently gathered data on the future time perspective of college students. College students are generally considered as being in late adolescence, and thus come under the eye of this chapter. As part of the measurement of future time perspective, subjects were asked when they expected certain events to occur, e.g., a cure for cancer or the end of the cold war. Platt and I were struck by the number of subjects who felt the cold war would never come to an end, or that it would take longer to end than any of the other events. Some subjects gave "infinity" as their answer to this question, suggesting that they felt that it would always be with us. Since these students have grown up with the cold war as a constant part of their lives, they are unable to imagine any other kind of world. If asked to participate in a cross national discussion aimed at peace, these students would feel defeated before they started, since they seem convinced that the end of the cold war is extremely unlikely.

This cynical, hopeless, or alienated feeling is often seen in adolescents, but is not peculiar to them. Instead, it may pervade a whole society and is related to the changes Mills (1951) and others have discussed. Of course, adolescents may be particularly prone to adopt a feeling of alienation, since their potential creativeness is almost never called upon. As far as the making of responsible decisions is concerned, ours is an adult-centered society, and the adolescents are left to their games and diversions. It may be true, as Coleman (1965) has contended, that the adolescent culture is mostly social and athletic, with little emphasis upon more serious topics. If true, it would be difficult to think of adolescents as making informed choices from this life style. The adolescent is given little responsibility in society, is expected to inhibit his sexual drive, and is further expected to conform to the wishes of his parents. This intense socialization is not likely to lead to more mature independence in the adolescent. The vicious-circle phenomenon is also apparent here. Having adapted to such a frivolous life, the adolescent is not in a very good position to shift to a more serious responsible life style, even if such were made available to him. Perhaps a parallel can be seen in the problems inherent in attempting to bring democracy to nations which have experienced years of non-democratic rule. Attempts to shift governments from authoritarian or quasi-authoritarian forms to democratic ones are likely to fail unless the change is made gradually rather than overnight.

It is hoped that the reader has now eschewed some of the easy explanations for adolescent behavior, such as "Adolescents are just rebellious, that's all there is to it," or "adolescents can't accept responsibility," or "adolescents don't have any values." These pseudoexplanations are all similar in that they suggest, implicitly or explicitly, that the cause of the social ills associated with adolescence is the immaturity or irresponsibility of the adolescent. It is often claimed that if adolescents would just grow up and accept responsibility everything would be all right; or that adolescence is just a difficult age and there's not much that can be done about it. Both of these answers oversimplify the issues involved and make the adolescent the scapegoat for what are complex social problems. There are no simple answers available but it is possible to recognize the complexity of the situation and then attempt to understand this complexity in its relationship to the youth of our society.

VALUES

The foregoing discussion has considered many of the values and dilemmas in adolescence. We shall now be concerned more directly with values *per se*. First, let us consider a typical adult stereotype of the adolescent, viz., "Adolescents just don't have any values." While perhaps overstated, such a view is held by many educated and uneducated people. The basic point seems to be that adolescents, teenagers, or whatever they are called, fail to have higher values and show an amazing lack of concern for vital issues. What is the evidence for such an assertion?

We have already reported the Coleman (1965) claim that today's youth are oriented to a peer culture which stresses social and athletic values to the exclusion of more serious considerations. To the extent that Coleman is correct, it can be said with some accuracy that adolescents do not have many serious values, or at best that their serious values exert less influence over their everyday behavior than their peer-oriented values.

Jacob (1957) has reviewed the studies concerning the degree to which adolescents absorb the values they find in college. His conclusions are that our colleges and universities exert remarkably little influence on the values of their students. In addition, he found a depressing homogeneity as a characteristic of American youth. Jacob was surprised that, considering the diverse backgrounds of the students studied, there was so little difference in their value orientations. Most were concerned with personal success (tie this in with Johnstone and Rosenberg's chapter) and had little fear of the probability of failing. An abundance for all seems to be what youth envisages. While the students were tolerant of diversity, they had little inclination to do anything about discrimination. Instead, they were simply willing to accept change as it came without getting personally involved. These and other values of the American college student led Jacob to conclude that students are uninvolved, cheerful conformists in many ways. He admitted that their values, or lack of them, are possibly due to a shift away from the previous Puritan emphasis upon hard work. Contemporary students may be the forerunners of a new society with different values. One could add that *different* does not necessarily imply bad. However, despite these qualifications, Jacob's overall view of the value profile of American college students is a negative one. Before the reader becomes completely disillusioned, he should again remind himself to read the Block, Haan and Smith chapter on activist youth. It will add perspective to Jacob's findings.

There is some support for Jacob's contention about the uninvolved life style of the average college student. I hasten to add that this uninvolvement is with many of society's higher ideals (political democracy, nondiscrimination, etc.) and not uninvolvement in general. Students are certainly involved with questions relating to sex mores and the like. However, the basic point is that contemporary youth has responded to these issues, but has not taken any firm position on them. As Jacob characterizes them, the students happily accept the status quo. I was recently surprised to find that students at two quite different colleges responded most similarly to a test of moral judgments (Eisenman and Smith, 1966). The test was devised to confront subjects with situations which would commonly be considered immoral, but which also involved mitigating circumstances. One of the items is: "C. L. stole a loaf of bread to eat because he was very hungry and had no money." Subjects were asked to rate each statement on a scale of 1 to 7.

In the first study with the moral judgments scale, we were concerned with the relationship between severity of moral judgment and the complexity of a drawing of a person (which all subjects did). We had all kinds of reasons for making a specific prediction. Unfortunately for our prediction, our subjects overused the middle rating categories to a marked extent. In other words, most of these students (who were at the University of Georgia) did not reveal themselves as being either particularly harsh or particularly liberal in their moral judgments. They chose the middle ground. One is led to suspect that the students may not have been too concerned with moral judgments, since their lives may not be guided by a deep concern with right vs. wrong (Jacob, 1957; Coleman, 1965). The students took a middle-of-the-road position. Perhaps they would have been more susceptible to what the peer group felt was right or wrong if we had engineered a situation such as this and had then demanded their opinion (Riesman, 1950).

It occurred to me that this middle-of-the-road approach may be more true of Southern students at the University of Georgia than of students from, say, the North. Thus, the same moral judgments test was given to students in three classes at Temple University, in Philadelphia. Did these students reveal a liberal approach in contrast to their Southern peers? Such regional differences might be anticipated, but the fact is that the results were virtually identical to the earlier study. The vast majority of students chose a rating near the midpoint of the rating scale and thus avoided either a liberal or conservative position (Eisenman, 1967b). It may be that the test is invalid and that everyone, no matter how intensely involved he is with higher moral standards, simply tends to choose middle categories. However, my hunch at present is that both the Georgia and Temple students have indicated their lack of involvement in issues of right or wrong, and that they would have been much more responsive to pressures for conformity than to a task which asked for a moral judgment. For what it is worth, some of my colleagues looked at this data and their observations are consistent with this view of contemporary youth as being uninvolved and "middle-of-the-roaders" on issues of value.

There have been recent attempts to point to civil rights demonstrations and anti-war demonstrations as negating this stereotype of uninvolved youth. But the issue of civil rights is losing its short-lived popularity as a cause, and peace demonstrators are looked upon in a negative light by many who fear the loss of their status quo. Consequently, the recent tendency to point to student involvement may be fading somewhat, with more and more commentators of the American scene returning to their previous stereotype of the uninvolved and uncaring American youth.

PERSONALITY AND SOCIAL FORCES

A more sensible approach (in contrast to a cyclical swing which first derogates and then defends youth) would be to appraise each particular issue in terms of a broad consideration of personality and social correlates and causes. The attempts to stereotype the adolescent typically involve only his personality, and neglect an attempt to understand how social phenomena contribute to his development. Thus, as previously noted, many adults remain in the center on issues and continue to be uninvolved. This may well be due to the social forces which tend to reject the individual who does not conform. Certain personality types may respond to these forces more so than do others, but this does not justify the frequent failure to consider the interaction of the person and his society in attempting to account for observed behavior.

Jacob's (1957) profile of values on the American college student suffers, in part, because of his emphasis upon values and his neglect of attitudes. Or, to put it in other terms, Jacob has focussed on many ways in which adolescents are homogeneous but has neglected basic personality differences. For example, it may be that most adolescents (or even most people in general) will give highly similar responses to questions about the best form of government, or about how moral a given situation is. This does not mean that this homogeneity of values reflects all that is of importance to these respondents. To the extent that the society exerts strong pressures for conformity we may expect many of society's general values to be similar. This is not by way of apology, since it is frightening to think of such mass acceptance without more intellectual rumination. Nevertheless, the society may instill certain basic beliefs and certain tendencies to become or remain uninvolved to most of its members. Of at least equal importance are personality characteristics. It is at this point that adolescents and people in general might not appear so homogeneous.

Consider the future time perspective study mentioned previously. It was pointed out that many college students felt the cold war would never end. With regard to this issue there was much agreement. But there were many individual differences with regard to this time perspective. Some students had a great deal of future time perspective, and will probably prove to be excellent planners who are capable of seeing long range consequences. Other students seemed very low in this quality, and are likely to be the impulsive types who are not going to delay gratifications even if immediate gratification has very negative long-term consequences. This is certainly one of the problems of the disadvantaged adolescent as discussed in Kohrs' chapter. I have only chosen one personality attribute, future time perspective, to make my point. Many more examples could be given. Students differ in anxiety, in their perception of reinforcement as internally or externally controlled, and in a host of other variables typically subsumed under the label of personality. In other words, adolescents may be homogeneous with regard to many things, and it may be most unfortunate that there is not more diversity, especially with regard to moral judgments, higher values, and the like. But, it is a mistake to think that this tells the whole story about contemporary youth. They also differ in many personality characteristics. Today's adolescents are not all robots responding in exactly the same way, although there is a modicum of truth in such a stereotype which is certainly worthy of consideration. It should be remembered that in many kinds of endeavor, what you find depends upon what you study.

LIBERALIZATION OR HOMOGENEITY?

Those who have reviewed changes in students generally conclude that students tend to become more liberal in their attitudes with increased education. This would seem to stand in contrast to our more negative findings about adolescents, and would further seem to suggest that many of the characteristics of adolescents are subject to change with increasing maturity, information, exposure to others, etc. For example, in their review of personality changes in college students, Webster, Freedman, and Heist (1962) referred to studies which suggest that there are changes in information and values as a result of education. Students become more liberal and accepting of differences in others with increased schooling.

The Webster *et al.* conclusion is a typical one for those who look at studies of changes in ethocentrism, authoritarianism, and the like. It may come as no surprise to find Jacob (1957) again the devil's advocate, when he claims that students do not become more liberal with increased education. Jacob feels that the term "liberalization" is a misnomer, and that what really happens is that students are socialized into accepting a particular viewpoint, which happens to be one of tolerance of diversity. Those who cannot adjust to this socialization pressure often drop out of school, and thereby avoid having to undergo liberal indoctrinization. Jacob's point would seem to be twofold: first, the finding of increased liberalization with increased education is in part an artifact due to the dropping out of students who are too rigid to make the adjustment to the college pattern of beliefs. Consequently, those who stay are those whose opinions can be manipulated in the direction demanded by the college. They are not more liberal after four years but simply have been changed in comparison to those who dropped out. Secondly, the so-called liberalization is not a fundamental change. It is instead a minor shift in posture which sophisticated students can easily make.

Although there may be truth in both of Jacob's points (and there is statistical evidence for the homogeneous outlook of college students), it would also seem true that the liberalization has some real substance to it. If I know that Student X is a college graduate, I can predict, on the basis of the above studies, that he is more likely to be accepting of deviance than Student Y, a nongraduate. This would seem to be valuable information, since it may mean that Student X, the graduate, is less likely to punch me in the mouth or decide, as a juror, to send me to jail for some unpopular view I may possess. In other words, it would seem that there are real consequences of having more liberal attitudes, namely that one's behavior may reflect these attitudes and allow for more diversity. If there is this consistency between liberal attitudes and behavior then the gain for society is real, despite the reservations of Jacob. The point here is not that Jacob's criticisms are incorrect, but only that they do not tell the whole truth. Increased liberalization may indeed have important consequences, even though we may have wished consequences which were more far-reaching than those obtained.

CREATIVITY, PERSONALITY, ATTITUDES AND VALUES

Changes do not just occur during the college years. They also occur all along the road through high school to college. Perhaps this can be documented by some of my ongoing research on creativity. At this point we are not so much concerned with creativity per se, but rather with those aspects of creativity which parallel and are tied in with values and attitudes. The reader will find that Ellen Piers has presented a full discussion on the topic of creativity in the preceding chapter.

I have been interested in finding some means of testing personality variables which should, based on previous findings and theories, be related to creativity. A study by Child (1965) which was not concerned with creativity, has reported several tests which seem to tap areas of vital concern for our discussion. I shall present information about these personality tests and the findings with college students. We will then compare this data with similar information on high school students. Although the findings are unpublished and preliminary, they help to make the point that continuous changes do go on in adolescence.

Child presented six items from each of several tests. In all cases the six items were the ones which had the highest correlations with the total scale. I chose five of these scales as ones which should be related to creativity. This gave me a 30-item test. The tests chosen, with an example from each, are as follows.

Elements of Creativity, Personality, Attitudes and Values

Tolerance of complexity. This scale attempts to measure whether or not the subject appreciates the complexity of things, or whether he tends to have an overly-simple outlook. A sample item is: "Most of our social problems would be solved if we could somehow get rid of the immoral, crooked, and feeble-minded people." Subjects answer all items true or false, and in this instance, a false answer is scored in the direction of tolerance of complexity.

Tolerance of ambiguity, ambivalence, and unrealistic experience. This scale sounds similar to the first one, but is different in that the emphasis seems less on conceptual outlook, and more on sensory and perceptual experiences. "The expert ski jumper should enjoy the sport all the more if it remains a source of tension and even alarm." This is scored a plus for a true response.

Scanning. This refers to the tendency to notice things other than what one is immediately focussing upon, i.e., to take into experience a broad range of stimuli. "I rarely notice the color of people's eyes." Scored a plus for a false response.

Independence of judgment. Barron (1953) developed and validated a scale which would distinguish between conformers and non-yielders in Asch's (1956) famous conformity studies. "The unfinished and the imperfect often have greater appeal for me than the completed and polished." Scored a plus for a true response.

Regression in the service of the ego. This psychoanalytic concept is tested with items prepared by David Singer (according to Child). "I can detect in myself no strong anti-social impulses of the sort which, under certain circumstances, might lead to crime." Scored a plus for a false response.

Perhaps this brief sampling of items can convey some impression of the personality characteristics being measured. All are believed to be related to creativity. It should be apparent from the items that the creative person is seen as being open to new experiences and free of the inhibitions imposed by extreme social conformity. Before using the items in the combined 30-item scale, the test was given the innocuous title of "Personal Opinion Survey," and administered to 229 subjects for purposes of performing an item analysis. If the individual items failed to differentiate between the high and low scorers on the test, the items would be useless for inclusion in further research with the "Personal Opinion Survey." Most of the 229 subjects were college students, but a few laborers, secretaries, and professional people were also included. As it turned out, every one of the 30 items differentiated high from low scorers in the predicted direction and most to a significant extent. The 114 high scorers had a mean score of 22.07 out of a possible 30, while the 115 low scorers had a mean of 15.68. All five of the scales held up well, with the exception of *scanning*, where the differences were as predicted but relatively small.

The "Personal Opinion Survey" was next administered to 11th and 12th grade high school students. A preliminary analysis suggests that they score much lower than the predominantly college student sample. Few of the high school students even scored as high as 22, which was the mean score of the high group previously tested.

What interpretation can we offer? As a tentative interpretation let us consider the possibility that the same effect mentioned previously is again with us: as education increases liberalization of attitude increases. In this particular case, what seems to be involved is an increased movement in the direction of those personality characteristics which are associated with creativity. If this interpretation is correct, the many negative things mentioned previously about adolescent values and attitudes should be balanced somewhat by the implication of the present finding as well as those of other investigators. With increased education adolescents become more liberal, more open to experience, and thus are more likely to be creative persons. Such a ray of light is quite meaningful when compared to the rather dark picture of conformity, absence of values, etc., which has also been discussed. From the adolescent's standpoint, this shift toward more liberal or creative thinking also involves problems. Undoubtedly it will bring him into conflict with his more conservative parents or society. While I have presented the shift toward liberalism in a favorable light (reflecting my values), it will often create problems for the person who makes this shift and thereby antagonizes the more conventional and status quo segment of society.

SUMMARY

This chapter has presented considerable information which puts adolescents in a rather negative light. To offset this, I have attempted to show how many of the adolescent's negative characteristics cannot be understood without considering the ways in which his parents and society encourage or develop such behavior. I have not tried to present a summary of the vast body of literature on this topic, but have instead taken a position on some of the issues which are often clouded with stereotyped statements or by superficial analysis. In particular, attempts to indoctrinate the adolescent with society's values, including the sexual taboos, exert a strong effect and have much to do with ways in which adolescents behave. This does not mean that all adolescent behavior can be justified on the grounds that parents and society are implicated. Such a position would be too much like the argument of children who say: "You started it first."

What does seem necessary is some consideration of how both the adolescent and the parent, and the adolescent and society, interact. We have frequently viewed adolescence as a time of storm and stress which, in our culture, is often quite accurate. But, it is time we went beyond this superficial description of what adolescents are like, and considered the role of the greater society in adolescent development.

The values and attitudes of adolescents may be different, in many ways, from those of the adults. However, adults, and that abstraction we call "society" or "culture," play an important role in the formation, maintenance, and sometimes, in the change of values and attitudes.

REFERENCES

Asch, S. E. Studies of independence and submission to group pressure: I. A minority of one against a unanimous majority. *Psychological Monographs*, 1956, *70*, (Whole No. 416).

Barron, F. Some personality correlates of independence of judgment. *Journal of Personality*, 1953, *21*, 287–297.

Child, I. L. Personality correlates of esthetic judgment in college students. *Journal of Personality*, 1965, *33*, 476–511.

Coleman, J. S. The adolescent culture. In: Gordon, I. J. (Ed.) *Human Development*. Chicago: Scott, Foresman, 1965.

Eisenman, R. Scapegoating and social control. *Journal of Psychology*, 1965, *61*, 203–209.

Eisenman, R., and Smith, J. F. Moral judgment and effort in human figure drawings. *Perceptual and Motor Skills*, 1966, *23*, 951–954.

Eisenman, R. Scapegoating the deviant in two cultures. *International Journal of Psychology*, 1967, *2*, 133–138. (a)

Eisenman, R. Sex differences in moral judgment. *Perceptual and Motor Skills*, 1967, *24*, 784. (b)

English, H. B. and English, A. C. *Comprehensive dictionary of psychological and psychoanalytical terms*. New York: David McKay, 1958.

Jacob, P. E. *Changing values in college*. New York: Harper, 1957.

Mills, C. W. *White collar*. New York: Oxford, 1951.

Peskin, H. Pubertal onset and ego functioning. *Journal of Abnormal Psychology*, 1967, *72*, 1–15.

Riesman, D. *The lonely crowd*. New Haven, Conn.: Yale University Press, 1950.

Stone, L. J., and Church, J. *Childhood and adolescence*. New York: Random House, 1957.

Webster, H., Freedman, M. B., and Heist, P. Personality changes in college students. In N. Sanford (Ed.), *The American college*. New York: Wiley, 1962, pp. 811–846.

CHAPTER 9

Activism and Apathy in Contemporary Adolescents[1]

Jeanne H. Block, Norma Haan, and M. Brewster Smith *

DURING THE "EISENHOWER ERA" OF THE 1950's, COMPLAINT WAS frequently voiced about the apathetic, conforming, success-oriented youth on American campuses. As we write in the late '60's, quite other complaints predominate. Viewers, with alarm, wonder whether American colleges are becoming politicized like those of Latin America where the mounting of political protest often takes priority over educational goals. That there has been a change in public perception and in atmosphere can hardly be doubted. The underlying facts are, as always, harder to get at.

Political and social protest in the '60's, as previously, is carried out by a minority of students. But this committed and protesting minority

* JEANNE H. BLOCK is a Research Associate in the Institute of Human Development at the University of California (Berkeley). She has published a number of articles in the areas of personality development, psychosomatic medicine, schizophrenia, and cross-cultural child-rearing.
NORMA HAAN is an Assistant Research Psychologist in the Institute of Human Development. She has co-edited *Readings in Professional Education: An Interdisciplinary Approach.* She has also written several articles on intelligence quotient changes, and social mobility.
M. BREWSTER SMITH is a Professor of Psychology and the Director of the Institute of Human Development. He has co-authored or written: *The American Soldier; For a Science of Social Man;* and *Opinions and Personality.* His other contributions to the literature are on such topics as social psychology, attitudes, values, and mental health.

[1] This chapter was prepared in connection with our Institute of Human Development study of the moral orientations of student activists, supported by grants from the Rosenberg Foundation and the Foundations' Fund for Research in Psychiatry. We gratefully acknowledge the support of these organizations which, of course, are not responsible for our assertions and judgments here.

seems to contrast not only with the privatistic, conforming majority (who held the center of the stage relatively unchallenged in the Eisenhower years), but also with the activist minority of the Depression '30's. Ethos and action—sincerity, authenticity, purity of gesture—now seem to count for more than achievement and success (goals of the '50's) or ideological correctness and consistency, so valued in the '30's. The reactions of contemporary young people to American political and social institutions have some genuinely new elements. The present chapter attempts to identify the nature of contemporary protest, to provide a coherent conceptualization of the several varieties of activism and apathy and to summarize the results of recent empirical studies regarding the origins, correlates, and consequences of societal involvement or uninvolvement. We begin by a brief historical excursion to compare activism during the Great Depression and activism in the Affluent Society.

ACTIVISM IN THE THIRTIES AND IN THE SIXTIES

In both the Depression era and the present, student radicalism arose from the background of an immediately preceding period in which political apathy, concern for security, and passive conformity were pronounced. These periods, in turn, followed the two most calamitous wars in history. During the Depression, large numbers of young people were actively involved in radical organizations. The American Student Union, an amalgamated group encompassing most radical student groups of the time, claimed a membership of 100,000 students in a college population that then numbered one and a half million (Lipset, 1966a). Student protests of that time were oriented around two themes: radical revision of the social and economic order, and pacifism. Many of the activities in which radical students then participated were similar to those of today: they organized associations of the unemployed, they picketed, demonstrated, signed the Oxford Pledge refusing to bear arms for the United States, designated Army Day as an annual day of protest on which rallies were held and strikes conducted in the cause of peace. It has been estimated that more than 200,000 students took part in the anti-war parades of that period (Lipset, 1966a).

As of 1966 the combined memberships of the Student Non-violent Coordinating Committee, the Congress of Racial Equality, Students for a Democratic Society, and the Student Peace Union have been estimated to have involved only between 12,000 and 50,000 students in a college population of six million students (Munk, 1965; Peterson, 1966b; Braungart, 1966). For activists of the present generation civil rights and peace are the two consuming issues. Each of the activities of the '30's has a counterpart in today's protests: community organization of the poor in urban ghettoes, picketing, demonstrating, burning of draft cards, anti-Vietnam Days of Protest, and peace marches.

In their status as minorities of their student generation, in their anti-war commitments, and in some of the strategies of protest employed, these two generations of student activists—separated by thirty years—have important features in common. There are significant differences, however, that distinguish their preferred modes of protest and have led to different reactions on the part of the adult community.

The Depression years were a time when dissent was flavored and polarized in one way or another by Marxist ideology. Ideology and theory were often so important that differences of opinion within a particular organization could not be resolved. As a result, many splinter groups were formed, each homogeneous ideologically. In contrast, many of today's radical youth groups are relatively non-doctrinaire, oriented to specific issues or particular injustices. Concerned as they are with immediate moral tasks, they are not inhibited by ideological dogma from cooperating with groups whose values may be widely different from their own. The largest radical student organizations in the '30's were campus derivatives of adult political organizations whose programs were determined and dominated by the older membership. In contrast, most radical student organizations of the present generation have no affiliation with adult-sponsored organizations and operate autonomously.

Still another difference between these two generations, that is presently disconcerting to the adult society, is that protest today occurs at a time when, for large segments of the population, material affluence and financial security are at unprecedented levels. In this time of affluence, the leaders of youthful revolt come primarily from families in the upper economic and educational strata; as children they were financially secure; they have enjoyed material comforts and educational opportunities and can look forward to successful careers in high-status professions. Protest was more understandable and acceptable to society in the '30's when poverty, unemployment, hunger, disenchantment, and fear were rife. Greater countenance was given to the radical causes of that time by the New Deal government itself, which was modifying its doctrines and policies along liberal lines to accord with economic and social realities. In the '30's then, student radicalism was closer to the mainstream of opinion than it appears to be today.

The most dramatic difference, however, between the student activists then and now is not so much with respect to ideological emphasis as in strategy, specifically in the use of civil disobedience. Contemporary activist students have learned their most valued technique from the civil rights demonstrators in the South who successfully used tactics of civil disobedience to fight segregation of buses, restaurants, parks, and other public facilities. Student activists have extended the use of civil disobedience into other areas of dissent and have engaged in sit-ins to effect changes in society. Ordinary citizens find civil disobedience disconcerting; it is challenging and upsetting to established institutions and procedures. The tactics employed by today's activists have estranged many in the adult world who, as the activists see it, value security, image, and conformity; but who, in their own eyes, value order, due process, and civility. It is difficult for adults to understand a commitment so strong that one is willing to risk arrest and subsequent penalties and possibly forego the tangible fruits of the affluent society.

The attention drawn by young activists—in public anxiety, in controversial articles, and in research—has been disproportionate to their actual numbers, since a rather small minority of students on a relatively few campuses is centrally involved in protest. But to dismiss this small, vocal group as atypical is to miss the point. They speak for many not so articulate as themselves, as was shown on the Berkeley campus during the by-now-famed sit-in at Sproul Hall and by new events occurring at Berkeley as we write. During the free speech rebellion, for every student sitting-in there were twenty-one sympathetic students who approved—either mildly or strongly—of the Free Speech Movement (FSM) (Gales, 1965). The university, particularly the selective campus that aspires to intellectual leadership, provides one of the few institutional bases in American society for cultural criticism and social renewal. What happens on campuses, therefore, matters very much, particularly when it is realized that some of the most selective universities have been the scenes of greatest student unrest and protest. In the campus microcosm, as in the larger world, it takes only a minority to set the spirit of an age.

THE SCOPE OF STUDENT ACTIVISM

Almost all research studies that have been concerned with social action and protest have limited their inquiry to the incidence of activism in the college population. The findings we cite, therefore, do not include younger adolescents nor do they reflect the majority of young people in the late teens who do not continue their education. The studies of Coleman (1961, 1965) and of Musgrove (1965) indicate that in the United States and in England, secondary school youth for the most part are not conscientious critics of society. Held off by adult society from full participation in it, "teenagers" participate instead in a "youth culture" that is, in good part, an exploitative adult creation. Aspects of the youth culture might be seem as implicitly critical of the adult world of "square" respectable values. But, in contrast with the college youth with whom we are concerned, "teenagers" have not to our knowledge engaged to any marked extent in conscientious protest activity. Their rebellion tends to merge, in adult eyes, with delinquency. We turn, then, to recent college studies.

The most thorough recent study assaying the scope of organized student protest is that of Peterson (1966a), who surveyed Deans of Students in all regionally accredited, four-year colleges existing in the United States in the fall of 1965. A number of conclusions can be drawn from the questionnaire returns received from 85% of the Deans.

Local issues of civil rights were most apt to provoke student protest. Complaints about food service and parietal rules governing personal conduct were cited as the next most frequent causes of student dissent. The Vietnam war ranked next, while educational reforms and issues of academic freedom were the categories least often cited as student concerns. Only the off-campus issues of civil rights, the Vietnam war, and disarmament showed variation in protest by type of institution. Private secular universities and liberal arts colleges and large public universities tended to report student protests involving these issues more frequently while public liberal arts colleges, religiously sponsored institutions, and technical and teachers' colleges reported little student activity in these spheres. A positive relationship was found between institutional quality as indexed by the proportion of faculty doctorates and the frequency of protest over off-campus issues. Colleges in the South report substantially less student protest over off-campus issues: civil rights and American foreign and military policies. In Peterson's study, only one in four Deans report the presence of any radical student groups on their campuses, and only six of the 849 colleges included estimated the number of student radicals as exceeding five per cent.

Peterson (1966) and Braungart (1966) agree in estimating the number of *organized* students *actively* engaged in social protest at fewer than one per cent of the total college student population. However, when the definition of activism is broadened to include politically unaffiliated students participating in social protest, a far larger percentage of students is included. In a national sample of college students polled by *Newsweek* magazine (1965), 18% said they had participated in picket lines, presumably for civil rights. In our own study on the Berkeley campus, 18% of a randomly selected sample of sophomores, juniors, and seniors indicated that they had engaged in picketing and 16% responded that they had participated in peace marches and demonstrations. When we extend the definition of activism to include reconstructive behavior that does not directly challenge the status quo, we find on the Berkeley campus that 11% of the randomly selected sample of students had at one time or another been engaged in tutoring children in economically distressed areas, a figure that is consistent with extrapolation made from current roster of participants in the tutorial programs. Katz and Sanford (1966), in their research on the Stanford and Berkeley campuses, concluded that the number of socially involved students totals about 15% of the student body.

What, then, of the majority of students on the campuses today? According to Katz and Sanford (1966) both freshman and senior students at Stanford are typically uninterested in participation in local affairs or in working toward improving our national or international relations. Students rationalized their lack of involvement in the larger community by explaining that they were not "crusaders" and that their primary life concerns in the present were in the areas of personal and emotional development. The achievement of emotional well-being, respect, love, and affection in the present were more important than political-social involvement, financial success, or the realization of intellectual or artistic values. The students anticipated that after graduation their greatest concerns would be about their careers, marriages, and future families. Katz and Sanford conclude from their investigations that the great majority of students are not involved in political or social issues. They suggest that colleges, instead of being disturbed by occasional vivid expressions of student "activism," should encourage students to assume reponsibility in the realm of public affairs.

Although the common concerns of young people center around a search for personal identity, this search takes many different forms. Some direct themselves quite determinedly toward future goals and the achievement of adult roles and status; others take a tortuous, circuitous path as they attempt to challenge the values of a society whose goals do not conform to their sense of humanity or insistence upon justice. In the next section of this chapter, we explore the development of activism and apathy in terms of the tasks of adolescence, the parental values that have been inculcated, and some socio-moral discrepancies that affect youth as they seek to establish an authentic place for themselves in a complex and sometimes compromising adult world.

THE DEVELOPMENT OF POLITICAL-SOCIAL SENSITIVITY

To construct a firm sense of identity and to fashion a set of values consistent with the self, consonant with one's history, and worthy of commitment, are the work of adolescence (Erikson, 1963). The young person entering adolescence has not only to respond to the changes occurring in his physical state and stature, but to encompass a rapidly expanding world as his psychological life space and his actual, geographic environment enlarge in diverse ways. New, extended perceptions of the world, the development of complex cognitive skills (see Elkind's discussion), and the emergence of different, intense affects typify the experiences that are to be integrated during adolescence.

The scope of the physical environment enlarges because newly acquired competencies and mobility permit the early adolescent to range beyond the boundaries of his immediate neighborhood into the larger, outlying world. Junior and senior high schools widen the range of his encounters with students and teachers and confront him with subject matter that now leaves room for opinion and interpretation. The greater freedom to discover and explore presents the middle-class adolescent with a diversity of situations, people, and ideas from which he was earlier insulated, geographically or by parental prohibitions. The adolescent needs to digest these new perceptions and awarenesses in a way that is consonant with his own sense of emerging integrity. However, marked discrepancies with his own earlier values and attitudes and those of the significant people in his childhood are likely because the adolescent is confronted with the contemporary values of a world that has dramatically shifted during his and his parents' lifetimes.

The adolescent period is marked not only by a broadening of experiences and a heightening of awareness, but by an increased capacity for dealing with cognitive complexity so that hypothetical, reflective, abstractive, and future-oriented thinking become possible. According to Piaget, most children prior to the age of eleven conceive of themselves in concrete, definitional, empirically given terms and have not yet developed abstract notions of self or ideals. Beginning between the ages of about 13 to 15, a new affective component enters when the adolescent becomes able to experience feelings about himself relative to certain abstract ideals (Piaget and Weil, 1951). The development of an ideal concept is possible only when the individual is capable of future-oriented reflective thinking, thinking about thoughts, and when he is able to differentiate between the real and what could possibly be true (Inhelder and Piaget, 1958). With the development during adolescence of propositional, hypothetical thinking, it becomes possible to articulate a set of ideals based upon what could be real for one's self and one's society and to evaluate oneself relative to those ideals.

As the young person becomes capable of hypothetical thinking and begins to anticipate the character and qualities of his own and his generation's future within the society, he may come to find it wanting. He begins to think in terms of daring possibilities, often dedicating himself to effecting changes in societal values and institutions. Inhelder and Piaget (1958) call this developmental juncture the "idealistic crisis," and suggest that commitment to concrete cognitive attainments by taking a job or starting professional training turns the idealistic reformer to the realities of the adult world, leading him away from the dangers of purely formalistic, hypothetical thought.

The cognitive capabilities emerging during adolescence are accompanied, influenced, and sometimes exaggerated by other, future-oriented necessities. The adolescent aspires to define himself as a person who knows himself, not only in terms of what he is, but equally emphatically, in terms of what he is not. Individuation of one's self cannot occur in an unpeopled vacuum, and the future adult and citizen-to-be frequently casts his self-examination in terms of comparative similarities and contrasts between himself and his family, and between himself and his society.

This scrutiny of self in relationship to historically significant mentors and previously unquestioned and unexamined social institutions is a daring maneuver emotionally that is not handled with skill or grace by many adolescents. Some do not even venture to probe at all. Some may parry the hazards and gambles that self-definition entails by avoidance, either by not thinking or only thinking concretely of the next best thing to do. These avoiding adolescents, consequently, have little occasion or reason for criticism of self or society. They define their roles and goals without serious self-examination.

Questioning adolescents, however, are in a stage, aptly described by Erikson (1963, 1964) in rich detail, that involves a central and essential preoccupation with establishing a sense of *fidelity*. Fidelity concerns the articulation of ideals, interpersonal and social values, and qualities by particular human relationships worth the devotion of one's self. In constituting a sense of fidelity, the adolescent wonder's whether he can trust himself to behave reliably, that is, predictably and consistently. He tests to see whether he can esteem himself in terms of his own humanity, veracity, courage, or other components making up his ego-ideal. If he is to persuade himself to enter his society as a full-time participant, he must examine his past, his forebearers, his society and its institutions to determine the quality of their intentions toward him and his generation. His scrutiny involves at least a three-sided question: can I find fidelity within myself; can I find it in my parents in spite of our generational differences; and can I find it in my society? Adolescence is thus a time for examination and testing of self, parents, and society. If all goes well between the adolescent and his elders, the emergent adult knows who he is, who he is not; and he has made differentiated, informed commitments to some aspects of his society and selected those causes which he will continue to support.

Constituting a sense of fidelity is both an internal matter for one's self and an external matter for one's society, one's parents, and one's own generation. The adolescent's choice in committing himself to the making of his own generation's history depends upon the tolerance of his society for dissent and also upon the adaptive strength of his personality for dealing with dissonance. Some societies and some parents cannot afford, and will not allow, the scrutiny involved in establishing fidelity. Some adolescents cannot pose the questions, protecting themselves with the shared code of peer group uniformism (Blos, 1962), or conformity. Other young people pose their questions in a nonnegotiable manner so that the answers are merely self-fulfilling prophecies. In these instances, growth may be impaired since, as Erikson (1964) suggests, fidelity is a matter acutely relevant to the ego's adaptive strength, essential for continued growth and greater personality differentiation. Young people who cannot manage this difficult task constructively, either because their own resources are insufficient or because their social predicament is too formidable, not only foreclose their own potentialities for growth; they also deprive society of one of its major sources of creative change, the push from each new generation to make society more responsive to its needs.

In the favorable case, the outcome in late adolescence is a shift in emphasis from experiencing, questioning, and experimenting to *integrating*. In Erikson's terms, such a resolution involves the development of an *historical perspective* that relates to an understanding of the irreversibility of events and the significant cause-and-effect relationships in society. Adolescent ideals become tempered by the knowledge of the intransigencies of reality. The adolescent adjusts to outer reality as he comes to recognize aspects of his own self and life that cannot be changed or helped. The realistic integration comprised in such an historical perspective does not merely represent compromise with the world as it has always been. Rather, the maturing person's efforts to effect social change become more differentiated as they are directed toward making society more responsive to the needs of each new generation of youth.

The development of political and social sensitivity is, for the individual adolescent, a derivative of his confrontation with life and of the disparities and contradictions that he notices and has to integrate to the conflicts aroused by his perceptions of the discrepancies between the professed values and ideals of society and the actual societal context may, however, take a variety of forms, which we will now consider.

ADOLESCENT REACTIONS TO THE SOCIETAL CONTEXT

To avoid the terminological confusion that seems to prevail in much discussion of adolescent political-social behavior, we need to introduce some conceptual distinctions. Young people engaged in protest against contemporary social institutions have been variously termed "protesters," "rebels," "radicals," "activists," "demonstrators," "beatniks," or young people engaged in "pro-social action." These terms obviously vary in the extent to which they are pejorative and confuse degree of social involvement with acceptance or rejection of social institutions, ideological orientation, and the nature of protest, pro or anti-social in form. Similarly, in the descriptions of uninvolved youth, important differences are obscured when such labels as "alienation," "lack of commitment," "passivity," "disaffiliation," and "resignation" are used interchangeably. Two dimensions seem useful to us in conceptualizing the political stances and social reactivity of the adolescent. The first dimension is the *degree of involvement* with contemporary political-social issues. At one extreme we find uninvolved, socially indifferent or apathetic youth while at the other end of the continuum we see the involved, active, dedicated young person with a sense of instrumentality. In the political-social sphere this dimension is reflected in the degree to which an individual feels that he can make a difference, can be an instrument of change in his society.

The second dimension relates to the degree to which the adolescent *accepts or rejects the traditional values and the institutional authority of the society*. At one end of this dimension we encounter the young person who accepts the prevailing values of society and conforms readily to its institutions. At the other extreme is the young person who rejects traditional societal values and flouts legitimate authority.

How involvement or uninvolvement is conjoined with acceptance or rejection of traditional values and authority has widely different implications for the quality of adolescent behavior. Before we attempt to coordinate these two dimensions, the reader should note that we are maintaining *ideological orientations* as a conceptually independent dimension. Although there has been a tendency to equate social involvement and political activism with liberal politics, we have been impressed by the existence of an active protest group with a conservative political philosophy. The continuing presence of such individuals requires that activism be defined independently of political ideology if we are to extricate the correlates of activism *per se* from those of liberalism *per se*.

In the discussion that follows, we talk of adolescent political-social behaviors in terms of typologies for reasons of expository convenience. It should be understood, however, that continua are presumed.

Politically Apathetic Youth

Young people in this group are distinguished by their lack of political-social involvement and their readiness to accept the societal status quo. Judging from the studies of Katz and Sanford (1966) on the present day college generation, this group represents the majority of contemporary youth. These young people have identified with and accepted the values of their parents, which are largely within the mainstream of societal opinion. They have tended to handle whatever conflicts may have arisen from perceived discrepancies between their own and the larger world by minimizing the discrepancy and by retreating to their own small portions of society in which career, success, marriage, family, and financial security are the overriding considerations. They tend to accept the status quo, perhaps with a pessimistic attitude about the possibility of change. Focusing primarily on their own individual lives, these young people are little concerned with the long-term problems of society. We may describe these young people as politically apathetic.

Alienated Youth

Adolescents in this group have rejected the traditional values of society, rebel against institutional authority, and are uninvolved, nonparticipants in the political-social arena. Unlike the youth described above, these young people do not accept the prevailing leitmotifs of the culture. They reject its values, refuse its roles, and elect to escape from the culture by "opting out." This is the "beat" or "hippie" position, well described by a Berkeley student in the campus newspaper:

> "If you radicals see the disgusting nature of present society and see how unlikely it is that anything you do will change it, why waste your time trying? We agree with you that no sensitive human being wants to be a part of that society, but why worry about changing it at all? All that will happen is that you yourselves will waste your youth in an impossible struggle that may well leave ugly blemishes on your soul. Give up the struggle, try to love as much as possible, take a few trips and forget about it all" (Lerner, 1966).*

These young people have much in common with those described by Keniston (1965) who studied alienated Harvard students in the late 1950's. Keniston's alienated students had an approach to life that was primarily egocentric and aesthetically oriented. They concern themselves with a search for adventure, the creation of experiences, and the pleasures of sentience and unmediated responsivity. The alienated

---

* Quotation marks are Lerner's: this is Lerner's characterization of the "hippie" position and not an expression of his own position.

are relatively unideological, having no positively formulated set of values. They live in the present and their personal present may have little continuity with their personal history. These young people value their individuality and freedom. They distrust commitments which imply submission of the self to long-range compromising goals. Their regard for self-expression, their pessimistic evaluation of society, their concern with existential experience, and their patent refusals to accept the hypocrisies they project into adulthood combine to produce an adolescent sub-culture bent on escape from the conventional society and deeply involved with experiencing. It is not surprising that "consciousness-expanding" drugs and other forms of mystical experiences are sought by some of these adolescents who feel estranged from society and judge issue-oriented protests to be meaningless. We confine the term *alienated youth* to include young people who are both uninvolved and rejecting of societal values.

Individualist Youth

Young men and women who are involved with political-social issues and accept the traditional American values and authority structure are our concern under this rubric. The political-social commitments of these adolescents are directed to maintaining the *status quo* or even to restablishing an era of unhampered individualism. Their activities may include petitioning, letter-writing campaigns, active support of conservative candidates and policies, and techniques of counter-protest as they seek to reinforce the positions of traditional institutional authority. Although participants in demonstrations or members of picket lines, these young people confine their activities to legal forms of protest, rejecting the notion of civil disobedience.

This group is not ideologically homogeneous. Some present-day conservatives have been influenced crucially by the writings of Ayn Rand (1957, 1964) in which individualism and autonomy are stressed. These young people may endorse seemingly radical causes requiring only that they be consistent with individualistic principles. Less extreme student groups, influenced by the politics and morals of the conservative position, direct their energies toward maintaining the traditional values that they see as responsible for America's growth.

Both conformity and the strong political involvement of these active conservatives are suggested in the term *obedient rebels* that has been given them by Schiff (1964). While some of the young people studied by Schiff expressed conservative values and commitments consonant with those of their parents, others had reached the conservative position by "conversion." He reports important differences among the converts to conservative causes depending on the timing of the attitudinal changes (Schiff, 1966). Those adopting the conservative position in late adolescence came to be converted as a result of shock, repulsion, and anxiety as they encountered the larger adult world. Conversion, according to Schiff, represents an attempt to escape from and deny the possibility of real change. For these adolescents the structure and status of the conservative movement provide security and ideological content is secondary. For the early convert to the conservative position, on the other hand, the philosophy itself seems to meet important personal needs. Conversion in early adolescence is not an attempt to avoid questions, but to seek answers. The organizations attracting conservative youth tend to have a highly formalized and hierarchical authority structure. The young conservatives are likely to depend on adults for direction and program. Young people who adhere to traditional values and institutions, rely on individualism as a basis for choice, and devote themselves to work actively in support of their beliefs are designated as *individualists*.

Activist Youth

These young people have rejected major values of contemporary society and have dedicated themselves to fight, demonstrate, and protest actively against policies and institutions of mainstream American society that violate their ethic and sense of humane justice. Heterogeneous in ideology, they unite for action on common causes. Their rejection of authority extends to their selective willingness to engage in civil disobedience in the face of possible arrest and probable incarceration. These young people reject "liberalism" as misguided. They are not optimistic about the effects their protests will have on society. Although their protests seek to dramatize social issues, their behavior is based on a concern for personal integrity and authenticity. They feel compelled by their need for fidelity to speak out forcibly on issues they view as morally wrong; not to do so would be to participate in what for them is common hypocrisy. They deplore the dehumanizing forces of a technological society and reject authoritarianism and centralism in favor of a commitment to "participatory democracy" in which political power is placed in the hands of those affected by decisions. Unlike the apathetic, conforming adolescent for whom social concerns are irrelevant, a substantial part of the lives of the young activists is regulated and determined by the issues of current concern. Although sharing the disenchantment with American society and influences of existential philosophy that characterizes the alienated, the activists are more concerned with the existential *act* as a way of achieving integrity whereas the alienated have been more concerned with existential *perception* as a route to a sense of oneness. This difference in orientation toward the outer or the inner world fundamentally separates what we here call the *activists* from the alienated.

Constructivist Youth

As we move to another point along the acceptance-rejection continuum, we encounter a cluster of adolescents not yet described that overlaps to some extent with the activists. These actively committed adolescents occupy an intermediate position on acceptance or rejection of authority but are highly involved with political-social problems. They devote themselves to restitutive work in volunteer activities: in mental hospitals, in work with physically handicapped, in tutoring children from urban ghettoes, and so on. Enlistment in the Peace Corps, Vista, and Acción also represents a kind of commitment to effect social change in ways that involve working *within* the existing framework of society. Although these young people may have formulated an ideological position for themselves, they show little homogeneity except in their common altruistic concerns. They lack the zeal of the revolutionary but feel committed to work constructively to alleviate the ills of society. They are prepared to undergo discomfort, physical hardship, isolation, or even physical danger in order to contribute to the betterment of the human condition. They differ from the activists primarily in that they tend to be task-oriented, do not categorically reject authority, and work in ways that do not necessarily challenge the institutions of society. Young people falling in this group we will call the *constructivists*.

Anti-social Youth

The rebellion of the delinquent differs from the other cases we have considered in its lack of moral-ethical justification. Socio-political involvement is obviously minimal. The extent to which delinquency in fact represents revolt against societal standards—or rather, conformity to a particular sub-culture—is itself a topic of controversy. The subject of adolescent delinquency is beyond the scope of the present chapter but is touched upon, elsewhere, in Kohrs' discussion of the *Disadvantaged and Lower Class Adolescent.*

Having made these conceptual distinctions, we are now ready to consider the findings of relevant research studies in these terms.

AN OVERVIEW ON RESEARCH ON ACTIVISM

Most studies have been concerned with the Activists, the involved, rejecting students. This emphasis doubtlessly was accelerated by an interest in the participants in the Free Speech Movement (FSM) on the Berkeley campus and impelled by the incidents of protest at other major universities. The researches to date have been conducted largely on the elite university campuses of America where intellect, inquiry, and criticism are reinforced. Their findings are largely consistent but may not hold for other college environments.

Student Activists

Student activists have been studied at Berkeley in three investigations. Watts and Whittaker (1966) collected biographical and questionnaire data from students who sat in at Sproul Hall and examined the academic records of a sample of FSM participants. These researchers compared the academic status and questionnaire responses of FSM students with a sample of randomly selected students on the Berkeley campus. Heist (1965) compared a sample of students actually arrested in Sproul Hall with a randomly selected cross-section of Berkeley students in terms of their backgrounds and responses to a personality inventory. His research has focused on the intellectual dispositions and academic history and achievement of his subjects. Eighteen months later he conducted follow-up interviews with a sub-sample of FSM arrestees to determine their academic status at that time and to evaluate the stability of their political-social commitments over time. The present authors are conducting a study, which was undertaken a year after the FSM crisis erupted, that contrasts a sample of arrested FSM students with a randomly selected sample of Berkeley undergraduates and with samples of politically active students representing different ideological positions (Young Democrats, California College Republicans, Young Republicans, Cal Conservatives for Political Action) who were on campus during the FSM crisis. The study is currently being extended to Peace Corps volunteers and to comparison groups on another campus (San Francisco State College). Biographical information including political-social activities, descriptions of actual and ideal self, evaluation of ethical principles used in resolving moral dilemmas, and descriptions of the students' perceptions of their parents' child-rearing practices were obtained from each of the several hundred participants in the study.

At the University of Chicago, Flacks and Neugarten (1967) have compared activist with non-activist students, defining activism by extent and nature of participation in particular political-social causes. They have matched some of their sub-samples on a number of social characteristics (socio-economic class, sex, religion, and type of college attended) and have extended the scope of their research to include some parents of activist and non-activist students as well.

At Pennsylvania State University, Westby and Braungart (1966) have compared members of the "left" (Students for Peace) and the "right" (Young Americans for Freedom). Membership in either organization was the sole criterion for inclusion, and degree of participation in social or political causes was not taken into account.

Braungart (1966) extended the research on membership in extreme "left" and "right" student organizations by collecting questionnaire data from delegates to two national conventions, the Students for a Democratic Society and Young Americans for Freedom. The questionnaire data, obtained from more than 300 activists, provided information about social, political, attitudinal, and other background factors that might relate to activism.

Solomon and Fishman (1964) obtained questionnaire responses from a large randomly selected sample of participants in the 1962 Peace March on Washington. Interviews in depth were conducted with a small sample selected from the larger group to provide more information about personological characteristics of these young pickets for peace. Counter-protest demonstrators who were picketing in support of administration policies were also included in the research.

Family background. The origins of student activists are in the economically, educationally, and socially privileged strata of American society. Whether measured by family income, occupational prestige of parents, socio-economic indices, or the amount of education of parents, the families of actively committed students are more advantaged than those of other college students (Flacks, 1967; Braungart, 1966; Westby and Braungart, 1966). The difference seems most striking for the mothers of activist students.

The parents of activist students themselves tended to be politically liberal. The radical positions of these youth can thus hardly be interpreted simply as a rebellion against parental values. Committed students may chide their parents for failing to act in accordance with their political beliefs; they may accuse the older generation of having "sold out" to the "Establishment" and the comforts of suburbia. However, in terms of ideological content, the two generations show considerable agreement. Because the political values of parent and child have much in common, it is essential to distinguish two facets in contemporary rebellion. Rejection of major *societal* values does not necessarily imply rebellion against *parental* attitudes. Although placing themselves squarely in opposition to many of the prevailing views and practices of the culture, the activists have identified with and accept many of their parents' values.

Most young people engaging in protest describe themselves as nonreligious. In terms of parental religious traditions, a higher number of Jewish students are involved in protest than might be expected. Different investigators estimate from 20% to 37% of student activists are Jewish (Flacks, 1967; Solomon and Fishman, 1964; Watts and Whittaker, 1966). The over-representation of Jewish students in activist organizations and the findings of Flacks showing a preponderance of immigrant parents among activist groups may relate to the emphasis on intellectual values in the Jewish culture as well as to an historically determined identification with the oppressed.

Other findings about the family backgrounds of activists are less consistent. Some studies suggest that girls are disproportionately represented in activist groups (Braungart, 1966; Watts and Whittaker, 1966), and other studies point to the seemingly high number of oldest or only children in their activist samples (Schiff, 1964; Solomon and Fishman, 1964). These data are difficult to interpret because of the "base-line" problem. Schachter (1963) has shown that first-born children are over-represented in colleges and universities, particularly among the high achievers in elite educational institutions. Nichols' chapter in this book is of interest on this point.

Academic achievement. Not only have the parents of student activists achieved higher educational levels, but the students themselves have strong intellectual orientations and superior academic records in their colleges and universities (Flacks, 1967; Heist, 1965). Heist found in his thorough studies of intellectual disposition and academic achievement among the FSM participants at Berkeley that the FSM sample scored higher on the intellectual scales in the Omnibus Personality Inventory than did his random sample. He found also that the cumulative grade point averages of FSM participants computed after the semester in which the FSM had preempted much student time and energy exceeded the all-university undergraduate grade point average. Heist concludes that the students arrested in Sproul Hall were well qualified young people with strong commitments to intellectual values who maintained excellent academic records at a highly competitive university.

Personality characteristics. In the researches to date, the personality correlates of activism have been less the subject of systematic inquiry than the sociological and demographic characteristics. In terms of questionnaire responses on a standard instrument, the FSM students at Berkeley presented themselves as intellectually committed, esthetically reactive, expressive young people who are independent and relatively free from their cultural and institutional past (Heist, 1965). Specifically, Heist found that FSM members received significantly higher scores on scales reflecting non-authoritarian attitudes and independence of authority, skepticism about conventional religious beliefs and a tendency to reject them, tendency to express feelings and impulses directly; and four intellectual dispositions: Theoretical Orientation, Thinking Introversion, Estheticism and Complexity (Heist, 1965).

In the study we are now conducting, the FSM men described themselves as significantly more critical, curious, idealistic, individualistic, impulsive, informed, moody, perceptive, rebellious, and restless than did those in the randomly selected sample. In contrast, self descriptions of males in the random sample indicated greater concern with conventionality and achievement, as suggested by their higher scores on the following adjectives: conventional, optimistic, practical, responsible, ambitious, reserved, foresightful, considerate, self-controlled, and orderly.

Essentially similar results are obtained when the FSM women were compared with women in the randomly selected sample. FSM girls described themselves as significantly more informed, perceptive, loving, doubting, rebellious, and restless. In contrast, the women students in the random sample described themselves as significantly more conventional, ambitious, competitive, self-controlled, foresightful, orderly, responsible, and feminine.

These findings appear to be congruent with Heist's. The activists see themselves as less conforming and conventional, admit to restlessness and rebellion, value knowledge, interpersonal perceptivity, spontaneity, and tend to be idealistic. At the same time, they are less concerned about ostensible concrete achievement and success.

Value systems. In our study at Berkeley, FSM participants differed substantially from the randomly selected students in their value systems as reflected in the adjectives with which they described their ego-ideals. The so-called "Protestant ethic" is spelled out strongly by the items more characteristic of the ego-ideals of the randomly selected students: ambitious, self-denying, conventional, competitive, self-controlled, foresightful, orderly, responsible, and so on. In contrast, the FSM participants were more likely to proclaim values that are concerned with self-expression, intellectual orientation, and a sense of community with and responsibility for one's fellow man: curious, idealistic, altruistic, creative, impulsive, tolerant, perceptive, rebellious, empathic, responsive, restless, and so on.

Using a ranking procedure, Flacks (1967) found, similarly, that dedication to work for national and international betterment and interest in the world of ideas, art, and music were ranked as most important personal values for his activist students. Those scoring low on activism tended to place marriage and family and career in the highest ranked positions of importance.

The values of actively committed students reflected their concerns about Man, their intellectual interests, and their stress on personal honesty. They reject many of the values implicit in an achievement-oriented, competitive, individualistic society—values that are, however, endorsed by non-activist students.

Parental child-rearing practices. Many young activists in contemporary America were reared under the influence of Benjamin Spock (1946) who, as an articulate pediatrician, led a revolt against the more authoritarian, rigid, constraining child-rearing practices characteristic of an earlier generation of American parents. The Spock-oriented mothers of the forties substituted inductive reasoning for insistence upon blind obedience, corrective discipline for punitive discipline, flexible responsiveness for rigid scheduling, and reasonable limits for arbitrary prohibitions. It may be argued that the emergence of a dedicated spontaneous generation concerned with humanitarian values and personal authenticity is a triumph of Spockian philosophy and principles. Others have suggested, in a less benign interpretation, that activism is the consequence of excessive parental permissiveness, a failure to teach respect for authority, and an unfortunate submission to the needs and feelings of the child. What do research data tell us about the relationship between activism and permissiveness?

The parents of activist students do appear to have been more permissive than those of non-activist students. Parents of activists were described by their children as more lenient, less intrusive into the lives of their children, and milder disciplinarians than those of the non-activists (Flacks, 1967). Confirmatory data were obtained from the parents themselves: parents of activists rated themselves as more permissive than did parents in other groups.

In our own study, FSM participants as compared with the randomly selected sample described both parents as less authoritarian and more permissive. They perceived their parents as having a closer affective relationship with their children and as placing less emphasis on prohibitions, restrictions, and punishment.

The most characteristic parent-child relationship described by FSM students was, however, complex. While attributing closeness and warmth to the relationship, the FSM students also admitted conflict with parents. While subscribing to many of their parents' values and views, they were less likely than the randomly selected students to rate themselves as in agreement with their parents with respect to choice of occupation, religion, politics, and friends.

Stability of commitments.   Activism appears to represent a relatively enduring personality disposition rather than an isolated, impetuous, ephemeral behavioral act. The students engaged in protest apparently make a relatively long-term commitment and direct their activities toward a number of issues. Solomon and Fishman (1964) found in 1962, relatively early in the days of activism, that 72% of the participants in the Peace March had been previously involved in political or social action. A follow-up study of participants found a large majority still involved in some kind of political or social cause. Heist (1966) also reports that, eighteen months after the sit-in at Sproul Halls, 94% of the FSM participants sampled were engaged in activity oriented around political or social issues. Our own data corroborate these results and suggest that the large majority of FSM participants were engaged simultaneously in a variety of other activities challenging the *status quo*.

Summary. The results of the relatively few available studies of student activists yield quite consistent results. These position-taking young people are superior students from socially and educationally advantaged homes. To a large extent, their political values and social ideals are consonant with the values of their parents who themselves are politically liberal. The activists describe their parents as permissive and stressing a rational approach in their child-rearing practices. Perhaps because they were reared in child-centered homes where communication and understanding were important, these young people value dialogue and expect that social institutions, like their parents, will listen and be responsive to their concerns. They feel supported by their parents as they challenge the values of modern society. For most, acts of protest were not impulsive, isolated episodes but were part of a pattern in which their sense of authenticity seems to require that they speak out on social issues that offend their image of man and society.

The Individualists

The research findings on individualist students actively engaged in conservative causes have been somewhat inconsistent. There have been fewer studies concentrating on these young people, and the samples on which conclusions are based have sometimes been small. The groups have been defined in several ways: by actual participation in counter-protest demonstrations (Solomon and Fishman, 1964; Flacks, 1967), by membership in conservative activist organizations (Schiff, 1964; Westby and Braungart, 1966), or by delegate status to national conventions of student conservative organizations (Braungart, 1966). There have been differences, also, in the ideological positions of the conservative groups studied. Finally, some inconsistencies in findings may relate to the nature of the groups against which the individualist is contrasted, a normative group or an activist group.

Family background. Apart from agreement that active conservative students tend to come from Republican families who are predominantly

Protestant (Solomon and Fishman, 1964; Braungart, 1966; Westby and Braungart, 1966; Flacks, 1967), there is little consistency in findings and no conclusions can be presently drawn.

Academic achievement. No evidence of significant differences in academic performance has been offered.

Personality characteristics. Few investigators have systematically assessed the personality characteristics of young people who are actively committed to conservative causes. There is some evidence that these students are more submissive to authority and tend to exert greater control over expressions of impulse and anxiety (Schiff, 1964). Interestingly, and contrary to stereotype, no evidence of greater prejudice or ethno-centrism was found by Schiff in his evaluations of student conservatives. We find at Berkeley that the individualists (as contrasted with the random sample) describe themselves in ways that emphasize their independence, unwillingness to compromise, egocentricity, and unconventionality, traits highly prized in Ayn Rand's (1957, 1964) individualistic philosophy that has influenced many conservative activists at Berkeley.

Value systems. The values of the individuals studied at Berkeley as they are reflected in their distinctive characterizations of their self-ideals are oriented to matters of personal integrity and individualism. These students ascribed less value to interpersonal relationships and were less oriented to altruistic or humanistic values than were other groups. Flacks (1967) found that his counter-protesters ranked *marriage and family* and *career* as first and second in order of personal importance, while ranking low interest in the arts, abstract ideas, or involvement in improving world conditions.

Parental child-rearing practices. The parents of individualists appear to expect much of their children and to place high value on achievement and characterological "goodness," according to our results and those of Schiff (1964). When parental expectations are not fulfilled, the mothers of conservative activists tend to react with anger and disappointment while their children respond to the pressures with feelings of resentment and failure. Particularly for the males in the conservative sample, there was an emphasis on the mother's use of guilt-arousing techniques of control. The mother-son relationship was described as more impersonal, less affectionate, and less appreciative than that depicted by the randomly selected sample. The father-son relationship appeared to differ little from that typical of the random sample. However, our sample was small, and these findings obviously need corroboration.

Summary. The information available regarding the individualists is sparser and less consistent than that available for the activist groups. Several factors contributing to the discrepancies in findings have been cited. The conclusions one can draw about active conservatives are very tentative.

One finding that does appear with special clarity is greater parental pressure in the direction of achievement in a child-rearing context that relies on authoritarianism and is relatively lacking in emotional warmth. The values expressed by the conservative students reflect an emphasis on individualism, integrity, and consistency. The nature of the conservative movement itself may satisfy the adolescent's needs for structure, certainty, and reliance on authority.

The Alienated

Alienated, estranged, politically apathetic adolescents have stimulated relatively little research beyond the intensive study conducted on a small sample of Harvard students by Keniston (1965) in the 1950's. On the basis of psychological test responses, Keniston selected twelve Harvard undergraduates who manifested the "alienated syndrome." These were students who rejected the dominant values, roles, and institutions of contemporary American society, expressing their ideological disenchantment in disaffection and disaffiliation. The twelve students were intensively studied over a three-year period. Keniston learned to know these young men well and has provided an incisive portrayal of them as people, of their cultural and familial heritages, with an insightful analysis of the social context predisposing toward alienation.

The reader should remember than Keniston describes the alienated syndrome in a very atypical group of young people, upper middle-class students at one of the most prestigeful private universities in this country. The fact that most of these young people were able to maintain student status over a three-year period indicates that their rejection of traditional American achievement values was discriminating rather than total.

The Keniston sample of alienated college males, like most Harvard men, came from upper middle-class and upper-class socio-economic backgrounds. Their fathers had attained high professional status and prestige. Their parents had been well-educated and were involved actively in the social and cultural affairs of their local communities.

The alienated young man, according to Keniston, regards his mother as a talented woman whose career was sacrificed to marriage and family. He expresses a special sympathy for his mother's unrealized potentials and identifies with her unhappiness. His desire for a close, dependent relationship with his mother is countered, however, by his resentment of her domination, possessiveness, and neuroticism. The father image portrayed by the alienated Harvard students is of an inhibited, constricted, cold, withdrawn man oriented to success, status, and security. Fathers of the alienated are pictured as men who, in their youth, had visionary dreams and idealistic hopes. Under the stress of parental and societal pressures for achievement, the fathers of the alienated abandoned these dreams and, in the perceptions of their sons, "sold out" their noble aspirations to the demands of the marketplace. Keniston's alienated young men were not overtly hostile toward their fathers but were condescending and accorded them little respect.

In early childhood, the alienated described themselves as "shy" and "reserved" and were oriented to the intellectual world of books and ideas. The adolescence of the alienated was marked by turmoil accompanied by strong negative feelings about sexuality. During mid-adolescence, these alienated-to-become began questioning the values of their parents and of society at large. It was not until later adolescence, however, that these students overtly rejected parental, community, and cultural values.

The rejections of the alienated are many. They refuse to orient themselves and their lives toward long-range goals because of an inherent pessimism about the future. They reject the puritan virtues of self-control, self-denial, order, responsibility, insisting on the values of spontaneity, expression, intense confrontation with experience, and personal freedom. They reject the conventional adult role with its attendant responsibilities, inevitable compromises, and the expectation of adult sexuality. The positive values for the alienated young men were in experiencing, deeply, freely, and appreciatively.

Keniston concluded that the rebellion among the alienated Harvard students is not directed at their parents but rather at a society whose premises and values they cannot accept.

In a recent paper, Keniston (1966) distinguishes between two types of alienation, the activist (similar to our conception) and the disaffiliate. The disaffiliate is non-political, culturally alienated, and rejecting of societal offerings and values. The demonstrations of disaffiliates, according to Keniston, are private rebellions manifested in Beatnikism, Bohemianism, or psychedelic withdrawal from the mainstream of public life. Keniston finds little political participation in this group but occasional peripheral involvement in protest movements. Their rejection of American society is based less on idealism and outraged indignation, Keniston postulates, than upon temperamental opposition to the requirements and rewards of American society—and to their fathers who epitomize this society for them. The disaffiliate is estranged from both family and society.

Estrangement from family and friends has been found also by Watts and Whittaker (1966b), who studied disaffiliated non-students living on the fringes of the Berkeley campus. These investigators recruited their research volunteers from the coffee shops and book stores adjacent to the University. The group was extremely heterogenous, ranging from students temporarily out of school in order to work for one semester to others who never were students and were unemployed. For this sample, rejection of contemporary society, personal isolation, estrangement from family, and experimentation with drugs were more frequent than in the contrast sample of students Watts and Whittaker studied.

Summary. The alienated, like the activist, is engaged in a repudiation of traditional societal values. He differs from the activist, however, in a passive pessimism, in keeping with which he concerns himself with the extension and intensification of subjective experience rather than with active protest. Another basic difference between the alienated and the activist is in terms of attitudes toward parents and family. The activist tends to identify with many of the values of his parents. The alienated, however, has developed a disparate set of values, inconsistent with those of his parents, that may elicit disapproval and strain communication.

The Constructivists

Young people directing their energies to constructive programs of action *within* existing societal institutions have not been the object of much research inquiry. Gelineau and Kantor (1964) assessed a number of Harvard and Radcliffe student volunteers in a large public mental hospital and find them little different in social background from the typical Harvard or Radcliffe student. The only distinguishing features were: (1) a larger number had attended public schools and (2) a disproportionate number of volunteers were from Jewish backgrounds while Catholics were somewhat under-represented. Gelineau and Kantor found the volunteers to be intelligent, secular, sophisticated, idealistic, and valuing of creativity. They were motivated by their interest in human contact and an altruistic desire to be helpful to others.

In a study of Peace Corps volunteers, Smith (1966) suggested three main factors as motivating enlistment. A "psychosocial moratorium" (Erikson, 1956) providing time out for self-discovery and evaluation of life goals was important to the volunteers. They required, however, that this moratorium be constructively earned by devotion to something intrinsically worthwhile. The opportunity in the Peace Corps for direct personal action toward good ends was an important motivational component. Opportunities for adventure and experience in foreign cultures was a third, but lesser reason for the appeal of the Peace Corps. Volunteer service contributes to the adolescent's need to establish an identity for himself and to test his skills and competence in a way that does not directly confront or challenge authority. Altruism, in this context, provides a safe outlet for the expression of doubts about the adult society and a channel for the adolescent's idealistic desires to effect changes in that society.

Our survey of research findings will not include politically uninvolved young people who accept most of our prevailing societal values. This group includes the typical adolescent whose developmental and personological characteristics have been described in other chapters of this book. We proceed now to consider briefly some of the factors predisposing to activism in today's society and some explanations that have been offered for the recent re-emergence of a vital student movement.

SOCIO-CULTURAL FACTORS
PREDISPOSING TO ACTIVISM

The unpredicted change in the ethos of youth from the "silent" generation of the 1950's to the "protesting" students of the 1960's has challenged sociologists and social psychologists for explanations. The traditional historical forces previously associated with the emergence of radical youth movements—limited occupational and economic opportunities, the breakdown of traditional authority under the impact of industrialization—seem insufficient explanations for the development of contemporary protest. Several hypotheses have been offered and these will be summarized.

Sociological Explanations

Keniston (1965) has posited that intensification of technological change in our country and in much of the modern world has relegated human values to lesser importance. The stress in our technological society is upon empiricism, pragmatism, efficiency, and production. The absence of articulated social goals and the deification of technological progress at the expense of social concerns has dehumanized society. The very rapidity of change makes the past irrelevant to the present and the continuity with history that eases the task of identification and adaptation is weakened. The "generational gap" is widened by accelerating changes so that communication between generations becomes increasingly difficult. Patterns for the solution of today's problems cannot be found in the experiences of the past. The protest of youth against this "dehumanizing" process is a part of their struggle for identity and integrity.

Psycho-social Factors

Flacks (1967) has extended the explanations of rebellion in terms of disjunction between values and expectations of the traditional nuclear family and those prevailing in the occupational sphere of society (Eisenstadt, 1956; Parsons, 1963). Although discrepancies between family and societal values are inevitable in modern industrial society, Parsons suggests that these differences are lessening in middle-class America. Flacks goes on to propose that within middle-class society there is a segment of well-educated families whose stress upon democratic, egalitarian principles, on permissiveness, on values other than achievement does not accord with the prevailing values and expectations in the occupational sphere. Young people reared according to these precepts should find it difficult to accept the traditional social values that require submission to authority, competition, ambition, and self-control. Their questioning of the social norms, instigated by their parents, has been reinforced by their selectively chosen friends, by their experiences in progressive schools or camps, and by their reading. The customary rewards and incentives of the occupational sphere have only limited effectiveness for these young people who have already achieved status and affluence by virtue of their family origins. Flacks suggests that the abstract concern with democratic and egalitarian values of the parental generation, expressed in their child-centered approach to rearing, has become embodied in their children as personality traits. In this way, adolescents engaging in protest are not rebelling in a conventional sense but are expressing the values according to which they have been reared. Further, the non-authoritarian stance of their parents releases these young people to react to the problems and significant people of their own time rather than having to adhere to the guidelines of the past.

The Existentialist Attitude

The young people of today have been reared at a time characterized by the omnipresent and ominous pressure of the uncertain nuclear stalemate. Many cogently wonder, along with their elders, whether mankind will be able to get by "by the skin of its teeth." These bleak uncertainties, in the face of the waning voice of traditional religion, have made many youth responsive to the Existentialists' call for individual commitment and responsibility. At first or second hand, the Existentialist formulations of Sartre, Camus, and Kierkegaard have served to crystallize attitudes that differentiate thoughtful youth of the present generation.

The existentialist call to "being," "actualizing," or "becoming" appeals to many. In an age of mass society and impersonal technology, its emphasis upon an enlarged and acute sense of personal responsibility is refreshing. Sartre (1957) holds that man is responsible for himself, for his own individuality, and is responsible also for all men. He emphasizes that the future will be as man decides it is to be. He exhorts man to involve himself in the decision-making which will determine his future.

If the existentialist posture in its version of human dignity repudiates the cosmic reassurances of traditional religion, it has equally little use for the rationalism of the scientific world view. In its romantic subjectivism, it offers no guidelines, no criteria for meaningful choice in a world of "absurdity." All depends on inner conviction, on freely willed choice. What is chosen in full consciousness and freedom is "authentic," and authenticity is a principal virtue. Depending on one's personal bent, one may seek authenticity in the intensification of inner experience and spontaneity (as do the alienated) or one may, like the activists, find meaning in the existential act of making a stand against injustice and hypocrisy. To the extent that youthful protesters conceive of their activism within a generally existentialist outlook, they will not feel the need for rationally elaborated or logically consistent theory as manifested by the non-ideological, undogmatic character of New Left protest. By the same token, they become the less accessible to rational dialogue with their elders.

Retreat of the Protestant Ethic

With the increasing secularization of America, religion has declined as a determinant of behavior. Psychoanalysis, existentialism, and the influence of the scientific method have encouraged the development of a more rational ethical system concerned with honesty, authenticity, and personal responsibility for one's acts. Freed from the taboos of the Victorian era and impelled by the dictates of a rational conscience, today's youth find that their struggles for authenticity often require dissent. At the same time, the consumption-oriented values of an affluent society have further eroded the foundations on which the traditional future-oriented achievement-centered ethos of Benjamin Franklin rested (Riesman, 1950).

Child-rearing Factors

Flacks has stressed the importance of permissive, democratic child-rearing practices in the development of the young activist. It is not just with matters of respect for the child and encouragement of self-regulation that we are concerned in this section. It seems to us that the very *techniques* used by parents who have rejected authoritarian methods of control encourage the development of empathy and concern for others. When categorical enforcement of arbitrary rules by implacable authority is abandoned in favor of more rational methods of discipline, several things happen. First, the reasons behind parental demands are explained to the child so that they no longer appear quite so arbitrary. Second, these reasons are usually based on welfare concerns. The mother prohibits the child from actions, not because they are inherently "bad," but because they are potentially harmful to himself or others. Third, the child is encouraged to see the relationship between his own actions and their subsequent effects on other people. These "other-oriented" mechanisms of discipline are associated, along with affection, with the development of a "humanistic conscience" (Hoffman, 1964). The development of empathy and a humanistic orientation make it probable that a young person will concern himself with the plight of others. The relationship between activism and humanism is supported by our results on value systems reported earlier.

Child-training practices viewed in this way highlight the continuity between parent and child generations, explain to some extent the support accorded to protest by parents of activists, and rationalize the frustrations felt by activist youth when confronted by arbitrary authorities who refuse their invitation to dialogue.

SUMMARY

In this chapter we have discussed and examined the activist and the apathetic adolescent who raises his voice, or who does not raise his voice, in political and social protest. The activist youth has voiced his dissatisfaction with contemporary society. This has produced tensions. However, tensions between generations and between youth and society are inevitable because the older generation stands as gate-keeper to the opportunities and aspirations of the young, and because the choices and commitments of youth have the power to either confirm or negate the values of their elders and of their society. If man and society are to change and grow, the adult world not only has to provide guidance for its youth, but also must be able to hear and profit from the perceptions, indignations, and insights of its youth. The "rejuvenations" (Erikson, 1962) of society and the older generation come from the vitalism, idealism, and dedication of the young.

REFERENCES

Block, Jeanne. The child-rearing practices report. Institute of Human Development, University of California, Berkeley, 1965 (Mimeo).

Blos, P. On adolescence: A psychoanalytic interpretation. Glencoe: The Free Press, 1962.

Braungart, R. G. SDS and YAF: Backgrounds of student political activists. Paper presented at the Annual Meeting of the American Sociological Association, Miami, Florida, August, 1966.

Campus '65. *Newsweek*, March 22, 1965, p. 54.

Coleman, J. S. *The adolescent society: The social life of the teenager and its impact on education.* Glencoe: The Free Press, 1961.

Coleman, J. S. *Adolescents and the schools.* New York: Basic Books, 1965.

Eisenstadt, S. *From generation to generation.* Glencoe: The Free Press, 1956.

Erikson, E. H. The problem of ego identity. *Journal of the American Psychoanalytic Association*, 1956, *4*, 55–121.

Erikson, E. H. Reality and actuality. *Journal of the American Psychoanalytic Association*, 1962, *10*, 451–474.

Erikson, E. H. Youth: fidelity and diversity. In: Erikson, E. (Ed.) *Youth: Change and challenge.* New York: Basic Books, 1963.

Erikson, E. H. *Insight and responsibility.* New York: W. W. Norton Co., 1964.

Flacks, R., and Neugarten, Bernice. The liberated generation: An exploration of the roots of student protest. *Journal of Social Issues*, 1967, (In press).

Gales, Kathleen. Berkeley student opinion: April, 1965. (Mimeographed paper, 1965).

Gelineau, V. A., and Kantor, D. Pro-social commitment among college students. *The Journal of Social Issues*, 1964, *20* (4), 112–130.

Heist, P. Intellect and commitment: the faces of discontent. Center for the Study of Higher Education, University of California, Berkeley, 1965. (Mimeo)

Heist, P. The dynamics of student discontent and protest. Paper presented to SPSSI Symposium, American Psychological Association Annual Meeting, New York City, September, 1966.

Hoffman, M. L. Techniques and processes in moral development. Mimeographed report, 1964.

Inhelder, Bärbel, and Piaget, J. *The growth of logical thinking from childhood to adolescence.* New York: Basic Books, 1958.

Katz, J., and Sanford, N. Causes of the student revolution. *Saturday Review*, December 18, 1965, 64–67.

Katz, J., and Sanford N. 17 to 22: The turbulent years. *Stanford Today*, 1966, *15*, 7–10.

Keniston, K. *The uncommitted: Alienated youth in American society.* New York: Harcourt, Brace and World, 1965.

Keniston, K. Faces in the lecture room. *Yale Undergraduate,* 1966, *11,* 2–16.

Lerner, M. Hippies and radicals. *Daily Californian,* October 27, 1966, 6.

Lipset, S. M. Student opposition in the United States. *Government and Opposition,* 1966, *1,* 351–374. (a)

Lipset, S. M., and Altbach, P. G. Student politics and higher education in the United States. *Comparative Education Review,* 1966, *10,* 320–349. (b)

Munk, M. New left: Background of young radicals. *National Guardian,* September 18, 1965, 3.

Musgrove, F. *Youth and the social order.* Bloomington, Indiana: Indiana University Press, 1965.

Parsons, T. Youth in the context of American society. In: Erikson, E. (Ed.) *Youth: Change and challenge.* New York: Basic Books, 1963.

Peterson, R. E. *The scope of organized student protest in 1964–1965.* Princeton, N. J.: Educational Testing Service, 1966. (a)

Peterson, R. E. Organized student protest in 1964–1965. Paper presented at APA Symposium: Unrest and Protest on the American Campus. New York, September 3, 1966. (b)

Piaget, J., and Weil, A. M. Le developpement chez l'enfant de l'idee de patrie et des relations avec l'etranger. *Bulletin International des Sciences Sociales* (UNESCO), 1951, 3, 605–621.

Rand, Ayn *Atlas shrugged.* New York: Random House, 1957.

Rand, Ayn *The virtue of selfishness.* New York: New American Library, 1964.

Riesman, D. (with R. Denney and N. Glazer) *The lonely crowd: A study of changing American character.* New Haven: Yale University Press, 1950.

Sartre, J-P. *Existentialism and human emotion.* New York: Philosophical Library, 1957.

Schachter, S. Birth order, eminence and higher education. *American Sociological Review,* 1963, *28,* 757–767.

Schiff, L. F. The obedient rebels: a study of college conversions to conservatism. *The Journal of Social Issues,* 1964, *20* (4), 74–95.

Schiff, L. F. Dynamic young fogies, rebels on the right. *Trans-action,* 1966, November, 30–36.

Smith, M. B. Explorations in competence: a study of Peace Corps teachers in Ghana. *American Psychologist,* 1966, *21,* 555–566.

Solomon, F., and Fishman, J. R. Youth and peace: a psychosocial study of student peace demonstrators in Washington, D. C. *The Journal of Social Issues*, 1964, *20* (4), 54–73.

Spock, B. *The commonsense book of baby and child care.* New York: Duell, Sloan and Pearce, 1946.

Watts, W. A., and Whittaker, D. N. E. Free speech advocates at Berkeley. *Journal of Applied Behavioral Science*, 1966, *2*, 41–62. (a)

Watts, W. A., and Whittaker, D. N. E. Students of life: a study of the Berkeley non-student. Paper presented to Sixth World Congress of Sociology, Evian, France, September, 1966. (b)

Westby, D., and Braungart, R. Class and politics in the family backgrounds of student political activists. *American Sociological Review*, 1966, *31*, 690–692.

CHAPTER 10

The Role of Educational Institutions in Adolescent Development

F. Glenn Macomber ✳

THERE ARE MANY INSTITUTIONS WHICH HAVE AS THEIR CHIEF PURPOSE the education of adolescent youth. Boy and Girl Scout organizations, for instance, are dedicated to the education of the early adolescent and have advanced programs for the high school student as well as the children of junior high school age. Their announced purposes often include the development of effective citizenship and ethical character, and their programs are designed to attain this end. The home itself can be seen as an institution existing primarily for the reproduction, protection and development of the human being from infancy on through the adolescent years. To these institutions which have a real concern for the education of adolescent youth, could be added the church, the YMCA and YWCA, various denominational youth organizations, Junior Red Cross, and many others. This chapter will confine itself primarily to the public school as an educational institution. This is not because I attach lesser importance to other institutions having the development of the adolescent as a major concern, but rather because of space limitations. Even within this narrowed focus I can only discuss a few of the more important aspects of the role of the school in adolescent development.

✳ F. GLENN MACOMBER is Superintendent of Schools in Coupeville, Washington. He is also Dean Emeritus of the College of Education of Miami University in Ohio. Dr. Macomber has authored and co-authored: *Psychological Factors in Education; Teaching in the Modern Secondary School; Principles of Teaching in the Elementary School;* and a wide range of articles on topics such as the public school curriculum, and large group teaching at the college level.

PUBLIC EXPECTATIONS OF EDUCATION

At first glance, it would seem that there should be a near consensus of opinion on the purposes of an institution as old and as nearly universal as the American secondary school. This is not the case. There is general accord that the basic aim of education is to contribute in a major way to the development of youth into effective members of the democratic society in which they live. Here the agreement ends. There is much disagreement regarding the nature of the society in which we live, particularly when we consider the nature and needs of the society which present day adolescents will help to shape. It is obvious to any thinking person that we are in the midst of social, economic, industrial and scientific revolution and that the world is changing at a pace never before dreamed possible. Unfortunately, we know much more about the nature of the change itself than we do about the implications of change for the education of youth. There is not only a great lack of agreement as to the direction of education, but there is also even greater disagreement as to the means of education. A few illustrations will make this clear. Ask any ten academicians from the humanities faculty of a major university what the character of secondary education should be, and you will get general agreement that intellectual training is the one and only sure means of developing the capability to effectively solve the problems of the world in which we are living. Many academicians cling to the old theory of mental discipline, insistent that the mind of the individual as such can be trained, and that intellect so disciplined can then cope with problems of various and sundry natures; including, for instance, social, political, scientific and philosophical problems. Education to the Hutchins, the Mark Van Dorens, and to a surprisingly large number of professional men in every community, should consist primarily of this kind of "intellectual training." Many sincerely believe this to be the sole function of the school, and consider personal and social integration to be aims achieved through this means. Non-intellectual activities are important, but they are the concern of the home, the church, and industry—not of the school.

Again, ask a dozen college professors from the social sciences, mathematics, and the physical and biological sciences what role the school should play in the development of youth. This time you may receive a discourse on the importance of the student's developing a depth of understanding of the basic disciplines into which the world's knowledge is organized. The best education, from this viewpoint, is that which develops the highest degree of mastery of the separate disciplines which make up the social sciences, the humanities, the physical and biological sciences, and mathematics. There is a marked agreement among the classicists that such subjects as agriculture, home economics, industrial arts and family relations are as extraneous to the real function of the school, as are athletics and driver training.

Again, ask several industrialists what they consider to be the function of secondary education and you will get lectures on the importance of knowing the value of hard work, or of being able to communicate well and correctly, or of having a high regard for the value of work and property. The ability to get along with people and adjust to new work situations will also be stressed, and knowledge of the so-called basic skills will be emphasized as will ambition and the desire to get ahead on a job.

This process could be carried on indefinitely. Ten parents from different walks of life and different educational and social backgrounds would differ greatly in what they expect from the school. The same disagreement would be found if ten secondary school students were asked what they believed to be the most significant functions of the school. Answers would be colored significantly by the social and economic backgrounds of the students and by their own educational goals.

In these United States there is no institution which holds out to the public greater hopes for the "salvation" of future generations than the public school system. In many states this now includes the junior or community colleges. Education, probably more than any other single factor, is given credit for having made America great. It is education which possesses the potential to fulfill our basic national goals of the future. This belief is so intense it is almost a blind faith. The State of Washington, as an illustration, on March 24, 1967, passed House Bill 548 which provides that:

> The purpose of this Act is to provide for the dramatically increasing number of students requiring high standards of education either as a part of the continuing higher education program or for occupational training by creating a new independent system of community colleges which will (1) offer an open door to every citizen regardless of his academic background or experience at a cost normally within his economic means; (2) insure that each community college district shall offer thoroughly comprehensive edu-

cation, training and service programs to meet both the needs of the communities and students served by combining, with equal emphasis, high standards of excellence in academic transfer courses; realistic and practical courses in occupational education, both graded and ungraded; and community services of an educational, cultural, and recreational nature. . . .

The Act goes on to state that:

> Each community college district shall maintain on open door policy to the end that no student will be denied admittance because of the location of his residence or because of his educational background or ability; that, insofar as is practical in the judgment of the college board, curriculum offerings will be provided to meet the educational and training needs of the community generally and the students thereof; and that all students, regardless of their different course of study, will be considered, known and recognized equally as members of the student body. . . .

The American secondary school, which had its beginnings in the Latin grammar school and the academies of the Colonial and early Federal period of American history, has long ago given up its highly selective function. What began as an institution primarily dedicated to the preparation of a very select few for entrance to college has become the comprehensive American secondary school. Today, high schools and junior high schools are dedicated to the education of all youth, and possess as great a concern for those who are not college bound as for those who are. More and more, a high school diploma has come to mean merely that the holder has remained in high school in good standing for a period of four years. He has completed the specified number of courses for a particular program, and has been graduated from the school. For at least the last three or four decades, and increasingly during the past twenty years, youth has been under severe pressure from compulsory attendance laws. There has also been family and social compulsion, and economic pressure, to enter and to remain in high school until the coveted diploma is received.

The community college, which began as the junior college of the "thirties" and which with certain notable exceptions was primarily dedicated to offering the lower division courses of a four-year college program, is rapidly becoming a comprehensive institution for furnishing two years of work and study beyond the high school for all students. Pressures upon youth are already building up to the point at which the two years of community college will become a part of every normal educational program.

THE ROLE OF THE PUBLIC SCHOOL

There is no commonly accepted philosophy of the function and purpose of the school and, consequently, no generally accepted idea of the role of the school in the development of the adolescent. Rather, there are differences of thought in regard to the role of public-school education with three major emphases exercising considerable influence on programs for public education. Stated in an over-simplified manner and with no attempt to attach identifying names or labels to these emphases, we find: (1) Those who believe that the school exists primarily to bring about the intellectual development of children and youth. They believe that essentially all of the activities of the school should be dedicated to this end; (2) Those who believe that education is and should be primarily a mastery of the content of formally organized disciplines; and (3) Those who believe that education should be primarily concerned with all of the developmental aspects of the individual. While the development of intellectual capability is a highly important purpose of the school, the school must also be vitally concerned with the physical, social, and emotional development of the individual. Most preschool and primary teachers belong to this latter school of thought; i.e., those who believe that the school must be seriously concerned with all aspects of the development of the child.

As one moves upward through the intermediate grades and into the secondary school, there is a definite swing toward the idea that mastery of the formally organized disciplines is the stuff out of which education is made. There are, of course, notable exceptions and even within a given secondary school there are considerable differences in governing policies. For instance, most teachers of the strictly academic areas are committed rather fully to the study of the disciplines as disciplines. This is not generally true of those who teach vocational courses, nor of those who are charged with school guidance. These indivduals are governed more by the concept of the indivisibility of the learning personality. At the college level, and to a considerable degree at the community college level, a professor is hardly respectable in the college community unless he is committed, heart and soul, to his subject matter and to the idea that his job is to insure that his students develop a reasonable degree of competence in his discipline. Those who believe that intellectual development is the sole purpose of education are to be found among the disciples of most disciplines. Especially they are to be found among the classicists who see their classical studies as being the best approach to intellectual development.

The highly restrictive concept that the nature and purpose of education should be defined in terms of intellectual development is in part responsible for the popular notion that what a pupil learns outside the classroom in high school and college is more important to his later life than what he learns in the classroom. The fact that a considerable majority of students in both high school and college have non-academic goals is also supportive of this point of view. Society reinforces the conviction when personal status is measured by financial earnings and social affiliations rather than by the individual's intellectual capability or achievement.

Probably most of those educators who are seriously concerned with child development, and who are also in some sense students of the society in which the child lives, believe that the chief function of education is that of contributing materially to integrating the learner and the society in which the learner lives. It is obvious that there is no such thing, nor can there be any such thing as the intellectual learner, the social learner, the emotional learner or the physical learner. Similarly, there can be no separation of any individual into the home child, the church child and the school child. What the child is becoming through home and church influences and experiences determines to a large degree what he is like in the school. Conversely, what he is becoming in school continually affects his behavior in the home. There is a considerable body of evidence which indicates that the experiences of the child during his initial formative years (prior to entrance into the kindergarten or first grade) are of more significance in determining what he will be academically and intellectually than the forces of the school. Nichols develops this point in detail in an earlier chapter. Certainly the school can play a significant role in adolescent development. To fulfill this role the school must be concerned with all aspects of human growth and development. Hopefully, in some measure this will result in the achievement of such goals as good citizenship and effective parenthood.

It should be emphasized here that this does not mean that the school must be equally responsible for all aspects of development. Nor does it mean that the school must take over the responsibilities of the home, the church and the community. There is no doubt that intellectual development is a major concern of the school, while social and physical development are major responsibilities of the home. The ideal educational process however, would develop in a situation where each of the institutions responsible for adolescent development would recognize the interdependence of all phases of behavior. Thus while each might accept a major responsibility for a particular domain, as an example, in intellectual development, each would recognize the extent to which it is highly dependent upon all the others for success in its own developmental contribution. Optimum intellectual development is almost impossible to bring about in young people with serious emotional disturbances. Similarly, a child coming from a home in which many of the activities are intellectual in nature has a much greater chance of successful academic development than does a child of comparable potential living in a non-intellectual home environment.

The school of today is being forced into accepting a major portion of the responsibility for almost all aspects of human development. The great majority of the youth of this nation (raised as they are in urban areas from city slum to elite suburbia) have known little of the work experiences and all-round family participation which were characteristic of rural life in past decades. Highly commercialized entertainment, the ease and frequency of divorce, the modern phenomenon of women working outside of the home and away from their children—each contribute to a greatly changed pattern of life in the United States. All of these factors have operated to cause schools to accept willingly, or unwillingly, a greater and greater responsibility for the ethical, moral and physical development (in addition to the intellectual development) of the student. Regardless of what one believes the role of the school in adolescent development should be, any realtistic appraisal of the function of the school makes it clear that almost no phase of human growth and development can be totally ignored.

THE SCHOOL AS AN INTEGRATIVE
AGENT FOR THE ADOLESCENT

In the "progressive" educational circles, one often hears that the integration of the individual is the chief and the guiding aim of education. Unfortunately, there is a great deal of misunderstanding (or lack of understanding) of the concept of integration, both social and personal. A person is generally thought to be a well-integrated individual when he is capable of facing the major problems he encounters and finds reasonably satisfactory solutions to them, or when he succeeds in making livable adjustments to the problems and pressures of modern society. A great deal has been written about the needs of children and youth in our dynamic society and there has been considerable research—some good, some poor—conducted to determine the nature of these needs. Too often in actual practice, teachers have failed to differentiate between immediate desires and basic underlying needs. Consequently, we have seen a number of "core" courses developed, particularly at the junior-high-school level, in which such problems as: how to act on a date; how to use the family car; how to be well liked and well groomed; how to be accepted into one's peer group in the school and how to conduct oneself in the family situation so as to secure peace and harmony, are seen as problems of such significance as to require a major share of the time alloted to the total school program. These problems are mostly immediate problems *growing out* of certain basic needs rather than being the basic needs themselves. To get at the nature of the more basic needs one has to go to the studies of psychologists, physiologists, cultural anthropologists, sociologists and other life scientists. When this is done, we arrive at a listing of needs which may include statements such as the following: All youth need to develop a relatively high degree of effectiveness in communication, so that they become better able to express themselves well both orally and in writing, and can better understand the communicative efforts of others through both reading and listening. All youth need to understand reproduction and the ways in which the family functions as an institution for the reproduction, protection and development of human beings (See the chapters by Staton and Bell). All youth need to learn to appreciate the beautiful in nature and to develop their own capabilities as creative individuals in the various media of artistic expression. All youth need to set goals which become motivational and to experience some success in the achievement of these goals. All youth need to develop satisfactory working relationships with others of their peer groups, and to feel that they are making worthy contributions to the achievement of group goals.

These are only a sampling of the possible basic needs of the human organism but are illustrative of the "stuff" out of which education should be made. A youth does not necessarily become a well integrated person merely because he has mastered the basic facts and principles of the organized disciplines. It is equally true that he cannot make a worthy contribution to the society in which he is living (nor can he develop a successful personal life) unless he has developed a reasonably high degree of understanding of the operations of his government and of the manner in which his economic system operates, and has developed some sensitivity to ways of living successfully with other human beings. This latter includes the members of his present family and of the family which he himself may help to found at a later time in life. Similarly, it is a serious error to believe that a person can become well integrated in this complex, scientific world in which we live without having attained a certain level of understanding of the phenomena of science, or without having developed a rather high level of competency in mathematical reasoning. Taking into consideration all of these needs, we may conclude that the aims of education should be formulated in terms of the kind of behavior patterns required for the individual living in society. The means through which such behavior becomes possible requires, among other things, a great store of knowledge about the world and the ability to utilize this knowledge in achieving one's own goals. The schools are the most powerful agency committed primarily to this function.

THE SCHOOL'S ROLE IN
INTEGRATING SOCIETY

A social group, like an individual, is continuously under heavy pressures and strains, some of which tend to weld the groups together and others of which threaten to tear them apart. At any given time in any large society, there are forces at work which are integrative in their effect upon the society, and forces which are disintegrative in their effect. For instance, in many communities of the United States and in Congress itself, the racial issue tends to pit elements within the community (or within the legislative body) against each other in a bitter struggle to achieve or prevent racial equality under the law. This struggle constitutes a disintegrative force of considerable magnitude. While religion is an integrative force in that it tends to bring members of the same religious faith together, it often is highly disintegrative in its effect in that it may create fear and distrust among groups of different religious beliefs. For instance, a major difficulty in developing social integration in the nation of South Vietnam lies in the competition between two religious groups for supremacy in the government. The history of the world is to a large degree a history of religious, racial and economic strife. A major aim of education is thus the development of social integration through achieving increasing understanding and compassion within and among various groups. This understanding and compassion should be with respect to the problems which tend to create distrust and strife among these groups. The healthy and full development of individuals within the minority segments of the lower socio-economic classes is to a high degree dependent upon resolving the conflict among racial groups and among economic classes in the larger society. The development of *social* integration can, therefore, be seen as a very important factor in the development of integration of the pupil and a real concern of the school.

THE NEEDS OF SOCIETY AND
THE GOALS OF EDUCATION

Any large group of people who function together as an organized society, have needs that must be satisfied. The needs of the individual and the needs of the society are so interrelated that it is difficult to separate them even for purposes of discussion. The individual, however, has certain needs which must be satisfied, regardless of the nature of his social group; for instance, the need for food and water and some form of protection against extreme weather conditions. Likewise, there are needs of the society which go beyond the needs of the individual, for instance, the need for developing some system of exchange whereby the goods or services of one individual group, or region can become available to others. An individual living alone has no particular need for communication but as a member of a group, he has a very great need for communication. In the same manner, the group itself cannot function well except as there is a common means of communication within and among the members of the group. A common language is, for this reason, a highly important integrative force within any society; lack of a common language encourages disintegration of the group. It is not the purpose here to present a listing of social needs, but rather to illustrate some of these needs and to consider their significance in the development of the individual and in their effect upon the program of the school. Again, to determine the basic underlying needs of a society, the research studies and writings of social scientists are utilized. A statement of social needs may include such statements as the following: A society must produce goods and services to meet the needs of the society and of individuals within the society. A society must develop some means of education so that the mores and institutions of the society may be perpetuated and improved. A society must develop means of transporting goods and services within and among subgroups and regions. A society must develop improved means of communicating both in terms of language itself and in terms of the processes through which communication is achieved. A society must develop an organization for governing. A society must conserve its resources, both human and non-human.

The above do not constitute a complete list of needs but, rather, a few illustrations of what these needs might include. The ability to satisfy such needs determines to a large degree the extent to which integration of the society can be achieved. Education must be seriously concerned with both the integration of the individual and the integration of the society. Neither can exist without the other as man on the one hand is a social animal, and on the other, society itself is made up of individuals. The disintegration or integration of either seriously affects the other.

EDUCATION AND PERSONAL AND SOCIAL INTEGRATION

It is a serious error to believe that a school, dedicated to the development of social and personal integration as major aims, is soft in its approach to education. To the contrary, if it hopes to be successful at all it has to be characterized by firmness, but firmness based on intelligent understanding of both the individual and the society in which he lives. It calls for highly intelligent and well-informed teachers dedicated to continuous efforts to improve the educational process. There are no greater challenges in our society than those of striving for more satisfactory solutions to our racial problems, to our dealings with the forces of communism, and to finding peaceful ways of utilizing the discoveries of the atomic age. The adolescent needs to learn how to date, how to drive the family car safely, how to get along with his family as a cooperative member and how to develop the kind of habits and attitudes which will make him effective as a technical or a white-collar worker. But far more than this, he needs to develop an interest in applied science, in international relations, and in the ways in which the community can solve its many problems of social, economic, political, racial, and religious living.

The modern age is a space and nuclear age; it is also an age of awakening for many of the less advanced nations of the world. It is an age that needs a highly intelligent and well-informed citizenry in all nations. Unfortunately, however, a large percentage of young people and adults alike lack the motivation or the capabilities to become successful contributors to the solution of the major social problems. It is equally unfortunate that large numbers of our schools are operated in such a manner that they fall far short in making the needed contributions to personal and social integration. Professional educators, for instance, have known for several decades that children of a given chronological age differ so greatly from one another in their ability to learn in every learning field, that it is highly ineffective to try to keep them all at the same learning level for any great period of time. It is only in the last few decades that curricular organization and content have been developed which may challenge the student of high capability and yet at the same time make it possible for the slow-learning student to move along more slowly but still successfully. Many adolescents of high academic potential are capable of doing college-level work by the time they are in the 11th year of the public school, and a few at an earlier time. These students should be permitted to accelerate so that their intellect is challenged by difficult and abstract concepts and ideas. At the same time, the slow-learning student must have a curriculum developed at his level of ability so that he can achieve; otherwise the psychological effect of repeated failure may be disastrous. On the other hand, the student of high ability who regularly receives high grades for mediocre effort may also suffer. Academic programs which will stimulate and challenge, yet which are within the reach and ability of all individuals, are the goals for which we should strive. It must of course be recognized that social and biological development does not necessarily progress at the same rate as intellectual development. Thus, a person of low academic ability may have a high degree of neuro-muscular coordination, so that he achieves easily on the athletic field or in other areas requiring physical skill. Also, young people develop socially at different rates. The student who is least capable academically, for instance, may be more mature biologically and socially than the others (or she may be less mature). One of the complicated problems of education is how to organize the curriculum so that highly capable youth in the later adolescent period may be working with and competing with students of adult intellectual capability and at the same time not be forced into adult social relationships. The precocious 7th grader who probably should be studying science and mathematics with students three or four years his senior, may not be suited to this group either biologically or socially. The development of an educational program which will fit each aspect of education to the capability and maturity of the student is one of the big challenges facing public schools today.

SCHOOL STRUCTURE AND ADOLESCENT DEVELOPMENT

The American school system for several decades prior to 1910 was organized as an 8-4 system (eight years of elementary education followed by four years of high school). During the year of 1909-10 junior high schools were organized in Columbus, Ohio, and Berkeley, California with the new 6-3-3 plan which was seen as better related to the period of early and later childhood, early adolescence and later adolescence. Much of the initial justification for the organization of the junior high school was the desirability of providing an orientation to the high school program by providing a "middle school" to secure a more gradual transition from the self-contained elementary-school classroom to the highly departmentalized high school. The chief justification during recent decades, however, has been based upon the desirability of having grouping closely related to the social and physical development of the pupil. Junior high schools generally are organized and housed separately from senior high schools and this is arranged primarily to provide physical and social activities which are in harmony with the developmental stage of junior-high pupils. This avoids the distractions of senior high school activities which are in close proximity. During the past four or five years there has been some shift toward a so-called "middle" or "intermediate school" which would include grades 6, 7 and 8. There are several reasons for this regrouping, one of which is pure expediency; however, there seems to be some psychological support for the argument that children of grades 6, 7 and 8 form a better social grouping than children of grades 7, 8 and 9. This is particularly true with respect to the girls who tend to date older pupils as they reach grade 9. Another, and an often compelling reason for the change in organization, at least in small school systems, is to make it possible to include 9th grade boys on athletic squads. Regardless of whether or not there should be a greater shift toward the intermediate or middle school, it is still a fact that the organization into a 6-3-3 plan or a 5-3-4 plan does nonetheless have as its chief justification, the value of forming groups of pupils of somewhat comparable physical and social development. It provides an institution dedicated to activities which are suited to this developmental group.

SUMMARY

Adolescent development is influenced by many educational and quasi-educational institutions. Chief among these institutions is the public school. But there is no general assent—either among the academic or among the lay public—as to what exactly the role of the public school should be. Though such a determination is actually made through the cooperation of many groups and individuals, what has been presented in this chapter is a standard rationale for determining the school's role. It is used widely among professional educators who look for an integrative approach which considers all the developmental aspects of adolescents. This can be done by seeking to integrate both the individual adolescent and his society. Such a task is too large for one institution, but it has nevertheless been thrust upon the public schools. This is frequently done without considering the larger partner (society) of which the school is but one representative.

The integrative task which the school should undertake must have a base in social-scientific accounts of the nature of the adolescent, if it is to be grounded in anything more stable than personal opinion. It is quite true that, even when such evidence is taken into consideration, the final goal, stated as a developmental need, is a value judgment. If such a judgment is rejected, however, for whatever reason, it must be replaced by another, for the schools must have *some* base for their guiding policies.

The task of the schools with respect to integrating the individual adolescent involves determining those skills, attitudes, learnings, etc., which constitute the necessary conditions for effective living in our society. The suggestions made along this line have purposely included the personal goals of individuals. These have been illustrated in such a way that the more immediate, transistory, and historically arbitrary "needs" have been excluded. Competence and understanding in communication, government, economics, science (broadly construed), and family living have been suggested as defensible paradigms for the needs of youth.

The school's task with respect to integrating society appears to be substantially that of creating, in all individuals and groups which make up the society, an understanding of that society—locally, nationally, and internationally—and of promoting tolerance toward other individuals and groups. With respect to our own society, the needs for production of goods, distributive services, a common language, some method of transmitting culture, a government, etc., were used as examples of social needs which must influence the formulation of educational policy. But such needs cut two ways: they are social necessities which necessarily involve individuals. Thus we can see the interdependence of individual and societal needs.

With respect to the levels of education and their relation to the developmental levels of adolescents, schoolmen have tried to align the two, at least superficially. The historical organization of the levels was 8-4, while the 6-3-3 pattern has increasingly been adopted in response to research. The 5-3-4 plan is the newest proposal and is designed to further improve education as a function of our most recent information concerning social and biological development in adolescents.

Collectively, the public schools have tried to take into account the development of adolescents, physiologically and psycho-sociologically, while attempting to satisfy what educators and lay persons together have construed as distinctly educational aims. A school dedicated to such aims is an organization committed to very high stndards. The challenge of determining and building the appropriate curriculum for adolescents of diverse achievement levels and capabilities looms as a monumental task for today's educators.

For those interested in pursuing a more detailed account of the different topics of this chapter, the following references will present an excellent beginning.

REFERENCES

Association for Supervision and Curriculum Development. *What shall the high schools teach?* Washington, D.C.: National Education Association, 1956.

Conant, J. B. *The American high school today.* New York: McGraw-Hill, 1959.

Conant, J. B. *Slums and suburbs.* New York: McGraw-Hill, 1961.

Conant, J. B. *The comprehensive high school.* New York: McGraw-Hill, 1967.

Elam, S. (Ed.) *Education and the structure of konwledge.* Fifth Annual Phi Delta Kappan Symposium on Educational Research. Chicago: Rand McNally, 1964.

Ford, G. W. and Pugno, L. *The structure of knowledge and the curriculum.* Chicago: Rand McNally, 1966.

McNeil, J. D. Principles of curriculum and instruction. In: Kneller, G. F. (Ed.) *Foundations of education.* New York: John Wiley, 1967.

Phenix, P. H. *Realms of meaning.* New York: McGraw-Hill, 1964.

Tyler, R. W. New dimensions in curriculum development. *Phi Delta Kappan,* 1966, *48,* 25–28.

CHAPTER 11

Sex Education for Adolescents
Thomas F. Staton *✶*

LITTLE RESEARCH, IN THE ACADEMIC SENSE OF THE WORD, HAS BEEN done on sex education. The subject, indeed, is one that does not lend itself, under the limitations of our cultural standards and mores, to conventional methods of scientific investigation. Most reports involve the number of instances in which this is done or that is done in a program of sex education. The reports by Kinsey and his colleagues (1948; 1953), Masters and Johnson (1966a), and dozens of other researchers give us voluminous information on the physical occurrence of sexual behavior, but Dorothy Rogers' (1962) observation that little study has been made of the emotional aspects of sex still holds true. Ehrmann (1957) states that there are relatively few actual knowns of sexual behavior in human beings in general, and Americans in particular. Significantly missing are studies of the emotional aspects of sexual behavior. It is possible to cite opinions, but conclusions reached must be viewed as tentative.

It is reasonable to consider, however, that the opinions of clinical psychologists, psychiatrists, and counselors, based on years of experience in psychotherapy and counseling, possess some validity; so such opinion is often cited in this chapter as evidence as to the psychosexual dynamics active in some area.

THE OBJECTIVES OF SEX EDUCATION

⌐The subject of sex education cannot be treated meaningfully apart from value judgments.⌐ Education on the *physical* aspects of sex can; but when we enter the area of education regarding sexual behavior,

✶ THOMAS F. STATON is a Professor of Psychology and Head of the Psychology Department at Huntingdon College. He has written: *How to Study; How to Instruct Successfully; Dynamics of Adolescent Adjustment; R. S. V. P.: A Dynamic Approach to Study;* as well as a number of articles in psychology and education.

248

it is unrealistic to teach other than in terms of behavioral objectives. Then the question of values arises: *Whose* objectives?

It seems to me to be reasonable to teach those behavioral objectives which seem to maximize the likelihood of good mental health and social adjustment and minimize the likelihood of emotional trauma or social injury. I suggest that a marriage in which partners can enjoy their sexual relations, uninhibited by feelings of conflict or anxiety which may arise from earlier sexual experiences or psychic scars from past episodes, is a worthy aim. The enjoyment of sexual relationships with one's wife or husband is not only a solid pillar for a marriage but one of its greatest pleasures. This should not be jeopardized by earlier sexual activities which might injure the married relationship. I will grant that in America today there is a considerable divergence between the lip service rendered the traditional standards of sexual morality and the sexual behavior of the nation. Nevertheless, it seems to me that the behavioral objectives taught in a program of sex education for adolescents should be in consonance with the professed moral ideals of the society in which the adolescents will live.

The fact that some adolescent sub-cultures offer rewards in popularity and position for a girl's granting sexual favors, and that others are tolerant of all degrees of sexual license, should hardly be taken into consideration in deciding what standards of sexual behavior and values should be the objective of a program of sex education. After all, it is a sad but well-known fact that many of our adolescent sub-cultures exert group pressure on members to experiment with narcotics and participate in tests of daring, such as driving automobiles recklessly on traveled streets. The realistic adult recognizes the difficulties involved in attempting to dissuade adolescents from those behaviors which are undesirable from his viewpoint when these behaviors are not only tolerated but actually rewarded within the adolescents' peer group. This does not call for abandonment of standards that are perhaps higher than those of the age group we are trying to educate. Rather, it calls for the most effective use of education, adult authority, and the helpful elements of peer group values to bring boys and girls through to maturity. Hopefully, this maturity will contain standards and values which are more in keeping with the professed mores of society than the ones they and their peers would have developed if left alone.

Behavior is determined largely by the attitudes of the person(s) involved. Therefore, although aimed at the ultimate objective of behavior control, effective sex education must work through the medium of attitudes. It must attempt to control the behavior of adolescents by developing in them appropriate attitudes on crucial subjects.

Marital Happiness: The Objective

My frame of reference regarding sex education can be briefly sketched: (1) Good sex education maximizes the likelihood of married partners' achieving greatest happiness in their sexual relations with each other; and (2) In current American society, premarital promiscuity, or even occasional premarital experiences, may produce effects on the personalities of boys and girls which lessen their likelihood of optimum marital adjustment.

Any adequate program of sex education must be designed to provide instruction and understanding in two major areas: the physical aspects of sex and the psychological aspects. Of course, these areas and instruction intertwine and overlap. Nevertheless, the program should make conscious provision for each as a distinct element.

EDUCATION IN THE PHYSICAL
ASPECTS OF SEX

In an education program for adolescents on the physical aspects of sex, content should include instruction on the reproductive system and process, the nature and bases of heredity, chemical and glandular functions related to sex, and anatomical differences in the sexes. In addition, boys and girls should learn of the changes that take place in their bodies as they grow from childhood to adulthood, and the causes and effects of these changes. All this should be taught, not as subject matter to be learned as an academic discipline, but from the standpoint of developing in adolescents an understanding and appreciation of the significance and implications of these phenomena for their lives and functions as men and women.

Most textbooks in elementary psychology contain excellent expositions of heredity. In books on child psychology can be found discussions of the reproductive processes and systems that are suitable as a basis for this aspect of sex education for adolescents. Elementary texts in physiology, biology, and anatomy provide adequate source material for instruction in the anatomy and physiology of sex; and most textbooks on adolescent psychology present substantially what an adolescent should know about the changes taking place in his body during adolescence (see Garrison's discussion within this book).

EDUCATION IN THE PSYCHOLOGICAL
ASPECTS OF SEX

Innumerable articles and texts are available presenting the physiology of sex in a form easily adapted to a program of adolescent sex education. However, as might be gathered from our earlier discussion of the topic, relatively little of practical value on the psychology of sex has been published for this education. To convince yourself of this, pick up at random a dozen textbooks on adolescent psychology and see the extent to which the authors explore such topics as dominance— submission in boy-girl relationships, the role of love in sexual desire in the girl as opposed to the boy, and the influence of conversation on sexual behavior. In the area of psychosexual education there is a notable dearth of readily available material covering facts and concepts which are essential to a program of sex education if it is to equip boys and girls with the knowledge and understanding they require. With the stipulation, therefore, that education on the physical aspects of sex is an essential part of any program of sex education, the remainder of this chapter will be devoted to an exploration of psychosexual factors which also are an essential, but often neglected, part of any adequate program. The psychosexual dynamics postulated in the chapter are drawn from the writings of many clinical psychologists, psychiatrists, sociologists, and counselors, substantiated by my own clinical and counseling experience.

Sexual Desire in Humans

The simplest, most elemental and universal manifestation of sexual differentiation is the mating urge. In lower animals, the mating drive generally becomes urgent only when the male is stimulated by the female's periodic condition of sexual receptivity called estrus or "heat," and the female is only receptive during that period. In humans, the male's mating urge, his sexual desire, is unrelated to the biological condition of the female, and her receptivity is little (although somewhat) dependent upon the stage of her fertility cycle. In humans, sexual desire, while it has its origin in bodily chemistry (as it does in the lower animals), arises and becomes intensified not primarily as a result of biological conditions but as a result of psychological factors. These factors are principally attitudinal and emotional.

The fact that human consciousness of and reaction to sexual stimuli are primarily emotional rather than chemical in origin is easily confirmed by dozens of examples. A brother typically is not stimulated sexually by his sister under circumstances which would produce arousal if another girl were involved. A physician typically is not sexually excited by the sight of a female patient whom he is examining or treating. And, although more exceptions may be found in this example, it is still a matter of record that male artists characteristically look on nude female models without sexual arousal. If the reaction were fundamentally biological and chemical, sexual arousal of the males in the foregoing illustrations would be universal. It is universal among male animals of lower species when bodily chemistry decrees it.

The fact that the mating urge, manifested as sexual desire, is primarily psychological, rather than precipitated by biological conditions, is vital to any intelligent treatment of the subject of human sexual affairs. In educating adolescents to adhere to desired patterns of sexual behavior, it means that we must think in terms of their mental and emotional lives; of the experiences which will have one or another effect on their emotions at a given time; of their desires, aspirations, and fantasies; and of the invisible but terrific force of peer group opinion and behavior. We have to consider, and lead them to understand, how their imaginations can trigger their endocrine systems to action under certain conditions. This is more important than the objective facts of the situation in which the adolescent is involved.

Thus, in considering and in leading adolescents to consider *realistically* anything pertaining to sex, we must think, and show them how to think, in terms of the psychology of a situation. The same portion of a girl's leg may be visible as a result of wearing shorts or of having her skirt become disarrayed. Objectively speaking, the part of the leg seen is the same in both situations. The effect on a boy seated beside her at a drive-in movie may be vastly different. Whether this is the first or the fifth time it has happened also will influence the boy's reaction, although it would not alter the objective, physical situation of the moment. The mind of the boy or the girl does as much to determine the sexual significance of an act, statement, or circumstance as does the actual nature of the act, statement, or circumstance.

It is important for boys and girls to appreciate the implications of this fact. Some of those implications will emerge in our further exploration of the needed content of psychosexual education, and still others will be noticed frequently by the perceptive adult working with adolescents.

In the last analysis, sexual behavior depends principally on the attitudes held by the individual involved. As pointed out by McKinney (1960), the biological sex urge is seldom so powerful that it seizes control of the adolescent and dominates his behavior without its first being stimulated by psychological factors and/or deliberate physical manipulation. When fanned to a fever heat by prolonged petting, sex-oriented conversation, infatuation on the part of the girl or wish-fulfillment fantasies on the part of the boy, the sex urge can, indeed, become temporarily overwhelming. But it was built to this pitch of influence by the minds and emotions of the people involved. It did not become so as a naturally functioning biological process. The intensity of the sex urge, and the extent to which it controls behavior, are infinitely more influenced by the emotions aroused by the attitude-directed behavior of a boy or girl than by the biological nature of either.

A program of sex education should contain information on sex that boys and girls will not receive in the process of everyday living but that they need to have in order to know how to manage their social relationships wisely and constructively. Each course should feature those aspects of most concern to the sex involved. Thus, girls need receive only brief instruction on the phenomena of erections and nocturnal emissions, but considerable instruction on the menstrual cycle. The emphasis for boys would be reversed. In the succeeding discussion, the relative need of each sex for different topics will be apparent.

Meanings Attached to Premarital Sex

One example of male-female behavior dramatizes a social attitude and a psychological fact that are basic to the philosophy of an effective program of sex education. Characteristically, boys feel proud and boast of sexual conquests, while girls often suffer loss of self-respect and incur feelings of anxiety or guilt from having engaged in sexual intimacies outside the marriage relationship. This fact reveals a fundamental difference in male-female relationships to premarital sex and carries with it profound implications for a program of sex education for adjustment.

Except in an occasional sub-culture (usually an unsavory one), the girl who engages in premarital sexual activities loses status and respect if the fact becomes common knowledge. The boy who is known (or believed) to have achieved sexual relations with many girls is not correspondingly derogated by his peer group. Why? Because the boy has mastered, made a conquest, demonstrated his masculine appeal and virility. These are causes for pride, if altruistic values are ignored. The girl, on the other hand, has not conquered or seduced by her irresistible femininity. (It is commonly understood that a girl does not have to possess fascinating femininity to make her desired sexually by a male—she only has to be female.) In another generation, she was said to have "fallen"; today, she has "been had," given in, submitted, been used, or surrendered. The whole language of sexual intercourse (scientific, colloquial, and slang) emphasizes that the boy wins and the girl surrenders or is defeated in the contest that ends in their having sexual intercourse. Thus, sexual promiscuity by the adolescent girl has a diametrically and fundamentally different effect on her ego and self-concept from that on the teenage boy. To him, it is a source of pride. To her, it is having been used, having let herself be conquered and exploited.

Kinsey (1953) reports that 18 per cent of unmarried women who reported having had sexual intercourse admitted more than minor regret for their actions, with 13 per cent reporting minor regret. Blood (1962) indicates that these figures may be misleadingly low, and I believe the consensus of counselors and psychotherapists would support his conclusion. It is reasonable to assume, for instance, that a much larger percentage of people suffering from guilt feelings about premarital intercourse would fail to report having had intercourse than would be the case among those who had intercourse and felt no regrets. Clinical psychologists and psychiatrists find frequent instances of *unconscious* as well as *unadmitted* anxiety and guilt deriving from premarital sex experiences. They have repeatedly commented on the number of girls encountered in their clinical practice who, underneath a veneer of sophisticated "emancipation" and sexual equality, were suffering from severe feelings of guilt and loss of self-respect as a result of having let themselves be "used" sexually. "I'm only a body to him," is the bitter remark often heard in such circumstances, and such a feeling is destructive to self-respect and pride.

Eventually, of course, the girl may overcome such feelings and regard her sexual submission as merely her contribution to a social relationship, analogous to the boy paying for the theater tickets. Such sophistication, however, is rarely encountered in adolescents. It is more typically a defense gradually built up as a girl grows older, in an attempt to rationalize her degraded self-esteem back into self-respect. Kinsey (1953) reports that the more a girl had engaged in premarital intercourse, the less likely she was to regret her actions. This is hardly surprising.

Because of social attitudes and a girl's frequent emotional reaction (totally apart from any moral considerations or the danger of pregnancy), much can be said in favor of chastity in the adolescent girl. It is important to her self-concept, self-respect, self-esteem, and mental health. It should not be forgotten that this chapter is concerned with optimum sex education for adolescents, not for adults who presumably might have greater experience, greater capacity for self-restraint and self-discipline, and the superior capability of intelligent self-determination.

Aside from the disapproval that they, too, will encounter from some portions of society, boys do not escape completely unscathed from sexual promiscuity. The sexually promiscuous male develops the attitude of exploitation, of self-centeredness, and of disregard for the welfare and happiness of members of the opposite sex as long as his own pleasure is achieved and his own desires are satisfied. This attitude is not a good background on which to build a happy family life. It will inevitably affect his adjustment with the girl he marries. One cannot exploit others—deliberately subject others to injury and danger —without injury to one's own integrity and mental health. Penal reformers have claimed, and psychologists substantiate their claims, that floggings ultimately injure the man who gives them as much as they injure those who receive them. The effect of service as guards in concentration camps (or even repeated observation of humiliation inflicted on others) on the natures of men has been generally recognized, and vividly described by Frankl (1963). The ruthless, the inconsiderate, the opportunists and exploiters, as seducers or otherwise, are undergoing damage less obvious but as real as that which is suffered by the other parties in the relationship.

Even an initially reluctant girl, her inhibitions broken down, may be cooperative and experience pleasure in the throes of sexual passion. This fact does not alter the effect on the boy's nature of having used his powers to persuade another to act in a manner potentially harmful to her, for his own momentary pleasure. The adolescent boy who uses his assets and desire for personal pleasure to overcome the moral resistance of girls is building a pattern of attitudes and values which may cripple him in all of his relationships with humanity. The self-centeredness and ruthless using of others, frequently developed by a boy in sexual promiscuity, are not likely to limit their scope to the girls he enjoys. They may also be transferred and reveal themselves in his activities in the community, on the job, and in his home.

I believe, from 25 years of clinical experience, that the effects of sexual promiscuity on boys' and girls' personalities, and on their prospects of good mental health and marital adjustment, constitute more than adequate grounds for making continence prior to the marriage relationship a valid and desirable objective of sex education.

The investigations conducted by Kinsey and his staff (1948; 1953) substantiate the clinical judgment I expressed in an earlier treatise on adolescence (1963). Males and females are quite different in their psychosexual constitutions. This is important for boys and girls to learn. It is human nature to assume that others think and feel much as we do, and attach much the same significance to things that we attach to them. The fact is that sexual desire in boys has a vastly different emotional base from sexual desire in girls, and an act or circumstance often has a completely different sexual implication to members of the different sexes. Knowledge of some of these instances of difference can spare the girl the embarrassment of having a boy attach a different meaning than she intended to some act of hers. It will also spare the boy the embarrassment of seeming to be crude or vulgar.

Sexual Stimuli

The Kinsey (1948; 1953) studies confirm the common observation that masculine nudity does not, characteristically, serve as a sexual stimulant to, or arouse sexual desire in, a girl. The sight of feminine nudity, on the other hand, is usually all that is necessary to arouse active sexual desire in a boy. Any movement suggesting nudity (e.g., taking off a dress under which a swimsuit is worn, unfastening the back of a halter to sun while lying face down, adjusting a stocking with hands hidden under the skirt) may have erotic significance to boys, even though they are done quite innocently by girls, with no consciousness of their erotic significance. Of course, there is considerable psychological evidence to suggest that brief swimsuits, tight shorts, and short skirts, while ostensibly worn innocently and without self-consciousness, in reality represent girls' unconscious if not conscious attempts to attract erotic attention. But there are such things as completely unintentional actions by girls (especially adolescent girls lacking extensive social experience and sophistication) that hold much erotic significance to boys.

Romance and Exploitation

One area of psychosexual difference in boys and girls is in the emotional bases of their sex urge. Ehrmann (1959) succinctly summarizes his research in this area as follows: Males are erotic, females, romantic. The emotional roots of the boy's sexual desire seem to lie in the desire to possess, and the feeling of mastery and strengthening of his self-concept that accompanies his achieving intimacy with a girl. This fact has been commented on by clinicians such as Deutsch (1944), and their observations substantiated by the research of Lindzey and Goldberg (1953) and Ehrmann (1959).

Also, the boy's physical desire is aroused early in circumstances of physical intimacy, or even in the intimacy of conversation about sexual matters. This physical desire spurs on his attempts to achieve more intimacy, and the greater intimacy achieved in turn increases the intensity of his physical desire. Love plays a minor and incidental part (if any at all) in the arousal, intensification, and satisfaction of his sexual desire. His sexual desire is erotically oriented, not romantically oriented (Grant, 1957), although he may cultivate the trappings of romance because of their appeal to the girl.

On the other hand, as Stone and Church (1957) point out, a girl's sexual desire springs primarily from a feeling of love for the boy. It is compounded by a desire to make him happy, which appears to be absent in the boy's feeling of sexual desire for the girl. Rarely does her physical desire for sexual relations become a driving force in her behavior, and then only after extensive preliminary psychological and perhaps physical stimulation. The fondling and kissing, snuggling and caressing, are to her things of pleasure and, more often than not, satisfactory ends in themselves. To her they signify love and romance. They give her pleasure, and she is happy in the belief that she is giving equal pleasure to the boy. Her sexual nature is attuned to love and romance. Physical appetite usually makes an appearance late, if at all, and dominates her behavior only in the last stages of love play.

Failure to understand and appreciate these vast psychosexual differences often leads to frustration and unhappiness for both boy and girl. Interestingly, both boys and girls seem slow to comprehend the truth from personal experience. A boy often feels that girls are "teases." They lead him on, raise his hopes of achieving intercourse, excite him to the point of agony, and then unreasonably stop him or even become offended when he attempts to carry the intimacy to what is (for him) the only possible rational conclusion.

The girl, however, has thoroughly enjoyed what was to her the romance of shared lips and caresses. She has been happy in the thought that she is affording equal happiness to the boy toward whom she feels, at least at the moment, so tender, if not actually loving. Now she finds that he is pressing for an intimacy which she never intended, which shocks her, in which she perceives danger to herself and a violation of her code of behavior. Unlike the boy, she had not considered the petting a prelude; a means to an end that was inevitable if satisfaction was to be achieved. To her the kissing, caressing, and whispered endearments were ends in themselves, inducing a state of supreme happiness and contentment. Suddenly, as in a case described by Kanin (1957), her sweet companion is no longer a sweet companion but a wolf, and a slavering, snapping one at that! She does not know why he "changed" so. She does not realize that he considers that *she* is the one who suddenly changed, suddenly contradicted her former behavior. The boy is frustrated and angry, feeling he has been led on and made a fool of. The girl is shocked, angry, sometimes hysterical. She did not know her behavior was, in the eyes of the boy, a clear go-ahead signal.

Sex education has failed when misunderstandings such as this arise. The *situations* may arise despite good psychosexual education (although it is probable that they would arise less often), because adolescent boys and girls occasionally will get themselves into such predicaments. But the bafflement, the misunderstanding, the outrage and feeling of being cheated can be prevented. Through an understanding on both sides of what has happened, the boy and girl are better equipped to avoid developing a harmful distrust or contempt for the opposite sex, and a recurrence of such a contretemps.

Closely related to the erotic-romantic relationship just described is the different relationship between love and sexual desire in boys and girls. An old saying sums up the situation succinctly and with only moderate distortion: "A gentleman will try to seduce every girl except the one he loves, but a nice girl will not be seduced by any man except the man she loves." Every clinical psychologist working with adolescents has heard girls say, " I *loved* him . . . that's the only reason I let him do it. I thought he loved me, too. Why did he want us to do that if he didn't love me?" Blood (1962, p. 131), interpreting research data, concludes, ". . . it seems fair to say that *most* of the premarital intercourse of college men is exploitive in nature rather than an expression of love."

Knowledge of this fundamental sex difference in the relationship between love and sexual desire will not change the behavior of all girls. People tend to believe what they very much want to believe, even though the rational portion of their mind tells them it is not true. The girl who loves a boy wants his love to equal hers. Therefore, when he uses the claim of his love for her as a device to assist in seduction, she often will believe him because she so desperately *wants* him to love her. She disregards evidence in order to believe that he does. Knowledge of this fact, too, is a proper part of a girl's sex education.

The different relationship between love and sexual relations is logical—not mysterious or paradoxical, but rational and reasonable—when we further examine the psychosexual structure of males and females. Both from the standpoint of biology and society, a girl runs a greater risk of inconvenience, embarrassment, and tragedy for engaging in sexual reactions outside of marriage. It is natural that if she is of normal emotional and social adjustment she would be reluctant to accept such a risk, and inclined to do so only to bring happiness to one she loved. Ideally, a boy should be unwilling to subject any girl to such eventualities for his pleasure. Certainly, if he is emotionally mature, sensible, and responsible, he would be reluctant to subject a girl he genuinely loved to possible social censure and personal tragedy. In a momentary surrender to blind sexual fury he might do so, but at such a time he would not be an emotionally adjusted and rational being. Certainly, he would not subject a girl he loved to these attendant dangers through deliberate, planned seduction.

Thus, it seems fair to say that in consenting to premarital sexual relations a girl is, at least in many instances, "proving her love" (although, of course, she may feel just as strong a love but nevertheless refuse to violate her self-concept and standard of behavior). On the other hand, the boy's insisting on sexual intimacies suggests a lack of mature love rather than its presence.

Understanding all these things enables a girl to understand the psychodynamics of her attitudes and actions and those of the boy. Properly appreciating these factors allows her to choose her course of action accordingly. That is to say, she does not act on a gross misinterpretation of the motives and attitudes of her partner.

Dominance and Submission

Another psychosexual difference between boys and girls that Ehrmann (1959) discusses is worthy of note. Boys characteristically possess the male urge to dominate, while girls have the characteristic female tendency toward submission. This distinction is well nigh universal among lower animals, and shows itself prominently in primitive cultures. As man becomes more humane, develops a greater grasp of the concept of social justice, masculine domination of the female declines. In contemporary American culture, the decline of masculine dominance has progressed to a degree where there are so many exceptions in individual person-to-person contacts that it cannot be applied accurately as a generalization. However, this decline in masculine dominance is conspicuously greater among adults than among children or adolescents. In other words, masculine dominance tends to exist until social maturation diminishes or eliminates it. This tendency of the male to dominate and the female to submit is often responsible for the common situation of a girl persisting in her infatuation with a boy who pointedly humiliates, neglects, and socially misuses her; who, in short, "treats her like dirt." Perhaps this is more often the correct explanation than is her having a feeling of genuine affection for the boy. It is an atavistic tendency of the weak (or merely insecure) to seek security through submitting to the strong, and rudeness or brutality is easily confused with strength by the insecure.

This dominance-submission tendency, not yet "socialized" out of adolescents, accounts for much of the trouble parents have in preventing their teenage daughter from running frantically to the street when summoned by a preemptory blast on the horn by her boy friend. The male summons and the female comes. Even when the girl seems to take the initiative, to be the aggressor in the relationship, it is almost always apparent to the observant adult that in actuality she is trying to maneuver the boy into a position of displaying possessive behavior toward her. An understanding of these mechanisms of the two sexes will help the girl to consciously combat her submissive tendencies when they may lead her into dangerous situations. It may also help the boy who is basically goodhearted to understand himself and his girl and to refrain from importunities exploiting his strength and her weakness.

Separation of the sexes for instruction in sexual matters (which is discussed in more detail later in the chapter) serves as an example in giving boys and girls a comprehension of the relationship between sexually oriented conversation or discussion of sexual topics and sexual arousal and desire. Kinsey (1953) found that adolescent boys, and many adolescent girls, have experienced the arousal of sexual excitement, if not passion, as a result of reading accounts of sexual activity or participating in discussions of sexual topics. With such sexual arousal mutually experienced, there is greater difficulty in a girl controlling her own behavior as well as the advances of her companion. Experienced boys and men often employ suggestive and subsequently more directly sexually oriented conversation as a means of arousing sexual interest in a date and gradually lessening her inhibitions. The girl who engages in sexually oriented conversation to show her emancipation, or for a thrill, is encouraging the development of urges and passion in both herself and her date that almost inevitably leads the boy to attempt physical intimacy. The adolescent girl should know that unless she wants to lead her date into physical intimacies on the sexual level, she had better not engage in suggestive or sexually oriented conversation with him. Words may be as effective as sights, or even physical contact, in arousing and intensifying erotic urges.

Controlling the Situation and Environment

In this connection, it may be noted that Ehrmann's (1952) depth interviews with girls on the psychodynamics of petting revealed that the crucial point at which limiting further physical intimacies became most difficult was when the girl permitted caresses beyond a simple embrace. Psychologists had theorized that probably the degree of intimacy which made it most difficult for a girl to call a halt to the progression of erotic activities was after she had permitted the boy's hand to caress her inside her clothing. From interviews with adolescent and late-adolescent girls, Ehrmann found that the girl permitting the boy's hand to caress her below the shoulder level, even caressing her breasts outside her clothing, triggered the erotic forces in each party that were most likely to constitute the point-of-no-return. Failure to comprehend this can result in a girl letting her relationship with her date get out of her control before she realizes she has entered the danger zone of sex play.

The mother who admonishes her child not to get wet, but does not warn him away from an inviting stream beside the picnic grounds, has not effectively guided his behavior. Similarly, a program of sex education that fails to acquaint adolescents with circumstances which get them into situations where unwise behavior is likely to take place is not as effective as it should be.

Robert Burns summarized the ingredients of a situation leading to sexual indiscretions as follows: "A well-lov'd lad, convenience snug, a treacherous inclination." When a boy and girl find themselves in a situation of privacy for a considerable period of time, and most especially if it follows an experience encouraging feelings of romance in the girl or erotic arousal in the boy (such as a dance, a party, a romantic movie, or any emotion-arousing activity), the temptation to follow the urgings of psychological and biological nature is strong.

"If you drink, don't park—accidents cause people" is a paraphrase I have heard young people use to express two other factors promoting sexual activity among adolescents. The lowering of moral and other inhibitions under the influence of alcohol is too well known to merit elaboration. Both psychologists (Wattenberg, 1955) and sociologists (Kanin, 1957) have noted that an automobile parked in a secluded place promotes sexual intimacy. Adolescent girls should be aware of the difficulty they may have in handling a situation that can develop when an automobile ride eventuates in the boy parking the car in a place of undisturbed privacy. It is hard to get away from such a spot if the girl finds she is the only one who wishes to leave. It would have been more effective for her to object to going there in the first place. The same opportunity and temptation exist, often intensified, when adolescents are permitted prolonged privacy in one of their homes or at a party. In fact, Kinsey (1953) reports the girl's home as the prime location for premarital intercourse, the boy's home and automobile being major secondary locations.

Parental requirements that dating adolescents come home within a short time after leaving a scheduled activity or group function, and prohibitions against late dating hours or extended periods of privacy for a couple in the home, seem wise. The adolescent who protests, "If we were going to do anything wrong, we could do it in ten minutes as well as in an hour," either does not know the dynamics of sexual intimacy on dates or is pretending ignorance. Except in the case of a boy and girl who have become habituated to sexual intimacies from long practice with each other, boy-girl sexual behavior almost invariably follows a well-defined and time-consuming course, from kissing to necking to petting to intercourse, with considerable time spent in each activity. Kinsey (1953) found that even an interruption is likely to terminate the progression (through one person becoming alarmed or self-conscious) or at least "set back" the progress that had been made.

Extended time in considerable privacy is conducive to the development of intimacies. This is true even though the couple has not deliberately sought for and planned these intimacies. The boy or girl who winds up engaging in sexual activities that were not premeditated usually has spent a considerable period of time working up to the level of involvement. Without the prolonged erotic and romantic play, final intimacy would not have taken place.

It was said earlier in the chapter that the biological urge for satisfaction of the sex drive seldom becomes overwhelmingly powerful unless cultivated by deliberate physical or psychological stimulation. However, once cultivated by prolonged petting or conversation of an erotic nature, the sheer biological urge to mate is capable of becoming so powerful in both sexes that few adolescent boys and girls have the mature self-discipline to resist it. Given sufficient help and cooperation, nature can, indeed, establish a point-of-no-return in the relations of an adolescent boy and girl. Both time and privacy, in considerable quantities, usually are required for this point-of-no-return.

The time a boy and girl spend in intimacies has a cumulative effect. That is to say, they carry over from one date to the next. This is one of the dangers (although probably not the chief one) of adolescents "going steady." A boy and girl who think enough of each other to be together repeatedly, especially to the exclusion of dating other people, become increasingly familiar with each other's bodies as well as personalities. Increasingly intimate physical contact comes to be taken for granted. For them, the starting point for romantic or erotic activities becomes petting of greater and greater intimacy, with little or no time being spent in the preliminary conversation and kissing as is the case of a boy and girl not yet thoroughly familiar with each other.

You can almost say that every romantic interlude takes up where the last one left off, and goes on from there.

Sex and Sexuality

Masters and Johnson (1966b) draw an interesting and valid distinction between sex (by which they mean an aspect of physiology) and sexuality (which involves the whole complex of personality factors and social relationships having their origin in the reproductive drive). Sex is innate in the human being. Sexuality must be learned. As far as is known, the learning of sexuality follows the same principles of learning as does the learning of other attitudes and habits. Learning theory, as well as common sense, suggests that a reaction once given is more readily given in a subsequent, similar situation. Thus, it is an unusually safe prediction that the more a boy or girl has taken part in sexual intimacies, the less likely he or she is to refrain from similar actions when another opportunity or temptation occurs. A very real danger of what is euphemistically called a "single mistake" (which certainly should not be considered as smirching the adolescent's character) is that from all that is known of learning theory, it predisposes repetitions. Certainly, it is my own view that the danger of premarital sexual intimacies between a boy and girl in love with each other lies as much in the fact that habit patterns thus formed will have a tendency to prevail in other situations involving other people as in the fact that such premarital intimacies may injure their own future relationship. Perhaps all this can be summarized as follows: Premarital intercourse is not necessarily promiscuity, but certainly increases the likelihood of promiscuity developing.

HOW SHOULD SEX EDUCATION BE CONDUCTED?

Sex education, like education in correct grammar or good manners, is not something that can be satisfactorily achieved through formal teaching. It must be accompanied by general life experiences which support and reinforce the more formalized portion of education. Adults in every area of adolescents' lives (parents, teachers, clergy, coaches, counselors, scout or recreational leaders) should be alert to seize every opportunity to enhance the boy or girl's sex education. Noteworthy news events, situations encountered in the study of literature or history, current civic happenings, or circumstances in the adolescent's own experience can make important concepts in sex education more real and of greater practical significance to boys and girls.

Certainly, in the average family, it is good for parents to give their children as much instruction in all aspects of sex education as they are capable of giving. Statements of Drucker (1952) and Lee (1952) are representative of the opinions of psychologists on this point. The intimacy existing between a parent and young child affords ample natural opportunities for instruction in these fields to be given gradually and naturally, in the normal processes of family living. Information and guidance can be given in response to the child's questions or other expressions of curiosity about his body or the bodies of others. This would cover reproduction or other directly sexual topics. The amount of information and degree of detail can be adjusted to the child's level of interest and understanding. Finally, the intimacy existing between parent and child can be used in the process of imparting information on sex to emphasize that this is not a topic one discusses casually in social conversation.

In the normal and wholesome family environment, this basic information on sex will have been given by the parent before the child reaches adolescence; but, as Rogers (1962) points out, the amount of information regarding the physiology and psychology of sex that the average parent *can* give is extremely limited. It usually is confined to the most elementary explanations of the simplest facts of sexual structure and reproduction, because few parents retain (even if they once learned) the degree of knowledge of psychology and biology required to give the adolescent a clear understanding of the psychological and biological aspects of sex. It is even more important and more difficult to build an appreciation of the significance of this information in the lives of people.

It is both practical and in keeping with the modern concept of the responsibility of our schools for the school to assume considerable responsibility for giving the adolescent an understanding and appreciation of the anatomy, physiology, chemistry, and biology of sex. This should also include the psychology of sex and the significance of sex in a person's life.

Education by Sex on Sex

As may have been inferred from earlier statements, I take what I fear is very much a minority position on how sex education should be presented in the school. However, my position is based on many years of working with boys and girls in both clinical and school settings. It is my conviction that sex education in the school *should not* be scheduled primarily in groups where both sexes are present. Sex education will be more effective, and assume its more appropriate place in the thinking and value systems of boys and girls, if given to separate groups. Physical education classes seem to me one logical answer.

I completely agree with those who contend that segregation of the sexes for purposes of sex education makes sex something of a taboo, something that is not accepted and dealt with matter-of-factly (e.g., the circulation of the blood or the hunger drive). But it seems to me that the people advancing this contention miss the whole point of sex education; or, perhaps their objectives are different from mine. Sex is *not* just another physiological process, not just another craving. It is a most unique thing, carrying with it wonderful as well as dangerous potentialities. Treating it as an impersonal thing like the function of the liver, or just another emotion such as sibling jealousy, is unrealistic. This is true because the psychological forces (social sanctions and taboos, the potential for emotional satisfaction or disturbance, and social adjustment or maladjustment) associated with it are so much greater, more complex, and more contradictory than in the case of other physiological and psychological functions.

The mode of sex education should recognize the uniqueness of its subject and assist the adolescent to develop the concepts of privacy and reserve properly associated with sex. It is difficult to teach such reserve, by admonition, in a setting that contradicts the admonition. The fact is that our attitudes and feelings tend to follow the patterns of our thoughts and speech about as much as our thoughts and speech follow the patterns of our feelings and attitudes. I believe any serious student of semantics will agree that lessening the inhibitions in discussion of a subject will lessen the inhibitions of the majority of discussants in their behavior regarding the subject. Adolescent boys and girls cannot discuss with true inner (as opposed to apparent) scientific detachment a subject that exercises on them such profound, provocative, titillating emotional stimulation, as does sex. Therefore, unless the objective of sex education is to lower the barriers of reserve between adolescent boys and girls, segregation for sex instruction and especially for discussion of sexual topics and problems is essential.

The Self-Concept and Sex Education

In my own experience I have found one approach to influencing adolescent sexual behavior notably more effective than any other. It is my observation that the boy or girl who has a strong self-concept and who recognizes a type of behavior as inconsistent with that self-concept characteristically will avoid that behavior. This is congruent with Stagner's (1961) emphasis on the role of the self-image and self-respect in bringing consistency into behavior. I have found that a girl who thinks of herself as master of her behavior, who takes pride in being a person who cannot be manipulated by others, and who feels that being used for someone else's pleasure is beneath her dignity and standards, is unlikely to indulge in behavior that would injure that self-concept. Similarly, the boy who thinks of himself as a responsible person of honor and integrity, who feels contempt for preying on weaker or less knowledgeable people, who takes pride in the honesty of his dealings with everyone, is unlikely to attempt to persuade a girl to engage in activities which might expose her to injury or criticism.

Consequently, my approach to influencing behavior through sex education is principally an attempt to get boys and girls to form self-concepts of themselves as people who are above anything that would lessen self-respect (especially for girls), or would take advantage of another to that person's possible hurt (especially for boys). Adolescent boys and girls respond amazingly to discussions that help them acquire firm, clear pictures of themselves as people of pride, honor, and integrity, as people who will not act out of character from the self-concepts they develop and want to maintain.

In this respect, society lends us a helping hand. Although society is tolerant of immorality (of other kinds, as well as sexual), Remmers and Radler (1957) conclude that sexual misbehavior becoming known lessens the respect a girl is accorded in all societies save a few subcultures previously mentioned. Even in the case of the boy, investigators have found that adult society, as a whole, possesses values such that he cannot trespass them morally without some injury to the respect and regard in which he is held. This lessened respect will result in injury to the boy's or girl's self-concept. Adolescents are not independent of prevailing social values and standards. They are influenced by them and are unable to avoid evaluating themselves to some extent in terms of them. Stagner (1961), indeed, states that self-respect appears to be chiefly our introjected conception of the respect of others; and Gordon (1963) emphasizes the self-concept as including the individual's response to the evaluation placed on him by society. Boys' and girls' self-concept are injured if they fall below those standards. Make an adolescent sufficiently conscious of a good self-concept, and you will influence his behavior profoundly. The self-concept approach to teaching morality ties powerful emotional pressures within the boy and girl to certain modes of behavior rather than giving them only an intellectual concept with which to resist the emotions and pressures toward promiscuity that they will encounter.

The best way I have found to help adolescents develop strong self-concepts is through group discussions. Where sex is not the *primary* subject involved, mixed groups may be used under some circumstances. Self-consciousness minimizes the expression of values and standards violating good morals and ethics in such a group and maximizes exploration of positive values and behavior. Thus, participants get a feeling of group endorsement of high moral standards and sound values, and tend to accept them. Accepting them, they can be motivated to try to live up to them to avoid degrading their self-concepts or tacitly admitting their inferior standards.

Much of the content of a sex education program has to be presented first as a lecture or reading assignment, to get the requisite information to boys and girls. Some elements of it (such as the physiology of sex and the biological processes) may need nothing more than a lecture or reading assignment and a period in which questions can be asked to clarify wherever needed.

Where attitudes regarding sex are to be developed, however, or behavior change is desired, use group discussion to explore the significance and implications of the facts and concepts within the subject. By going through the process of thought on a topic himself, by putting his thoughts into words, by hearing himself talk about a subject, and by attempting to follow and understand the thoughts of his peers, the adolescent boy or girl achieves a relationship to facts and concepts that is infinitely more effective in crystallizing attitudes or producing behavior change than is reading or hearing a lecture on the topic. Particularly when the group reaches conclusions on pertinent issues and shows substantial agreement on certain standards and values, those conclusions, standards, and values are much more likely to be incorporated into the self-concepts of the boys and girls participating than if they were formulated and handed out by an adult.

If boys and girls can be found who are capable of leading the discussions, this is all the better. A good role for the teacher or counselor in such a discussion is that of resource person, one who can supply facts and guide reasoning when needed. Because, of course, the discussions must in fact result in sound conclusions, establish sound values and standards, to be effective. If we can assume that high moral values and standards *are* sound, it follows that sound reasoning will reach them, and the teacher should not hesitate to volunteer information or concepts that set straight a discussion that is straying into invalid patterns of thought and reasoning. Of course, this should be done as briefly, unobtrusively, and non-dictatorially as possible.

As an example of what is meant here, I sat with a group of college men and women who were discussing a philosophy, propounded by a widely known writer, of complete sexual freedom, with mutual consent and pleasure the only criteria of morality. Discussion was centering on the advantages of such a moral system, substantiation of the man's reasoning, and challenging the reasons usually advanced in support of conventional morality. I asked how the writer's system operated in his own heterosexual relations. In fact, as some members of the group had read and brought out, he apparently used a girl as a convenience and status symbol. By reason of his personality, virility, position, or all three, he had no difficulty in getting attractive girls to live with him on his own terms. When he tired of one, he terminated the relationship and sought another. The girls involved seemingly had little to say about anything pertaining to the relationship other than their original acquiescence to it. The group quickly determined that, in fact, the "mutual consent" involved was more apparent than real, and proceeded to a discussion of whether mutual consent could reasonably be depended upon as the sole regulator of an association such as the extremely closely knit and emotionally charged relationship between two people that tends to develop along with complete and prolonged intimacy. A question had started the group on a line of thought that led to more realistic perception and accurate reasoning than the one they were pursuing.

SUMMARY

Sexual behavior in the human being is regulated more by attitudes than by biological forces. Sex education, therefore, should aim more at attitude formation than at a simple imparting of knowledge. The development of a strong self-concept, of seeing one's self as a self-disciplined, responsible, and honorable person, is a relatively effective means of controlling behavior. It is thought that the desired attitudes are more likely to be produced by group discussions (generally with only one sex participating) than by other formal educational procedures.

The sexes differ radically in their psychosexual make-up and dynamics. Girls are romantic and boys are erotic. Girls' self-concepts tend to be injured by sexual relations outside marriage and their social standing compromised if their sexual activities become generally known. Boys' self-concepts are more likely to be enhanced by their sexual "conquests," and they incur much less social disapproval if their sexual activities become known. Both the boy and the girl, however, are likely to suffer psychological injury through sexual behavior which violates the professed standards of society.

REFERENCES

Blood, R. O., Jr. *Marriage.* New York: Free Press of Glencoe, 1962.

Deutsch, Helene. *The psychology of woman: A psychoanalytic interpretation.* New York: Grune & Stratton, 1944.

Drucker, A. J., Christensen, H. T., and Remmers, H. H. Some background factors in socio-sexual modernism. *Marriage and Family Living,* 1952, *14,* 334–337.

Ehrmann, W. W. Student cooperation in a study of dating behavior. *Marriage and Family Living,* 1952, *14,* 322–326.

Ehrmann, W. W. Some knowns and unknowns in research into human sex behavior. *Marriage and Family Living,* 1957, *19,* 16–22.

Ehrmann, W. W. *Premarital dating behavior.* New York: Holt, 1959.

Frankl, V. E. *Man's search for meaning.* New York: Washington Square Press, Inc., 1963.

Gordon, J. E. *Personality and behavior.* New York: The Macmillan Company, 1963.

Grant, V. M. *The psychology of sexual emotions: The basis of sexual attraction.* New York: Longmans, Green and Co., Inc., 1957.

Kanin, E. J. Male aggression in dating-courtship relations. *American Journal of Sociology,* 1957, *43,* 197–204.

Kinsey, A. C., Pomeroy, W. B., and Martin, C. E. *Sexual behavior in the human male.* Philadelphia: W. B. Saunders Company, 1948.

Kinsey, A. C., *et al. Sexual behavior in the human female.* Philadelphia: W. B. Saunders Company, 1953.

Lee, M. R. Background factors related to sex information and attitudes. *Journal of Educational Psychology,* 1952, *43,* 467–485.

Lindzey, G., and Goldberg, M. Motivational differences between male and female as measured by the Thematic Apperception Test. *Journal of Personality,* 1953, *22,* 101–117.

McKinney, F. *Psychology of personal adjustment.* New York: John Wiley & Sons, Inc., 1960.

Masters, W. H., and Johnson, Virginia E. *Human sexual response.* Boston: Little, Brown & Co., 1966. (a)

Masters, W. H., and Johnson, Virginia E. A defense of love and morality. *McCall's* XCIV, 2, November, 1966, 102–173. (b)

Remmers, H. H., and Radler, D. H. *The American teen-ager.* Indianapolis: Bobbs-Merrill Company, Inc., 1957.

Rogers, Dorothy. *The psychology of adolescence.* New York: Appleton-Century-Crofts, 1962.

Stagner, R. *Psychology of personality.* New York: McGraw-Hill Book Company, Inc., 1961.

Staton, T. F. *Dynamics of adolescent adjustment.* New York: The Macmillan Company, 1963.

Stone, L. J., and Church, J. *Childhood and adolescence.* New York: Random House, 1957.

Wattenberg, W. W. *The adolescent years.* New York: Harcourt, Brace and Company, 1955.

The Marital Expectations of Adolescents

Robert R. Bell *

ONE OF THE MOST STRIKING CHARACTERISTICS OF THE AMERICAN POPULA-
tion is that we are marrying at younger ages and in greater numbers
than ever before. This is true even though many middle-class males
are not entering their adult occupational roles until older ages. For the
first time in any society we are encouraging and supporting marriage
for many of the young well before they are able to operate as self-
sustaining economic units.

For many adolescents, marriage implies adult status. With most adolescents anxious to reach adulthood, marriage is often seen and sought
as a clear symbol of being an adult. It is not that the young adolescent
necessarily wants to get married, but that he often wants to move into
the male-female relationships that are the prelude to marriage—
engagement, and especially, going steady. To be involved in relationships as "adult" as going steady or engagement may be symbolically
very important to him in a world where he sees himself treated as a
child.

In this chapter our main focus is on the marital expectations and
roles that children and adolescents develop, and on the importance of
these expectations and roles for the future adult years. We will look
first at love and marriage as symbols of adulthood; secondly, at the
social process of mate selection; and finally at some of the ways in
which parents serve as marriage role models for their children.

* ROBERT R. BELL is an Associate Professor of Sociology at Temple University.
His books include: *Sociology of Education: A Sourcebook; Marriage and Family
Interaction;* and *Premarital Sex in a Changing Society.* He has also written a num-
ber of articles on the sociology of the family and sexual behavior.

LOVE AND MARRIAGE AS ADULT SYMBOLS

For most Americans, love and marriage go together as do the prover-
bial horse and carriage. However, love as the reason for marriage is a
recent social invention. This change was closely related to the shift of
emphasis from the family as a group to the family member as an individual. When the family group had greater control in choosing the
marriage partner, premarital love was not nearly as important. The
main values stressed in the selection of a mate were meant to satisfy
the needs of the family unit, not the particular needs of the individual
who was to be married. However, with mate selection increasingly in
the hands of the individual, love became an important factor. Loving,
and being loved, satisfied the ego-needs of the two individuals involved.

Most Americans believe that marriage must be preceded by love and
that the only satisfactory consequence of being in love is to marry.
If two people in love cannot marry for some reason, it is generally
viewed as a tragedy by the individuals and as unfortunate by society
at large. American literature is full of stories of individuals who have
led lives of misery and unhappiness because they could not marry their
beloved. The reactions of society to unfulfilled love seems to vary as a
function of society's value judgments. If a woman chooses against love
and marriage and pursues a career, she receives little sympathy from
society, and her "basic womanliness" is often subject to question. If
she does not experience love and marriage because she must care for
an ailing or aging parent, it is a different story. She is now treated with
respect and sympathy (Bell, 1963).

Love as Learned Behavior

Love, its importance both in and of itself, and as a prerequisite to
marriage, is learned behavior. People are born with the capacity for
all kinds of social learning, including the capacity for love. However,
people must learn to love as they must learn, for example, to hate. They
must also learn ways and means of controlling and expressing their
love. That is to say, they must learn the general patterns of when and
how to express love (with some room for individual variations) within
the social patterns of their society.

The American culture regards some form of love relationship as an
ideal for all periods of a person's lifetime. The newborn infant will,

with some socialization, presumably enter into a love relationship with his parents. Since the socialization of the child affects his preparation for future adult love relationships, the early participation in, and learning of, love becomes a significant cultural factor. If young children are conditioned to marriage as a future adult expectation before they learn of love as the prerequisite to marriage, it may be because marriage and marrige roles are easier to identify with and grasp than the more abstract concept of love. Children usually learn to perceive love and marriage as basic adult characteristics. They learn to believe that these values are as natural to their future as their growing to an adult height.

When children reach adolescence, the part that love plays in their lives increases. They hear others telling about their love experiences (often imaginary) and begin to anticipate these experiences for themselves. Because love is thought of as "grown-up," and because adolescence is a period of age-role insecurity, love is yearned for as a proof of attaining adult status. Some implications of these pressures are pointed out by Kirkpatrick (1955, p. 273) who writes: "Young persons of dating age fully expect that sooner or later they will be caught in the magic spell of love and experience the pangs and delights which seem as inevitable as growing older or being mortal. It is well-known that cultural expectations produce real results."

To what extent adolescents seek out love for its own sake and to what extent they seek it out for its symbolic adult attributes is hard to say. No doubt both influences are operating. Another pressure is added if the *mode* of the peer group is to fall in love. Few other groups in American society demand as much conformity as the adolescent subgroup. Thus, the adolescent is simultaneously reaching for and being pushed into a new role. Oftentimes when the adolescent feels he has found love, his new self-image becomes very important to himself and to anyone else who cares to observe it. As Morton Hunt (1962, p. 374) puts it, the "jaunty step, new-minted optimism, and smug contentment of the adolescent in love means that he has found two things to be of great value—his beloved, and himself." He has attained that which society has taught him to seek and attain.

In the United States, the cultural conditioning is often so effective that the adolescent, and many times the adult, believes that when he has fallen in love, he has discovered something distinctly unique—something unknown to others, past or present. When the individual who has fallen in love thinks of his experiences as unique, mysterious, and without precedent, it is usually the result of cultural learning

(Waller and Hill, 1951). He has so well internalized his cultural values into his personality structure that he has come to believe that they have originated within himself.

As the young person reaches late adolescence and enters the early adult years, there is an increase in the various pressures that help propel his internalized value of finding love. Because marriage is of great importance in the American society, especially for the girl, love must be encouraged to develop so that marriage will occur during the accepted age period. Goode (1959) argues that because love, as related to marriage, is so important to society, it must be controlled before it appears. Therefore, the constant early emphasis on the value of love is closely related to the future marital choice. Parents frequently pressure the young person to fall in love; more specifically, they try to direct their children to fall in love with the "right kind of person." When parental pressure starts early in adolescence, parents are often able to control the children's choice of a love partner. As Goode (1959, p. 43) has so aptly put it: "[Parents] threaten, cajole, wheedle, bribe and persuade their children to go 'with the right person,' during both the early love play and later courtship phases." The degree to which this pressure is exerted will vary, of course, with the parents and with the cultural or sub-cultural group to which the family belongs.

The adolescent's age peers can support or undercut parental influence, depending on whether the general values of the parents and the peer group are alike or different. When the values are essentially the same, the individual will, presumably, suffer only minimal conflict in finding an appropriate love partner. But when parents and peers differ, the potential for conflict is great and depends upon the influence and meaningfulness of each of the pressure groups for the individual.

Pressures intensify during the age period when an increasing number of the individual's age peers are finding love and marriage. The peer group splits sharply between the "chosen" and the "unchosen." Increasingly concerned with his negative *unchosen* status, both the individual and his parents may actively try to wipe out the stigma.

During adolescence there often emerges a rather sharp attitudinal sex difference. Girls are generally much more preoccupied with thoughts of marriage than are boys of the same age. One important reason for this difference is that marriage is seen as far more meaningful for the future adult role of the girl than for the boy. It is our contention that the most important adult role for the majority of American girls continues to be that of wife-mother. For her to achieve this role, it is customary to first fall in love. The achievement of the boy's most important adult role, that of choosing and entering into an occupation, is not dependent upon his being in love. In fact, the boy may view love as a threat to his occupational achievement. He fears that marriage and parenthood may either restrict his needed education or not allow him to direct his full energies toward achieving success in his occupation.

Let us look further at the differential learning experiences of boys and girls with regard to love and marriage. Parents, at the time of their child's birth, subject the child to some important socialization differences which are dependent upon the child's sex. These general child-rearing differences for boys and girls are reflected in their eventual views on love and marriage. For example, during early childhood, boys and girls are consistently taught their sex roles. This is done in dress, the toys they are given, how adults interact with them, and so forth. It is of interest to note that the toys given to young children are often related to their future adult roles. Boys frequently receive toys related to romantic versions of adult occupations, e.g., sports equipment, soldiers' suits, and so forth. Girls are given such toys as dolls, miniature household appliances, etc., that are closely linked to the expected roles they will play as a wife-mother-housekeeper.

Henry (1963, pp. 149–150) suggests that when children enter school, the "boys' society pivots on games requiring teams, and there are few boys' games of any prestige that can be played individually." It is difficult for young boys to avoid group life and team life. Henry goes on to say that by contrast "little girls play with their dolls, their sewing, their cut-outs, or their jacks, and their talk is not about rules of the game, about trying hard and winning, but about the trivia of their semi-isolated play." The most important factor, with respect to the difference in play for young boys and girls, may be that the boys' group *provides* the setting for him to validate his sense of developing masculinity. However, the girl seeks her developing sense of femininity *with reference to* the boys and not as a part of any girls' group. Therefore, in contrast with the boy, it is not until much later, when the girl enters dating and courtship, that she has the opportunity to validate her basic sex role.

One of the problems during adolescence is that in the boy-girl relationship, the girl has more of an investment than does the boy. This greater female investment is a pattern that continues on through the adult years. That is, boys are often increasingly concerned about school work, going to college, and their future occupations. By contrast, girls are more concerned about dating, meeting the right boys, and interpersonal problems (Adams, 1964). As Henry (1963, p. 169) says, ". . . boys ruminate about their place in society and girls ruminate about boys" during adolescence.

The greater importance of dating and courtship for the girls than for boys is also reflected in the significance given to boy-girl relationships by the parents. The girl finds that her parents, especially her mother, are very much interested in her dating and her future marital possibilities. The greater importance of the parents for the daughter is reflected in Henry's (1963) finding that girls often mentioned their parents in connection with their courtship activity. On the other hand, in the same area, not one boy mentioned his parents.

We know that it is common for many young people to regard love and marriage as highly idealistic or romantic. Staton, in another part of this book, discusses this point with respect to sex education. He notes that it is usual for the girl to focus on the romantic aspects of love. It is not surprising then, to find that when the adolescent girl projects her thoughts into her future marriage, she may have an unrealistic view of the role she will fulfill. For example, adolescent girls can identify with the future roles of wife and mother, but not that of housekeeper. Hunt (1962, p. 144) writes that "the modern girl likes to envision herself as a slim, girlishly appealing young mother, mistress of a charming immaculate home, and perhaps part-time teacher or author—but not as her own housemaid."

Age and Marriage

Out of the complex of values about love and marriage in American society come general approval and encouragement for young marriage. This is reflected in the fact that a greater proportion of Americans than ever are marrying at earlier ages. In 1890, the median age at first marriage in the United States was 26.1 years of age for males and 22.0 years for females. By 1964, this figure had dropped to 23.1 years of age for males and 20.5 years for females (Rodman, 1965). This change also reflects a decrease in the age difference between husbands and wives from 4.1 years in 1890 to 2.6 years in 1964.

It appears that the lowest age for marriage was reached around 1950 and that since that time it has leveled off (Burchinal, 1965). Burchinal (1960) found that very young marriages usually involve young girls and their slightly older husbands, involve premarital pregnancies in between approximately one-third to one-half of all cases, and disproportionately involve persons with lower or working-class backgrounds. Another study of young marriages (Moss and Gingles, 1959) indicates that girls who marry young are emotionally less stable than those who marry later. They also have less satisfactory relationships with their parental families.

There is some slight evidence that the frequency of young marriages may be decreasing. Any decrease may be at least in part influenced by more extended formal education. Burchinal (1965) suggests that greater high school and post-high school attendance should lead to some reduction in the young marriage rates. As evidence, he points out that among 17-year-olds, school dropout rates declined from 32 per cent in 1950 to 24 per cent in 1960.

THE PROCESS OF MATE SELECTION

We have discussed adolescence as a period of increasingly involved boy-girl relationships which may result in mate selection and marriage at young ages. Even when young marriage does not occur, the dating relationships of adolescents are important to the later choice of a mate. Therefore, in this section we will look at some of the major forces that influence the adolescent's choice of a husband or a wife.

In all cultures, a number of persons of the opposite sex are theoretical marriage mates; yet, in no culture is the selection of the marriage partner one of random choice. There are always restrictions that limit or affect the final decision. All cultures have social, and most cultures also have personal, restrictions. The social restrictions relate to such factors as the person being of the proper age, not already married, not too closely related, and so forth. The personal factors involve the individual's satisfaction of his ego-needs, as in the United States where reciprocal love is of great importance.

In most cultures, the selection of a mate has not usually rested with the young person entering into marriage. Often the possible mates are determined by the parents, usually the father, or other elder males connected with the family. The parents limit the choice of a marriage partner for a number of reasons. Two of the most important of these are that in a patriarchal society, the father makes most of the important decisions; and secondly, the choice of a marriage partner is often related to economic factors which are of importance for the family. Through the use of a bride price and a dowry system, marriage relationships are based on economic alignments between families. When the young person selects a mate, the limits of choice have usually been set up in advance by the father. In spite of all these considerations, when the final choice of a specific mate is made, most cultures have given the young person at least some say in the procedure.

The shift from a patriarchal family to one more democratically oriented has been related to the emergence of love as a prerequisite for marriage. In the United States today, a great stress is placed on the individual's right in the determination of his spouse, and the rationale of romantic love seems to provide the individual with an orientation for mate selection. A possible explanation for the importance of romantic love is that it "has filled an ideological vacuum, caused by the disappearance of arranged marriages" (Stephens, 1963, p. 206).

However, in the United States, parents still have some influence on the selection of their offspring's spouse. Parents influence their offspring by passing on the values that affect his selection of a mate. Parents more directly influence this process when their children discuss their choice of a marriage partner with their parents. It is of some interest to note that today, in contrast with the patriarchal system of the past, the mother is more apt to be consulted than is the father. Burgess and Wallin (1953) have found that the mother is consulted by 62 per cent of the men and 70 per cent of the women. The father was consulted by 44 per cent of the men and 32 per cent of the women. Discussion with a friend or friends by the male was as frequent (43 per cent) as discussion with his father, and the daughter was more apt to consult her friend or friends (42 per cent) than her father. While the evidence indicates that parents continue to play a part in their offspring's mate selection, it seems safe to assume that the young person is more often the ultimate selector today than he was in the past. The Burgess and Wallin study also found that 51 per cent of the men and 42 per cent of the women did not consult anyone on the wisdom of their choice. We will discuss in a later section the influence of parents on marital decisions as a function of how the parents play their own husband and wife roles.

It is known that mate selection for most people in the American society is a gradual process that starts with dating and moves through the courtship process. It does not usually happen to the individual "all of a sudden," but rather is the culmination of the young person's preparation over a number of years. Determined by his previous experiences and ego-needs, a person reaching the age of marriage starts to focus on a particular individual. The person's values have been pretty well established at the age of marriage, and the general type of person he will marry has, within reasonable limits, already been determined.

The experience and values leading up to mate selection are a combination of emotional and rational factors. Waller and Hill (1951, p. 195) write: "A man does not select the type of woman who will make a good wife, all things considered; he almost necessarily selects the sort of woman with whom he can fall in love, and women likewise select husbands on the same gloriously irrelevant basis." The direction, whether romantic or rational, will vary with different individuals. Regardless of individual variations, the young person who is selecting his own mate places far greater importance on the personal and emotional factors than do his parents when they are aiding in the mate hunt.

The anthropological data illustrates that when free mate selection becomes a part of a culture, it is proceeded by courtship based on personal needs and values. Stephens (1963, p. 187) writes: "If people are free to choose their own spouses, then individual motives come into play: romantic love, sexual desire, loneliness, desire for children and full adult status, or more exotic motives. (One motive for marriage among the Siwai is the desire to raise one's own pigs.)"

Parental Influence on Mate Selection

In our culture, what has happened has been a breakdown, to a high degree, of control by parents over the marital choices of their offspring. As previously mentioned, this is not to suggest that parents are no longer influential in their children's marital decisions, but rather that their influence over mate selection is now less direct and more subtle. Therefore, in this section we will look at some of the ways in which parents of the American middle class continue to influence their children in their dating, courtship, and eventual choice of a marriage partner.

In traditional societies, a part of the importance of the older generation, and especially that of the father, was based on the need for generational continuity in the family. In the past, questions of inheritance, kinship ties, alignments through marriage, family name, and overall respect and responsibility for the older generation were important in permitting two individuals to enter into a marriage. Also, in traditional patriarchal societies, there was little free recreational time for the younger generation. Even if they had free time, the distance between families in a rural society, as well as the limited means of transportation, made social interaction outside of the family difficult.

However, over the past 50 or 60 years the rate of social change has been extremely rapid. That is, urbanization, new methods of transportation, and mechanization have greatly altered the traditional family structure. They have also made many of the traditional values, which supported family continuity, of little importance. During this period the younger generation has been, for the most part, removed from the work force and kept in school. As Borow discusses some of these trends and problems within a separate chapter, we shall not consider them further here. Suffice it to say that for the last 20 years, the middle-class adolescent has been supported by his affluent parents. He has had free time and money to spend, and as a result has developed new patterns of dating, going steady, and earlier marriage. These changes have been generally made possible by an American economy that can afford to maintain a noneconomically contributing middle-class adolescent and young adult population. With respect to the values of this group, Johnstone and Rosenberg's chapter will be of interest to the reader. They have interviewed almost a total population of 16-year-olds in one community (Webster Grove) and report on their findings.

While the adolescent population is limited in its productive capacity, it is a highly important consumer segment of the American buying population. It is estimated (*Newsweek*, 1966) that when allowances and incomes from part-time and summer jobs are combined, the 1966 income for the nation's teenagers was about twelve billion dollars. This averages out to be an income of about $670 per teen per year. It seems clear that for many middle-class adolescents, their life is characterized by both social *and* economic freedom from their parents. It would appear then, that many adolescents can have their cake and eat it too. That is, they are economically supported by their parents and yet can, to a great extent, live a daily life quite independent of their parents. For many young people, emancipation from parents occurs quite abruptly at the time they marry. (Of course, for others it does not occur even then.) It is somewhat ironical that many single young people, who have a freedom made possible by the economic support of their parents, reach full fledged adult status through marriage only to discover that they have to give up many of their single freedoms. For the majority, however, this pattern of breaking the bonds of parental authority through marriage is a common experience. As Stephens (1963, p. 395) says: "Our society is unusual in the joining of marriage with sudden, radical emancipation."

While our social norms have been altered to the extent of giving adolescents greater freedom in their heterosexual relationships, we still maintain legal control over the adolescent who wishes to marry at too young an age. Generally speaking, the rule in the United States is that before 18 for the boy and 16 for the girl, neither they nor their parents can allow them to marry. Next there is a span of several years where we say in effect that the young are old enough to marry but not old enough to make the actual decision. There is generally an age range from 18 to 21 for the male, and from 16 to 18 for the female, where they can marry only if their parents give their legal consent. Once the upper age limits have been passed, the parents have no legal control over their children marrying.

As suggested earlier, there are a variety of highly important and often subtle ways in which parents influence their children's views about courtship and eventual mate selection. The parental influences are based on the fact that the parents have close control over their children from birth on, to teach and influence, both consciously and unconsciously, a vast range of values, norms and roles. The fact that the parental involvement is usually one of high emotional interaction, with a minimum of competition during the early years of childhood, makes the impact of the parents very important.

For many years there has been the argument that children grow up to seek a mate similar to their parents of the opposite sex (see Beller's discussion of the psychoanalytic viewpoint in the chapter on theories of adolescent development). Recent research indicates that the development of an ideal mate image in the mind of the young is not necessarily influenced by the parent of the opposite sex. The ideal mate tends more often to resemble the most loved parent. Therefore, the basis for an ideal mate image is not an automatic, instinctive, affectional response to the parent of the opposite sex. It is rather due to the conditioning of the affectional response patterns in early childhood (Waller and Hill, 1951). Assuming then that a close parental relationship is important, from where does this ideal image for a future mate come? The answer would seem to be that the child's idea of the most desirable traits to seek in a mate is most frequently influenced by his mother. This is because the mother is usually the closest parent to her children of either sex. Prince (1963, p. 95) concludes that the "influence of parental image on the ideal mate concept shows that the ideal mate for both men and women is one with qualities similar to those of mother."

Over the long run, it may be that parents do not actually serve as direct role models for the ideal images which their children develop, but that the parents' values orient and possibly circumscribe the direction in which their children's romantic interests will ultimately go. Parents may also influence their children's values in a variety of indirect ways. For example, parents may encourage their children to interact with one group of children and discourage their interaction with other groups. The various groups of children may differ by social class, religion, race, ethnic background, neighborhood and so forth. Or when children become involved with "undesirables," the parents may directly forbid their continued interaction or use techniques of withdrawal of privileges or love to enforce their wishes. These overt and direct attempts to control the dating and courtship behavior of their children often reflect parental desperation. In all probability, the attempts are also doomed to failure. To accomplish the same goal, an undoubtedly far more effective technique is the transmission of parental values so that ultimately the children will refrain from dating certain people because they, the children, make the choice.

All the current concern with so-called adolescent rebellion and the flouting of parental values appears to be minimal in the area of mate selection. By that, I mean that the vast majority of young people grow up and select a mate well within the range of acceptability to their parents. Ideally, probably no mate is good enough for one's child; realistically, most mates are quite acceptable. One piece of evidence for the indirect influence of parents on their children is that during adolescence most young people feel they have a high degree of freedom from parental demands. A nationwide survey of teenagers (*Newsweek*, 1966) found that 86 per cent felt that their parents minded their own business. The ultimate and strongest proof for the indirect influence of parental values is that the vast majority of young people do eventually marry within the same social class, race, religion, and ethnic background as their parents.

THE PARENTS AS MARRIAGE ROLE MODELS

Probably the most important impact that parents have on their children's future marriage is that generally the parents are the only adults that children have to observe in the wide range of intimate values and behavior associated with marriage. Most children grow up to learn how a husband performs and how a wife acts, both independently and in relationship to one another, from observing their parents' marriage.

The importance of the parents as marriage role models is seen when we realize how few alternative marriage role models are available to children. The marriages of other relatives and friends are almost always limited as a source of observation. Furthermore, this limited interaction means that one's chance to observe other marriages is usually limited to the "public" side of that marriage. Rarely do we see the private nature of marriage role relationships—except in the case of our parents' marriage. While parents have a private side to their marriage that their children never (or seldom) see, it is obvious that this private dimension is more available for inspection than it is in most other marriages.

Mass media, particularly movies and television, often project an image of marriage and marriage roles, but it is doubtful if this projection has any real influence on the younger generation's development of marriage role expectations. When one realizes that the type of marriage given the greatest publicity is that which is unhappy or ends in divorce, it would appear that our mass media have had little causal impact. In fact, the "soap opera" view of courtship and marriage may have a positive result for many viewers, giving them a chance to compare their personal marital experiences with those miserable marriages portrayed, and leading them to feel that their marriages are better off by comparison.

The impact of parents on their children's development of marriage role models for themselves and their spouses may be shown in several ways. One is to look at the manner in which children grow into marriages which follow patterns similar to those of their parents. Over the years a number of studies (e.g., Kirkpatrick, 1955) have indicated that children coming from homes where their parents' marriage has ended in divorce have had a greater probability of their own marriage ending in divorce; i.e., greater than did children coming from homes where their parents' marriage had remained intact. There is some evidence that a young person has a better chance of success in his own marriage if his parents' marriage was successful (Waller and Hill, 1951). Research also shows that children from homes where their parents' marriage ended through death have a higher probability of divorce than do children from homes where the parents' marriage remained intact (Kirkpatrick, 1955).

The higher divorce rate among children of divorced parents may be caused by several factors. Having experienced their parents' use of divorce as a means of dealing with marital problems, the children have a familiarity with this type of a "solution." That is, for many there undoubtedly continues to be a stigma associated with divorce because it seems too foreign to themselves and their "kind." But for those who have grown up with it, through their parents' experience, divorce is not foreign and is a pattern of behavior that is sometimes used by their "kind." It should not be overlooked that for some children of divorces quite a counter reaction may occur. They may decide that they are not going to have their marriages end in divorce under any condition.

If the marriage of the parents' ends while the offspring is a child or adolescent, it often means that the remaining parent is not only no longer filling a marriage role, but is now playing a combined parental role. That is, whether the marriage ended through divorce or death, the parent rearing the children is doing so as an isolated parent (as long as he or she does not remarry). In most cases the continuing parent is the mother, and she is often called upon to fill a combined parental role. One consequence is that the mother becomes much more responsible and forceful than she would be if she still had her husband present. The children growing up under these circumstances may develop an image of the woman's role (both as mother and as a wife) as being very responsible and forceful. If they take this image into their own marriage, and the person they marry has an image of a more balanced set of responsibilities for the husband and wife, there is a definite potential for marital difficulty. While we have examined this problem within the context of parental death or divorce, it is, of course, not limited to these situations. If for any reason the marital role expectations of the newly-wed young couple are different, for example coming from homes with differing emphases on the dominance of the husband or wife in the marriage, it might be expected that this would be a potential source of conflict.

SUMMARY

We have suggested that when adolescence is reached in our society, there is an increasing concern about marriage. This concern may not be with marriage as such, but rather with marriage as it is viewed by the adolescent as symbolizing full adult status. We have also suggested that while parents continue to have control over their children's selection of a mate, this has been greatly reduced in that the parents' influence is usually indirect. It is now exerted through the socialization of the child as he grows toward maturity and in the way in which the parents serve as marriage role models. By the time most young people reach late adolescence, their values with regard to mate selection and marriage roles have been shaped to a marked degree by their parents. During adolescence, the marriage values which children have acquired from their parents may be supported by their age peers. Whatever the sources of the various influencing forces, each individual must ultimately be responsible for his own mate selection and the fulfillment of his own marriage role.

REFERENCES

Adams, J. F. Adolescent personal problems as a function of age and sex. *Journal of Genetic Psychology*, 1964, *104*, 207–214.

Bell, R. R. *Marriage and family interaction.* Homewood, Ill.: The Dorsey Press, 1963.

Burchinal, L. G. Research on young marriages: implications for family life education. *Family Life Coordinator*, 1960, 9, 6–24.

Burchinal, L. G. Trends and prospects for young marriages in the United States. *Journal of Marriage and Family*, 1965, 27, 243–254.

Burgess, E. W. and Wallin, P. *Engagement and marriage.* Philadelphia: J. B. Lippincott Co., 1953.

Goode, W. J. The theoretical importance of love. *American Sociological Review*, 1959, 24, 38–47.

Henry, J. *Culture against man.* New York: Random House, 1963.

Hunt, M. M. *The natural history of love.* New York: Harper and Row Publishers, 1959.

Hunt, M. M. *Her infinite variety.* New York: Harper and Row Publishers, 1962.

Kirkpatrick, C. *The family as process and institution.* New York: Ronald Press Co., 1955.

Moss, J. J and Gingles, R. The relationship of personality to the incidence of early marriage. *Marriage and Family Living*, 1959, 58, 592–595.

Newsweek. The teenagers. March 21, 1966.

Prince, A. J. and Baggaley, A. R. Personality variables and the ideal mate. *Family Life Coordinator*, 1963, *12*, 38–42.

Rodman, H. *Marriage, family and society.* New York: Random House, 1965.

Stephens, W. N. *The family in cross cultural perspective.* New York: Holt, Rinehart and Winston, 1963.

Waller, W. and Hill, R. *The family.* New York: The Dryden Press, 1951.

CHAPTER 13

The Disadvantaged and Lower Class Adolescent

E. V. Kohrs *

THE POOR, FREQUENTLY REFERRED TO AS "THOSE ON THE OTHER SIDE OF the tracks," cannot be confined in our thinking to any one locale or ethnic group. Geographically, a large percentage would be called Southerners. Many are concentrated in urban slums. Others are found in the less visible rural areas, migrant labor camps, and reservations.

Thirty years ago poverty was regarded as an ordinary condition of life. Prior to this, the poor were the Oriental, Central and Eastern European, German, Irish and Scandinavian immigrants who lacked special skills. The goal of many of these individuals was to remove themselves from the strings of poverty as the economy advanced. The *new poverty* is found in the pockets of second and third generation urban, rural and slum poor. These individuals represent the *hidden American* who has not been able to succeed and is now faced with limited opportunities and ability to adapt to the discipline of our modern economic world.

Technological change, with its effect on entry level jobs for youth (see Henry Borow's chapter), cannot be considered apart from the culture of poverty in which the teenager has lived. It is scarcely necessary to support the hypothesis that the economic conditions of youth are determined to a measurable extent by those of their parents. The problem of accommodating these products of the post-war boom is reflected in some alarming statistics. There are nearly one million unemployed youth who represent a third of all jobless workers and between 12 to 15 per cent of the labor force (Howard, 1965; U.S.

✳ EL DEAN V. KOHRS is the Director of the Passaic (New Jersey) Children's Bureau. Prior to this he was the Administrator of Counseling at the Kilmer Job Corps, Center. He has published several articles in the area of psychological testing.

287

Department of Labor, 1966). This rate approaches 60 per cent for Negro teenagers, and as high as 70 per cent for minority males from the city slums who do not have a high school diploma (Conant, 1961; U.S. Department of Labor, 1966).

Associated with the concern about unemployment has been the rate of disqualification for military service. One-third of all young men in the nation turning 18 would not qualify if they were examined for induction into the armed services. One-half of these rejections would be for medical reasons, the remainder for inability to qualify on the mental test (President's Task Force, 1964). McNamara (1965) reported that of those who failed for mental reasons, 60 per cent are not working and 40 per cent had dropped out of school to support families. Forty per cent of their fathers are unemployed, and of those employed, 25 per cent hold unskilled jobs.

Another perspective is provided by the typical adolescent enrolled in the Job Corps (Office of Economic Opportunity, 1965). Typically, he is 17 years old, unemployed, and looking for work. He has finished the eighth grade, been out of school eleven months, and has a median reading ability at the fifth grade level. He is seven pounds underweight. As a group, 80 per cent have never seen a dentist or physician professionally. Sixty per cent come from substandard housing; 57 per cent from over-crowded living facilities; 63 per cent from families where the primary wage earner is unemployed; 40 per cent from families on relief; and 68 per cent from families in which the parents hold unskilled jobs.

There have been a number of descriptive studies of the various poverty sub-cultures. For example, Heller (1966) has written about Mexican American youth. The problem of the rural youth who lacks the social, educational and vocational resources to live in an urbanized society has been extensively discussed by Burchinal (1965). Life in Boston's "West End" slum neighborhood, distinguished by a female-based family, is described through the eyes of a participant-observer (Gans, 1962). An understanding of the Appalachian culture with its life of individualism, family tradition, and fatalism has been presented by Weller (1965).

The most extensively studied group has been the Negro (e.g., Frazier, 1949; Karon, 1958; Clark, 1964; U.S. Department of Labor, 1965). Discrimination and the splintering of the family, which dates back to the effects of slavery, have set the Negro apart from other groups. The matriarchal pattern, resulting from a high divorce, separation, or desertion rate, has been considered to have had a profound influence on the adolescent—particularly the Negro male. It has been noted that the female is preferred by Negro mothers or mother substitutes and receives a better education. The Negro boy, on the other hand, often has no adult male with whom to identify (Dai, 1949). His maleness is deprecated in the home and white community, and he unwittingly identifies with maternal authority (Ausubel, 1965).

Part of the unemployment problem for the Negro adolescent can be explained by the higher birth rates and the lower death rates which have increased the size of the younger age group; however, a larger part can be attributed to education. The U.S. Department of Labor (1965) found that at the ages of 16 and 17, nearly 40 per cent of nonwhite boys still enrolled in school are retarded a year or more below grade level. Furthermore, two-thirds of the 18-year-old Negroes (as compared to slightly less than 20 per cent of non-Negroes) who took the Armed Forces Qualification Test, failed (Neufville and Conner, 1966). The consequence is that the Negro adolescent male is further barred from an experience where he is treated as an equal in a masculine world. To the Negro adolescent, the cause of his plight is his skin color; rather than his education, the shrinking number of jobs, or his lack of parental support.

Interestingly, the Negro adolescent may be more capable and less disturbed than his white counterpart at the lowest level of social class. As an explanation for this it might be argued that the Negro, because of discrimination, has remained in a state of poverty, while the white youth who is at the lowest rung of the economic ladder is more often there because of lack of competence or motivation.

Studies between Negroes and whites, with social class levels equated, have generally shown that the similarities are greater than the differences (Pierce, Reid and King, 1959; Herzog, 1963; Rosenhan, 1966; Schmuck and Luszki, 1966). In a discussion of Italo-Americans, Negro-Americans and American Jews, Ianni (1964) notes that it is not the ethnic association or adolescent subculture alone that produces norms, but rather a blending process whereby the cultural norms learned as a child filter through and blend with norms of adjustment to life in general.

It is commonly agreed that a culture of poverty does exist whose inherent qualities are a matter of public knowledge and record. The problem, however, is the lack of precise differentiations and criteria for the classification of this group. Non-middle class, the poor, the lower class, the working class, the deprived, the underprivileged, and so forth, are terms which are often used interchangeably. There is more agreement as to the existence of the "poor" than on how he should be classified. At times, the "lower class" will refer to the population which suffers from severe poverty as the result of unstable employment and unskilled work. At other times, the "lower class" title is used to designate those higher paid service workers in stable employment sometimes classified as "lower middle" or the "working class." Few studies have made distinctions between the low working class and the lower lower class.

When one uses criteria for classification which place stress on culture and the importance of social and psychological problems, it leads to a discounting of class variables. Yet, concern with economic deprivation discounts the importance of status variables. Typically, research on the lower classes has not utilized a design based on a typological approach (e.g., Miller, 1964) which recognizes the differences that might occur as a result of an economic as well as a style of life criterion.

In the guideline issued by the U.S. Department of Health, Education and Welfare (1966), the phrase disadvantaged youth is defined as "culturally, economically, socially, and educationally handicapped youth." The emphasis here is with the environmentally disadvantaged young person who lives in neighborhoods or communities characterized by large numbers of out-of-school, unemployed youth; by family incomes at a poverty level; by high rates of unemployment and low levels of occupational skill; by adults with limited formal schooling; and by a high proportion of substandard, overcrowded, and inadequate housing.

HISTORICAL RESEARCH

Interest in deprived youth is not a recent phenomenon. Examples of philanthropic and moral concerns are seen in the "Sunday School" movement of the early 1800's, organized by Robert Raikes of Gloucester, England; and Jane Addams' Hull House, which was founded to deal with the problems of immigrant and economically deprived youth (Addams, 1910). The early depression years saw the publication of three major works dealing with the effect of industrialization on youth: a classical work on distinct youth subcultures (Thrasher, 1927), an autobiography of a young delinquent (Shaw, 1929), and a study of the effect of family life, gang associations and neighborhood conditions on the development of a criminal career (Shaw, 1931). Subsequent years saw the application of cultural anthropology to the study of a mid-western industrial city (Lynd and Lynd, 1937), the social life of a southern town (Dollard, 1937; Davis, et al., 1941) and a New England town (Warner and Lunt, 1941, 1942).

While these earlier studies contained descriptions of adolescents from various socio-economic classes, the classic work is the intensive study of 735 Elmtown youth who graduated from the eighth grade in a midwest community between 1938 and 1941 (Hollingshead, 1949). Using case histories to investigate the relationship between class level and such things as school attendance and career expectations, support was found for the hypothesis that the social behavior of adolescents is functionally related to the position of the family in the social structure of the community. In addition, it was found that the lower class is divided into two groups. The "upper-lower" class contained, for the most part, semi and unskilled workers who earned regular wages but who did not associate with the "loafers" or the "criminal class." One-third were from homes broken by divorce, separation, or death. The families were larger and begun earlier. They were not religious and did not belong to organizations or churches. The "lower-lower" class was the lowest class rank in the community. Their work was menial, low paying, and irregular. Parents, children and in-laws lived in two or three rooms; marriage took place in the middle teens for the girls and in the early twenties for the boys. Seventy-eight per cent of the mothers gave birth before 20 years of age (Hollingshead, 1947). Exploitive sex relations were frequently found between these girls and the boys from higher classes. Twenty to 25 per cent of the children were born out of wedlock. The odds against a boy finishing high school were 230 to 1 while for the girls they were 57 to 1. About two-thirds of these youth did not attend dances, plays, or parties. Only girls from the lower class worked in restaurants as waitresses or in stores as clerks.

A companion study of 16-year-olds from Elmtown reveals a positive correlation between social class and character reputation (Havighurst and Taba, 1949). However, social class position was not as important as conformity to the middle-class students of the school. The intelligence quotient, achievement, and reputation were more highly related to social class than were values.

The conclusions coming from a more recent, longitudinal, study by

Havighurst, *et al.* (1962) are of interest. In the lowest class, only two of 57 boys went to college and half were drop-outs from the public school. Fifty per cent of the delinquents also came from this group. The authors conclude that one-third of the River City youth who drop out have started school with cultural handicaps and inadequate encouragement. This helps to build up a record of failure and frustration, which in turn, drives them out of school.

Gottlieb and Ramsey (1964) have noted that the aforementioned studies have all used a common methodological approach. It has consisted of classifying the social class of a stratified sample, coding responses, comparing responses between the social strata, and finally, noting the significance of social class once a relationship is found. This type of analysis has led to a confusion of relationships with causative factors; or treatment of classifications as real rather than the devices imposed by researchers to handle continuous dynamic factors (Mayer, 1953).

Nevertheless, these intensive community studies have pointed up the inequality of rewards in our society and have provided descriptive information with respect to the lower class adolescent. They have also laid the groundwork and hypotheses for much of the research which has followed. In the following sections of this chapter, we shall consider some of this research under the headings of: education, vocational development, socialization, and delinquency or anti-social behavior.

EDUCATION

There is common agreement that school failure is frequently associated with impoverished circumstances. The lower class youth is more likely to drop out of school, have lower tested achievement and intelligence, and have greater reading and learning difficulties. Sexton (1961) reports that this group will attend schools having larger classes, more teacher substitutes, less experienced teachers, and poorer educational programs. The lower class youth is less likely to go to college even when his ability is high (Flanagan *et al.*, 1964); is likely to be older than his higher status classmates (Coleman, 1940); and is likely to have lower predicted college achievement (Hewer, 1965).

Studies have linked up the lower class adolescent's difficulty in school with home finances (Perella and Bogan, 1964), school retardation and low intelligence (U.S. Department of Agriculture, 1960), dissatisfaction with school (Bledsoe, 1959; Reis and Rhodes, 1949), and value conflicts between the school and parents (Davie, 1953). From these references it should become apparent that no single cause but rather a multiplicity of factors are involved.

Different Values

A number of investigators have been concerned with the effects of values on cultural sub-group educational achievement. Public education is permeated with middle-class values which are foreign to the lower class student (Havighurst and Neubauer, 1949). Consequently, the lower class adolescent who brings his parental values with him is penalized and rejected. In a study of teachers' reactions, the lower class adolescent was felt to be more difficult to discipline and teach because his behavior was not morally acceptable (Becker, 1952). Compounding the problem is the antagonism of the parents who may fail to support the school (Toby, 1957). In an effort to escape these pressures, the lower class adolescent withdraws from the school; thus giving up whatever opportunity he has for social mobility through education.

Types of Achievement

Another school of thought focuses on achievement rather than parental values. Coleman (1962), in a study using a sample of Elmtown high school students in 1957, found familial identification and parental social class to be less important than qualitative types of achievement (such as athletic recognition) in determining status (also see: Parsons, 1959). Using these leads, Gottlieb and Ramsey (1964) studied these influences on student educational and occupational aspirations. Contrary to previous findings (Hollingshead, 1949; Kahl, 1953), only a third of the lower class boys mentioned their parents. In addition, they received their greatest support, with respect to achievement, from the school personnel.

Preparation for Learning

A third point of view is presented by those who reason that the disadvantaged is a poorer student because he has a qualitatively different preparation for the learning process (Deutsch, 1964). While the initial differences between the lower class individual and other students are small during the first years of school, a cumulative deficit develops as a function of time. For example, Vane (1966), in a study of high school students, found that achievement is set early in school and that few students improve after making a poor start. Furthermore, Negro and white tend to achieve on levels which are commensurate with their socio-economic standing.

Although he is sometimes quite articulate, language development and auditory discrimination is often lacking in the disadvantaged youth (Riessman, 1964). Consequently, words are used to impress others rather than as concepts; and there is a greater sensitivity to the reactions of others rather than to ideas (Gans, 1962). Argument is not by common sense, but by a series of anecdotes. Strang (1966) argues that an important effect of this cumulative deficit is the development of a reading disability which leads to school failure. The inability to read, in contrast to his apparent verbal fluency, is a threat to his self-esteem. The fear of failure or of being overpowered by the teacher results in the dropping out of school because of the difficulty of expressing ideas in school language.

Learning Capacity

Considerable attention has been given in the 1960's to the learning capacity of the minority student (Katz, 1964). The Negro has not performed well on mental ability tests (Dreger and Miller, 1960; Pettigrew, 1964; Shuey, 1966). Some studies have concluded that there are real racial differences (Shuey, 1966). Others, noting that test scores for whites in isolated, restricted environments (e.g., Appalachian regions) are also low, believe the differences are due to environment. Clark (1965) has argued this point persuasively, and Coleman (1966) has presented documentation that segregation in the South and conditions in the ghetto of the North have resulted in grossly inferior education. Roberts (1946, 1950, 1963) has provided data to show that few Negro graduates of segregated high schools meet entrance requirements of nonsegregated colleges; however, over a period of two years they were able to increase their test scores. Those from Northern high schools, with a somewhat higher average level, also increased their scores.

Despite the difficulty of obtaining a good matching of groups for study, several investigators have used designs which have supported the contention that environment is the important factor. Canady (1951) and Fifer (1964) found differences in test performance between middle and lower class samples within ethnic groups. Also, test differences were found in Negroes and whites at the seventh and eighth grade levels but not in the first grade when the subjects are matched for sex and intelligence (Tehan, 1965). There is not space for an extensive discussion of this problem within our chapter. Suffice it to say that, at the present time, the evidence does not seem conclusive on either side of this important issue. The reader will find that Nichols' chapter on *nature and nurture in adolescence* definitely gives this issue a new look.

Rehabilitating the Educationally Disadvantaged

There have been a number of programs aimed at meeting the needs of the disadvantaged adolescent. New York City has undertaken a demonstration project to provide better quality education (Board of Education, 1961). Socially deprived boys and girls entering the high school academic program were placed in small classes and given remedial and psychological assistance. At the end of their senior year they were compared with preceding classes. Superiority was shown in the per cent graduating from high school, completing academic programs, and continuing their education beyond high school. In the process, their average intelligence quotients rose from 92.9 in the ninth grade to 102.2 in the twelfth grade. Sloats and Butterfield (1965), using a token system of reinforcement while giving 40 hours of reading instruction, were able to dramatically increase the reading level of 14-year-old Mexican American delinquents who had a long history of school failure.

Several programs have been developed for the older student. These programs have recognized that as the student moves further along in school, the cultural and educational differences become more pronounced. One of the more important programs is "Gateway English." This program has been developed by the Project English Curriculum Study center of Hunter College (New York City) under a grant from the United States Office of Education. It is not conceived as being remedial or clinical, but rather aimed at the disadvantaged whose reading abilities are several levels below their grade.

The Manpower Development and Training Act has provided counseling, job development services, and training in institutional and on-the-job programs. A high percentage of the "graduates" were employed, mostly with the employer who gave the training. Although a number subsequently left employment, those remaining represented significant successes (U.S. Department of Labor, 1966).

Several programs for 16 through 21-year-old youths have grown out of the War on Poverty. The Neighborhood Youth Corps brings together unemployed youth and unfulfilled needs within the community. Financial assistance and work experience are provided (Howard, 1965).

The *Job Corps* is an operation which has focused on residential training for youth who are out of school and out of work. Two types of centers have been used to capitalize on the beneficial effects of a change in living environment. The *urban center* is located on an unused military base. The program is contracted to private corporations, state agencies, and universities who provide work in reading and mathematics along with vocational training. The vocational training emphasizes those fields which are anticipating increased employment in the coming years; e.g., automotive repair, culinary arts, and business machine repair. The *rural center,* located on Government operated public lands, has stressed remedial education at a lower educational level as well as conservation work. The rural center is smaller than the urban center and has provided only limited vocational training. The urban center (1000 to 2600 youth) has been more flexible and encouraged to develop its own training program so that the effectiveness of various approaches might be evaluated.

Although the conception of the Job Corps contained many sound ideas, the high cost of training per "graduated" enrollee, the large dropout rate, behavior control problems, and inadequate administration have seriously jeopardized the continued existence of the program. A number of issues have been raised as well. These issues are: Is a residential program more effective than a community based program? Should the program reflect middle-class values? Can large numbers of youth be housed together regardless of race, geographic background, age, or urban-rural classifications? Should training be primarily vocational, educational, or both; and should the emphasis be on rehabilitation or training?

Two years after the opening of the first urban Job Corps Center in 1965, the enrollment and number of training programs offered at a number of these centers had been reduced to half. The Job Corps, while offering the best opportunity for creative experimentation with the educational and vocational training of the disadvantaged which this country may ever see, has had in the opinion of the writer, most disappointing results.

VOCATIONAL DEVELOPMENT

Occupational choice for the lower class adolescent is frequently forced on him by the attitudes and teaching methods used (Becker, 1952), the lack of encouragement provided in school (Hollingshead, 1949), and the concentration of the particular social classes in the school attended (Wilson, 1959). A number of authors have stressed the many faceted importance of the family's influence on the vocational choice of the adolescent (Rogoff, 1953; Super, 1957; Roe, 1956; Ginsberg, *et al.*, 1961). Because the level of occupation is frequently used as a determiner of social economic class and considered the best predictor of the latter, the inherited effect perpetuates employment in low level occupations. There is a feeling on the part of many vocational counselors that the product from a culturally deprived urban slum or rural shanty dwelling does not fit the *mold* presented by vocational theorists. Resignation, inability to resolve problems of vocational choice within the limitations set by parental income, and a number of other factors are instrumental in encouraging counselors to ignore or disregard theory and to operate on the basis of their own biases. It is frequently easier to encourage the entrance of a young person, from this background, into the low "inherited" vocational level of his subcultural group. Certainly this is easier than making an attempt to build programs where more positive self-concepts will be developed.

Justification for a lack of attention to the lower-class adolescents' vocational development and decisions is frequently sought in studies which indicate a relationship between social stratification and the level of aspiration (Youmans, 1954; Himmelweit, 1955; Sewell, 1957) or unrealistic vocational preferences and inability to adjust to jobs (Amos, 1964). These studies give little insight into the nature of this difference or to the possibility that there is no single type of aspiration that can be considered to be absolutely related to class status.

Several researchers have indicated the importance of social mobility as a factor in motivation. Hieronymus (1951) found that the social and economic expectations of tenth graders, and the anxiety generated by this expectation, are more important than the factor of intelligence (at least as we presently measure it). Rosen (1956) has extensively studied achievement motivation and found that social mobility can be explained in terms of the differing motives and values of the social classes, and that no one demographic factor explains achievement motivation; although motivation scores are generally lower in the lower classes (1961). Kahl (1953), concerned with the large variances that existed in the prediction of the vocational aspiration of high school boys, even though I.Q. and family status had been controlled, found that those aspiring to higher occupational status came from families who were dissatisfied with their position. These families encouraged their sons to seek higher opportunities. A related study by Ellis and Lane (1966), using a group of lower class Stanford University matriculants, found that the upwardly mobile lower class youth resembled his middle-class counterpart but tended to consider more compromises; i.e., he considered occupations of lower prestige. These were based on his uncertainty of excelling in his chosen field or in achieving success as an adult.

Other reports have indicated that the lower class youth shares the general values of society, but not to the same degree (Caro, 1966). He aspires to get ahead, but not at the same absolute level as the higher status youth (Empey, 1956). Further, he shows a high concensus of agreement with respect to aspiration, but a lowering of his expectations when it comes to educational plans (Stephenson, 1957). Herriott (1963) found support for the hypothesis that the aspirations of adolescents vary with the level of their self-assessment in relation to others and with the level of expectation which they perceive as being significant for others to hold for their behavior. Out of the dynamic experience of social situations, concepts of success and failure develop. Those who perceive the chances of success as small, or have repeated experiences of failure, stop trying or reduce their levels of aspiration.

Rosen and D'Andrade (1959) have claimed that there is a difference in achievement motivation between Negroes and whites. Smith and Abramson (1962) matched 33 Negro and white high school students for age, sex, intelligence and social status. They found that Negroes do not differ in achievement motivation but do have significantly higher educational and vocational aspirations. In a somewhat related manner, Henderson (1966) argues, on the basis of an exploratory study of 200 adolescents in Detroit's first anti-poverty target area, that differences between middle and lower class Negroes are not in their achievement motive but in the available opportunities to achieve their goals. While very little difference was shown in *ideal* aspirations, large differences appeared in *real* aspirations between middle and lower-class youth. Most lower class youth expected to enter semi-skilled or clerical jobs, but the middle-class youth expected to be engaged in professional or managerial occupations.

Similar differences were reflected in a study using measured vocational interests. Pierce (1959) found a definite relationship between the socio-economic status of eleventh grade students and their interests as measured by the *Kuder Vocational Interest Inventory*. The lower class preferred mechanical, domestic service, and clerical jobs, while the higher status group preferred social activities and jobs with high prestige value and responsibility.

The author performed a visual inspection of several hundred of Clark's *Vocational Interest Inventory* profiles of Kilmer Job Corps enrollees and observed that a majority of their interests were similar to employees in the food service or truck driver occupations. Preliminary studies run at the same location by the author revealed that the typical adolescent male in this group has a low maturity score on Crites' *Vocational Development Inventory*. The answers of the group indicate a lack of occupational information and knowledge of their own ability. These observations raise some intriguing questions as to whether vocational choice reflects a basic oral and mobility need, a lack of occupational information about other fields, a belief that only certain occupations are open, or merely another facet of the general cumulative deficit which characterizes the lower class adolescent.

SOCIALIZATION

Numerous articles and books have documented the lower class adolescents' feeling of alienation from society. These adolescents are less likely to participate in intellectual hobbies or extracurricular activities, hold office in a socially recognized organization, or be the recipient of positive community recognition.

Sexual Behavior

Fatalism and a feeling of powerlessness also characterize sexual behavior. The lower class adolescent does not regard himself as an active chooser of a mate (Rainwater, 1960). Selection of a partner is influenced by residential proximity, and courtship is frequently of short duration and accompanied by a lack of planning. This adolescent can be described as being lax, promiscuous, and unable to defer immediate gratification of sexual impulses. It has been found, for example, that in the lower class, 40 per cent of the girls become pregnant before marriage (Hollingshead and Redlich, 1958). Whyte (1943) has reported a strict sexual code which limits the acceptable forms of sexual behavior to the specific girls sanctioned by the group. Kinsey (1948), on the other hand, concludes that it is not gratification *per se* but rather the manner of expressing it which differentiates between the socioeconomic classes. In the lower class, premarital intercourse is more likely to be tolerated as a sexual outlet than masturbation. Studies dealing with this aspect of social class behavior generally lack methodological sophistication since sexual experience is not well defined, nor are illegitimacy studies controlled in terms of knowledge of contraceptives or the rate of illicit coitus.

Poverty and Personality

An important interest of psychologists has been focused on the effect of poverty on psychological characteristics. Although personality constellations have been found to be associated with cultural training (Milner, 1949), when the effect of such variables as the size of the family and the marital status of the mother have been controlled, class status was found to be an insufficient explanation for the individual differences (Nye, 1951). Contrary to the findings in other age groups, no significance was found between mental disorders and class position for the ages between 15 and 24 (Hollingshead and Redlich, 1958). Similarly, Haan (1964) found that ego functioning as an adult had little relationship to socioeconomic status as an adolescent. More important to adult coping behavior were personality variables in the adolescent which were related to social mobility.

While lower class boys are generally considered to be more aggressive (Pope, 1953), caution must be exercised in generalizing. Klausner (1953) found the lower class to be aggressive as a reaction to inferiority and insecurity. Added to this should be Mussen's (1953) observation that while Negroes feel aggression from the environment and have little interest in maintaining a friendly relationship with others, the Caucasians feel rejection and see others as interested in establishing friendly relationships. Although this study did not control for social class differences, my experiences with adolescents in the Job Corps suggest to me that these findings can be generalized to the lower class.

Self-concept studies have also added support to the findings of social class differences. Carroll (1945) and Smith (1952) found that lower class Negroes emphasize such things as happiness, glamor, and beauty more than do upper class Negroes. However, when the effects of sex and race are controlled, social class differences on *ideal* and *self* ratings tend to disappear (McDonald and Gynther, 1965).

The most comprehensive and systematic survey of adolescent self-images has been conducted by Rosenberg (1965). This study involved approximately 5000 students from eleven public schools in New York State. Although dropouts from the junior and senior high school years were not included, it is the most definitive work available on adolescent self images. Data on ten independent variables, including an index of socioeconomic status, were gathered and extensively analyzed. In addition to the usual finding that the lower class strata are less likely to accept themselves, an important norm of family relationships involving father-son closeness was isolated as having a profound bearing on self-esteem. When the upper and lower groups are equated for father-son closeness, the expected self-esteem differences were greatly reduced. In fact, those with low self-images in the upper class had a lower self-image than those in the lower class when the father-son variable was held constant.

Peer Relationships

It is commonly agreed that an important developmental task is the transition from a parental to a peer group frame of reference. In the lower class, it is believed that this transition occurs early because of greater freedom, laxness of restrictions, and an earlier, more abruptly terminated relationship with the parent. In order to determine the psychological effect of this phenomenon, Maas (1951) observed a small group of early adolescent boys and girls and concluded that the lower class were more dependent in their relationships within the peer group primarily as a result of inadequate communication with their parents.

A crucial issue in the socialization process, however, is the role played by the peer group. Davis (1944) has argued that the organization of the peer group and its values is highly influenced by years of subtle indoctrination along class lines and that the peer group merely enforces these values. The close parallelism found between adult and adolescent attitudes in various social strata (Centers, 1950) might be considered as support for the parental influence theory. Because *class* was defined in terms of *class identification,* the Centers' study more correctly supports the view that those who regard themselves as being of a certain class exhibit attitudes similar to others who make the same class identification.

Contradictory findings were obtained by Coleman (1962) in an important study which indicated that the adolescent has his own set of values and lives more and more in a society where the home has less and less ability to mold him. This point of view, indicating that character reputation is more related to conformity to school than to the home, was suggested by the study of character development in 16-year-old *Prairie City* youth (Weckler, 1949).

Phelps and Horrocks (1958), in a multifactorial study, found that the lower class adolescent formed informal groups as a reaction to a predominately middle-class moral and social orientation. These groups offered a form of recognition and status that they were unable to obtain in school. Furthermore, lower class status was associated with the factors of early assumption of adult roles, and identification with their own social class peers while rejecting those of more fortunate means.

From another point of view, the peer group becomes a crucial medium for maintaining class stratification (Kahl, 1957). The reactions to situations and the solutions adopted by lower class adolescents may appear unsocialized to those holding middle-class standards. For example, the lower class youth may avoid the permanent ties of marriage because his economic deprivation prevents him from assuming financial responsibility and stable roots (Rodman, 1964).

The peer group of the *West Enders'* adolescent serves as an *outlet* for action-seeking as contrasted with routine-seeking patterns (Gans, 1962). Because the lower class male had not been prepared for work, he turned to action-seeking gratification within his peer group. The group represented action through competitive encounters in card games, athletic contests, sexual adventure, and attacks on the adult world.

The Sherifs (1964), using the concept of reference groups, hypothesized that individuals who experience common motives enter into repeated interactions which over a period of time are stabilized into status and role positions. In addition, norms are set which regulate the behavior of the group. These reference groups were intensively observed in their natural setting over a five to seven-month period in order to determine if there were differences in the behavior of adolescent boys; differences, that is, based upon their association with low, middle, and high social neighborhood groups. The Sherifs' findings reveal that while there are variations between social groups which are related to characteristic differences in the neighborhoods, there are also common values which are related to membership in a larger society. All groups engaged in socially unacceptable behavior, had common desires for material symbols of success, and contained a critical dimension of power. The differences for the lower group were primarily in goals which did not extend as far as for the other groups. The most tightly knit groups were in neighborhoods where the boys had the most time on their hands. They were also less mobile in these areas and more frequently labeled "asocial."

DELINQUENCY AND ANTI-SOCIAL BEHAVIOR

Delinquent behavior is generally considered an adolescent phenomenon which occurs during the period when the individual is freeing himself from pre-puberty parental authority in an effort to achieve adult status. This factor alone, however, does not account for the rise of the norm-violating adolescent behavior which has been the focus of many popular articles. While the teenage population rose only four per cent in 1964, the number of delinquency cases handled by juvenile courts increased 14 per cent.

The public has noted the climbing delinquency rate with alarm and has related it to a myriad of causative factors. Research on delinquency prevention and control has typically pointed out the lack of opportunity for healthy recreation, undesirable environments, low moral values, and pattern of criminal behavior (Glueck, 1966).

As a group, the juvenile delinquent has been characterized by high rates of drop-out and poor school adjustment (Kvaraceus, 1945). There are also a number of studies which relate social class to delinquency. Wattenberg and Balistrieri (1950) report that the socioeconomic factor is the best predictor of repeated offenses in gang members. Palmore (1963), in a study of children from families receiving financial assistance from Aid to Families with Dependent Children (AFDC), found higher delinquency rates in the lower socioeconomic group. The factors most related to delinquency were being non-white, male, less intelligent, or a school drop-out. When class, age, race, and sex were controlled, little or no association was found between AFDC aid and delinquency.

Several studies support the thesis that class differences will disappear when other variables are controlled. Short and Nye (1957) compared institutionalized training school boys with a high school population. The moderately high correlation usually found between delinquency and socioeconomic status disappeared under these circumstances. Although the highest rate of delinquency was found in those census tracts of San Diego which combined low family status, low economic status, and a high concentration of non-whites, no evidence could be found to show that the rate of delinquency was based on class factors when family status and racial status were held constant (Polk, 1957). Nye and others (1958) could not find sufficient evidence to reject the null hypothesis that "there is no significant difference in the delinquent behavior of adolescent boys and girls in the various social economic strata." Scarpitti (1965) reports that a negative perception of middle-class values and feelings of blocked opportunities do not result in delinquency in lower class boys if the boys see themselves in terms of a healthy self-image.

Pine (1965) has discovered a strong relationship between social mobility (but not class level) and delinquency. Adolescents moving downward in the social structure commit more delinquent acts. Those whose aspirations are in an upward direction are the least involved. The lower class youths were involved in proportionately more serious offenses, but the upper middle class students were found to be involved in alcohol offenses and collective delinquent activity. Academic performance and educational aspiration appeared to have a significant bearing on where a youth fell on the continuum of norm behavior (Pine, 1964). Pine's study would appear to accentuate the importance of the school system as an agency that both aids and impedes the mobility process.

The importance of the interplay between social class striving and the barriers to social and material goals was studied by Brennan (1963). In her sample of lower class Negro girls, Brennan argues that one must distinguish between the poor who accept middle-class standards and the poor who reject these standards. Because the lower class Negro girl has little hope of breaking established barriers, little or no impulse control is seen, as witnessed by the pattern of attack on lower class white girls, and in prostitution.

Difficulties in Research Design and Definition

Most investigators of delinquency have employed one of two approaches. The first research design has been to divide a community into high and low delinquency areas and then to compare the social and economic characteristics of each. The second design uses delinquent and non-delinquent subjects and compares them on the basis of economic, social or psychological variables. With either method, differences are considered to be the factors contributing to the causes of delinquency.

Confusing the investigations in the area of delinquency is the problem of defining delinquent behavior. In addition, the lack of consistency of reporting delinquent behavior by the police, social agency, or adults, presents difficulties for the investigator. What is considered norm-violating behavior by one person may not be so in the eyes of another. It is also well known that the treatment and reporting of delinquent acts by the police vary with the social and economic characteristics of the person or area. Because a relationship between slums and delinquency is expected, more police are concentrated in these areas with the likely result of a higher apprehension rate. All of these problems confuse research designs and the interpretation of the results. Consider, for a moment, the different definitions of delinquency which are implied in Tappan's (1949) list of twelve points at which delinquency can be identified:

1. All children's behavior.
2. Specific delinquent conduct.
3. Discovered delinquency.
4. Delinquency alleged to court.
5. Unofficial court delinquency.
6. Official adjudicated delinquency.
7. Delinquency resulting in arrest or report.
8. Delinquency resulting in court hearing.
9. Delinquency commitments to institutions.
10. Delinquency submitted to agency intake.
11. Cases of delinquency accepted for treatment.
12. Cases recorded by agency as delinquent.

Is it surprising that definitions and the results of research have frequently been more confusing than helpful in our understanding of lower class youth? The Sherifs (1964), noting the confusion over the conceptions of delinquency and wishing to avoid the problem of defining delinquent behavior, studied the actions of adolescents in terms of the group norms which were established in their various reference groups. They found that members of all social groups were engaged in socially unacceptable behavior, regardless of social rank. This has been a fresh approach, but we still have a long way to go before the confusion caused by different definitions and research designs is clarified.

Theories Explaining Deviant Behavior

Several theories have been advanced to explain deviant behavior among the lower class and disadvantaged adolescent. Writers have noted the effect of social disorganization, and cultural traditions and conflict. An early theory, reflecting the ideology of the mental health movement, considers deviant behavior an outgrowth of environmental frustration and social disorganization. Being deprived of "warmth," understanding, and standards of realistic discipline was thought to contribute to the "short run hedonism" on which these youth operated. The difficulty with this theory is that there has not been an adequate test of the hypothesis that the statistical differences noted between child rearing practices of the lower and middle classes account for the pragmatic differences in behavior at a later age. Whyte (1955) noted in his report on Cornerville, for example, that delinquent behavior was not caused by a lack of organization, but rather the failure of one social organization to mesh with another.

At least four different theories can be identified as growing out of recent studies of gang behavior. Several writers have associated the lower class delinquency with a masculine protest arising out of the effects of living in a female based household or the need to prove one's self as a man (Cohen, 1956; Gans, 1962). Toughness and the associated delinquent acts are not a clinical entity but rather a form of aggression which reassures the delinquent that he is tough. The Burton and Whiting hypothesis (1961) is an extension of this theory. Their review of studies about American, as well as primitive societies, suggests that the initiation rites of primitive societies, which brainwash and purge away the feminine identity, are comparable to the initiation practices of delinquent gangs.

Associated in some respects to the preceding discussion is the theory that delinquency is a product of the transition from adolescent to adult status (Block and Niederhoffer, 1958). Writers who follow this thesis generally emphasize that: adolescence is a time of storm and stress (see Beller's discussion in the chapter on Theories of Adolescent Development); definition of role and initiation to adult status is not understood nor clear; or, adult society delays entrance into their society by blocking participation in certain things while requiring it in others. With respect to this latter point, consider such things as drinking age, voting age, and military service. Under these circumstances it is assumed that the lower class youth is likely to exhibit more delinquent activity because of the conflict between his peer culture and the model provided for him by society.

In each of the previously mentioned theories, it is probable *that research conducted with adequate controls would reveal little or no social* class difference. It can be easily argued that the factors of stress, fear of not being masculine, and the lack of a "warm" family environment, can be found at any class level.

A second type of theory focuses on the basic disparity between class goals, values, and major concerns (Kvaraceus and Ulrich, 1959; Miller, 1958, 1965). Major characteristics of lower class youth are toughness, outsmarting others, seeking excitement, fatalism and autonomy. His clash with the middle-class values of restraint, ambition to get ahead, and being law abiding, get the lower class youth into trouble. This youth sees his surest route to prestige and status in his street gang and its norm violating behavior. Those who do not become delinquent are explained as being upwardly mobile exceptions who aspire to middle-class status (Kvaraceus, 1966). Support is offered for this theory by the Rim City, Massachusetts study of Gerald Pine (1965) discussed earlier.

The *differential opportunity theory* (Cloward and Ohlin, 1960) represents a fusing of the *differential association theory,* as developed by Sutherland and Cressy (1960), and the theory of a breakdown between goals and the legitimate avenues of access to them, as espoused by Merton and Nesbit (1961). This theory, unlike that of the culture conflict school of thought, assumes that lower class youth accept most middle-class goals but are prevented from pursuing them due to a discrepancy between aspirations and opportunities. While most middle and many lower class youth are able to achieve these goals through legitimate means, more lower than middle class youth have difficulties. Factors which influence this discrepancy are inadequate support from parents, poor study habits, lower intelligence, and discrimination in treatment at schools.

The differential association theory accounts for second and third generation AFDC children who, through a process of acculturation, learn adaptive modes and values which permit their survival in their culture of poverty. In the face-to-face interaction and communication processes of his primary group, antisocial delinquent behavior is learned. This theory would explain the popular notion that one gets into trouble by running with the "wrong crowd." The structural theory of Merton, on the other hand, regards deviant behavior to be a society's over-investment in certain cultural goals without providing simultaneous avenues of access to these goals.

These theories present fertile areas for future research. One point of view stresses lack of motivation and upper mobility aspiration as a problem. Others emphasize the problem of opportunity and capacity. The question of how to rehabilitate lower class delinquents is an essentially uncharted field (Peterson, 1966). Not only has it been difficult to establish delinquent personality types, but also, associated successful treatment prescriptions are in need of extensive study. What is recognized is that an adolescent's motivation, attitude, and self-image cannot be minimized, regardless of class status.

SUMMARY

The lower class adolescent, already molded by the effects of a legacy of poverty, faces an adult future of limited alternatives, insecurity, and a feeling of powerlessness to control his life. He is frequently characterized by poor educational achievement, a lack of positive vocational development, different socializing experiences, and the belief that all those in authority are "crooked." Increased sophistication of research is correcting long held impressions that lower class youth place no value on educational achievement, that they lack vocational aspirations, that they reject stable marriages, or that they exhibit more norm violating behavior.

We should expect the increased sophistication of research in this field to also point to new applications in training and in rehabilitation. Much of this has been and is being learned from the War on Poverty programs. Future research should require that clearly defined populations be drawn from the various subcultures of poverty, that a variety of data gathering techniques be used, and that statistical tests examine the variances within groups to determine the effect of such factors as dropping out of school, sex, and race. Fertile areas for research might be the role and importance of a masculinity drive, the effect of an alienated dependence syndrome, and the differences in sensory attentiveness in the educational setting. In programs aimed at the lower class adolescent, the emphasis will be on the use of the peer group itself to change attitudes. In addition, emphasis will be placed on physical and concrete approaches to learning and visible goals or opportunities which are attainable and lead to a material betterment of one's life.

REFERENCES

Addams, Jane. *The spirit of youth and the city streets.* New York: Macmillan Company, 1910.

Amos, W. E. Job adjustment problem of delinquent minority group youth. *The Vocational Guidance Quarterly,* 1964, *13,* 87–90.

Ausubel, D. P. Ego development among segregated Negro children. In: A. H. Passow (Ed.), *Education in depressed areas.* New York: Columbia University Teachers College Press, 1965.

Becker, H. S. Social-class variations in the teacher-pupil relationships. *Journal of Educational Sociology,* 1952, *25,* 451–465.

Bledsoe, J. C. An investigation of six correlates of student withdrawal from high school. *Journal of Educational Research,* 1959, *53,* 3–6.

Block, H. A., and Niederhoffer, A. *The gang: A study of adolescent behavior.* New York: Philosophical Library, 1958.

Board of Education. Demonstration guidance project. *Fourth Annual Report.* New York: Board of Education, 1961.

Brenman, Margaret. Urban lower-class Negro girls. In: Grossack, M. N. (Ed.), *Mental health and segregation.* New York: Springer Publishing Company, 1963.

Burchinal, L. G. (Ed.) *Rural youth in crisis: Facts, myths, and social change.* Washington, D.C.: U.S. Government Printing Office, 1965.

Burton, R. V., and Whiting, J. W. M. The absent father and cross-sex identity. *Merrill-Palmer Quarterly of Behavior and Development,* 1961, *7,* 85–95.

Canady, H. G. The American caste system and the question of Negro intelligence. *Journal of Educational Psychology,* 1951, *42,* 161–172.

Caro, Francis G. Social class and attitudes of youth relevant for the realization of adult goals. *Social Forces,* 1966, *44,* 492–498.

Carroll, Rebecca E. Relation of social environment to the moral ideology and the personal aspirations of Negro boys and girls. *School Review,* 1945, *53,* 30–38.

Centers, R. Social class identification of American youth. *Journal of Personality*, 1950, *18*, 290–302.

Clark, K. B. *Youth in the ghetto: A study of consequences of powerlessness and a blueprint for change.* New York: Harlem Youth Opportunities Unlimited, Inc., 1964.

Clark, K. B. *Dark ghetto: Dilemmas of social power.* New York: Harper & Row, 1965.

Cloward, R. A., and Ohlin, L. E. *Delinquency and opportunity: A theory of delinquent gangs.* New York: The Free Press of Glencoe, 1960.

Cohen, A. K. *Delinquent boys: The culture of the gang.* London: Routledge and Kegan Paul Ltd., 1956.

Coleman, H. A. The relationship of socio-economic status to the performance of junior high school students. *Journal of Experimental Education*, 1940, 9, 61–63.

Coleman, J. S. *The adolescent society.* New York: The Free Press of Glencoe, 1962.

Coleman, J. S., *et al. Equality of educational opportunity.* Washington, D.C.: U.S. Government Printing Office, 1966.

Conant, J. B. *Slums and suburbs.* New York: McGraw-Hill, 1961.

Dai, B. Some problems of personality development among Negro children. In: Kluckholn, C., and Murray, H. A. (Eds.), *Personality in nature, society, and culture.* New York: Knopf, 1949.

Davie, J. S. Social class factors and school attendance. *Harvard Educational Review*, 1953, *23*, 175–185.

Davis, A. Socialization and the adolescent personality. *Forty-third yearbook of the national society for the study of education.* Chicago: University of Chicago Press, 1944, Part I, 198–216.

Davis, A., Gardiner, B. B., and Gardner, M. R. *Deep south: A social anthropological study of caste and class.* Chicago: University of Chicago, 1941.

Deutsch, M. The disadvantaged child and the learning process. In: Reissman, F., Cohen, J., and Pearl, A. (Eds.) *Mental health of the poor.* New York: The Free Press of Glencoe, 1964.

Dollard, J. *Caste and class in a southern town.* New Haven: Yale University Press, 1937.

Dreger, R. M., and Miller, K. S. Comparative psychological studies of Negroes and whites in the United States. *Psychological Bulletin*, 1960, *57*, 361–402.

Ellis, R. A., and Lane, W. C. Social mobility and career orientation. *Sociology and Social Research*, 1966, *50*, 280–296.

Empey, L. T. Social class and occupational aspiration: A comparison of absolute and relative measurement. *American Sociological Review*, 1956, *21*, 703–709.

Fifer, G. Social class and cultural group differences in diverse mental abilities. Paper presented at Invitational Conference on Testing Problem. New York, 1964.

Flanagan, J. C., *et al. Project talent.* Final Report to U.S. Office of Education. Cooperative Research Project No. 635. Pittsburgh: University of Pittsburgh, 1964.

Frazier, E. F. *The Negro in the United States.* New York: Macmillan Co., 1949.

Gans, H. *The urban villager.* New York: The Free Press of Glencoe, 1962.

Ginsberg, E., *et al. Occupational choice: An approach to a general theory.* New York: Columbia University Press, 1961.

Glueck, Eleanor T. Distinguishing delinquents from pseudo delinquents. *Harvard Educational Review*, 1966, *36*, 119–130.

Gottlieb, D., and Ramsey, C. *The American adolescent.* Homewood, Illinois: Dorsey Press, 1964.

Haan, W. The relationship of ego functioning and intelligence to social status and social mobility. *Journal of Abnormal and Social Psychology*, 1964, *69*, 594–605.

Havighurst, R. J., and Neubauer, Dorothy. Community factors in relation to character formation. In: Havighurst, R. G., and Taba, H. (Eds.) *Adolescent character and personality.* New York: John Wiley and Sons, 1949.

Havighurst, R. J., *et al. Growing up in River City.* New York: John Wiley and Sons, 1962.

Heller, Celia S. *Mexican American youth: Forgotten youth at the crossroads.* New York: Random House, 1966.

Henderson, G. Occupational aspiration of poverty stricken Negro students. *Vocational Guidance Quarterly*, 1966, *15*, 41–45.

Herriott, R. E. Some social determinants of educational aspiration. *Harvard Educational Review*, 1963, *33*, 157–177.

Herzog, Elizabeth. Some assumptions about the poor. *The Social Service Review*, 1963, *37*, 389–402.

Hewer, Vivian H. Are tests fair to college students from homes with low socio-economic status? *Personnel and Guidance Journal*, 1965, *43*, 764–769.

Hieronymus, A. N. Study of social class motivation: Relationship between anxiety for education and certain socio-economic and intellectual variables. *Journal of Educational Psychology*, 1951, 42, 193–205.

Himmelweit, Hilde T. Socio-economic background and personality. *International Social Science Bulletin*, 1955, 7, 29–35.

Hollingshead, A. B. Selected characteristics of classes in a middle western community. *American Sociological Review*, 1947, 12, 385–395.

Hollingshead, A. B. *Elmtown's youth: The impact of social classes on adolescents*. New York: John Wiley and Sons, 1949.

Hollingshead, A. B., and Redlich, F. C. *Social class and mental illness: A community study*. New York: Wiley, 1958.

Howard, J. Breaking the poverty cycle: The neighborhood youth corps in action. *Manpower Training Facts*, 1965.

Ianni, Francis A. J. Minority group status and adolescent culture. In: Gottlieb, D., and Ramsey, C. (Eds.) *The American adolescent*. Homewood, Illinois: Dorsey Press, 1964.

Kahl, J. A. Educational and occupational aspirations of "common-man" boys. *Harvard Educational Review*, 1953, 23, 186–203.

Kahl, J. A. *The American class structure*. New York: Holt, Rinehart, and Winston, 1957.

Karon, B. P. *The Negro personality*. New York: Springer Publishing Co., 1958.

Katz, I. Review of evidence relating to effects of desegregation on the intellectual performance of Negroes. *American Psychologist*, 1964, 19, 381–399.

Kinsey, A. C., *et al. Sexual behavior in the human male*. Philadelphia: Saunders, 1948.

Klausner, S. J. Social class and self-concept. *Journal of Social Psychology*, 1953, 38, 201–205.

Kvaraceus, W. C. *Juvenile delinquency and the school*. New York: Harcourt, Brace, and World, 1945.

Kvaraceus, W. C. *Dynamics of delinquency*. Columbus, Ohio: Charles E. Merrill Books, 1966.

Kvaraceus, W. C., and Ulrich, W. E. *Delinquent behavior: Principles and practices*. Washington, D.C.: National Education Association, 1959.

Lynd, R. S., and Lynd, Helen M. *Middletown in transition*. New York: Harcourt, Brace, and World, 1937.

Maas, H. S. Some social class differences in the family systems and group relations of pre- and early adolescents. *Child Development*, 1951, 22, 145–152.

Mayer, K. The theory of social classes. *Harvard Educational Review,* 1953, *23,* 149–167.

McDonald, R. L., and Gynther, M. D. Relationships of self and ideal self descriptions with sex, race, and class in southern adolescents. *Journal of Personality and Social Psychology,* 1965, *1,* 85–88.

McNamara, R. S. Hearings on the employment opportunity act of 1964, subcommittee on the war on poverty program, committee on education and labor, House of Representatives, 88th Congress, Second session, March 18, 1964. In: Will, R. E., and Vatter, H. G. (Eds.) *Poverty in affluence.* New York: Harcourt, Brace, and World, 1965.

Merton, R. K., and Nesbit, R. A. *Contemporary social problems.* New York: Harcourt, Brace and World, 1961.

Miller, W. B. Lower class culture as a generating milieu of gang delinquency. *Journal of Social Issues,* 1958, *14,* 5–19.

Miller, W. B. Focal concerns of lower class culture. In: Ferman, L. A., Kornblug, J. L., and Haber, A. (Eds.) *Poverty in America.* Ann Arbor: University of Michigan Press, 1965.

Milner, Esther. Effects of sex role and social status on early adolescent personality. *Genetic Psychology Monograph,* 1949, *40,* 231–325.

Mussen, P. H. Differences between the T. A. T. responses of Negro and white boys. *Journal of Consulting Psychology,* 1953, *17,* 373–376.

Neufville, R. D., and Conner, Caryl. How good are our schools? *American Education,* 1966, *2,* 1–9.

Nye, F. I. Adolescent-parent adjustment: Socio-economic level as a variable. *American Sociological Review,* 1951, *16,* 341–349.

Nye, F. I., *et al.* Socio-economic status and delinquent behavior. *American Journal of Sociology,* 1958, *63,* 381–389.

Office of Economic Opportunity. Program development and analysis, dittoed report dated June, 1965.

Palmore, E. Factors associated with school dropouts and juvenile delinquency among lower class children. *Social Security Bulletin,* 1963, *26,* 4–9.

Parsons, T. The school class as a social system: Some of its functions in American society. *Harvard Educational Review,* 1959, *29,* 297–318.

Perella, Vera C., and Bogan, F. A. Out of school youth. *Monthly Labor Review,* 1964, 1260–1268.

Peterson, W. M. Delinquency: A re-evaluation of current concepts. Paper presented at American Psychology Association Convention. New York, 1966.

Pettigrew, T. F. *A profile of the Negro American.* Princeton: Van Worstrand, 1964.

Phelps, H., and Horrocks, J. E. Factors influencing informal groups of adolescents. *Child Development,* 1958, *29,* 69–86.

Pierce, J. J., Reid, J. B., and King, F. J. Adolescent racial and ethnic group differences in social attitudes and adjustment. *Psychological Reports,* 1959, *5,* 549–552.

Pine, G. J. Occupational and educational aspirations and delinquent behavior. *The Vocational Guidance Quarterly,* 1964, *13,* 107–111.

Pine, G. J. Social class, social mobility, and delinquent behavior. *The Personnel and Guidance Journal,* 1965, *43,* 770–774.

Polk, K. Juvenile delinquency and social areas. *Social Problems,* 1957, *5,* 214–217.

Pope, B. Socio-economic contrasts in children's peer culture prestige values. *Genetic Psychology Monographs,* 1953, *48,* 157–220.

President's Task Force on Manpower Conservation. *One-third of a nation: A report on young men found unqualified for military service.* Washington, D.C.: U.S. Government Printing Office, 1964.

Rainwater, L. *And the poor get children.* Chicago: Quadrangle Books, 1960.

Reis, A. J., and Rhodes, A. L. Are educational norms and goals of conforming, truant and delinquent adolescents influenced by group position in American society? *Journal of Negro Education,* 1959, *28,* 252–267.

Riessman, F. Are the deprived non-verbal? In Riessman, F., Cohen, J., and Pearl, A. (Eds.) *Mental health of the poor.* New York: The Free Press of Glencoe, 1964.

Roberts, S. O. Socio-economic status and performance of Negro college women, North and South, on the ACE. *American Psychologist,* 1946, *1,* 253 (Abstract).

Roberts, S. O. Socio-economic and performance over a four year period on the ACE of Negro college women from the "North and South." *American Psychologist,* 1950, *5,* 295 (Abstract).

Roberts, S. O. Test performance in relation to ethnic groups and social class. Nashville: Fisk University, 1963 (Mimeo).

Rodman, H. Middle class misconceptions about lower class families. In: Shostak, H., and Gomberg, W. (Eds.) *Blue collar world.* Englewood Cliffs, New Jersey: Prentice-Hall, 1964.

Roe, Anne. *The psychology of occupations.* New York: Wiley, 1956.

Rogoff, Natalie. *Recent trends in occupational mobility.* New York: The Free Press of Glencoe, 1953.

Rosen, B. C. The achievement syndrome: A psychocultural dimension of social stratification. *American Sociological Review*, 1956, *21*, 203–211.

Rosen, B. C. Family structure and achievement motivation. *American Sociological Review*, 1961, *26*, 574–585.

Rosen, B. C., and D'Andrade, R. The psycho-social origins of achievement motivation. *Sociometry*, 1959, *22*, 185–218.

Rosenberg, M. *Society and the adolescent self-image*. Princeton: Princeton University Press, 1965.

Rosenhan, D. L. Effects of social class and race on responsiveness to approval and disapproval. *Journal of Personality and Social Psychology*, 1966, *4*, 253–259.

Scarpitti, F. R. Delinquent and nondelinquent perceptions of self, values and opportunity. *Mental Hygiene*, 1965, *49*, 399–404.

Schmuck, R., and Luszki, Margaret B. A comparison of Negro and white students in several small midwest communities. *American Psychologist*, 1966, *21*, 663 (Abstract).

Sewell, W. H., Haller, A. O., and Straus, M. A. Social status and educational and occupational aspiration. *American Sociological Review*, 1957, *22*, 67–73.

Sexton, Patricia. *Education and income*. New York: Viking Press, 1961.

Shaw, C. R. *The jackroller*. Chicago: University of Chicago Press, 1929.

Shaw, C. R. *The natural history of a delinquent career*. Chicago: University of Chicago Press, 1931.

Sherif, M., and Sherif, Carolyn W. *Reference groups*. New York: Harper & Row, 1964.

Short, J. F., Jr., and Nye, F. I. Reported behavior as a criterion of deviant behavior. *Social Problems*, 1957, *5*, 207–213.

Shuey, Audrey M. *The testing of Negro intelligence*. New York: Social Science Press, 1966.

Sloats, A. W., and Butterfield, W. H. Treatment of nonreading in a culturally deprived juvenile delinquent: An application of reinforcement principles. *Child Development*, 1965, *36*, 925–942.

Smith, B. F. Wishes of Negro high school seniors and social class status. *Journal of Educational Sociology*, 1952, *25*, 466–475.

Smith, H., and Abramson, M. Racial and family experience correlates of mobility aspiration. *Journal of Negro Education*, 1962, *21*, 117–124.

Stephenson, R. M. Mobility orientation and stratification of 1,000 ninth graders. *American Sociological Review*, 1957, *22*, 204–212.

Strang, Ruth. The reading ability of disadvantaged adolescents. *Adolescence*, 1966, *1*, 60–69.

Super, D. E. *The psychology of careers.* New York: Harper and Brothers, 1957.

Sutherland, E. H., and Cressy, D. R. *Principles of criminology.* New York: Lippincott, 1960.

Tappan, P. *Juvenile delinquency.* New York: McGraw-Hill, 1949.

Tehan, Sally. An exploratory study concerning the effects of race upon school achievement. *Connecticut College Psychology Journal*, 1965, *2*, 13–23.

Thrasher, F. M. *The gang.* Chicago: University of Chicago Press, 1927.

Toby, J. Orientation to education as a factor in the social maladjustment of lower-class children. *Social Forces*, 1957, *39*, 259–266.

U.S. Department of Agriculture. Characteristics of school dropouts and high school graduates. *Agricultural Economic Report No. 65.* Washington, D.C.: U.S. Government Printing Office, 1960.

U.S. Department of Health, Education, and Welfare, Office of Education, NDEA Institute for Advanced Study. Title XI: *A Manual for the Preparation of Proposals.* Washington, D.C.: U.S. Government Printing Office, 1966.

U.S. Department of Labor. *Young workers.* Washington, D.C.: U.S. Government Printing Office, 1966.

Vane, Julia R. Relation of early school achievement to high school achievement when race, intelligence and socioeconomic factors are equated. *Psychology in the Schools*, 1966, *3*, 124–129.

Warner, W. L., and Lunt, P. S. *The social life of a modern community.* New Haven: Yale University Press, 1941.

Warner, W. L. *The status system of a modern community.* New Haven: Yale University Press, 1942.

Wattenberg, W. W., and Balistrieri, J. J. Gang membership and juvenile misconduct. *American Sociological Review*, 1950, *15*, 744–752.

Weckler, Nora L. Social class and school adjustment in relation to character reputation. In: Havighurst, R. J., and Taba, H. (Eds.) *Adolescent character and personality.* New York: John Wiley and Sons, 1949.

Weller, J. E. *Yesterday's people.* Lexington: University of Kentucky Press, 1965.

Whyte, W. F. A slum sex code. *American Journal of Sociology*, 1943, *49*, 24–31.

Whyte, W. F. *Street corner society.* Chicago: University of Chicago Press, 1955.

Wilson, A. B. Residential segregation of social classes and aspirations of high school boys. *American Sociological Review*, 1959, 24, 836–845.

Youmans, E. G. Social factors in the work attitudes and interests of 12th grade Michigan boys. *Journal of Educational Sociology*, 1954, 28, 35–48.

CHAPTER 14

Sociological Observations on the Privileged Adolescent

John W. C. Johnstone
and Larry Rosenberg *

DURING THE PAST DECADE FEW TOPICS HAVE RECEIVED MORE WIDESPREAD commentary than the character of contemporary youth and their relations with adults. Since the mid-fifties this age-group has attracted the attention of educators, psychiatrists, anthropologists, child psychologists, youth workers, criminologists, newspaper columnists, religious leaders, sociologists, and a variety of specialists who come into contact with young people in the armed forces, the labor force, the federal youth programs, or even as consumers of material goods. Moreover, American youth have been the subject of documentary films presented on all three major commercial television networks and of numerous feature articles in mass circulation magazines.

Although this increase in national attention must be attributed at least in part to the vastly expanded numbers of young people in our population, recent writings have not been primarily concerned with the problem of numbers. Instead, the central issue seems to be generational continuity—or rather the lack of it. Today's youth are viewed as different from those of previous generations not just in their numbers

✻ JOHN W. C. JOHNSTONE is the Senior Study Director of the National Opinion Research Center at the University of Chicago. He has written *Young People's Images of Canadian Society*, and *Volunteers for Learning*. In addition, he has authored a number of articles on the sociology of education, mass communication, and adolescence and youth.

LARRY ROSENBERG is an Assistant Professor of Sociology at Brandeis University. Prior to this he was in the Sociology Department at the University of Chicago. Dr. Rosenberg is the co-author of *Teaching Styles and Learning* and has written articles on topics having to do with the sociology of education, social interaction, and the sociology of mental disorders.

but in their values, morals, actions and general outlook on life. They are portrayed as increasingly involved in and vulnerable to the demands of the so-called "adolescent society" and "youth culture," as increasingly out-of-touch with adults and adult influences, and as disenchanted with the models of adulthood provided them by the parental generation. Few observers dissent from the view that the worlds of youth and adults are further apart today than they have ever been in the past; and many feel that the gap is widening. In a recent study of alienated college students, for example, Keniston (1965, p. 228) observed that "increasing numbers of young Americans find themselves so distant from their parents that they can neither emulate nor rebel against them." This is reflected, he observed, not so much by increased rebellion against parents as by a more widespread "vision of parents and those in their generation as irrelevant, as merely old fashioned or 'square.'" This situation, moreover, is not seen as limited to underprivileged or culturally deprived youth, nor to racial and ethnic minorities in the process of assimilation of upward social mobility. The subjects of Keniston's study were all from the more affluent sectors of American society, and other observers such as Blaine (1966) have gone so far as to cite the wealth of our society itself as a major cause of damaged communication between generations. Indeed, the very emergence of a youth culture is often attributed to affluent economic conditions. Eisenman's general discussion of the values and self-concept of the adolescent (within this volume) will do much to fill out the knowledge of the interested reader in this area.

Other explanations and interpretations of generational discontinuity are plentiful. They range from broad theories concerning age-grading in pre-industrial and industrial societies, to interpretations based on the influence of recent changes in such institutions as the family or the school, to more mundane influences such as television or the automobile. Most writers, however, do hold recent social changes of one sort or another as responsible for a widened gap between generations. Concern over the state of youth has been voiced in practically all societies and ages, but no era as yet seems to have produced the volume of attention currently encountered in our own society. This suggests that large segments of the population experience a sense of isolation from other age-grades, that a good many parents and adults feel uncomfortable with young people perhaps even fearful of them, and that significant numbers of adolescents and young adults are in one sense or another alienated from their elders.

Yet it is not at all clear whether recent public attention on this issue accurately represents the experiences of the population. In many cases these conclusions have been based on little if any solid empirical evidence, and most of the empirical studies which have been done are of non-representative groups of youth. There is also little question that deviant youth, whether delinquent, radical, or Bohemian, have gained a heavily disproportionate attention from the mass media in recent years. The portrait of severed adult-youth relations in American life, in short, is an image for which appropriate empirical support is seriously lacking. Moreover, in spite of a number of researches demonstrating the existence of an elaborate social structure among high school and college-aged youth (e.g., Hollingshead, 1949; Gordon, 1956; Coleman, 1961; or Wallace, 1966), the overall degree to which involvement in the youth culture removes adolescents from adult influences has never been satisfactorily established. In this regard, Turner (1964, p. 143) has noted that the extent of peer rivalry and antagonism has often been underestimated and that "youth-adult tension is more a consequence of youth subculture than its cause."

In this chapter we will present a general overview of the life situation and outlook of young people from the more affluent sectors of our society. We draw widely from past writings and researches on youth and also introduce results from our own recent study of sixteen-year-olds in a prosperous midwestern suburb.*

CATEGORIES OF ADVANTAGED YOUTH

Our specific concern in this chapter is with youth from middle, upper-middle and upper class backgrounds. The view of the social structure we adopt includes just under half of the total population within these categories. At the top is a tiny upper class comprising about 1 or 2 per cent of the population and made up of extremely well-to-do families whose influence is derived primarily though not exclusively from inherited wealth. Little has been written about the distinctive features of adolescence for young people from these backgrounds, although insightful accounts are often found in novels about life in the private school, or in biographical or autobiographical materials. However,

---

* This research was conducted by the authors as the basis for a documentary film on adolescents. The film, "Sixteen in Webster Groves," was produced for CBS-News by Dr. Arthur Barron, and was first shown on the CBS national television network on February 25, 1966. The film depicts adolescent life in Webster Groves, Missouri, a suburb of St. Louis.

there have been no systematic empirical appraisals of adolescents with unambiguously patrician credentials. Most accounts of advantaged youth refer to a somewhat larger aggregate, one more properly designated as the upper-middle class. This refers to the ten per cent of the population made up of the more successful professional and business families. Today the upper-middle class is disproportionately concentrated within the suburban fringes of our largest cities, and its families are typically headed by college graduates who place a high premium on college education and established careers for their children.

Next in order is the middle class proper, sometimes further differentiated into the middle-middle and lower-middle classes. This is a much larger and more heterogeneous grouping covering about 35 per cent of the population and made up of less successful professional and business families, white-collar workers, and more successful manual workers. Most youth from these backgrounds graduate from high school, and many go on to college or receive specialized technical or vocational training beyond high school.

Our discussion is focused on adolescents from these backgrounds. Below this level, to complete the picture, we would identify a large *working class* (another 35 per cent of the population), and somewhat smaller *lower class* (perhaps 20 per cent). Although the precise boundary separating the middle and working classes is difficult to discern, the working class consists in the main of factory and semi-skilled workers who receive hourly or weekly wages rather than annual salaries. Today possibly half to two-thirds of working class youth complete high school, but few go much further. Finally, at the very bottom are those employed in the poorest paying semi-skilled and unskilled jobs, and the chronically unemployed. Few young people from these backgrounds complete high school, and many fail to enter. Most live in urban slums or near slums, or in depressed rural areas. These youth are discussed in considerable detail by Kohrs elsewhere within this book.

ADOLESCENCE IN CONTEMPORARY AMERICAN SOCIETY

Viewed sociologically, adolescence may be defined as a status which individuals occupy during the transition from childhood to adulthood. As is well known, the nature and duration of this status depend very substantially on cultural factors since different societies employ quite different criteria in according their young full rights, privileges, and responsibilities as adult members of the society. As Eisenstadt (1956) has noted, adulthood in most societies commences when individuals are accorded the right to establish a family, and not simply when they acquire the capacity or right to engage in sexual intercourse.

Two recent trends reflect the changing nature of adolescence as a life-stage in our own society. On the one hand, the median marriage age of our population has been declining steadily for several decades, while on the other hand the average number of years spent in school has been increasing. The first of these trends has worked to shorten adolescence as a life-stage, and the second to prolong it. What appears to have been occurring, however, is that youth who have been staying in school longer are not the ones who have been getting married younger. Even though marriage rates among college students are certainly higher today than 20 years ago, they are not nearly as high as many observers suggest, and don't even come close to the rates exhibited by youth already out of school. Among 20- to 24-year-olds in the 1961 class of graduating college seniors, for example, Spaeth (forthcoming) found that only 16 per cent had ever been married. By comparison, in 1962, 60 per cent of the total population in this age-group had been married at least once (U.S. Bureau of the Census, 1963). In other words, continued attendance in college works as a strong deterrent to early marriage, and thus tends to prolong adolescent status.

While it is not at all uncommon these days for sons of factory workers to attend college, one cannot but be impressed at the different rates of attendance among persons from various social class origins— even among those with equivalent scholastic ability. This situation has been documented repeatedly over the years, and though rates of college-going are generally higher today than in the past, the gap between social classes does not appear to have closed. On the basis of a national survey of high school seniors in 1955, for example, Rogoff (1961) found that among those scoring in the highest quartile on scholastic ability, intentions regarding college dropped from 83 to 43 per cent across five socioeconomic groupings. Moreover, social origin appeared to be a more important influence than talent: 53 per cent from the top social but bottom ability grouping planned to attend college compared with just 23 per cent in the highest ability but lowest socioeconomic group. And in a more recent study of high school seniors in the Milwaukee public school system, Sewell and Armer (1966) reported socioeconomic background to be among the strongest predictors of college plans. When they divided their sample into thirds on the basis of measured intelligence, rates of college plans among those in the top ability group dropped from 66 to 49 to 25 per cent across three socioeconomic levels.

One of the most striking features of middle- and upper-class adolescence in our society, then, is its duration: as a life-stage it simply lasts longer for these youth than for their generational counterparts from lower social origins. Middle- and upper-middle class youth stay in school longer, enter the labor force later, and marry older. As a consequence they are attached to the youth culture for a longer time than their working and lower class peers, who following the high school years tend to disappear rapidly into the adult world.

PROLONGED ADOLESCENCE AND
MIDDLE-CLASS SOCIALIZATION

As a social stage, adolescence makes many demands on its incumbents, but the most important one is to maintain student status. As Keniston (1965, p. 402) has remarked, "the price of admission and permission to stay in the youth culture is steadily rising academic performance." This not only requires individuals to be successful in the academic arena, but to be content with a status which denies them full economic and personal autonomy. On both these counts, middle- and upper-class youth are at an advantage—they do better in school and are more likely to have internalized values which are consistent with delayed adulthood.

A great deal has been written about the emphasis middle-class parents place on deferred gratification (for example, Schneider and Lysgaard, 1953; or Rosen, 1956) and it is generally agreed that a principal cultural difference between social classes is in regard to time orientation. It has been remarked, for example, that because of their concern with family heritage and tradition, the upper classes are oriented primarily to the past; the middle classes, with their emphasis on personal self-control and rational planning, live primarily for the future; and the lower classes, reflecting the adage "live for today and let tomorrow take care of itself," are oriented mainly to the present. This is an oversimplification, but the important point is that traditional middle-class values—personal control, rational planning, and the capacity to postpone short-run rewards for long-term gains—are highly congruent with the demands of extended adolescence.

THE WEBSTER GROVES STUDY

Our study of the youth from one suburban community provided evidence that young people from higher socioeconomic backgrounds do indeed incorporate expectations of a long-term adolescence. The results which we will report are based on a case study of 16-year-olds living in Webster Groves, Missouri, during October, 1965. The data for this study were collected in two ways: first, from questionnaires which were administered in the public and parochial high schools in the community (as well as to youth from Webster Groves who were attending parochial schools located elsewhere in the St. Louis area); and second, from observing and interviewing a substantial number of the teenagers who had filled out questionnaires. Useable questionnaires were completed by a total of 688 persons, an estimated 90 to 95 per cent of the 16-year-olds living in the community at the time of the study.

Although virtually all of these youth were solidly middle class, their backgrounds were sufficiently varied to permit comparisons, and we were able to divide them into three groups based on their father's occupation and the level of schooling attained by their parents. In the comparisons which follow, the *highs* are those with fathers in professional and managerial occupations and with at least one parent a college graduate; our *intermediate* group consists of those whose parents met one of these criteria but not both; and the *lows* are youth whose parents met neither. In terms of national norms, the *highs* are solidly upper-middle class in background, the *intermediates* are marginally upper-middle class, and the *lows*, the bulk of whose fathers were small businessmen, salesmen or skilled tradesmen, would be middle-middle or lower-middle class. To avoid confusing racial with social-class differences, the results presented here pertain to white students only. Of the 688 respondents, 35 were non-white.

How did these groups differ in their anticipation of adulthood? Table 14-1 summarizes three reactions of relevance here—aspirations to marry early, eagerness to launch a career, and the desire to own a car while still in high school. Since employment and marriage are the two main avenues of departure from adolescence, two of the measures clearly reflect a person's readiness to assume adult roles. Cars, on the other hand, are an important commodity of the youth culture itself, particularly for males living in non-urban settings, and the desire to own a car while still in high school does not necessarily mean that one is restless with the adolescent status. Having a car of one's own does

TABLE 14-1

ORIENTATION TO ADULT STATUSES

(A) *Marriage.* As far as you yourself are concerned, what would be the ideal age to get married—assuming you had found someone you wanted to marry?

	Boys Socioeconomic Background			Girls Socioeconomic Background		
	High	Intermediate	Low	High	Intermediate	Low
Per cent who wanted to be married by 21 or younger	12	18	27	20	26	39
Total N =	100	96	77	103	115	106

(B) *Career readiness.* Everyone likes to daydream a little bit. Suppose you had just finished up all your schooling and had the option of either taking off a year or two to do something you'd always wanted to do, or of starting in on a job that would enable you to begin building your career right away. Which do you think you'd rather do—take the time off or start right in on building your career?

	Boys Socioeconomic Background			Girls Socioeconomic Background		
	High	Intermediate	Low	High	Intermediate	Low
Per cent who would begin their career right away	47	59	62	42	48	58
Total N =	110	108	88	107	120	106

(C) *Car Ownership.* Do you have a car of your own? IF NO: Are you planning to get a car of your own before you get out of high school?

	Boys Socioeconomic Background			Girls Socioeconomic Background		
	High	Intermediate	Low	High	Intermediate	Low
Per cent who owned a car already or who planned to get one before getting out of high school	22	41	41	11	16	26
Total N =	110	108	88	106	118	107

indicate some degree of autonomy from parents, however, and a willingness to defer ownership until after the high school years implies reconciliation with adolescent dependency.

Marriage, Careers and Cars

From Table 14-1 it is clear that youth from the lower class levels in this community displayed a greater sense of urgency in all three of these areas. First, more than twice as many *lows* as *highs* hoped to be married by 21, and though at the same socioeconomic level more girls than boys were disposed to early matrimony, fewer of the *high* girls than *low* boys were oriented in that direction. In other words, while it is generally the case that women marry younger than men, it is also true that social class influences cut across these sex-linked propensities. It should also be noted, however, that in the community as a whole only the girls deviated from national norms in their views about when to get married. For boys in the study, the median age of aspired marriage was 23.1 years—a figure identical with the national median marriage age for males in 1964 (U.S. Bureau of the Census, 1965). For girls, however, the median was 22.4 years, almost two years higher than the 1964 national average of 20.5 years.

Thus, the first way in which economically advantaged youth—or at least girls—are oriented toward extended adolescence is that they are more ready to delay marriage until well into their 20's. In addition, they display a less pressing sense of urgency about establishing themselves economically. Although upper-middle class youth are certainly no less ambitious or success-oriented than their less affluent peers—indeed, their occupational and economic aspirations are considerably higher—the figures from Part 3 of Table 14-1 suggest that in this realm they are also more ready to live with postponement. When confronted with the alternative of diverting time at graduation from economic to non-economic pursuits, it was the *lows* who were most eager to get on with the business of a career. These results might also reflect levels of confidence about long-term career prospects, but they are not inconsistent with the interpretation that young people from affluent backgrounds are more attuned to late maturity.

A third difference between these groups was in the importance attached to owning a car: boys from the two lower strata were considerably more likely than the *highs* to own or have intentions of owning a car, and among girls ownership plans were consistently higher in the lower status groups.* This is not to say that driving was unimportant to youth from higher origins, for they were actually somewhat more likely to hold driver's licenses or temporary driving permits. The almost universal significance of cars is reflected in the fact that 89 per cent of the boys and 78 per cent of the girls were licensed to drive during their first year of eligibility.

The real difference between the groups, was in the importance of owning a car rather than simply driving one. This is demonstrated in Table 14-2 which compares the saliency of ownership among those permitted to use their family car freely (whenever their parents weren't using it) and those allowed access either on special occasions only or not at all. Although those from the higher strata did in fact enjoy relatively fewer restrictions on the use of the family car (or cars), it was not this which accounted for their lower aspirations regarding ownership. Table 14-2 shows very striking social class differences among those reporting unrestricted access. This confirms the relatively greater importance of ownership itself to those from the less affluent strata.

TABLE 14-2

IMPORTANCE OF OWNING A CAR

Per cent who already owned a car or who planned to get one before getting out of high school

	Boys Socioeconomic Background			Girls Socioeconomic Background		
Access to the family car	*High*	*Intermediate*	*Low*	*High*	*Intermediate*	*Low*
Unrestricted	21	33	51	10	17	26
Total N=	82	67	51	70	72	51
Restricted	26	50	26	12	15	27
Total N=	23	35	35	32	41	52

The results in this table also suggest that parental restrictions on cars had virtually no impact on the ownership aspirations of girls, but did influence boys' intentions in this regard, although in quite different

* Because rates of actual ownership were low among these youth, the measure combines owners with those who had definite intentions to purchase before graduating from high school. Rates of actual ownership, moving from high to low across the socioeconomic groups, were as follows: 6, 16 and 11 per cent among boys; and 7, 6 and 7 per cent among girls.

ways for those from different backgrounds. Use of the family car appeared to dampen the ownership needs of boys from *high* and *intermediate* backgrounds, but to have a reverse effect on the interests of boys from the *low* group. Why should this be so? The most likely explanation is that it reflects very real differences in the functions and uses of cars in the upper- and lower-middle class male youth cultures. Because upper-middle class youth are much more active in clubs, organizations, and athletic teams in the high school and other community institutions, much of their discretionary time is planned in advance and involves activities which require them to be in a specific place at a specific time. These youth have very busy leisure time schedules, and tend to stay home when they haven't planned a specific activity. Except for "making out" on dates, or for "letting go" after school, they use cars primarily to meet very predictable spatial-temporal leisure time commitments. For uses of this type, the family car is probably just as acceptable as one's own, and perhaps even more so since it would be more likely to guarantee reliable transportation. It seems plausible to us to suggest, then, that ownership becomes salient to upper-middle class boys only when access to the family car is restricted.

In the lower-middle and working class youth cultures, on the other hand, cars mean much more than simply transportation, for they provide both a context for group interaction and an important substantive activity as well. Driving around with friends for purposes of being seen or to see others (called "goofing around"), for example, is much more frequently cited as a favorite spare time activity by lower-middle and working class boys than by those from the upper-middle classes. Being less involved in organized spare time pursuits which follow a regular schedule from week to week, youth from these backgrounds tend to have much more constant needs for cars, and their patterns of usage are less amenable to advance planning. In a peer culture which uses cars as ends in themselves, in short, only personal ownership can guarantee a boy constant access to "wheels."

Getting into College

There are two prevailing images concerning the central character of American youth. The first emerges largely as a reaction to the values of the youth culture: it emphasizes hedonism and irresponsibility, an overriding concern with having fun, disdain of scholastic achievement, and a propensity to indulge in improprieties such as drinking, truancy and "making out"—in the sense of sexual conquest. The other pictures youth as hard-working, serious-minded, and committed to high educational and occupational ambitions.

Adults who hold to images of the former type tend to identify a serious "youth problem" in our society, and are concerned about the inability of adults to control youth and about the lack of respect of the young for their elders. Their concerns have undoubtedly been greatly heightened by the recent upswing of political activism among college students, by the Berkeley protests of 1964 (which, significantly, used the organizing slogan "don't trust anyone over 30"), and by the more recent emergence of a psychedelic movement. (See the Block, Haan and Smith chapter within this volume for a discussion of activist youth at Berkeley and elsewhere.)

Those who hold to the latter images, emphasize the strains which modern society places on youth, cite the vastly expanded fund of knowledge they must master in a technological age, and emphasize the increased competition they face in gaining admission to college.

While sociologists are usually able to locate subgroups of youth which fit reasonably well to one or the other of these characterizations, it is also true that most adolescents simultaneously endorse or hold values of both types. Keniston (1965, p. 405) for example, talks of the "double orientation" to adulthood held by most adolescents:

> On the one hand, they see themselves as participants in the youth culture, and by virtue of that fact committed to non-adult values and distrustful of the adult world. On the other hand, most take for granted that they will one day enter adulthood and see themselves as preparing themselves for it.

Most middle class high school students, in other words, are attached to a youth culture which rewards attributes such as athletic ability, personality and popularity with the opposite sex *and* at the same time holds high educational aspirations. Indeed, youth who are distressed when they receive mediocre or failing grades at school would at the same time rather be remembered for their popularity than their scholastic brilliance.

Getting admitted into college is perhaps the most serious problem middle class adolescents face today. They view college much more as an inevitability than a meaningful alternative. Most hardly question whether they will go: regardless of how well they are doing in school they expect to attend college, look forward to it, and have difficulty imagining not going. This situation is not without its problems. Critics of American education have suggested that mediocre students feel compelled to gain a higher education because of parental pressure which is frequently unreasonable. In a recent evaluation of American secondary schooling in deprived and advantaged settings, Conant (1961, p. 101) for example, emphasized the continuing problem suburban school personnel have in bringing parental ambitions into line with the abilities of their children.

> The parents are determined that at least the boys, regardless of ability, receive a degree from a college with high academic standards. The pressures mount . . . through the grades, increasing in severity so that all three parties—school, child, and parent—are aware of the importance of college board examinations and the day when the fateful letter from the college admission office is due.

Although in Webster Groves we did not interview parents on their attitudes regarding college for their children, there was little question that the students *felt* under pressure to attend. When asked, "Do your parents urge you to go to college?" for example, 72 per cent said they were urged "very strongly" and only 11 per cent indicated the decision would be left up to them. Yet very few perceived their parents' ambitions for them as different from their own: as many as 81 per cent said they would be disappointed if they didn't get to go, and only 3 per cent indicated a personal preference not to attend.

It was also evident that the young people in this community held an extremely pragmatic view of the function of higher education. They were well informed of the economic consequences of a college degree, and many expressed their desire to go to college in precisely those terms:

> I want to go to college because now-a-days all the books and slides say that the difference in jobs and their pay is due to college. College really counts . . . like they had the difference between how much a high school drop-out and a college graduate makes, and you know the difference might be $200,000 in a lifetime. So it's important that you go.

Although few viewed higher education in quite so materialistic a fashion as this, many felt compelled to go to college for fear of making a mistake that would have serious economic repercussions later in life.

For example, several of those we interviewed were ready to surrender adventurous and somewhat unconventional occupational ambitions for the security of a college degree.

> What I really want to do is fly . . . but as a career. Flying is the one thing I really want to do, but I'm going to college because I'm expected to. . . . Despite my love of flying it's better to get a college degree first and then maybe fly than the reverse . . . because if you don't like flying then you would be stuck without a degree.

Images of the occupational and economic consequences of college dominated the rhetoric of these teenagers. Their orientation to higher education was based neither on intellectual curiosity nor on an overriding interest in the extracurricular aspects of life on campus—although playground images of college-going were fairly prevalent too:

> I would like to go to _____ University because it is one of the few colleges which let freshmen drive a car and I don't think I could go to college and not have a car. That would kind of bother me. It's also supposed to be real lenient about dorm hours and things like that . . . and it's a real good school.

For most, however, thoughts about college were related to long-term career goals, and as such were basically serious rather than frivolous.

These concerns were also reflected in the students' responses to a check-list of reasons for wanting to go to college. From Table 14-3 it is clear that the boys viewed the value of college predominantly in terms of occupational payoffs: finding an interesting and well-paid job were endorsed much more frequently than any of the other reasons. The girls also rated the chance to discover an interesting line of work as the most important reason for going, but were much less concerned than the boys about the monetary consequences of a degree. By comparison the girls held much broader perspectives on the functions of higher education and were much more likely to view the college experience as one which would broaden their intellectual, personal, and social horizons. They were 29 per cent more likely than the boys to rate the acquisition of new ideas as important; they were 26 per cent more likely to look forward to meeting "new and interesting people" at college; and they were 24 per cent more likely to rate personality development as an important reason for going. In fact, the only functions of college cited more frequently by the boys were the monetary benefits

TABLE 14-3

REASONS FOR WANTING TO GO TO COLLEGE

	Per cent who identified each reason as "very important"	
The Chance to	Boys (N=306)	Girls (N=334)
(1) Discover a line of work that would really interest me	86	89
(2) Prepare myself for a job with a really good salary	85	65
(3) Learn more about subjects that really interest me	61	75
(4) Meet new and interesting people	59	85
(5) Develop my personality and become a more interesting person	59	83
(6) Make my parents proud of me	58	61
(7) Be stimulated by new ideas	44	73
(8) Prepare myself to make a real contribution to mankind	38	54
(9) Gain the social standing that comes from having a college degree	34	23
(10) Take part in campus activities and social life	31	45
(11) Get away from home and be on my own	30	34
(12) Find a mate	27	29

and social standing that they would accrue from having a degree (by 20 and 11 per cent, respectively).

However narrow these values may appear, they do reflect the different sex-role demands placed on young men and women in our society, and the fact that women gain their social position primarily through marriage (see Bell's chapter) while men must establish theirs in the world of work. To be sure, some of the expectations of college rated highly by the girls were in areas which would enhance their attractiveness as marriage partners, but the main reason for their broader point of view was probably the realization that they were not expected to use their education to enter the labor market. Given the social background of the boys in this study, however, it is a little surprising that they exhibited such narrow views; indeed, their reactions are much more in keeping with traditional working and lower class perspectives on education and learning than with those of the upper-middle class. In a recent national study of the educational behavior of American adults, for example, Johnstone and Rivera (1965, p. 252) noted how the meanings attached to education varied across different segments of the population.

> From the lower class point of view, education is valuable mainly because it leads to occupational success and job security. This emphasis is also primary in the middle socio-economic groups, although the monetary consequences of a good education are also recognized. Finally, the wealthier and better educated third of the population— or at least the younger portion to this aggregate—tends to value education primarily for its own sake.

In the eyes of the boys in this upper-middle class community, however, a good education was valued highly much more often because of instrumental payoffs to be realized later in life than for any intrinsic satisfactions attached to the learning process itself. In short, they viewed education very much as an insurance policy to success, the premiums being the acquisition of good grades and a college degree.

That middle class boys are subjected to a relatively greater pressure than girls to achieve high grades in school was also evident throughout

TABLE 14-4

ACADEMIC PRESSURE FROM PARENTS

Per cent who often disagree with their parents about how hard they were trying in school

A. Boys		Socioeconomic Background		
	Grades	High	Intermediate	Low
	High	21	19	10
	Total N=	58	32	21
	Average	35	39	31
	Total N=	26	36	26
	Low	52	50	44
	Total N=	23	40	41
B. Girls		Socioeconomic Background		
	Grades	High	Intermediate	Low
	High	7	12	8
	Total N=	59	52	40
	Average	15	24	24
	Total N=	34	37	34
	Low	46	34	19
	Total N=	13	29	32

our results. Table 14-4 reports one indicator of this, the rates at which boys and girls reported disagreements with their parents over their efforts at school. Here controls are introduced both for socioeconomic background and for academic performance during the previous year, and while tensions in this area were clearly related to actual performance, it is revealing that on all nine comparisons between the sexes it was the boys who reported them more frequently. Regardless of socioeconomic background or of how well they were actually doing in school boys were still more likely than girls to experience parental pressure to try harder.

Table 14-4 also suggests that it is upper-middle class parents who expect most from their children by way of academic performance. This is particularly evident in the responses of boys who had achieved high grades the previous year (a "B" average or better), and among girls whose performance had been below average (a "C" average or lower). When standardized on actual grades received, rates of disagreement in this area turned out to be 36, 36 and 28 per cent, respectively, for boys in the high, intermediate and low groupings; and 23, 23 and 17 per cent for girls in the comparable groups.

The data also suggest that parents from the lower-middle classes react differently if their daughters rather than their sons are doing poor work in school. Looking just at those youth who had received low grades the previous year, for example, Table 14-4 indicates that boys from the high socioeconomic groups were just six per cent more likely than girls to report tensions with parents in this area, while boys from the intermediate and low groups, respectively, 16 and 25 per cent more likely to do so. This would indicate that middle- and lower-middle class parents as considerably more invested in the academic futures of their sons than of their daughters, while upper-middle class parents are concerned about getting children of both sexes into college. This finding supports Bettelheim's (1961) clinical observations, and is also consistent with results which Stinchcombe (1964) turned up in his study of rebellious high school youth. Although Stinchcombe conducted his research in a much less prosperous community than Webster Groves, his conclusions on this point were remarkably similar to our own: he noted that lower-middle class boys found it harder to fail than did working class boys, and that it was working class girls who found it easiest to fail. Our own results suggest that the same conclusions could be extended to comparisons a notch or two higher on the social class ladder.

SUMMARY

The thesis that American young people today have widely rejected the standards, guidance and authority of their elders, and are alienated from the main currents of American life, as yet remains to have demonstrated validity for middle- and upper-middle class adolescents. Although 16 may be the wrong age at which to study disaffection from the cultural heritage, and one suburban community is indeed an insufficient base for global generalization, we were nonetheless struck at the low incidence of deviant and unconventional ideas and attitudes among these teenagers. In Webster Groves, rather, we found a youth highly committed to traditional middle class definitions of success, one highly oriented to the rewards of the future rather than to a "cult of the present," and one which essentially endorsed rather than rejected the values of the parental generation. As one of our respondents put it,

> I respect my parents very much because they have made it in the world. I don't rebel because, well, something has got to be right because they have made it.

It is our suspicion that middle class America is still reproducing itself very well.

REFERENCES

Bettelheim, B. The problem of generations. In: Erikson, E. (Ed.) *The challenge of youth.* New York: Doubleday Anchor, 1961.

Blaine, G. B., Jr. *Youth and the hazards of affluence.* New York: Harper & Row, 1966.

Conant, J. B. *Slums and suburbs.* New York: McGraw-Hill, 1961.

Coleman, J. S. *The adolescent society.* Glencoe: The Free Press, 1961.

Eisenstadt, S. N. *From generation to generation.* Glencoe: The Free Press, 1956.

Gordon, C. W. *The social system of the high school.* Glencoe: The Free Press, 1956.

Hollingshead, A. B. *Elmtown's youth.* New York: Wiley, 1949.

Johnstone, J. W. C., and Rivera, R. J. *Volunteers for learning.* Chicago: Aldine Publishing Company, 1965.

Keniston, K. *The uncommitted: alienated youth in American society.* New York: Harcourt, Brace & World, 1965.

Rogoff, Natalie. Local social structure and educational selection. In: Halsey, A. H., Floud, J., and Anderson, C. A. (Eds.) *Education, economy and society.* New York: The Free Press of Glencoe, 1961.

Rosen, B. C. The achievement syndrome: A psychocultural dimension of social stratification. *American Sociological Review,* 1956, *21,* 203–211.

Schneider, L., and Lysgaard, S. The deferred gratification pattern. *American Sociological Review,* 1953, *18,* 142–149.

Sewell, W. H., and Armer, J. M. Neighborhood context and college plans. *American Sociological Review,* 1966, *31,* 159–168.

Spaeth, J. L. *American college graduates.* Chicago: Aldine Publishing Company, 1964.

Stinchcombe, A. L. *Rebellion in a high school.* Chicago: Quadrangle Books, 1964.

Turner, R. H. *The social context of ambition.* San Francisco: Chandler Publishing Company, 1964.

U.S. Bureau of the Census, *Statistical abstract of the United States: 1963.* (Eighty-fourth edition), Washington, D.C., 1963.

U.S. Bureau of the Census, *Statistical abstract of the United States: 1965.* (Eighty-sixth edition), Washington, D.C., 1965.

Wallace, W. *Student culture.* Chicago: Aldine Publishing Company, 1966.

The Adolescent in a World of Work[1]

Henry Borow *

CHILDREN GROW UP IN A TASK-ORIENTED SOCIETY. ALL ABOUT THEM ARE men and women who, for compensation, perform socially valued services within a complex economic system. We would find it extremely difficult to explain the manner in which man organizes his society, develops his institutions, conducts his daily round, and carries out many of his beliefs and practices without considering the place of the work experience in his life.

The nature of the work world, of course, is changing dramatically. Because man today lives a more abundant life and because society is able to provide him with more leisure time and earlier retirement than his forebears enjoyed, it is tempting to conclude that work has assumed decreasing importance and meaning for adolescent youth in the contemporary American culture. Yet, as this chapter will show, significant aspects of adolescent behavior can be better understood by viewing them as attempts to achieve the wider psychological independence of adulthood. This is accomplished, in part, by developing a work identity or an image of oneself as a potential worker. That the adolescent strives, often unconsciously, to develop such a self-image is not surprising. His experience in the world teaches him that how and where he lives, what prestige he gains, who his friends are, and how he spends his time will depend to some degree upon

[1] Parts of this chapter have been adapted from several recent conference papers on vocational development by the author.

* HENRY BOROW is a Professor of Psychological Studies at the University of Minnesota. Books with which he has been involved as editor or author include: *Vocational Planning for College Students; General Education for Personal Maturity;* and *Man in a World of Work.* He has written numerous articles on topics such as counseling, occupational psychology, career development, non-intellectual factors in academic performance, and psychological testing.

his occupation. He hears other persons classify a stranger by his field of work and he realizes that he, too, will come to be placed by others according to the job he will someday hold.

TOWARD THE WORK ROLE: A HYPOTHETICAL PICTURE

Adolescence has been commonly seen as a critical psychological stage in the socialization of youth. It is a stage marked by the shedding of immature habits and values and a groping for new ones. It is a stage characterized by an acceleration in role exploration and reality testing. The adolescent, haltingly and with the limited skill born of inexperience, assumes a wider range of social roles, many of which hold for him the lure of increased personal freedom. These newer roles he continually tries out within the milieu of his own age group, his own sex group, his particular socioeconomic group, and within the larger adult society. How successfully he learns to handle his new roles (or more accurately perhaps, how he perceives himself as performing them as the relevant reference groups feed back to him their expressions of approval and disapproval) determines to a significant degree the quality of the revamped ego identity he will establish, the kind of unifying image he will form of himself. We say in the household language that he is "learning to grow up." We mean that he is developing techniques of coping behavior which will earn for him social approval, personal acceptance, and a secure place in adult society. In this developmental process, the role of worker-to-be is a crucial one. Much, although certainly not all, of the coming-of-age behavior of the adolescent is better understood when we try to view it as a search for vocational motives and the working out of an appropriate vocational role.

In attempting to establish a stable and unifying concept of self, the adolescent enlists the behavior of other persons who are significant in his life as *role models*. In an earlier chapter, Beller discusses this process in the development of adolescent marital expectations. Some of this social imitation is conscious, but much of it is unconscious. Whichever it is, there seems little doubt that the adults in the intimate experience of the youth who is himself deeply involved in the business of learning how to be an adult, serve as his exemplars (constructive and helpful, or otherwise, depending on who they are). Thus, for the adolescent, learning how to be emotionally independent and learning also how to be economically independent are crucially important developmental tasks. When he takes employment, even though it may initially be part-time work, he begins to sense his independence from the family. If he succeeds now, he does so impersonally through his own ability and efforts, not primarily through the protection and loyalty of his family. Given this picture of adolescent movement toward adulthood, we can agree with Freedman (1962) that "the successful transition from school to work is central to the process of coming to age in America."

Some Concepts of Career Development

To understand better the developmental process by which children move into adolescence and establish a vocational identity, we find it useful to borrow several principles from developmental psychology and personality theory. In current research, theoretical work, and in the study of career development, several such concepts are widely used. We shall, with brevity, consider these concepts for the interested reader can consult Beller's chapter for a more detailed discussion of developmental theory.

Life stages concept. Charlotte Buhler's (1933) notion of arranging the study of evolving behavior according to a sequence of psychological life stages has provided a development thrust to the analysis of occupationally relevant acts in youth. Vocational plans and decisions are now viewed not as single events but as parts of an ongoing process of development. Thus, today, we believe we can learn more about career behavior by studying the individual over an extended period of time. He is examined from childhood through adolescence and adulthood in order to discover how his concepts, awareness, and aspirations concerning occupational life grow. This process should be contrasted to the technique of studying a sample of behavior taken from a given point in time.

Vocational developmental tasks. Borrowing both from the life stages concept and from Havighurst's (1953) notion of the developmental task, the study of career development has moved from fixed preoccupation with the act of vocational choice toward an identification of the motives and related problem-solving behavior which typify the individual at each life stage in his particular social setting. When we shift our focus in this manner, we appreciate that it is not necessary to delay the study of occupational behavior in the youth until he confronts his first, formal choice point in the decision chain as, for example, the choice between the office practice, industrial arts, and college preparatory tracks at the end of the ninth grade. We can study with considerable profit the occupationally relevant behavior exhibited in younger subjects, and we can consider its lessons for the vocational guidance of youth, including the improved uses of occupational information.

One illustration of an arrangement of vocational development tasks by level of maturity is provided by the work of Super (1957a) and his associates, as adapted from an earlier, more generalized scheme provided by Stratemeyer *et al.* (1947).

Vocational Developmental Tasks*

Preschool Child
Increasing ability for self-help
Identification with like-sexed parent
Increasing ability for self-direction

Elementary School Child
Ability to undertake cooperative enterprises
Choice of activities suited to one's abilities
Assumption of responsibility for one's acts
Performance of chores around the house

High School Adolescent
Further development of abilities and talents
Choice of high school or work
Choice of high school curriculum
Development of independence

Youth Adult
Choice of college or work
Choice of college curriculum
Choice of suitable job
Development of skills on the job

Mature Adult
Stabilization in an occupation
Providing for future security
Finding appropriate avenues of advancement

* Reprinted with permission of the publisher from Donald E. Super, *et al. Vocational Development: A Framework for Research.* New York: Teachers College Press, 1957. Copyright 1957 by Teachers College, Columbia University.

Older Person
Gradual retirement
Finding suitable activities for skills to occupy time
Maintaining self-sufficiency insofar as possible

More recently, Havighurst (1964) has presented another interpretation of how normal developmental tasks at each successive age level are associated with the learning of an occupational role. The following outline includes the first four life stages in Havighurst's six-stage version of vocational development. It is apparent that, in his earlier life stages, the individual is confronting experiences and learning to master developmental tasks which have an important bearing on his later vocational choice and adjustment behavior.

Stages of Vocational Development	*Age*
Identification with a Worker	5–10

Identification with a Worker   5–10
Father, mother, other significant persons.
The concept of working becomes an essential
    part of the ego ideal.

Acquiring the Basic Habits of Industry   10–15
Learning to organize one's time and energy to
    get a piece of work done. School work, chores.
Learning to put work ahead of play in appropri-
    ate situations.

Acquiring Identity as a Worker in the   15–25
Occupational Structure
Choosing and preparing for an occupation.
Getting work experience as a basis for occupa-
    tional choice and for assurance of economic
    independence.

Becoming a Productive Person   25–40
Mastering the skills of one's occupation.
Moving up the ladder within one's occupation.

Career pattern concept.   Despite a durable popular myth, most individuals do not make a single, fixed career choice. They make several. Industrial sociologists such as Miller and Form (1964) have traced what is called the career pattern of industrial workers, that is, the movement from position to position within the career sequence. The career pattern concept is related to the study of occupational mobility but goes beyond it in that it assumes a causal chaining of the decisions in the pattern. This includes causes that are both internal (psychological) and external (socioeconomic). Moreover, the career pattern concept furnishes a perspective on the individual's occupational history and the character of his occupational adjustment that the study of isolated job choices does not afford. Vocational development theorists have extended the concept of the career pattern downward in time to include the tentative and often unstable choices and aspirations of childhood that may long precede the subject's formal entry into the labor force.

The taking of occupational roles. In the complex, time-extended process by which the child becomes socialized with respect to the values, customs, and expectations of his primary reference group and of the larger subculture, he must learn his behavior modes from those around him. As he grows, he imitates the behavior of older children and of adults who thus become his role models. In part he is learning to master his developmental tasks, and in part he is exploring roles and experiences to learn both the kind of person he is and the kind he aspires to be. Some of these role-taking experiences become important in shaping his emerging concept of self as a potential worker. It seems quite plausible that the manner in which he assimilates, values, and uses occupational information comes under the influence of the kind of person he perceives himself to be or the person he projects as his ideal self.

Reality testing. Most of the foregoing principles of career development can be understood in relation to a kindred concept, namely, the striving of the adolescent to establish his psychological autonomy and to discover himself by means of trying out a variety of personal roles and experiencing society's reaction. In contrast to his earlier child self, the adolescent has built an improved critical capacity to judge his own capabilities and limitations in terms of the "feedback" he gets from those about him, such as parents, teachers, part-time work supervisors, and especially his peers. Accordingly, many of his acts are instances of self-exploration in which he measures his varying successes in terms of the verdicts and standards of the significant persons in his life. He is, in short, testing himself out as a person. In the process, he acquires a set of feelings about his potentialities not only as a family member and as a member of an adolescent culture, but also as a future worker.

THEORIES OF VOCATIONAL CHOICE

As any society becomes less agrarian and increasingly industrialized and urban, as the geographic mobility of the population increases, and as young people are given more freedom in the management of their own lives, the problem of vocational choice-making takes on added social importance. Moreover, the selection of an occupation involves one of the most crucial of personal decisions. Psychologists and counselors have long been interested in identifying the factors which influence vocational choice and a number of theories have been advanced in recent years to explain the process by which young people select their careers. Three of the most influential theories will be briefly described.

Vocational Choice as the Implementation of a Self-Concept

Donald Super (1957a), whose writings and research have had a pronounced influence on contemporary thinking about vocational life, regards occupational behavior as a sequence of developmental experiences culminating not only in a vocational choice but in a lifelong career pattern. Thus, Super speaks both of vocational choice and of *vocational development,* a process which he describes in terms such as ongoing, continuous, orderly, patterned, and dynamic.

For Super, adolescence is a critical period for revamping and building a more stable picture of oneself, a new self-image or self-concept. Striving to make an appropriate vocational choice and to adjust to one's occupation are mainly matters of finding and assuming an occupational role in which one can express himself in a manner consistent with his concept of himself. Super believes that the vocational counselor should be guided in his work by this interpretation of vocational development. He accordingly defines vocational guidance as "the process of helping a person to develop and accept an integrated and adequate picture of himself and of his role in the world of work, to test this concept against reality, and to convert it into a reality, with satisfaction to himself and benefit to society" (Super, 1957b).

During the initial developmental stages, *formation* of the self-concept is shaped by one's social experiences and one's perceptions of the meanings of those experiences. With passing time, the adolescent finds himself in social situations which make it possible and, indeed, necessary for him to *translate* his maturing self-concept into occupational terms. Thus, his experiences with certain school subjects, part-time jobs, and active leisure-time activities help him progressively to understand his work potentialities more clearly and to build his vocational self-image. Ultimately, the individual *implements* his concept of himself by tentatively selecting an occupation, undertaking training for his field of work and, if successful, entering the field and moving through it (Super *et al.*, 1963).

Vocational Choice as Reflecting the Personality Type Resulting from Early Child-Rearing Experience

Anne Roe (1957, 1964) has identified several relatively distinct patterns of psychological climates descriptive of early parent-child relationships. Of special significance in each child-rearing pattern, according to Roe, is a characteristic parental attitude toward the child which shapes the child's personality in certain ways. Each personality type involves a cluster of psychological needs which the individual seeks to satisfy in his various life roles. In adolescence or early adulthood, these needs are expressed in part in the making of curricular and occupational choices. While research on the relation between child-rearing experience and subsequent selection of a career field has not furnished impressive support for Roe's notions, she has produced some evidence to indicate that certain atypical vocational choices may have been influenced by the interpersonal atmosphere in the child's home. She found, for example, that girls who chose engineering as a career generally had difficult family backgrounds in which they tended to identify with the father rather than the mother. Boys who chose social work had experienced a more stressful and less affectionate home life and, in Roe's interpretation, chose social work partly as a reaction to their early experience and as an attempt to establish more satisfying relations with other people.

Vocational Choice as a Compromise with Reality

Eli Ginzberg (1951), an economist, proposed a theory of vocational choice as a developmental process covering a minimum of six or seven years and, more typically, at least ten years falling mainly in the adolescent period. As a result of his studies of 64 subjects who ranged in school status from sixth graders to graduate students, Ginzberg concluded that individuals move through three principal psychological periods as part of the process of making vocational choices: *fantasy* period, *tentative* period, and *realistic* period.

During the fantasy period, which characterizes children up to about age eleven, the child's thinking about choices is not qualified by such practical considerations as needed ability, training and entrance requirements, and available employment opportunities. There is little distinction between what the child wants to be and what he believes he can be. He does not think in terms of the conditions of the actual world.

During the tentative period, covering most of the adolescent years, the child begins to consider the conditions and demands he must satisfy to make an appropriate choice of occupation. He considers initially his interests, beginning at about age eleven or twelve. At successive ages, according to Ginzberg, the youth considers the relevance of aptitude and education (ages thirteen and fourteen) and personal values and goals (ages fifteen and sixteen). About age sixteen or seventeen, the adolescent attempts to integrate the facts relating to his interests, competence, and personal values in reflecting about his vocational potentialities. At approximately age seventeen, he enters a transition stage between the tentative and realistic periods of the vocational choice-making process.

It is during the realistic period, beginning typically toward the end of the seventeenth year of life, that the youth begins to work more directly on the resolution of his vocational choice problem. During this period, he becomes more sensitive to the opportunities and limitations of the external social and economic world, and he attempts to accommodate his motives and personal qualifications, as he perceives them, to the requirements and conditions of the real world. Essentially, he undergoes a process of compromise with the demands of reality. Ginzberg divides the realistic period into the substages of *exploration* (testing oneself out vocationally by means of competitive life experiences, such as school courses), *crystallization specification* (further delimiting his choice of occupation within the broader field and taking the actions signifying at least a tentative commitment to the occupation).

Ginzberg's conceptual account of the process of vocational choice is based largely on his observation of adolescent boys. He believes, however, that his descriptions of fantasy period behavior and tentative

period behavior hold reasonably well for girls, also, although he con-
cedes that, as considerations of marriage and home life enter their
thinking, the reality period may assume a different and more complex
form for girls. Even for boys, it is important to bear in mind that the
history of occupational choice-making does not take place in the
straightforward, uniform manner that Ginzberg's generalized picture
might suggest.

The value of all serious theoretical accounts, including those of
Super, Roe, and Ginzberg, is that they: (1) provide a meaningful
way of portraying occupational choice as a developmental process;
(2) suggests that the making of vocational decisions is much more
complex than ordinarily believed; (3) identify many of the personal,
social, and economic factors that influence thinking about occupational
life; and (4) show that vocational choice can be profitably conceived
as a multi-stage task in which the individual strives to link his evolving
personal aspirations with the demands of reality about which he is
becoming increasingly aware.

EARLIER CHILDHOOD INFLUENCES ON ADOLESCENT VOCATIONAL DEVELOPMENT

Because it is not ordinarily until adolescence that students face formal
decisions involving courses, curricula, and occupations or that they
receive their first real vocational counseling, it is often assumed that
no occupationally relevant experiences occur before that time. Actually,
the degree of vocational maturity exhibited at any substage of adolescence, the educational and occupational aspirations held, the motivation to plan for the future, the attitudes toward work, and a variety of
work habits are to a significant degree the products of preadolescent
experience. While the systematic study of the vocational meaning of
early childhood activities has largely been neglected, it is clear that
we cannot adequately understand the origins of the vocational thinking
and decisions of the adolescent without reference to his earlier history.

Members of the young child's immediate family (who comprise his
primary reference group) are the most significant individuals in his
socialization. It is in his interaction with them that he chiefly learns
impulse control, his expected sex role, his earliest concept of self, and
his repertoire of coping techniques. The family establishes the "cul-

tural timetables" by which he meets new social experiences, acquires new skills, and becomes aware of what the world expects from him stage by stage (Slocum, 1967). The implications for later vocational life of his early socialization is noted by Super (1957b) when he states, "Habits and expectations of success in the childhood family constitute a basis for later vocational success. The person who grows up in a home in which he is given experiences of success (and) in which his successes are rewarded . . . develops habits of success which carry over into school, social life, and work."

The school soon enters the scene as the second main institutional agent under whose influence the child learns his cultural perceptions and practices. Complying with rules, carrying out assignments, performing competitive tasks, and relating to other people are all part of the learning experiences of the child in school. Out of these the child forms concepts of success and failure, acquires an awareness of what he can and cannot do, and develops the roots of his educational and vocational aspirations. Macomber discusses the school's role in an earlier chapter of this book.

Underlying the forementioned development in the child's ability to comprehend and cope with his environment and, simultaneously, in his potential for future occupational roles, are certain fundamental traits and dispositions. Each of these is generally learned in the flux of early childhood, and each is an important determinant of the degree of success the adolescent will subsequently attain in a variety of task-oriented social roles, including those of student and worker.

Three of these behavioral characteristics are briefly identified below. They are interdependent and may, in fact, represent somewhat different emphases and interpretations involving the same broad competencies.

Personal Autonomy in Meeting and Handling Everyday Tasks

Increasingly, since the 1940's, the goal of hygienic child-rearing in America, particularly in middle-class society, appears to have been training for independence. We want the child to be equipped to take over ever larger domains of task attainment and personal choice-making so that, in effect, he learns to rely on his own understandings, resources, and skills to meet and solve new problems. This growing capacity for independence will later serve the child's effectiveness not only in his generalized interpersonal relations but also in competitive, task-centered settings such as the classroom and the place of work.

Internal Controls on One's Own Behavior

Young children vary in the rate with which they learn impulse control and the ability to delay gratification of a desire until they feel they have earned gratification. We see an example in the behavior of a child who delays his playtime activities until he has completed his homework assignment or a parentally assigned household chore. The ability of the child to progress in the mastery of his developmental tasks and to make an outward, productive attack on his problems will depend significantly on the early and successful establishment of internal controls on his own behavior.

Achievement Motivation

Early in training in independence and the effective rewarding of independent behavior in solving problems appears to nourish the child's need to achieve at a superior level. Achievement motivation thus refers to the tendency to set for oneself high standards of excellence and to act consistently in such a way as to attempt to attain this standard. Mussen, Conger and Kagan (1963), have noted the stability of achievement-oriented behavior as a personality trait, and state that "The child who enters school with a desire to do well is likely to develop into the adult who is concerned with intellectual competence." There is good reason to believe that achievement motivation is similarly predictive of the general level of occupational aspiration and the quality of the career pattern.

THE OCCUPATIONAL OUTLOOK
FOR TODAY'S YOUTH

Adolescents stand on the threshold of a world of work which is vastly different from that which their grandparents knew or even that which their parents experienced at the same age. Among the conditions and characteristics that distinguish the work situation today are the following:

1. The healthy state of the economy in recent years has kept the national average unemployment rate at about four per cent of the labor force. Job opportunities for youth, especially those with average or above average schooling, are good, as are the opportunities for choice among an expanding array of occupational training programs (U.S. Department of Labor, 1966).

2. Despite the relatively bright employment picture, unemployment among teenagers in the country stands in excess of 12 percent. For minority and disadvantaged groups of young people, the percentages run appreciably higher (see Kohrs' chapter on these young people). Male nonwhite teenagers of labor force age, for example, show an unemployment rate approaching 23 per cent, almost double the rate for all teenage youth (U.S. Department of Labor, 1966).

3. Since the early years of the century, the percentage of professional jobs in the total economy has more than doubled, while unskilled jobs have dropped more than 50 per cent in the total picture. Only one job in 20 in today's labor force calls for an unskilled worker (Wolfbein, 1964).

4. Service jobs have become more common in the economy while goods-producing jobs have become much less so. A smaller percentage of jobs traditionally thought of as masculine and as excluding women are to be found in the current occupational structure.

5. Young women tend to marry earlier and are still comparatively young when their children enter school. Thus, many have a two-cycle work career, entering the job market for the first time typically as late teenagers and again at about age 35. Thus, Useem (1960) speaks about the "two lives" of women, that of homemaker and that of worker. The typical high school girl of today may expect to spend about 25 years of the remainder of her life in employment.

6. Formal education as a prerequisite for entrance into many occupations has assumed new prominence. By 1959, the unemployment rate of school dropouts had risen to about double that for holders of the high school diploma and more than three times the rate for those with some college training. Since fewer jobs are available today to those with limited schooling, the tendency is for youth to remain in school longer. The typical age of full-time entry into the labor force has risen steadily from about age 14 at the turn of the century to about age 19 or 20 today.

7. Occupational mobility is rising. Rapid technological change and the sharp increase in the rate of job obsolescence will probably mean that young people entering today's labor market may expect to change occupations three to five times, on the average, during their working careers. The chances for orderly and successful career patterns will be greater among youth who acquire transferable work skills.

8. Because of the fluid state of the occupational structure, much larger proportions of workers will need to be retrained for new positions. The sharp separation between school and work will be lost. The emphasis in training young people will be on adaptability and the willingness and capacity to continue to learn and adjust to change in the work setting.

9. The work week, which is currently only a little more than half as long as a century ago, will likely continue to shorten. Young workers who enter the labor force will need to find satisfying and useful ways of organizing their time around both work and leisure roles. They will continue to find their identity through the work role, in part, but will need to find it increasingly in non-work activities as well.

The Alienation of Youth from Work

Societal barriers increasingly wall youth off from early, full-time labor force participation. The principal restrictive mechanism is the demand for more education, but the related qualifications of age and previous work experience are also involved. Thus, early and direct experience with work is open to fewer youth, and they are much less commonly regarded as important economic assets to the family than was once true. Moreover, they find it difficult to know the meaning of the adult experience in the role of worker.

Increasing numbers of jobs are either more intricate and complex than hitherto or they have become fragments of larger work operations. In addition, large-scale organizations having an inscrutability and impersonality not found in the small, intimate setting of work, tend to account for increasing proportions of employees. The net effect of these trends has been to make the work of parents less visible to their children. There are fewer opportunities than formerly for children to witness parents firsthand at work or to talk with them comprehendingly about their work, much less the opportunity to work alongside them, as for example, in the case of the farm youth or the son of a small shopkeeper.

Ironically, the growing complexity of the occupational world and the rising divorcement of youth from work is accompanied by the broadened freedom available to youth for personal decision-making, including decisions about curriculum and vocational plans. The phenomenon of occupational inheritance is now a minor factor in occupational choice in America. In a study of 1,000 Chicago male subjects, Duncan and Hodge (1963) found only a ten per cent incidence of sons entering their fathers' occupations. In all probability, many if not most of those in the ten per cent group represent examples of "forced inheritance" by which conditions of restricted opportunity and cultural deprivation ensnare the young person and make it difficult for him to avoid entering the parent's low status occupation. For the majority, however, there is increased responsibility for personal choice-making concerning vocational plans at a time when the options have become more numerous and puzzling and when youth has comparatively limited acquaintance with the essential elements of choice. Knowing this, we are better prepared for the findings of several recent studies in which substantial proportions of high school graduates report the retrospective wish that their school had provided more career guidance.

MOTIVES UNDERLYING VOCATIONAL CHOICE

We have already seen that the search for a satisfying vocational goal can be linked with the adolescent drive toward increased personal autonomy and with the attempt to find a life role which is consonant with the image the young person projects of himself. In more specific terms, preference for one type of occupation over another can be viewed as an expression of the particular values which become clarified and ascendant during the adolescent years. Rosenberg (1957) has identified three constellations of values about which vocational decisions tend to cluster. These involve the individual's orientation toward: (1) helping people, (2) earning extrinsic rewards as, for example, high income or fame, and (3) self-expression, as exemplified by the writing professions and the performing arts.

When senior high school students are asked to specify the occupational conditions which they consider most important in the selection of a career, they typically name "interest in the work" with greatest frequency (Powell and Bloom, 1962). The desire for security is also prominently mentioned as a motive for choice. In comparison with adults, high school seniors, girls in particular, also identify interest in people and the opportunity to be of service to others as significant conditions of occupational choice.

There is doubt, however, that the majority of younger adolescents are clear about their interest and value systems or that they consciously evolve vocational plans with their personal values clearly in mind. Brighter youth and those who are academically and socially more successful are generally better able to provide a more rational and explicit account of their vocational choices in terms of values. Yet, on the whole, it does not appear that a deliberate and calculated concern about implementing a set of personal values strongly governs the particular choice. Many fortuitous and situational circumstances appear to affect vocational decisions in ways that are not always predictable. Thus, many youth, particularly those of lower socioeconomic class status and those with limited education, appear to "fall into" their job fields. It is out of consideration of such unplanned occupational behavior that contemporary vocational guidance has tended to center more directly on the need to assist young people over an extended period of time with problems of career development and, especially, with the need to clarify their own goals and to set rational vocational plans consistent with them. The following chapter by Hackman develops this in some detail.

It is becoming clear that, as part of the continuing socialization experience, children and adolescents form and internalize powerful stereotypes of many occupations which are related both to the prestige they command and the life style they open up to those who enter them (O'Dowd and Beardslee, 1960). Entering a high status occupational field, business management or medicine for example, may be seen as a way of attaining and insuring an enviable way of life extending to a high standard of personal living, a rich variety of leisure adventures, and attractive friends. Among some adolescents, including upwardly aspiring liberal arts college students, knowledge of the status-conferring power of an occupational field may be more accurate than knowledge of how one enters the field or of the specific duties one is expected to perform.

STABILITY OF ADOLESCENT
OCCUPATIONAL GOALS

Because society attaches considerable importance to the making of vocational decisions as a precondition of educational and personal plans, high school students sense considerable pressure to state their occupational choices. Among entering college freshmen, compliance with this social expectation comes in the form of selecting rather specific curricular fields or academic majors. Indeed, studies over many years have repeatedly demonstrated that newly admitted college students single out the occupational preparation function of the college experience as the primary one involved in their decision to accept higher education.

Evidence bearing on the foregoing point is provided by a recent study of approximately 18,000 college-bound high school students. These subjects constituted a representative 3 per cent sample of a population of 612,000, tested under the American College Testing Program between November 1964 and October 1965. When asked to choose from a list of ten options the one which represented their most important goal in attending college, slightly over half (51 per cent) chose, "To secure vocational or professional training." The alternative showing the second highest frequency was, "To develop my mind and my intellectual abilities" (Baird, 1967).

Those naming vocational goals as the primary motivating factor in their decision to enter college also tend, in substantially greater numbers, to cite the availability of a special curriculum as an important reason for their particular choice of college. Of course, valuing the occupational preparation function of college above other goals and having a particular vocational objective in mind at the time of entrance does not insure that the choice of occupation will remain fixed. The emergence of new curricular and occupational interests resulting from initial exposure to new courses in college or from the failure to earn satisfactory grades in required courses (e.g., freshman mathematics course in engineering) illustrates how vocational goals might undergo change. In the United States, the frequency of such shifts is substantial, even among entering college students who enroll in comparatively specialized curricula. It is nonetheless true that the persistence of stated occupational goals during adolescence increases with age. In this regard, the vocational goals of college students are appreciably more stable than those of high school students.

To the younger high school student, the problem of making a vocational choice often appears fearsomely complex and bewildering. Work motives and interests are in a relatively early stage of clarification, and knowledge of the external economic world, as we have seen, is seriously limited. It is not surprising, then, to discover that the occupational preferences and choices of younger adolescents tend to be transitory.

Seventh and eighth grade students express a great deal of uncertainty about their vocational plans. Even among the small minority (well under 25 per cent) who are able to specify a definite career field, considerable fluctuation will occur in the occupation named over the next several years of their lives. Douvan and Adelson (1966) found that the majority of fourteen-to-sixteen-year-olds view their vocational aspirations only as tentative and exploratory choices. Only five per cent of boys in this age range report a feeling of certainty about continuing to work toward the career goal they have named. More than one-half of the stated occupational goals of tenth-grade boys are likely to change in the interval between their sophomore year and six months following graduation from high school (Schmidt and Rothney, 1955). Even among high school juniors it has been shown that a substantial majority will shift occupational goals over the next two years of their life.

REALISM OF VOCATIONAL CHOICE

As we have already seen, children tend to become more sensitive to reality considerations in the vocational choice-making process as they mature. However, because there is much evidence that the occupational preferences of youth are often insufficiently based on accurate knowledge of relevant personal and economic characteristics and conditions, vocational psychologists and school counselors are likely to look beyond the fact of choice itself and to inquire about the appropriateness of the choice. The question of whether an adolescent's vocational plan is realistic generally rests on three considerations: (1) the degree to which he has related his personal characteristics to the requirements and demands of his preferred occupation; (2) the current and projected employment supply-and-demand status as it relates to his preferred occupation; and (3) the adequacy of the educational plan by which he intends to implement his career choice. Given these criteria, how realistic are the occupational choices and preferences of adolescents?

Inadequate Information

The occupational information possessed by adolescent youth, especially those of junior high school age, is both sharply limited and of questionable accuracy. As previously discussed, the increasing complexity and diversity of the occupational structure has made it more difficult for present-day youth to develop proper familiarity with the world of work. Owing to cultural restrictions, the range of occupations about which a rural youth has knowledge is even more limited than for an urban youth. In practical terms, this difference is manifested in the expression of preferences among rural youth for a slender array of unimaginative occupational preferences reflecting a comparatively low level of aspiration.

Occupational Supply-and-Demand Disparity

Because of the attractiveness of high status occupations and the parental and social pressures that lead youth toward these fields, a marked discrepancy often exists between the availablity of such jobs in the economy and the expectations of the youth who seek them. An estimated 12 per cent of jobs in the labor force are now classifiable as professional or technical. Yet the extensive Project Talent study found 62 per cent of high school senior boys and 52 per cent of high school senior girls naming occupations in these competitive categories (Flanagan *et al.*, 1964). This study substantiates the findings of a number of earlier research reports on this question. By contrast, only four per cent of early-teenage boys (ages 14 to 16) plan to take training in trade-level occupations (Douvan and Adelson, 1966).

Inappropriate Training Plans

It is not uncommon to find a high school student with measured abilities commensurate with the requirements of his chosen occupation but with education aspirations far too modest to permit qualification for entrance into the field. In Super and Overstreet's (1960) research, only about one-third of the ninth-grade boys studied revealed high school and post-high school plans appropriately related to their preferred occupations.

Evidence for Vocational Choice Realism

Not all the available evidence on the realism of adolescent vocational choices is negative. Some studies have probably misinterpreted the stated occupational plans of young people by failing to make a distinction between their hopeful preferences and their sober expectations. When adolescents of lower socioeconomic class status are asked to state their vocational aspirations, it is not uncommon to find nearly as high a percentage citing high status occupations as for upper-class youth. However, when specifically asked what fields of work they *expect* to enter (as contrasted with *preference*), lower-class subjects tend to name occupations which are lower on the level-of-occupational-aspiration scale and closer to the actual occupational status of their own parents.

It is important to observe, moreover, that employment opportunities are actually good in many high-status occupations and that the barriers to entrance more commonly concern the meeting of formal training requirements rather than any actual shortage of job openings. Inasmuch as young people customarily look to education as the chief means to upward occupational mobility, and since a broadened program of educational and training opportunities is now becoming available to disadvantaged youth, it may be argued that the vocational ambitions of children from lower-class families are not as unrealistic as is often charged.

Perhaps the soundest evidence of realism in the vocational planning of adolescents comes from comparative studies of career development. Such research is demonstrating that high school seniors are generally more aware of the need for rational planning for vocational life and more clearly understand the factors to be considered than is true of sophomores and juniors. Compared to young adolescents, older adolescents name fewer glamor choices and tend to base their occupational selections and plans more directly on the distinguishing characteristics and requirements of the career field in question. Furthermore, findings of the Harvard Studies in Career Development strongly suggest that a process of progressive clarification of self-concept appear to occur between the ninth and twelfth grades which prepares the individual for more reality-based personal planning and decision-making. Students during this period develop increasingly accurate estimates of their own abilities, interests, and personal values. Because they become capable of conceiving of choices less in terms of interests alone and more prominently in terms of personal attributes and competitive requirements, it seems reasonable to suppose that they are better prepared for counseling that has as its objectives the making of educational and vocational plans.

Unfortunately, society and our schools often obligate adolescent youth to narrow their occupational choices prematurely and to commit themselves to specific career goals before they are capable of doing so and, indeed, before they generally need to do so. Society's aim should be less concerned with the forcing of early choice and more concerned with creating occupational awareness in youth so that the process of vocational development can be nourished and facilitated.

SUMMARY AND IMPLICATIONS

The changing social, technological, and economic conditions facing contemporary youth which have been discussed in this chapter will constitute a continuing problem not only for adolescents themselves but also for their parents, teachers, counselors, and work supervisors. In view of what is now known concerning the nature of vocational development in our American culture, the following recommendations may be set forth as guides to educational and social policy and practice.

1. The curricular choices and work-related experiences of adolescents should be kept open-ended and treated as the necessary means for reality testing and self-exploration.

2. The vocational guidance aims of the schools and of counselors in particular should balance traditional concerns with problems of vocational choice with the challenge of helping youth find ways of investing their lives meaningfully through work. Specifically, the future objective of vocational guidance should focus more clearly on promoting the value of work as a social institution; and of cultivating a deepened regard for the world of work and especially for the work of others. These aims must, of course, supplement the fundamental one of promoting a sense of planfulness regarding one's educational and vocational future.

3. Planned part-time work experiences and work-simulation units will need to be more systematically developed as a way of combatting

the alienation of youth from the occupational community. Society and the schools must work toward the coordination of guidance and counseling activities with improved versions of the supervised work experience program, including such government sponsored programs as the Job Corps and the Neighborhood Youth Corps.

4. Special techniques will have to be utilized with culturally disadvantaged youth who have been denied contact with effective adult occupational role models and who have not developed achievement oriented behavior or useful habits of work. What is called for in the education of such students is an intensive program aimed at strengthening attitudes toward work, attitudes toward oneself as a potential worker, and a reservoir of work skills and habits upon which realistic vocational plans may be built.

5. Because interpretations of the meaning of work for modern man and significant concepts of the world of work can be introduced at many points in the school experience, it is likely that career development in the future will be increasingly fostered through the formal curriculum as well as through individual counseling contacts. The boundary between vocational guidance through counseling and through classroom experience will become less sharply delineated. Improvements in current practice and policy in this new synthesis will require that the school counselor play an initiating and catalytic role as a strategically placed member of the professional school staff.

6. Finally, closer cooperation must be established between counselors at different educational levels (elementary, secondary, college) and between school counselors and those in other settings (public employment service, social work agencies, rehabilitation centers). Vocational development is continuous and is not confined to one particular life stage or institutional setting. To the extent that there is general social recognition of this principle, a broad-gauged and coordinated program of guidance-related experiences can be provided with the objective of promoting the career development of youth.

REFERENCES

Baird, L. L. *The educational goals of college-bound youth.* Iowa City, Iowa: Research and Development Division, American College Testing Program, 1967.

Buhler, Charlotte *Der Menschliche Lebenslauf als Psychologisches Problem.* Leipzig: Hirzel, 1933.

Douvan, Elizabeth and Adelson, J. *The adolescent experience.* New York: Wiley, 1966.

Duncan, O. D. and Hodge, R. W. Education and occupational mobility: a regression analysis. *American Journal of Sociology,* 1963, *68,* 629–644.

Flanagan, J. C. *et al. The American high school student.* Pittsburgh, Pa.: University of Pittsburgh, 1964.

Freedman, Marcia In: *White House conference on children and youth.* Washington, D.C.: Government Printing Office, 1962.

Ginzberg, E., *et al. Occupational choice.* New York: Columbia University Press, 1951.

Havighurst, R. J. *Human development and education.* New York: Longmans, Green, 1953.

Havighurst, R. J. Youth in exploration and man emergent. In: Borow, H. (Ed.) *Man in a world at work.* Boston: Houghton Mifflin, 1964.

Miller, D. C. and Form, W. H. *Industrial sociology.* New York: Harper, 1964.

Mussen, P. H., Conger, J. and Kagan, J. *Child development and personality.* New York: Harper & Row, 1963.

O'Dowd, D. D. and Beardslee, D. C. *College student images of a selected group of professions and occupations.* Cooperative Research Project No. 562. Middletown, Conn.: Wesleyan University, 1960 (Mimeographed).

Powell, M. and Bloom, V. Development of and reasons for vocational choices of adolescents through the high school years. *Journal of Educational Research,* 1962, *56,* 126–133.

Roe, Ann Early determinants of vocational choice. *Journal of Counseling Psychology,* 1957, *4,* 212–217.

Roe, Anne Personality structure and occupational behavior. In: Borow, H. (Ed.) *Man in a world at work.* Boston: Houghton Mifflin, 1964.

Rosenberg, M. *Occupations and values.* Glencoe, Ill.: The Free Press, 1957.

Schmidt, J. L. and Rothney, H. W. Variability of vocational choices of high school students. *Personnel and Guidance Journal,* 1955, *34,* 142–146.

Slocum, W. L. *Occupational careers.* Chicago: Aldine, 1967.

Stratemeyer, Florence B., Forkner, H. L. and McKim, Margaret G. *Developing a curriculum for modern living.* New York: Teachers College, Columbia University, Bureau of Publications, 1947.

Super, D. E., *et al. Vocational development: A framework for research.*

New York: Teachers College, Columbia University, Bureau of Publications, 1957 (a).

Super, D. E. *The psychology of careers.* New York: Harper and Brothers, 1957 (b).

Super, D. E., *et al. Career development: Self-concept theory.* Princeton, N. J.: College Entrance Examination Board, 1963.

Super, D. E. and Overstreet, Phoebe L. *The vocational maturity of ninth-grade boys.* New York: Bureau of Publications, Teachers College, Columbia University, 1960.

U.S. Department of Labor, *Manpower report of the president.* Washington, D.C.: Government Printing Office, 1966.

Useem, Ruth H. Changing cultural concepts in women's lives. *Journal of the National Association of Women Deans and Counselors,* 1960, 24, 29–34.

Wolfbein, S. L. Labor trends, manpower, and automation. In: Borow, H. (Ed.) *Man in a world at work.* Boston: Houghton Mifflin, 1964.

CHAPTER 16

Vocational Counseling with Adolescents

Roy B. Hackman ※

THE PURPOSE OF THIS CHAPTER IS TO DISCUSS BRIEFLY THE VARIOUS aspects of one of the most important problems that the adolescent has to face. This is the problem of choosing a future occupation and the making of the decisions which ultimately lead the adolescent into that occupation. Counselors do not subscribe to the notion that students can or should pinpoint occupations and choose their life work once and for all. However, a start must be made during adolescence, and it will be made with or without help from the adult world. Whether the choice is realistic or even satisfying, only time will tell.

The question is, can we as counselors, teachers, or parents be of any real assistance to young people in the vocational area; and can we do this without dictating to them or making their decisions for them? Will they seek and accept our help, or will we again find ourselves on the periphery of a mystifying teenage world, which we do not understand and to which we simply close our eyes, our ears, and our minds?

My answer to the first question is, yes. Counseling and guidance, and in particular vocational guidance, can be and usually are very helpful to the adolescent. However, I immediately open myself (and all other counselors) to the demand—prove it! In answer to this, I do not intend to attempt a survey of the professional literature which purports to deal with this problem. While there is positive evidence which bears

※ ROY B. HACKMAN is a Professor of Psychology and Educational Psychology and is the Director of the Educational and Vocational Guidance Clinic at Temple University. He is co-author of the *Hackman-Gaither Vocational Interest Inventory*, has written a chapter in *Counseling and Guidance: A Summary View*, as well as a number of articles on counseling, vocational choice theory and decision making, and psychological testing.

on the issue, the techniques of scientific experimentation are extremely difficult to apply to counseling. This is due, in part, to the complexity of the problem, and in part to the techniques which are frequently irrelevant to the issue.

Thus, in my mind, the answer to the first question is clearly in the affirmative although I cannot point to any large-scale, long-term investigation which proves or disproves the validity or utility of vocational counseling. Perhaps the best proof of its value is the 50 years of vocational counseling which has pragmatically demonstrated its worth with an untold number of young people and adults. The next and equally important question is whether or not adolescents will seek out help. The answer here depends on *what* we have to offer and *how* we offer it.

The early emphasis in guidance was primarily on skillful interviewing, some job information, and a kind of unsystematic matching of personal qualities with job demands. It then progressed to a heavy reliance on the measurement of individual differences (by means of tests) to predict job success. Finally it evolved into a more systematic matching of people with jobs (the so-called Parsonian model of vocational guidance). This has changed. The modern approach is more dynamic, although we are still concerned with the vocational adjustment of people, whether it be in the present or in the future.

To give perspective to its use with adolescents, I shall attempt to show what vocational counseling and guidance is; what its objectives are; what techniques are used; some of the special considerations that need to be taken into account when working with adolescents; and some suggestions to non-counselors who wish to be of help in this very important area of adolescent life.

VOCATIONAL GUIDANCE VS. VOCATIONAL COUNSELING

A vocational counselor may do both vocational guidance and vocational counseling from time to time, even with the same person. However, I believe it is useful to distinguish between them because their approaches and techniques vary and their objectives are somewhat different. *Vocational Guidance,* from my viewpoint, is a generic term which encompasses all those activities in the school and the community which assist individuals in making realistic career choices and in implementing them through training and possibly placement. The ultimate goal is good vocational adjustment.

Vocational Guidance may be carried out in formal or informal settings, with individuals or with groups. It assumes that the adolescent or adult is able and ready to make a vocational decision, but does not know how to proceed and therefore needs and wants assistance. It also assumes that there are no other serious problems in the person's life (such as emotional problems) which override the vocational problem and require prior help. The process of vocational decision-making is considered to be a rational one and we therefore assume that the person is rational enough and intelligent enough to make this decision.

Choices are always made within the limits which are set by the total environment in which the individual finds himself. The counselor helps him to identify and formulate alternative courses of action and to set up and initiate specific plans to implement his decisions. The decisions may be investigatory or terminal. He assists him to set limits which are not too broad or vague and to expand limits that are too restrictive. The counselor may make a vocational diagnosis on the basis of the person's aptitudes, abilities, interests, and other significant traits. After this diagnosis he may help his client to select a definite goal and work out his career and training plans. The main techniques of vocational guidance are interviewing, testing, the presentation of occupational information, and job try-out. It may include vocational counseling, to some extent, but typically does not emphasize it. *Vocational Counseling* is the process of helping a person free himself and mobilize his inner strengths so that he can and will make a choice. He may know how to make decisions, but he does not do so. He is on "dead center" and he needs help to get moving. The counselor's purpose is to assist the person gain insight into his own need and value systems and his self-concepts, so that he will be motivated to make a vocational choice (and other related decisions), whose consequences, in and of themselves, are very likely to be therapeutic. The basic technique here is the interview.

Combining both Vocational Guidance and Vocational Counseling into a modern frame of reference results in a more dynamic approach. The purpose is to promote a person's understanding of himself (Tyler, 1961; Super, 1962)* and to motivate him in the direction of career

* References throughout this chapter will be illustrative, not exhaustive, of the types of resources and information with which the vocational counselor should be familiar.

planning, vocational maturity, and ultimately, a realistic vocational choice.

The process is intended to give the person, be he adolescent or adult, a more comprehensive and accurate view of the world of work over a wide spectrum of jobs and occupational milieu. The process illuminates the wide range of choices open to him as well as that of his own range of potentialities for achievement and satisfaction. It assists him to understand and use the decision-making process for choosing alternative courses of action under conditions of uncertainty and risks, where the consequences of his actions cannot be fully specified in advance. Moreover, it takes into account the person's self-concept, his value system, his needs and motivation, and relates them to the world of work (see Borow's chapter). Above all, it places the responsibility and the freedom of choice on the counselee. It is a developmental process which extends over a period of time, thus permitting revision and elaboration as needed.

Finally, the process seeks to help the adolescent or adult answer some basic questions about an occupation, such as: Can I do it, or learn to do it? (Aptitude) Will I like it and be satisfied? (Interests) How can I decide between this and some other job? (Decision-making) Will I amount to something? (Status) Will I be worth anything to myself and others? (Self-concept).

THE SETTING

Sometimes one wonders if there really is such a thing as late childhood or adolescence. The world is rushing on and by us at such a rapid pace that there seems to be little time for a young person to be truly young and carefree and full of the zest of life. In a way, he is being forced into becoming a frustrated, miniature 20th Century man or woman. To my mind, this is a very sad state of affairs.

In effect, society, or at least individuals within it, has been tampering with the process of maturation in many ways. The process has been telescoped, redirected, and channeled (the fashionable term today would be "programmed" or possibly "shaped") in ways that surely interfere with the psychosocial growth and development of young people. This in turn will shape their lives and affect the future course of our society (Parsons, 1964).

We have been preoccupied with such problems as: (1) the discovery of "talent" which usually means bright, middle-class, educationally oriented, but not necessarily creative or really talented students; (2) the elimination, or at least reduction, in the number of drop-outs (or "push-outs") from our schools, usually without changing the curriculum to fit their needs; (3) technological change, automation and programmed instruction; (4) the "new curriculum" or delinquency, LSD and "pot"; and (5) the myth of the powerful (which it is, commercially speaking) and terrifying teenage culture which "turns adults on and off." All this has had a deleterious and indeed shocking effect on our attitudes toward real people who happen to be in the age bracket we refer to as adolescence. We must somehow shift the emphasis away from these things which cause so much fear, anger, anxiety, frustration and, above all, abortive and ill-conceived "programs" for dealing with the so-called teenage or adolescent problem. While we cannot ignore them completely, they must be put into the proper perspective. We must, instead, focus our attention on boys and girls as individual human beings (Tyler, 1964, 1965), and not as members of an alien teenage culture in our midst.

We forget that in a way we are looking backward, through a darkened mirror, at ourselves. This is particularly true if we happen to be viewing our own children. We hold up goals and ideals which many of us never have attained and probably never will. Nonetheless, we still seek fulfillment for ourselves through our young people. In so doing, we always run the danger of forgetting them and thinking only of ourselves. We also forget that with a minimum of adult intervention and even well-intentioned advice or instruction, a great many young people will achieve within the limits of their own capacities and according to their value systems. After all, growing up does not occur in a vacuum, but within the framework of a society of which we are also members and which we certainly had and continue to have a part in shaping (Wrenn, 1962).

I am not trying to say that there is no teenage problem (although I am tempted to do so), but rather that these are individual boys and girls, some of whom do have problems and need special help from teachers, parents, friendly and interested adults, counselors or other members of the helping professions. We should be prepared to offer whatever special assistance is needed and at the appropriate time. Hopefully, the individual boy or girl wants help and can profit from it. We should never force it upon him or her. In a way, it is perhaps unfortunate that professional counselors tend to believe that you cannot assist a person who either does not want help, is indifferent to it, or becomes hostile when it is offered to him. This leaves counselors with a very difficult and somewhat embarrassing question. What should we do with an adolescent who obviously needs guidance but isn't about to seek it out or accept it? Should we let him "go down the drain" or should we put pressure on him to achieve and in so doing conform to the demands of society? This is an unresolved dilemma and I have no easy solution to offer. However, the application of the principles of learning as employed in behavior therapy (e.g., operant conditioning) eventually may be of great assistance in bridging the gap between the completely permissive and the completely directive point of view. Also, it is time that the lay public realizes that we should not use punitive methods to control behavior in the name of helping the individual involved. This is of paramount importance in dealing with the disturbed, anti-social, delinquent, hostile, or aggressive teenagers who are such a problem in our schools and communities.

We live in an ambivalent culture. On the one hand, it is permissive and it seeks to promote self-actualization and the good life for everyone. This is particularly true if middle-class values are accepted and followed. On the other hand, it is preoccupied with economic and technological problems which require manpower if they are to be solved, regardless really, of whether the individual desires to be part of such efforts or not. Here the *establishment* is in control. The individual is at best, secondary. It is quite apparent that a great many adolescents hate the establishment; most adults learn to tolerate it; hardly anybody really likes it.

A vocational counselor should be warm and permissive. Yet, he too is a part of the establishment (e.g., an educational system) which places demands on him which affect his counseling. As an example, he may be asked to select students for various training programs and then to motivate them to enter the programs.

I do not have any solution to this dilemma, although I think that most successful adults have somehow learned to live with it. Not so with teenagers. They do not see the problem clearly, and they certainly are ambivalent. They want freedom and yet they want limits. They are constantly being accused of being nonconformists because they fight the particular establishment in their lives; yet, they want conformity and togetherness and as a result conform to their peer group or some other value-loaded system. This sometimes gets them into serious difficulties. There are tremendous pressures put upon them (e.g., to go to college), and the decisions which they have to make are made earlier and are, in many cases, irreversible. Their problem is more acute today than it was in their parents' or grandparents' time. These are the paradoxes that must be reckoned with in vocational or any other kind of counseling.

It is no wonder that our young people complain that they have difficulty in finding some purpose in life at a time when it is questionable if they are mature enough to do so. Many adults have never found a real purpose in life, and yet they expect and even demand that young people know what they want to do. For example, they ask adolescents what occupation or type of work they want to go into after they finish school and become adults. It is strange how many parents, teachers and administrators want an adolescent to make a firm vocational choice because they think that having done so, he is now motivated to grow up and be successful in school and in the occupational world. Unfortunately, the mere act of stating a vocational choice often fails to motivate the person at all or it leads to failure and frustration because of its lack of realism.

We really must permit our young people to grow up. This takes time and varies from person to person. Too frequently, in my opinion, we try to force-feed them with all sorts of psychological, social vitamin pills (sometimes called reinforcers by psychologists) and special diets (such as programmed or computerized instruction). Sometimes we offer as incentives, synthetic and shallow rewards which are completely uninteresting to adolescents (e.g., grades in school). We fail, and we wonder why.

VOCATIONAL CHOICE

The process of vocational choice and career development does not begin or end in adolescence (Super, 1957). Whether they want to or not, adolescents often have to make conscious and deliberate (not necessarily rational) choices when they and their parents are faced with curricular decisions. These are intimately related to a wide spectrum of occupational goals. They also must make choices when they are dropping out or leaving school and seeking to enter the occupational world because they "need a job." On the other hand, they may passively float or drift like jetsam in the ebb and flow of events of their own life stream, never making decisions and getting nowhere. They become locked into a chain of events over which they have no control, or understanding, or even interest. They do not fight the "establishment" that life seems to be. Why fight the impossible? Why not seek some degree of satisfaction elsewhere, regardless of whether or not it is acceptable to the adult world?

However, the choice process is developmental (Nicholas, 1963) with many turning or branching points along the way. It begins in very early childhood and the forces which shape children's lives exist in powerful forms. The bulk of these forces and determinants are not subject to individual or family control or manipulation. In fact, the individual usually is not aware of them. It is no wonder that vocational choice is often viewed as accidental in nature and as a blind trial and error process. This is true because it is held that the individual has to respond to the realities of his life situation, regardless of his desires. Thus, for example, one could hold that the accident of birth determines the occupations of a large number (perhaps the majority) of workers, since it establishes family, race, nationality, social class, and to a large extent, cultural and educational opportunity. If carried to the extreme, this would be a devastating point of view which would immobilize education and the helping professions. I would prefer to take the position that these are important variables (some are irreversible) which must be reckoned with in counseling. But they do not establish the worth of an individual, nor do they shut the doors of opportunity to him.

Without succumbing to a deterministic or fatalistic philosophy, one cannot help but conclude that many young people fall into occupational niches or slots without much rational consideration on their part. Of those who do not, many will become members of a classless and faceless society composed of individuals who do not work or reap the benefit of our so-called affluent society.

If the environment (family, school and community) is benign and reasonably economically favored, the chances are good to excellent that adolescents will achieve some sort of occupational success. Members of this group (the advantaged) have excellent work potential and vocational guidance is very effective with them. At the middle to upper level of these adolescents are those described by Johnstone and Rosenberg in an earlier chapter.

According to one point of view, the normal person, if left alone, will make an adequate vocational choice, since he is impelled toward certain occupations because of his basic impulses. If in addition the adolescent is compliant (otherwise known as motivated, educationally oriented, well-adjusted, etc.), all will be well and he will automatically grow up to be a useful and happy citizen. It would follow, of course, that something must be basically wrong with the personality of the teenager who does not make a realistic choice at the appropriate time. It is felt that he must be abnormal or maladjusted or difficult or even that most horrible accolade of all, a *non-conformist*. This may be true in some cases, but mostly it is a dangerous myth which should be eradicated from our thinking. There are, in fact, many reasons why adolescents do not make vocational choices, not the least of which is that they are simply not ready to make them.

Alas, many normal boys and girls have difficulty in making and implementing curricular and vocational choices, as witnessed by the large number of dropouts in college (approximately 50% on the average) and by the considerable number of bright students who drop out of high school or who do not continue their education and training beyond high school. It has been my experience that people (including employers) tend to think of dropouts as: stupid, non-conformists, emotionally disturbed, or delinquents, and thus want no part of them. No wonder they have little confidence in teenagers and no wonder that teenagers want no part of adults. Worst of all, the facts do not warrant such assumptions.

Why do we insist that adolescents continually strive upward and onward toward the professions, technology, and the higher reaches of government and industry? Certainly status is closely tied to the work one does (particularly for males, and for those females who have or seek husbands), but to my mind happiness is not synonomous with job success. I have worked with too many clients who were successful vocationally, but who certainly were not happy in any true sense of the word. Ultimately each adolescent must seek his own happiness, using his own frame of reference and his own value system. For some this may be job success, for many others it is not and cannot be attained through work since many types of jobs in our economic world are purely *instrumental*. That is, in no discernible way do they lead to self-fulfillment. We talk to our young people about the dignity, not the joy, of work, but we do not help them to see that in all probability other areas of their lives will have to furnish satisfaction and self-fulfillment. Strangely enough, counseling in this area is definitely a part of Vocational Guidance (Hackman, 1964).

If the environment that adolescents live in is impoverished or malignant, their chances of occupational success are very poor indeed. For these adolescents there is no hope and no striving, because at best their expectancies of success are minimal and at worst completely negative. Here again, the adolescent who grows up in an urban or rural slum did not just get that way. One might say that his environment has trained him from birth. Of course, not all boys and girls from the "slums" fit into this category. It is also true that many innovative and creative programs are in existence whose task is to work on this problem. However, one conclusion seems inescapable: we must start long before adolescence to help these young people. They are extremely difficult to work with because they have experienced only failure in our schools. They need orienting and counseling which is not of the traditional formal approach, and they also need help from counselors and teachers who can relate to them and somehow forget their own middle-class, tradition-bound values. These boys and girls are often referred to as the "hard-core" group. To my mind this term has two bad connotations: first, that they are nasty and we really cannot do anything with them short of institutionalization or incarceration, and secondly that they are the root and the cause of all our troubles with the adolescent world. In both cases, nothing could be further from the truth. These boys and girls, if left without help, become alienated from our middle-class culture (not their own culture) and then go on to swell the ranks of the poor and the other disengaged segments of our society. It is true that we have done very little, really, for these adolescents via vocational guidance. Unfortunately, counseling such adolescents (particularly if they are in a minority group) is not the answer. The basic problems which exist in the individual's life require massive remediation and intervention before vocational guidance and job placement can become very effective. As Kohrs discusses this group and its problems in detail in an earlier chapter, I will not carry it further here.

Still another group of adolescents lives in a different kind of environment. These are boys and girls who grow up in homes and in communities which have a laissez-faire attitude toward the adolescent. The community is neither hostile nor loving and really, to all intents and purposes, does not care (at least so it seems to the teenager). If you ask a father what he hopes for his son or what he would like him to do, he will say something like "anything he wants to," or a mother might say, "I just want him to be happy." There is no attitude of concern expressed, in short, no apparent love. This happens very frequently with teenagers who do nothing bad or good to distinguish themselves, e.g., they are neither mentally retarded nor bright. To make matters worse, many of the same parents are themselves not interested in education and they give no encouragement to their children. They have obtained a self-satisfying life from skilled and semiskilled jobs and have no desire for anything else. Why should their children be different? No wonder so many boys drop out of school to work and so many girls get married and start families. Vocational guidance is difficult here because these boys and girls are frequently not educationally oriented; they have no special aptitudes or interests and they are not particularly interested in working. In the future the employment possibilities for this group are going to be more and more limited because of increasing automation. They are simply not suited for the increasing number of technical jobs in our society.

Young children are subject to all types of environments and they learn to react in fairly predictable ways. Many things in their environments bear on vocational choices and are thus important in vocational counseling. When we meet these children later as adolescents we are already looking at the end results of many forces which have "programmed" their behavior without their knowledge or consent.

As counselors and teachers and parents we need not expect to undo all of the deleterious effects of an adolescent's early environment. Some of its effects have very little harmful carry-over into the adult world. Not everything that happens to a child cripples him emotionally for life. He may even thrive. Also, as counselors we have very little control over the adolescent's present environment. For example, we can do very little to effect immediate changes in the school curriculum. Moreover, we can make only educated guesses as to what the adolescent's future environment will be. Of one thing we can be sure, however, and that is *that there will be change.* Counseling and Guidance would be a hopeless task were it not for the inner strength, the flexibility, and the growth potentialities of young people. The die is not cast at six, nor at sixteen, nor at forty-six. We start with the teenager where he is and we accept him and we listen to him and we help him learn to make sensible choices from among the alternatives available.

CHOOSING AN OCCUPATION

Before an adolescent can choose an occupational goal, he must know what alternatives are open (Samler, 1964). For any particular teenager, there are many possible vocational choices. Of the occupations he knows, some are questionable possibilities but should be realistically investigated. For various reasons, others are out of the question and should be eliminated from further consideration. Still others seem to be realistic and desirable and should be retained for consideration and possible choice. Here I am referring to those occupations which are visible, i.e., those of which he has some knowledge. Since this is usually a very small number of occupations (out of many thousands of different jobs in our economy), his range of choice is very narrow and it may not include many which ought to be considered (U.S. Department of Labor, 1966–1967; Hopke, 1967).

The answer to this problem lies in furnishing occupational information (e.g., job duties, employment outlook, etc.), beginning very early in adolescence, or even sooner (Hoppock, 1963; Baer and Roeber, 1964). In so doing, job information should first be presented and considered in terms of broad fields of work, such as *Business Contact* or *Technical* work. While it is true that there are jobs which cut across fields, most of them fall within one or another of the major areas. Each group of jobs has some important characteristics which are common to all of its members.

The student should first make a tentative choice in terms of the major field of his interest and how he sees himself as a future worker, i.e., his overall "vocational identity." Each major occupational field includes many different types of jobs which differ in terms of the ability needed, essential personal characteristics, and the extent and level of training needed for entrance.

Next, the student should focus his attention into one or more major sub-areas. These in turn can be narrowed down into specific jobs to be investigated further. This last step requires detailed occupational information which can be found in the various briefs, monographs, pamphlets and books available in most school libraries.

The process goes from the general to the specific. It is sequential and entails study and making choices at each major point mentioned above. Also, it involves determining a field of interest and the types and levels of specific jobs within it. As an example of how this might be done, let us start with some major occupational fields or groupings of jobs from which an adolescent might first consider and choose:

1. *Physical Science*, e.g., occupations in Mathematics, Astronomy, Chemistry, Physics, Geology, and Meteorology.
2. *Biological and Agricultural Science*, e.g., occupations in Zoology, Botany, Agronomy, Physiology, Entomology, Bacteriology, and Genetics.

3. *Social Sciences*, e.g., occupations in Psychology, Sociology, Anthropology, Economics, Political Science, and History.

4. *Medicine and Health*, e.g., such major occupational groups as Physician, Dentist, Veterinarian, Pharmacist, Chiropractor, Osteopath, Optometrist, Nurse, Dietician, Medical Technologist, Dental Hygienist, Physical Therapist, and Occupational Therapist.

5. *Engineering and Technical*, e.g., such major occupational groups as Engineer (with many specialties), Architect, Metallurgist, Surveyor, Draftsman, and Laboratory Technician.

6. *Business*, e.g., such major occupational groups as Accountant, Auditor, Purchasing Agent, Sales Manager, Public Relations Man, Personnel Manager, Job Analyst, Credit Manager, Office Manager, Store Manager, Appraiser, Foreman, Salesman, Bank Teller, Bookkeeper, and Business Machine Operator.

7. *Education*, e.g., such occupations as College Professor, School Superintendent, School Principal, High School Teacher (specializing in various subjects), Primary and Kindergarten Teacher, Industrial Arts or Vocational Education Teacher, and Special Education Teacher.

8. *Social and Welfare Work*, e.g., such occupations as Social Case Worker, Social Group Worker, Marriage Counselor, Director of Social Welfare, Parole Officer, Clergyman, and Recreation Leader.

9. *Special Talent*, e.g., such occupations as Writer, Editor, Translator, Commercial Artist, Designer, Photographer, Painter, Sculptor, Actor, Dancer, Musician, Radio and T.V. Announcer, Professional Athlete, Entertainer, and Graphic Art Work.

10. *Agriculture*, e.g., occupations in Farming, Ranching, Fishing, Forestry, and Hunting.

11. *Mechanical Work*, e.g., occupations in Machine Trades, Bench Work, Structural Work, Processing, Fabricating, Repairing and Equipment Operating.

12. *Service Work*, e.g., occupations in Domestic Service, Food Preparation and Serving, Personal Service, Amusement and Recreation, Building Service, and Protective Service.

Now, let us suppose that as a result of the first step, the adolescent boy feels that he wants to do something in *Business*. He has decided that he may want to acquire some specialized training before beginning his career. Also, on the basis of his investigation so far and his knowledge of himself, he feels that he does not want to work with people or deal with them on a face-to-face basis. He is more interested in the technical and administrative aspects of business.

His next task is to investigate further the field of Business and narrow his choice down into terms of the level of training (college, technical or vocational), and the type of work (duties and responsibilities) he would like to do and in which he feels that he could be successful.

He then looks at some of the major areas in the field of Business (excluding clerical work which he considers to be feminine), viz: Accounting, Purchasing, Sales and Distribution, Banking and Finance, Advertising, Public Relations, Personnel Management, Direct Selling, Market Research, Systems Analysis and Computer Programming and Data Processing. Once he has tentatively chosen one or more of these sub-groups, he can then investigate individual occupations and make one or more as specific (but tentative) choices.

He will soon discover many jobs in the business world which cut across occupational groupings. This is important, because in his case the business aspect of the job may be secondary to the type of work. He would like to be in Business, but actually the type of work (duties, job) comes first. For many people, the opposite is true. They are not so concerned with *what* they do, but *where* they want to work. Some examples of jobs from other fields that occur in Business are: Industrial Engineering, Sales Engineering, Commercial Artist, Applied Statistician, Economist, Corporation Lawyer, Industrial Physician, Industrial Psychologist, Advertising Copy Writer, and Training Director. Each of these jobs has a distinct type of preparation which is common to its field, but the application of the field of knowledge is in Business or Industry.

The point about urging the student to investigate these jobs, as well as the others, is not to add to his confusion and make his ultimate choice more difficult, but rather to expand his view of the world of work. He needs to know that specialized training can open many doors to him. That is, his role identity may be in business, but his job duties have much in common with other people who do not work in the commercial world. Both he and they can, and often will, move out of one and into the other.

This approach emphasizes versatility in training, rather than specificity. One first finds his own vocational identity and then makes a choice in terms of a fairly definite occupation with a fairly specific preparation. However, it will be found that the duties of the job can be performed in many different locations and in many different situations. Furthermore, with experience the individual has a great advantage (over the new job entrant) because he can readily learn closely related tasks and adjust to the new phases and innovations in industry as they occur. It is important to keep this in mind because of the changing aspects of our economy and of our uncertainty about what the occupational structure (types of jobs and their relative frequency) will be like when the adolescent enters the labor market.

Some alarmists would have us believe that the occupational world of tomorrow will be changed so drastically because of technology, e.g., automation, that vocational choice and vocational guidance with adolescents is impossible if not unethical and somewhat immoral. Possibly so, but I suggest that the changes will occur fairly gradually. In any case, enough so that we can educate young people to expect, prepare, and adjust for the changes when they occur. This task is of paramount importance for the future of our adolescents. Part of the primary responsibility for carrying out the task rests on Education and Vocational Guidance.

If today's adolescents shut their eyes to the necessity for training, and the need for vocational goals which are both broad and specific, they will be at the mercy of the economic forces which require and will find manpower. Again, I would like to point out that adolescents and adults do not have to make vocational choices (realistic or otherwise), but I submit that if they do not, somebody else will make them for them without worrying about self-actualization, job satisfaction, or need reduction. Our task as vocational counselors is to help adolescents, at various points along the way, make decisions which are in their best interests, as well as in the best interests of society.

Let us return to our adolescent boy who is investigating occupations in Business for the purpose of making a vocational choice. After studying the major areas, he finds that he is most interested in the following specific occupations: Advertising Man, Advertising Copy Writer, and Editor of Trade or Technical Publications. These are, of course, in the general Literary field (Special Talent) as well as in Business, and he should also investigate other related Literary occupations. He has now arrived at a tentative field of choice and some possible jobs in Business. He should keep an open mind regarding the environment in which he wants to work and he should definitely consider whether he has the special talent for any job which requires writing. He now needs information of a different type, i.e., information about himself and in particular, about his aptitudes for work in the literary field.

So far, in this particular discussion, you might feel that I have been proposing an old-fashioned "cafeteria" system of vocational guidance. A good occupational library, a program of steps for the student to follow and his ability to read well, would appear to be all that is necessary for him to make a realistic and satisfying vocational choice. Is this, you ask, all there is to vocational guidance? What about aptitude tests? What does the counselor do? Do we even need him? Why can we not handle all of this electronically and solve the whole problem instantaneously by giving our client a computer print-out when he needs it?

Of course, I have been talking about only one, but a very important, phase of vocational guidance. Before I discuss briefly some of the other aspects of vocational guidance, I would like to make it very clear that the proper use of occupational information is probably the most important and practical technique of vocational guidance. There are difficulties and drawbacks, but nevertheless, real vocational decision-making simply cannot occur in a vacuum. The adolescent has to have occupational information if he is to choose wisely. The only alternative is for someone else (perhaps on the basis of testing, interviewing, observation, or just sheer guesswork) to tell him what to do. Unfortunately, this latter approach to vocational guidance is still with us, but professional counselors certainly do not subscribe to it and they do not operate that way.

The problem with available occupational information is that it does not go far enough. It describes many things about jobs in terms of economic factors (salary), but it fails to cover adequately the psychological and sociological aspects of jobs. The student would like to know what it is like to be a worker at "X" type of work; what needs can be satisfied on the job, and what personal satisfactions (beyond economic rewards) can be obtained. Information on these things is woefully lacking in our occupational literature. People do work for wages and they need certain characteristics and potential skills for successful work performance. Much information on these matters can be obtained from published information and from contact with workers. The rest, unfortunately, has to be learned on the job. Our task as vocational counselors is to help adolescents eventually find work with which they are reasonably successful and happy.

Using the classic model of vocational choice theory (that of matching workers and jobs), we have so far looked at only one side of the coin. Turning to the other side, it is necessary to determine the characteristics of the person which bear on the problem of vocational choice. The theory was that knowing what the job requires in the way of aptitudes, personality traits, etc., and knowing what the person has, he or the counselor can then compare the two sets of data and pick out the occupation which is most suitable for the person. Since any rational person naturally will select the best "fit" of himself and the job (so the theory goes), the problem is solved and success and happiness is assured. Actually, there is some merit in this idea if it is not viewed and implemented mechanistically (theoretically it could be computerized very nicely). Unfortunately, it does not work very well in real life. I doubt if very many people actually choose jobs this way, and if they did, I do not think they would be very successful, even though superficially this approach looks simple and easy and perhaps even scientific. There are other ways of attacking this problem but, regardless of what theory of vocational choice one uses (Hackman, 1965), the personal characteristics of the adolescent are really the basic starting point. It is he who must choose on the basis of his own expectancies and his own value system.

Before going on, let me add a brief word picture of the hypothetical boy who was investigating occupational information earlier. He is in the eleventh grade in a comprehensive high school and is a C to B– student in the general academic curriculum. His best subjects are Social Studies and English and his poorest are Science and Mathematics. He is reasonably well adjusted, but somewhat quiet. His only extracurricular activity is writing for the school paper; otherwise he has evidenced no special talents or interests in school. He reads a great deal, but with little concentration in any one area. He has never been in trouble and he seems only mildly interested in school. He states he is not interested in four years of college although he is open to alternative suggestions. His teachers like him, but they do not really know him. His parents are interested in him and his future. There are no major financial obstacles to further education. This boy is a rather typical, undistinguished, middle-class adolescent who just does not know what he wants to do and is only mildly concerned about it.

If you were his counselor or advisor, would this information assist you in helping him make a vocational choice? Of course it would, but is it enough? Oh, you want to know his I.Q.? What about aptitude tests? What about College Board scores? What about his measured interests? How does he stack up on a personality inventory? How did he do on the comprehensive National Achievement Testing Program?

Why do you or I want to know these things? I grant at the outset that they would probably be useful (Cronbach, 1960; Goldman, 1961; Buros, 1965). The first and most important answer is that we want objective measures that will tell us concretely where our student now stands on the traits we have measured. The second answer is that we wish to predict how well he will do later on, all other things being equal. Whichever way you look at it, the purpose of any objective information is to assist us in helping our client, and its utility lies in whether or not it does so. The types of tests that are most useful in vocational guidance (looked at from a sequential point of view) will now be discussed.

Tests of General Intelligence and Scholastic Aptitude

These tests tell us something about the adolescent's scholastic promise, his level of trainability, and the degree of job complexity that he will be able to handle. This is a good starting point in vocational testing, if it is approached with caution and due regard for the pitfalls in intelligence testing. At best, intelligence tests measure the present level of the individual's functioning; at the worst, they can be misleading and damaging. Intelligence is not a single unitary trait. It can be broken up into subtraits such as concrete vs. abstract, verbal vs. performance, or verbal vs. quantitative thinking. Even so-called aptitudes may be considered to be special aspects of intelligence (or vice versa). As predictors of college success, scholastic aptitude tests leave much to be desired, since scores obtained from them do not correlate highly with grades. As a matter of fact, high school grades are still the best indicators of success in college.

In spite of the difficulties involved, the measurement of intellectual capacity and functioning is the first step in vocational testing. The level of the student's ability determines to a great extent the next steps in testing and counseling.

Achievement Tests

A student's pattern of achievement in various subjects (taking into account his reading ability) can tell us a great deal about his knowledge, ability, interests and drive, providing the tests are not just poorly disguised reading or intelligence tests. The individual's performance can be compared to both local and national norms. This shows, if you will, his competitive position in the educational market. Even more important, however, is that the profile (pattern of scores) shows his strengths and weaknesses in achievement. Whatever the reasons may be for his achieving in some areas and not in others (e.g., lack of interest or poor previous background), these differences are of great importance in planning further training. This, in turn, will help to indicate what occupational areas are the most suitable. Grades in school subjects should be considered as well since they reflect actual performance over a period of time.

Discrepancies often exist between ability (i.e., intelligence), tested achievement and school performance. In many cases underachievement stands out in bold relief, since the individual does not appear to be working up to his potential. As a result he is labeled, and his parents are told in no uncertain terms that he is, an *underachiever.* This shakes up everybody because they really do not know what to do about it. Worse yet, by this time the student may not even care. An underachiever is, quite simply, a student who is behind his age-class group of peers, or one whose test scores fall much lower on the norms than would be expected for his intelligence. A common example is a student who is "bright," and therefore would be expected to do well, but who is failing in school or just getting by.

Many people assume a very high positive correlation between the I.Q. and performance in school. Thus, for them, high I.Q. = high grades; average I.Q. = average grades; and low I.Q. = low grades (to use an oversimplified example). An individual student who does not fit this pattern (e.g., above average I.Q.—below average grades) is really exhibiting a negative correlation between I.Q. and grades, and this will never do! Parents, teachers, and counselors must remember that the correlation between intelligence and grades is far from perfect. It should come as no surprise that many boys and girls do not fit into this statistical schema of things at all and that they are not abnormal because they do not. There are other factors involved in achievement besides intelligence. It follows, therefore, that we should expect to find many underachievers in school and that we should not try to make all adolescents come up to the "national average" or some other mythical norm which is a generalization or statistical artifact. We should be more disturbed when adolescents do not come up to *their own level of aspiration,* whatever it may be. To my mind, this is real underachievement and it may reflect other and more serious problems than so-called underachievement. We seem to spend a great deal of time in attempting to raise the level of aspiration of students without really knowing or trying to understand these levels in the first place. We try to solve this problem by substituting higher goals which may well be inappropriate for the individual student. In addition, because of our own middle-class value systems, we attempt to change the direction of the aspirations (e.g., toward academic achievement and away from automobile mechanics) without regard for the desires of students. No wonder they rebel and retreat or perhaps sidestep our efforts so adroitly. The stigma attached to being labeled an underachiever is real and often devastating. In fact, it frequently immobilizes all who are concerned with the person so labeled.

Underachievement is a baffling problem, since the reasons for it are so varied and often so difficult to determine in an individual case. Generally speaking, adolescents do not suddenly become underachievers due to a sudden traumatic change in their lives. Failure has a way of feeding on itself. As time goes on it becomes a way of life and finally results in a complete breakdown from an educational point of view.

Vocational counselors are concerned with underachievement and with academic failure when other indications point to success within the range of abilities of the student. Lack of success in school has a direct bearing on subsequent job training and occupational success. Failure to complete high school, or even grade school, permanently restricts the employability and placeability of an individual in today's job world. At best, it results in occupational as well as educational failure. There are a large number of young job seekers today who have dropped out of school and who cannot find any kind of permanent work. Without help, their chances of ever being employed in good competitive jobs in industry are close to zero. This is a great challenge for vocational guidance and education.

When achievement testing reveals discrepancies such as those we have discussed, one should stop in the process of sequential testing and tackle these problems before going on to further testing or other guidance procedures. As for the particular problem, lack of achievement, one must look at the antecedents, the present situation, and the probable consequences. Problems of lack of achievement, underachievement, and dropping out of school involve educational diagnosis and remediation before vocational guidance and counseling can proceed with any hope of success.

Aptitude Testing

Aptitude refers to potential ability to learn and perform certain kinds of tasks. It does not depend on training to a marked degree. One tends either to have it or not to have it. Aptitude tests are a kind of "quickie" substitute for actual vocational try-outs, which are too slow and too narrow in their application. Thus a high score on a "mechanical" aptitude test purports to predict success in mechanical work of some kind. Early researchers hoped to analyze jobs in terms of the aptitudes needed, and then to construct tests which were predictive by accurately measuring these aptitudes. Thus, with a profile of needed aptitudes for the job being considered, and a profile of the individual's scores on the corresponding aptitude tests, one could proceed to match the worker to the job. Many years of research on this problem have failed to fulfill this expectation. As a matter of fact, the correlations of aptitude tests with the criteria of job success are actually very low. In fact, the correlations are so low that very little confidence can be placed on the power of a single aptitude test to predict success on the job. With the exception of the General Aptitude Test Battery of the United States Employment Service, even multiple aptitude test batteries are not much better. I do not deny that aptitude tests are useful at times, but I want to emphasize that we do not have a large number of aptitude tests which actually predict job success. The public still thinks that aptitude testing is a kind of magic that the vocational counselor uses to advise his client. The commonest inquiry we receive at our Vocational and Educational Guidance Clinic is, "Do you give Aptitude Tests?" not, "Do you do vocational counseling?" If used cautiously by trained counselors, aptitude tests are useful, but they have a limited value in counseling. There is no simple, objective technique for determining an individual's overall vocational potential or vocational satisfaction. A one-shot battery of tests simply does not give enough information about the development of the person, his present situation, or his probable future status.

Personality, Needs, Values and Interests

This is the most difficult area in which to apply the measurement approach. Personality inventories are commonly used in vocational guidance for three basic purposes. The first is to assess the temperament pattern of the individual as it relates to jobs. While there is no one-to-one relationship between temperament and job performance, nevertheless, the tasks and the climate of jobs do differ. For example, some people are best suited, temperamentally, to dealing with people, others to working alone. Personality inventories give some information which is useful here. The second purpose is to assess the overall personality adjustment, stability, lack of pathology, etc., of the person. Inventories should be followed up with more clinical approaches (such as interviewing and projective techniques) before steps are taken for referral or treatment by professional personnel. The employability of a person is closely related to his personality characteristics and his way of coping with his environment. This is particularly true when he is in a work situation where good interpersonal relationships are basic to his success. Personality maladjustment is a basic cause and heavy contributor to vocational maladjustment. If we can detect incipient trouble in this area for adolescents and get aid for them, we can help to prevent maladjustment and failure on the job later. Lastly, the personality inventory is used to assess the need and value systems of the individual. Since much of this area of an adolescent's life is unconscious, or at least non-verbalized, we sometimes use specialized inventories to obtain information which is pertinent to the problem of vocational choice. While we cannot change the economic world, it is very helpful for the counselor and his client to work through this problem in terms of reality. Adolescents must learn that needs can only be satisfied within limits. This is particularly true in the work setting where many of an individual's needs (such as self-actualization) simply cannot or may not be satisfied.

Personality measures are extremely useful in the hands of trained counselors. They are really clinical instruments, and as such, are of value in dealing with an individual adolescent only if the counselor knows a great deal about the boy or girl with whom he is working. They are sometimes criticized because they can be faked. This deception on the part of the person taking the inventory is minimal if rapport has been established with him, if he understands the purpose of the testing, and if he is undergoing it voluntarily. The biggest and most serious criticism of using personality "tests" is that they invade the privacy of the individual, often without his consent (Amrine, 1965; 1966). I agree entirely that this can be true in mass testing or testing for employment or selection. For this and other reasons I do not recommend the wholesale use of personality inventories in schools. I believe that their use should be restricted to trained counselors and school psychologists and that they be used on a one-to-one basis in a clinical setting. They can be very useful, but in the wrong hands and with the wrong people they can be useless and even dangerous. However, let us not throw the baby out with the bath water. Used properly, personality assessment devices are of great value.

Another type of test (actually an inventory) is the *Interest Inventory*. These are used to help the individual think about and react to a wide variety of job titles and job descriptions. They do not and are not intended to predict success on the job. They help to predict what type of work will be of interest to the student. If used in conjunction with occupational information, they are among the most valuable tools in the vocational counselor's kit.

Let us return to our hypothetical adolescent. He has narrowed down his vocational choices, through the study of occupational information, to work which requires writing, possibly in the field of Business. In addition to what we already know about him as a person, let us add some further items of testing information.

		Percentile	
1.	*Intelligence*	70	(Above Average)
2.	*Achievement*		
	Mathematics	45	(About Average)
	Social Studies	70	(Above Average)
	English	90	(High)
	Reading	85	(High)
	Science	35	(Below Average)
3.	*Aptitude*		
	Mechanical	5	(Very Low)
	Clerical	30	(Below Average)
	Mathematical	20	(Low)
	Art	80	(High)
4.	*Interests*		
	Business Contact	Above Average	(Mild Interest)
	Business Clerical	Very Low	(Strong Dislike)
	Outdoor	Low	(Dislike)
	Social Welfare	Below Average	(Mild Dislike)
	Scientific Technical	Very Low	(Strong Dislike)
	Mechanical	Very Low	(Strong Dislike)
	Service	Very Low	(Strong Dislike)
	Aesthetic		
	(Special Talent)	High	(Strong Interest)
5.	*Personality*	Average	(Well-adjusted)

The reader can put himself in place of the counselor and arrive at a recommendation if he chooses. Although this is a hypothetical, but fairly typical case, I would only suggest that the evidence seems to be quite consistent. The tests are useful in that they seem to corroborate the other information we have at hand. It suggests that this boy should be encouraged to go to a specialized school or a community college for more work in writing. It may turn out that he will decide to continue his education in a four-year college. In any case, he can aim at occupations which involve doing some kind of writing in a business (publishing) or semi-technical field. He is not likely to set the world on fire (few of us do), but he should be a competent and solid citizen on the job.

SUMMARY

We must *first* make sure that adolescents are exposed to a wide spectrum of reliable and valid information about the world of work. We need to help them look at occupational information realistically and not to just ignore it or incorporate some part of the information into a private world of fantasy and wishful thinking.

Secondly, we must assist individual adolescents to evaluate their own characteristics (such as aptitudes, interests and temperament traits) and relate them to the economic needs and realities of society— both present and future, insofar as this can be done.

Thirdly, we need to help young people learn how to make decisions which are, on the one hand, appropriate for them, and on the other hand, realistic and flexible. This means that they need to know what alternative courses of action are open to them; what the consequences and risks of choosing each of them are; and how these factors relate to their own system of values. They need to become aware that the ultimate responsibility for making choices rests with them, but that we stand ready to help them in the decision-making process.

Lastly, we need to (and indeed we must) "motivate" adolescents to make the choices, educationally and vocationally, which are feasible for them at their stage of development.

It seems to me that the most significant role we as teachers, counselors and parents can play is to do everything we can to make our young people (see Macomber's chapter) educationally oriented. We should encourage them to get everything they can from their school experiences. Above all, we should constantly reinforce the importance of high school graduation. We should stress the importance of good ability in reading, writing, speaking, and arithmetic; for these are the qualifications that employers look for at the entry level of jobs, rather than the specific vocational skills which are usually learned at work. Boys and girls who are deficient in these basic skills are seriously handicapped, both educationally and vocationally. Special remedial programs should be set up to handle this problem. However, we need new approaches and new techniques which are not rejected by the student because he sees only more of the same "old stuff." After all, who needs more failure?

We must help disadvantaged young people of all types (not just the so-called economically disadvantaged) to realize the importance of acquiring the basic educational skills which are needed in a modern society. We in turn need to realize that these young people have potentialities which are of value. New approaches to education are needed to develop these potentialities. Our schools are struggling with this problem, but until our curricula and instructional techniques change markedly, these boys and girls are not going to be helped very much and their economic future is very grim. Furthermore, vocational guidance is not likely to do much, either.

All of us who are interested in young people must work together on the problem of vocational development. No single group of people in the helping professions, in education, in industry, in the community, or the family can solve this problem alone. Vocational Guidance and Vocational Counseling can be of great help, but let us remember that it is only one approach. It is not a magic formula, nor is it a panacea which will solve the "adolescence problem" by itself.

REFERENCES

Amrine, M. (Ed.) Testing and public policy. *American Psychologist*, 1965, *20*, 857–993.

Amrine, M. (Ed.) Camelot and psychological tests. *American Psychologist*, 1966, *21*, 401–470.

Baer, M. F., and Roeber, E. S. *Occupational information: The dynamics of its nature and use.* Chicago: Science Research Associates, 1964.

Buros, O. K. (Ed.) *The sixth mental measurements yearbook.* Highland Park, New Jersey: Gryphon Press, 1965.

Cronbach, L. J. *Essentials of psychological testing.* New York: Harper and Brothers, 1960.

Goldman, L. *Using tests in counseling.* New York: Appleton-Century-Crofts, 1961.

Hackman, R. B. Manpower—untapped wealth: The role of the counselor as a social engineer. In: *Manpower for changing health needs.* Proceedings of the 14th annual conference of the Pennsylvania Health Council. Harrisburg, Pa.: Pennsylvania Health Council, 1964.

Hackman, R. B. The problem of vocational choice in vocational guidance: An essay. In: Adams, J. F. (Ed.) *Counseling and guidance: a summary view.* New York: The Macmillan Co., 1965.

Hopke, W. E. (Ed.) *The encyclopedia of careers and vocational guidance.* Chicago: J. G. Ferguson Publishing Co., 1967.

Hoppock, R. *Occupational information.* New York: McGraw-Hill, 1963.

Nicholas, Phoebe O. Vocational development. In: Jersild, A. A. *The psychology of adolescence.* New York: The Macmillan Co., 1963.

Parsons, T. Youth in the context of American society. In: Borow, H. (Ed.) *Man in a world of work.* Boston: Houghton Mifflin, 1964.

Samler, J. Occupational exploration in counseling: A proposed re-orientation. In: Borow, H. (Ed.) *Man in a world of work.* Boston: Houghton Mifflin, 1964.

Super, D. E. *The psychology of careers.* New York: Harper and Brothers, 1957.

Super, D. E., and Crites, J. O. *Appraising vocational fitness.* New York: Harper & Row, 1962.

Tyler, Leona E. *The work of the counselor.* New York: Appleton-Century-Crofts, 1961.

Tyler, Leona E. Work and individual differences. In: Borow, H. (Ed.) *Man in a world of work.* Boston: Houghton Mifflin, 1964.

Tyler, Leona E. *The psychology of human differences.* New York: Appleton-Century-Crofts, 1965.

U.S. Department of Labor. *Occupational outlook handbook.* Washington, D.C.: Superintendent of Documents, U.S. Government Printing Office, Bulletin No. 1450, 1966–67 Edition.

Wrenn, C. G. *The counselor in a changing world.* Washington: American Personnel and Guidance Association, 1962.

AUTHOR INDEX

A

Abramson, M., 298, 315
Acheson, R. M., 58, 65
Adams, J. F., 1-12, 277, 286, 386
Addams, Jane, 290, 309
Adelson, J., 354, 355, 359
Adler, A., 89
Allen, L., 136, 156
Altbach, P. G., 230
Altus, W. C., 107, 123
Ames, Louise B., 99, 147
Amos, W. E., 297, 309
Amrine, M., 382, 385
Anderson, C. A., 336
Anderson, H. H., 176-177, 179
Anderson, J. E., 173
Andrews, E. G., 171, 179
Andrews, M., 180
Armer, J. M., 322, 336
Armstrong, M. D., 122, 123
Asch, S. E., 195, 197
Astin, A. W., 104, 123, 175, 180
Aub, J. C., 68
Ausubel, D. P., 71, 98, 289, 309

B

Baer, M. F., 372, 385
Baggaley, A. R., 286
Baines, E., 100
Baird, L. L., 353, 359
Baldwin, 50
Balinsky, B., 134, 155
Balistrieri, J. J., 303, 316
Barker, R. G., 22, 42
Barron, F., 159, 163, 179, 180, 195, 197
Bayley, Nancy, 49, 50, 65, 132, 155

Beach, F. A., 49, 66, 127
Beardslee, D. C., 352, 359
Becker, H. S., 293, 297, 309
Bell, R. R., 87, 239, 272-286, 332, 338
Beller, E. K., 34, 70-100, 185, 282, 307, 339
Benedict, Ruth, 95, 98
Berkowitz, B., 134, 156
Bettelheim, B., 334, 335
Bilbro, W. C., 110, 126
Blaine, G. B., 319, 335
Bledsoe, J. C., 292, 309
Blewett, D. B., 111, 113, 123
Block, H. A., 306, 309
Block, Jeanne H., 82, 184, 189, 198-231, 329
Blood, R. O., 254, 259, 270
Bloom, B. S., 106, 107, 123
Bloom, V., 352, 359
Blos, P., 71, 98, 206, 228
Bogan, F. A., 292, 313
Borow, H., 281, 287, 337-360, 364, 386
Boswell, F. P., 43-44, 65
Bradway, Katherine P., 136, 155
Braungart, R. G., 200, 203, 214, 215, 219, 220, 229, 231
Breckenridge, Marian E., 56, 65
Brennan, Margaret, 304, 309
Britt, S. H., 137, 156
Bronson, Wanda C., 17, 41
Brown, N. H., 67
Bruner, J. E., 160, 179
Bryan, A. H., 47, 65
Burchinal, L. G., 277, 278, 286, 288, 309

387

SUBJECT INDEX